The Development of

CLINICAL

PSYCHOLOGY

THE CENTURY PSYCHOLOGY SERIES

Richard M. Elliott, Gardner Lindzey & Kenneth MacCorquodale

EDITORS

The Development of

CLINICAL

PSYCHOLOGY

By JOHN M. REISMAN

Rochester Child Guidance Clinic

&

The University of Rochester

NEW YORK

APPLETON-CENTURY-CROFTS

Division of Meredith Publishing Company

To
My Parents, Margo, and Our Children

PREFACE

THIS BOOK BEGINS in the late eighteenth century with a climate of ideas receptive to the development of clinical psychology, and proceeds to trace its growth in theoretical systems, techniques, practices, and professional organization. After the first chapter, which sets the stage for what follows, each chapter is devoted to a particular decade and is divided into these sections: a brief sketch of events, mostly outside psychology, to give a hint of the *Zeitgeist;* concepts and theories concerning "normal" personality functioning and some of the persons who advocated them; the major diagnostic techniques employed and the people who devised them; diagnostic formulations which were influential and those who conceived them; treatments proposed and used and those who practiced them; and the development of the profession and those who promoted it.

I should like to thank the Editors of The Century Psychology Series, Gardner Lindzey, Kenneth MacCorquodale, and especially Richard M. Elliott, for their many helpful comments and suggestions. Similarly, I wish to express my gratitude to those persons who make up that corporate entity "the publisher" for their assistance in making this book possible. Samuel Beck and Carl Rogers were generous in providing biographical material, and thanks are also due The University of Rochester Library, which provided most of the references used in this work.

J. M. R.

CONTENTS

1

Roots

Since the end of World War ii, there has been an enormous increase in the number of clinical psychologists. These men and women have joined a branch of psychology which, in a relatively brief period of time, has succeeded in making a significant contribution to the understanding that man has of himself. Yet this very success, the very fact that this field has grown so rapidly and that clinical psychologists are in positions which may profoundly affect the lives of others, has raised questions about the identity of this profession, questions that perhaps can be answered best by a consideration of its development.

This book is a history of the development of clinical psychology, and its purpose is not only to describe its many years of continuous growth but also to set down the reasons for its robust vitality. However, before we proceed to find when, how, and where it had its origins, let us consider briefly what clinical psychology is.

Clinical psychology is defined here as a branch of psychology devoted to the search for, and the application of, psychological principles and techniques that contribute to the understanding of individuals and that may be used to promote their more effective functioning. This definition has three implications.

First, it implies that clinical psychologists share with other psychologists the aim of becoming able to make accurate predictions about human behavior in situations of every kind. Through their observations, both controlled and natural, clinicians attempt to isolate, and often to measure, variables that affect the functioning of men, women, and children. Yet, clinicians are not content with statements of general relationships but focus whatever information they can obtain to the task of comprehending and helping a particular client or patient. Thus their special interest in the predictability of human behavior lies in acquiring sufficient understanding to be of service to specific human beings.

Second, the definition implies that clinical psychologists recognize the inherent value of the individual, the person's uniqueness and his right to be unique. For this reason, if for no other, each person is a challenge to the understanding of the clinician and to his ability to be of help when his assistance is indicated.

Third, the definition implies that clinical psychologists believe that every individual is entitled to function as effectively as possible, and, more particularly, to live his life and express his uniqueness in ways that are undistorted by misconceptions, anxieties, and fears. Certainly people who are in distress and are aware that they have psychological problems furnish the most ready examples of those to whom the services of clinical psychology are addressed. However, the recognition that one needs help is not a prerequisite for obtaining it. For example, children, the intellectually retarded, and criminals may deny that they wish psychological assistance; still, the energies and skills of clinicians are made available to them. Furthermore, clinicians are engaged to some extent in the area of primary prevention (as distinguished from secondary prevention, which refers to early diagnosis and effective treatment, and tertiary prevention, which refers to rehabilitation), i.e., the communication of psychological principles and insights to the public so that the incidence of conflict, unhappiness, and maladaptive behavior may be reduced and so that the best functioning of each person is encouraged. With this breadth of interest it is small wonder that clinical psychology has affected, more or less, the lives of most persons living in Western Europe and North America.

A BEGINNING

A history has no definite beginning or end. Rather than being confined by indisputable boundaries, it is a record and an interpretation, carved and constructed with deliberation and judgment from all the available information concerning its subject. At first glance, it would seem that our narrative might begin quite appropriately with the happenings and ideas current during the last decade of the nineteenth century. There were many events of outstanding importance that occurred in the 1890's— the publication of William James' *The Principles of Psychology,* Sigmund Freud's pioneer investigations into the causes and treatment of neuroses, the founding of the American Psychological Association, the opening of the first psychological clinic at the University of Pennsylvania, and the considerable activity evidenced in devising mental tests. However, to appreciate the significance of these ventures and why they met with success, we must consider the intellectual and social climate in which they took place. The fact is that a requisite favoring climate had been slowly developing throughout the eighteenth and nineteenth centuries, one that bore increasingly the stamp of values and attitudes of clinical psychology as we know it today.

So let us go farther back and begin with a contest. In 1749, in France, the Academy of Dijon announced a prize for the best essay on whether the arts and sciences had improved morals. The answer submitted by the contestant Jean Jacques Rousseau (1712–1778) was an impassioned negative. Far from improving morals, Rousseau asserted that society and civilization had corrupted man's native goodness. He went even further. In matters of importance, he argued, men should not be guided by rational thought but by their instincts and feelings. This would be the natural way to arrive at a decision and thus would be superior to any conclusion reached by mere reason.

Rousseau won that contest, an outcome which immediately indicates that his ideas were not found too shocking. Similar attacks on organized society had found eloquent expression in the writings of Locke, Voltaire, and Montesquieu. But what distinguished Rousseau from his fellow intellectuals of the Enlightenment was that where they condemned unnecessary restrictions imposed by the social order, Rousseau deplored the distortions it produced on man's natural development; where they extolled reason, Rousseau railed against it.

In what is perhaps Rousseau's most charming work, his propagandist novel *Émile,* he engagingly describes the education of a boy into manhood. By removing Émile from civilization, by permitting him to experience the natural consequences of his acts, by accepting him and allowing him to grow freely, a happy, confident, self-reliant young man is produced. Admittedly, any person reared in this manner would be no scholar, and his progress in Rousseau's world, as well as our own, would be difficult. For that matter, Rousseau acknowledged it was impossible, in a practical sense, to raise a child as the fictional Émile was raised. But he wished to communicate his principles of freedom in child-rearing and the value which he felt society should place on guilelessness and naturalness in expression. That he was successful in profoundly influencing educators is attested to by the founding of the Jean Jacques Rousseau Institute in Geneva in 1912.

Unfortunately, although Rousseau conceded there were times when reason might be necessary and even superior to feelings in guiding behavior—for example when attempting to deal with and master the complexities of a culture—he had a predilection for making rash statements: "I venture to declare that a state of reflection is contrary to nature; and that a thinking man is a depraved animal." Pronouncements like that, understandably enough, antagonized the intellectuals of his time and provoked Voltaire to remark: "No one has ever been so witty as you are in trying to turn us into brutes; to read your book makes one long to go all fours."

In part, Rousseau's extreme position in favor of the supremacy of instincts over intellect was an attempt to justify a felt need for God's existence in the face of logic and ever-increasing scientific advances. However, it is not necessary to adopt Rousseau's radical stance in order to see that there was value in much of what he said. Here was a revolutionary who believed that the natural inequalities of men in native endowments or talents are good and should be developed, while differences between them based on social inequalities of position and wealth are evil and should be eliminated. A revolutionary who regarded as best those systems of society and education which interfere least with the natural impulses, desires, and interests of the individual. One who asserted that all men possess virtue and common sense, and that these endowments are capable of evaluating and dealing effectively with all the issues that arise in a society. One who believed each person is entitled to respect for his opinions and to an equal voice in political affairs. Many budding revolutionaries were favorably impressed by Rousseau's advocacy of majority rule in government and freedom of expression, and were encouraged and stimulated by his philosophy in acquiring a questioning attitude toward established institutions, a spirit of reform, and an idealistic conception of society.

The considerable number of his contemporaries who listened to Rousseau generally shared his troubled feelings about these same issues. It was no secret that the existing aristocratic social order with a pampered royalty at its head was despised both by those who spoke of liberty, justice, and the rights of man and by those who fought to obtain them. Subsequently, the American and French Revolutions were expressions of these ideals, and yet as we know, despite a large measure of success in their outcomes, the ideals themselves were not hurriedly and lastingly enacted into reforms.

In the newly-independent United States the "self-evident" truth that "all men are created equal" was not intended to extend to Negro slaves. Apparently, Thomas Jefferson simply did not think of Negroes as being men, and this attitude among his contemporaries was not a particularly strange one. People in general, the masses, the common people, were regarded in terms of unflattering stereotypes. James Madison thought they were too impulsively violent to be trusted, Jefferson spoke of them as "panders of vice," and these views were shared by many of the founding fathers of the nation. Therefore, as checks on the rule of the majority, the Constitution was made to provide that Senators were to be selected by state legislatures and that the President was to be chosen by an electoral college. In England, under King George IV, voting was in the main confined to affluent property-holders, and a majority of the House of Commons was appointed or selected by local magnates or members of favored guilds. In France, under Louis Philippe, only 200,000 Frenchmen had the privilege of casting a ballot. When leaders of the working classes appealed to Premier Guizot for recognition of their rights to the franchise, his response was, "Get rich."

What we see, then, in the early part of the nineteenth century, is a general feeling of suspicion on the part of the rulers of countries toward the masses of their citizenry. They had good reason for their uneasiness. In a large part of the presumably civilized world a majority of the people were shamefully abused and exploited, while the French Revolution had demonstrated the explosiveness with which a populace might rebel and the ruthlessness with which they might take revenge when in possession of power. Thus it was thought most prudent to maintain an air of political conservatism.

The conservative view, since it represented the position of those parties at the top of the heap, quite sensibly regarded the rights of the individual as subservient to the needs of the state and to the preservation of order. In part to justify a resistance to social change, the prevailing attitude of government officials toward the poor seemed to imply a belief that the impoverished were not so much unschooled and deprived as they were stupid and lazy, that their complaints and restiveness were not so much a reaction to injustices as they were evidences of emotional instability, or at the extreme, innate depravity. Yet change was inevitable.

The official attitude was attacked from a variety of quarters: in literature, by political movements which opposed the status quo, by scientists armed with facts and expressing ideas that challenged traditional views, and by aroused, indignant individuals. Together, they created an atmosphere conducive to the enactment of reforms. We shall consider each of these areas of influence, starting first with the pressures brought to bear through literature.

THE IMPETUS WITHIN LITERATURE FOR REFORMS

Rousseau's philosophy dominated the arts during the first thirty years of the nineteenth century. This was a period of romanticism, in which its exponents worshiped nature, venerated the poor, burned for sweeping reforms, and often seemed in danger of becoming overwhelmed by their emotions. Shelley and Byron made impassioned pleas for freedom and justice. François de Chateaubriand saw a "holy innocence" in the poor, and William Wordsworth described England as "a fen of stagnant waters" in need of "manners, virtue, freedom, power."

Though romanticism continued to find expression throughout the nineteenth century, the major literary stream became that of realism. Sentimentality was largely abandoned in favor of a hard, unsparing examination of life as it is. In this literature, persons belonging to the middle and lower classes were usually cast as heroes in plots that portrayed their struggles against an oppressive environment as well as describing their inner conflicts. For example, Victor Hugo, in his epic *Les Misérables,* indicted the cruelty of man to man and dramatized the redemption of a "criminal" through heroism and suffering. Balzac and Flaubert, Zola and Dickens, Meredith and Mark Twain, Melville and Turgeniev, Dostoievski and Tolstoi illustrated in their writings that:

1. Virtue and vice are not the exclusive property of any one social class.
2. Men are driven by passions and are not by any means entirely rational in their behavior.
3. The poor are human beings with conflicts, feelings, aspirations, and sensitivity.
4. There are features of the social system which drive men to despair and which cry for rectification.
5. A better life is possible for all men if they will but examine themselves and look with sympathy upon their fellow man.

Ralph Waldo Emerson characterized the age as one of introversion and new respect for the individual: "The literature of the poor, the feelings of the child, the philosophy of the street, the meaning of household life, are the topics of the time. . . . Give me insight into to-day, and you may have the antique and future worlds."

These convictions, presented forcefully, dramatically, and directly through the media of novels, poems, essays, and plays influenced public opinion and pricked at consciences. However it would be an oversimplification to attribute any reforms that were made to their effects alone, even though occasionally such an oversimplification is offered in the form of a gracious gesture to an author. (In this category is Lincoln's remark upon meeting Harriet Beecher Stowe: "So this is the little lady who started this big war.") It is highly probable that of more immediate effectiveness in producing change than such writings were the impatient demands of the people and the threat that these demands posed to those in positions of authority.

THE POLITICAL PUSH FOR REFORM

With the growing power of the proletariat, a number of political movements arose to champion their cause. Socialism was expounded by Louis Blanc, communism by Marx and Engels, and anarchism by Pierre Proudhon and Mikhail Bakunin. Clearly these movements arose in response to, and gained their strength from, failures to rectify legitimate grievances. Despite the existence of booming industries, wealth tended to become concentrated in the hands of a relative few, while the vast population of laborers struggled to survive on barely adequate wages.

The growing strength of these radical political factions forced governments to effect reforms in order to stave off civil unrest, and, as it were, to "steal the thunder" from the opposition. For example, in England the combined Reform Acts of 1867 and 1884 extended the franchise to almost all male industrial and agricultural workers. But these improvements did not bring matters to a rest. On the contrary, with more people enfranchised, governments were compelled to be more responsive to the demands of larger segments of their population, thus setting the stage for additional reforms.

However, not all political reforms were in the nature of concessions. Another force influencing governments to better the lot of their citizenry was nationalistic self-interest. Social legislation was enacted that was intended to keep all classes loyal, healthy, and fit to fight in time of war. This was Bismark's prime motivation and he bluntly admitted it. To this end, between 1883 and 1884 he pushed through a program which limited the employment of women and children, fixed maximum hours of labor, and insured workmen against incapacity. The German example was soon followed by other countries on the Continent, notably Austria and France.

From our point of view, we can see that the political push for reform moved governments in two favorable directions. One, it caused officials to consider seriously the responsibilities of society for the care and protection of the mentally retarded and sick. Two, it made public funds for meeting these responsibilities available.

While these political pressures were being exerted, whole branches of science were developing which were attacking the problems of understanding man and his social organization. The advancement of technology was revolutionizing ways of working and living, and at the same time increasing the tempo of change. There were steamships and locomotives, the mechanical reaper and the telegraph, Bessemer steel and aniline dyes, thousands of new ideas, new discoveries, new inventions. A nation's technology was fast becoming a measure of its strength. To those living in the nineteenth century it must have seemed a most exciting and challenging period, one which had never been equalled in the number of marvels of man's inventiveness.

THE INFLUENCE OF SCIENCE
IN PRODUCING REFORMS

Virtually dead was the old rationalist tradition that the most valuable truth was to be derived from reasoning in the abstract, or "arm-chair philosophy." Empiricism now was dominant, and it claimed that truths are gained through sensory observations and experimentation. This emphasis on doing, testing, and experiencing something about a subject, rather than just thinking about it, was salutary, and it is reflected in the major developments in science from the beginning of the 1800's until approximately 1890, the period to which we are here confining ourselves.

Particularly outstanding was the progress made in the biological sciences. In 1809, the French biologist Jean Lamarck published his evolutionary hypothesis concerning the inheritance of acquired characteristics. The significance of his hypothesis was that it dared openly challenge the traditional beliefs of religion, and that it gave first importance to the influence of the environment in the generation of new species of animal life.

Karl Ernst von Baer, in 1830, announced the law of recapitulation: that during the embryonic period and youth, each member of a species reproduces the various important stages in the developmental history of the species to which it belongs. In 1835, Theodor Schwann pointed out that all living things are composed of cells, and a few years later Hugo von Mohl discovered that all these cells are composed of essentially the same complex substance, which he named protoplasm.

Lamarck's evolutionary hypothesis was called into question in 1859 when Charles Darwin published *The Origin of Species,* which contained his twin hypotheses of genetic variation and natural selection: that environmental conditions act in such a way as to select out over countless generations those variants among offspring which are best fitted to survive and reproduce. Darwin subsequently applied his evolutionary concepts to man as well as other animals, while his most enthusiastic proponent, Thomas Huxley, not only vigorously publicized them but also extended them to social institutions and moral ideals.

In 1865, Louis Pasteur advanced bacteriology as a science by attacking the theory of spontaneous generation and by formulating the law of biogenesis: all life comes from pre-existing life. That same year Joseph Lister introduced antiseptic surgery. The germ theory of disease made further strides when Robert Koch demonstrated that anthrax was caused by tiny, rod-like organisms in the blood of the diseased animal, and when he succeeded in discovering the bacilli of tuberculosis and Asiatic cholera.

The list of proud accomplishments in biology and medicine was not unique. An equally impressive itemization can be made for physics. In 1810, John Dalton, an English schoolmaster, revived the theory that all matter is composed of atoms; he argued for it so persuasively that it was soon accepted as a basic scientific premise.

Working on the basis of earlier discoveries by the Englishman James Joule, Hermann von Helmholtz formulated, in 1847, the principle of the conservation of energy. Later, in 1851, William Thomson (Lord Kelvin) systematically expounded the second law of thermodynamics and maintained that, while the total energy of the universe is constant, there is a continuous diminution in the amount available for work. The experiments of James Clerk Maxwell and Heinrich Hertz forced revisions on the then current theories of light by showing that light behaves in much the same way as electromagnetic waves. Finally, toward the close of the century experiments by Albert Michelson and Edward Morley, which failed to detect absolute motion, served as a significant prelude to Albert Einstein's construction of the universe.

Similar listings could be prepared for other areas of science, but the two just enumerated are sufficient to demonstrate that the biological and physical sciences were making great advances. Not only were the established branches of knowledge rapidly growing, but new disciplines were being developed. In 1813, James Prichard, an English physician, published *Researches into the Physical History of Mankind,* a milestone in the founding of anthropology. In 1830, Auguste Comte published the first of the six volumes of his *Cours de Philosophie Positive,* in which he coined the term *sociology,* defined it, and gave it both a systematic structure and a dynamics. And in 1879, Wilhelm Wundt founded the first psychological laboratory at Leipzig, aiding in the recognition of psychology as a science worthy of independent status.

One of the major effects of all this scientific activity was the shaking of cherished beliefs. Paradoxically, as man increased his knowledge of the world he grew more aware of his limitations and more suspicious of those who claimed to know with certainty. An air of skepticism and intellectual humility replaced the old dogmas. Such attitudes are seen in Huxley's doctrine of agnosticism: a frank confession that neither the nature nor the existence of God nor the ultimate character of the universe is knowable, though to many this appears to be in its own way a manifestation of the very dogmatic attitude it despised.

A second effect was an increased tendency to hold a relativistic conception of truth. The theory of evolution applied to man and his products indicated not only a continuity between man and other forms of life, but suggested that both he and his beliefs would be ever-changing.

A third effect was that many scientists openly supported the theory that all things are composed of matter or a mechanistic interpretation of the universe. These views helped pave the way for viewing man himself mechanistically and for asserting that his behavior is determined by physical laws; hence actions are predictable when we fully understand the circumstances under which they occur.

A fourth effect was prompted by the discovery of micro-organisms which produce disease. Physicians were given new hope that previously inexplicable maladies, such as mental illness, might prove to have a physical cause that could be isolated and treated quickly. The stigma attached to the mentally ill was thus being gradually removed by scientific advances in understanding the disease process.

At the same time that scientists by their gains fostered an atmosphere of change, uncertainty, and optimism, characters were portrayed in literature whose psychological sufferings were presented sympathetically; governments became responsive to pressures to provide at least semi-adequate care for the mentally ill; and humanitarian considerations prompting societies to assume the responsibility for those psychologically disturbed were promulgated by a few outstanding individuals, of whom the work of four was of special significance and fruitfulness.

FOUR INDIVIDUALS WHO EFFECTED REFORMS

Philippe Pinel, William Tuke, Eli Todd, and Dorothea Dix were, of course, products of their times, and yet they helped to shape them. Their accomplishments indicate that they did not stand alone; for they could not have been successful in crystallizing thinking and directing it into forceful action if others, in literature, in politics, in science, had not shared their convictions or received their ideas favorably. This is not to imply their tasks were easy. In each case they encountered resistance. At times this resistance was based on an unwillingness to spend enough money in this area, at other times it was based on a feeling of futility that little if anything could be accomplished, but all too often it was based on prejudices and fears concerning the nature of mental illness.

In order to appreciate better the obstacles they sought to overcome, we must recall that at the beginning of the nineteenth century there was still a lingering feeling that the insane were "possessed" by witches and demons, and that through their own devious actions those possessed had brought their afflictions upon themselves. These views were not shared by the medical profession of that era. Among physicians, the mentally ill were regarded as suffering from an oversupply of blood to the brain (this idea dated back to Hippocrates around 400 B.C.) and/or brain lesions. With the public, however, the medical profession shared the opinion that the mentally ill were strangely different from other people and that their condition was incurable. Therefore, it made sense to pay as little attention to them as possible, and this indeed was common medical practice.

At "Old Bedlam" (St. Mary of Bethlehem Hospital) in England, a physician would visit once a year to prescribe treatment: bleeding of all patients in April, purges and "vomits" of all surviving patients in May, and once again bleeding of all patients in October. At smaller private institutions, where medical care was usually even more sporadic, a physician might visit once in ten years to prescribe a regime of treatment for the next decade. As a continuing feature of institutionalization, patients were chained to posts in dungeons, whipped, beaten, ridiculed, and fed only the coarsest of slops.

Philippe Pinel (1745–1826), who is called the father of scientific psychiatry, was one of those who led in trying to alter the conditions just described. He was the son of a simple country physician in Saint-Paul, France. Since early in life he gave the appearance of being studious, introverted, and sensitive to suffering, it was planned that he should enter the priesthood. But Pinel abandoned plans for such a career when he came under the influence of the liberal and anticlerical writings of Voltaire and Rousseau. He decided to follow his father's profession, and at the age of twenty-two enrolled at the University of Toulouse, receiving his medical degree in 1773.

For two years Pinel tutored children in Latin, Greek, and natural history. He then went to Montpellier for further studies in comparative anatomy and the classification of diseases. Still unsettled, he left in 1778 for Paris. There, his scholarliness and and humility impressed his colleagues but repelled those among his prospective patients who were aristocratic and had become accustomed to expect elegance, charm, and entertaining gossip from their physicians. For fourteen years he remained obscure, impoverished, and studious; tutoring, translating books, and writing papers on medicine, physics, and philosophy.

With the second phase of the French Revolution in 1792, Pinel was appointed a municipal medical officer of low grade. His position required him to be present at beheadings: a duty which, understandably enough, he found repulsive. However, he saw in the principles of humaneness espoused by the leaders of the Revolution an opportunity to alleviate the sufferings of the mentally ill and, perhaps, a chance to do something that would isolate him from the violence in Paris.

Therefore, Pinel went to Thouret and Cabanis, administrators of the hospitals of Paris. He appealed to them to apply the benefits of Liberty and Equality to the insane. They were sufficiently impressed to appoint him, in 1793, to head the lunatic asylum of the Bicêtre.

What Pinel found in that old gray-stone house on the outskirts of Paris was the customary dismal combination of squalor, cruelty, and neglect. His first plan was to remove the chains from the patients. However, he was informed by the custodians that he would need the permission of the Commune before they could carry out his order. Pinel went before Georges Couthon, President of the Commune, and made his appeal, but found him suspicious that aristocrats and enemies of the Revolution might be hidden among the insane. Nevertheless, Couthon did not wish to be unreasonable; although a paralytic, he had himself carried to the Bicêtre so that he might personally interrogate the patients. Their responses to his queries, as one might imagine, caused him to wonder about the sanity of the man who wanted to unchain such "animals," but he left without forbidding Pinel to do as he wished.

Accepting this omission as permission, Pinel had the chains removed from a few patients, and eventually, all patients were unchained. Pinel saw to it that they received better food and were not beaten. Each day he would pass among them offering kindness and encouragement. "The mentally sick," he said, "far from being guilty people deserving of punishment are sick people whose miserable state deserves all the consideration that is due to suffering humanity." To most of the people of Paris, Pinel's words sounded like the ravings of a madman.

For the next three years, Pinel worked at the Bicêtre. During that time he was almost lynched by a mob which accused him of causing a cholera epidemic by poisoning wells. Luckily, he was saved by the heroism of one of his former patients. Thereafter, when not engaged in eluding ropes and lampposts, Pinel continued to write and study. His major aim was to make psychiatry more scientific. He introduced the practice of taking case histories and keeping records, and attempted to formulate a nosology, or systematic classification of mental illnesses; however, the last did not prove to be a significant contribution.

Following his success at the Bicêtre, Pinel received an appointment to take charge of the Salpêtrière. There, too, he ordered chains removed and initiated a program to train personnel in his humane methods of treatment. In 1799, Pinel was called upon to examine the Wild Boy of Aveyron. Considerable interest had been aroused in the populace by this feral child. According to Rousseau's ideas, since the boy had been unspoiled by civilization, he should have grown to be noble and virtuous. Instead, he was found to grunt like a beast, to display offensive table manners, and to be in general not at all winning in his behavior. Pinel pronounced him an idiot.

Since the mentally retarded in those days were thought to be incurable and untrainable, usually nothing was done to improve their condition. This would have been the fate of the Wild Boy of Aveyron had it not been for Jean Itard, one of Pinel's students. Itard believed the mentally retarded could learn and asked that he be allowed to attempt to educate the boy. For five years he labored with infinite patience to do so. Though his efforts were not as rewarding as he had hoped, they were not as futile as Pinel had predicted; the boy was taught to dress himself and to read simple words, though he never learned to speak. Of even more significance, Itard's dedication and methods inspired and encouraged others, even much later as Lightner Witmer, in the education of the retarded and the deaf and mute.

Pinel continued to teach "moral treatment" to his fellow psychiatrists over a span of about twenty years. He himself embodied the humane ideals he sought to inculcate in others, and richly deserved the fame posterity has accorded him. Yet his career ended unhappily. Accused of harboring priests from the authorities, he was removed from his teaching position and spent the remainder of his life in official dishonor.

At about the same time that Pinel was fighting for his reforms, an

English Quaker tea merchant, William Tuke (1732–1822), was listening to a strange story. Some of Tuke's friends had gone to visit a relative who was a patient in the Lunatick Asylum in York. The overseer had denied them permission and turned them away from the asylum. A few days later they were informed that their relative was dead, and they had reason to attribute the death to beatings. They had come to Tuke for advice.

Tuke was a respected member of his community and known for his generosity. He was also close to sixty years old and comfortably settled, and so it would have done him no discredit to simply refer his friends to someone else. Instead, Tuke talked the situation over with his son Henry, and decided to investigate further. He visited the Lunatick Asylum and similar institutions and was amazed, horrified, and angered by what he saw. He resolved to do something about it.

Appealing to the Society of Friends, personal acquaintances, and town physicians, Tuke enlisted their interest and support in planning "a place in which the unhappy might obtain a refuge." Years of laboriously soliciting funds followed. Finally, in 1796 the "place," the York Retreat, opened its doors to patients. Tuke built the retreat to resemble a farmhouse, set it in the countryside, and surrounded it with a garden and some cows. Conspicuously absent were bars and gratings on the windows, and fetters and manacles on the patients. The treatment was simple: respect, good food, recreation, exercise, expressions of religious values, and friendliness in personal contacts. Tuke had consulted with the medical profession about a treatment program but felt their recommendations of bleedings and purges were out of keeping with his own personality and sense of right. Thus these practices were not employed at the retreat. His principles assumed the dignity and worth of every man, and tolerated only kindness and decency in dealings with others.

Tuke devoted the remainder of his life to the York Retreat. He had the satisfaction of seeing it grow and serve as an example for hospitals in Europe and the United States. The humane work begun by him was continued with devotion and courage by his son, grandson, and great-grandson.

While Tuke and Pinel were working for better treatment of the mentally ill, each pursued his objective without knowledge of what the other was doing. Each encountered resistances, but of greater significance, each also encountered support and lived to see his efforts serve as models for emulation. Their ideas were not new; humane treatment for the mentally ill had been urged by Juan Luis Vives and Johann Weyer during the sixteenth century. But the voices of Vives and Weyer were ahead of their times and thus had little effect. In contrast, the voices of Pinel and Tuke were part of a growing chorus which sang of individual rights and social responsibility.

Eli Todd (1762–1832) was part of that chorus. A graduate of Yale in

1787, he was rich in everything but money. He had a fine family, good looks, and a brilliant intellect, but derived little income from his work as a country physician in Connecticut. Moreover, his daily rounds were often personally distressing experiences as he became aware of the unhappy consequences traceable to the lack of facilities for the mentally ill. At the beginning of the nineteenth century only three states, Pennsylvania, Virginia, and Maryland, had hospitals providing for their care. Accordingly, people were forced to improvise their own means for dealing with the mental illness of a member of their family; and since they felt ashamed about the condition, all too frequently their improvisation took the form of hiding the relative from the public in one pathetic way or another. Todd saw that all those concerned suffered, and had cause to be particularly sympathetic to such cases, for his own father had died insane and his sister, Eunice, was afflicted with melancholia. Yet at that time there was little that Todd felt he could do about it.

In 1819, he moved with his family to Hartford where medical practice was more lucrative. There, fees for visits had been increased from 50 to 75 cents. He quickly became a leading physician in that community, and one night in 1820 at a meeting of the Connecticut Medical Society, he told his colleagues of the work of Pinel. Todd pointed out that in a democracy men's hopes for success are raised high, and that for many the disappointment of not attaining their goals caused insanity. It seemed, therefore, that the community had some responsibility to provide humane care for the insane, and he urged that they consider the needs within their state: "Gentlemen, it is our duty as civilized men to attack this disease. Let us make inquiry and find out how prevalent it is and then establish an institution for its treatment and cure."

His colleagues gave Todd their enthusiastic support. Funds were solicited throughout the state and, in 1824, an institution called the Retreat was opened in Hartford with Eli Todd as physician in chief. The care he provided, "moral management," was based on respect for the individual and the strengths that the person still possessed. Insofar as was possible, each patient's case and the treatment he was to receive were frankly explained to him. Every effort was made to treat the patients as rational beings: "To allow them all the liberty and indulgence compatible with their own safety. . . . To cherish in them the sentiments of self-respect. . . . To occupy their attention, exercise their judgment and ingenuity, and to engage them in useful employments, alternated with amusements."

By 1826, only two years later, the news of Todd's methods and of his amazing success in treating insanity spread. There were a number of important positions offered to him, but Todd refused them all and remained at the Retreat. Nevertheless, his influence was extended by his followers who employed moral management in institutions that were arising in Massachusetts, Vermont, and New Jersey. Probably his most eminent disciple was Samuel Woodward, who became superintendent of the Worcester State Hospital and first president of an organization that was later to become the American Psychiatric Association.

For us, Todd's significance is threefold: he worked for adequate facilities for the treatment of the mentally ill; he offered a psychological explanation of illness and formed therapeutic relationships based on feelings of respect for the patient's competence and dignity as a human being; he considerably weakened the belief that all insanity was incurable. It was the last contribution that had a seriocomic effect, for it soon became fashionable for hospital superintendents to compete with one another in the percentages of patients they claimed to have cured.

By 1830 five states, Virginia, Maryland, Kentucky, South Carolina, and Ohio, had publicly supported hospitals for the mentally ill, and four states, Pennsylvania, Massachusetts, New York, and Connecticut, had private institutions. Yet the general system, or lack of system, persisted that each community should bear the responsibility for the care of its sick. Into jails and alms-houses were herded all those who, for whatever reason, had to be institutionalized. It was this hodgepodge system that Dorothea Dix attacked.

Dorothea Lynde Dix (1802–1887) was born in Hampden, Maine, to a father described as a shiftless religious fanatic and to a mother epitomized as submissive. At about the age of twelve she left them to go to Boston to live with her more well-to-do paternal grandparents, who maintained a proper and Puritanical atmosphere. By the age of fourteen young Miss Dix was gainfully employed as a teacher, and by twenty she was running a school which catered to the daughters of wealthy and prominent Bostonian families. Even at that age she evidenced her concern for the less fortunate by tutoring the children of the poor at her home.

After a few years her health failed, and she became the victim of recurring attacks of tuberculosis. During this period, 1824–1840, she attained some success as a writer of stories and books for children, re-established her school for girls, fell ill once again, and finally became financially independent and able to devote herself to philanthropic activities when she inherited some wealth from her grandmother.

The year 1841 found her teaching Sunday School in a jail in Boston. She was appalled by the neglect and brutality in the prison and by the fact that the mentally ill and retarded were housed among the criminals. Starting with nothing but indignation and a fierce conviction that she was right, she proceeded to virtually terrorize the consciences of government officials.

For over forty years Dorothea Dix traveled from state to state and abroad. Her bearing was quiet, gentle, and dignified, but her tactics were overwhelming. She would arm herself with unshakable facts concerning the quality of the mental health facilities of a particular area, rally public support through the press, and win key legislative spokesmen to her cause by her knowledge, persistence, and dedication. Relentlessly, she preached a gospel of humane treatment and adequate facilities for the retarded, insane, and criminal.

New Jersey was the first state to respond to Dorothea Dix by erecting a hospital for the mentally ill in 1848. In the years that followed, more than thirty state institutions were built or enlarged as a direct result of her efforts. Her work also bore fruit in France, Great Britain, Italy (where she told Pope Pius IX that the insane asylum in Rome was a "scandal and disgrace"), Japan, Austria, Denmark, Holland, Russia, Greece, Sweden, Germany, Norway, Turkey, and Belgium. Seldom in history has a single person catalyzed such widespread reform.

AN APPRAISAL

It is possible to characterize the nineteenth century in terms of a caricature of the attitudes of the Victorian era: prudishness, propriety, and an emphasis on good breeding. From our vantage it is readily seen that these attitudes may be interpreted as attempts to maintain stability in a world whose social order and beliefs were radically changing. Civil unrest and agitation existed in England, as well as in France, Germany, and the United States. The established order, whether democratic or autocratic, was assaulted by demands for justice and continuously reminded of its vulnerability by revolutions and assassinations.

Essentially, the movement was for an amelioration of social conditions on the basis of the dignity and rights of the individual. Its theme was as old as the golden rule, but the popular support it was given was new and historically important. From literature came an evaluation of men and women of all classes as sensitive, passionate, conflicted, and oppressed. From science came the distressing news of empirical findings and concepts that challenged cherished dogmas and traditions. From governments came reforms, not only in order to maintain themselves and because of the practicality and the eventual savings that came from meeting the demands, but also because the demands were recognized as legitimate. Such developments may be considered the roots from which clinical psychology, in all the ways in which it seeks to understand and help individuals, was able to grow.

References

Boring, E. G. *A History of experimental psychology*. New York: Appleton-Century-Crofts, 1950.

Burns, E. M. *Western civilizations: their history & their culture.* New York: Norton, 1947.

Durant, W. *The story of philosophy.* Garden City, N.Y.: Garden City Publishing Co., 1927.

Flugel, J. C. *A hundred years of psychology: 1833–1933.* New York: Macmillan, 1933.

Gauss, C. Rousseau, Jean-Jacques. In A. H. McDannald (Ed.) *The encyclopedia Americana.* Vol. 23. New York: Americana Corp., 1946. Pp. 723–725.

Itard, J. M. G. *The wild boy of Aveyron.* New York: Appleton-Century-Crofts, 1962.

Knoles, G. H. & Snyder, R. K. (Eds.) *Readings in Western civilization.* New York: Lippincott, 1951.

Lewis, N. D. C. *A short history of psychiatric achievement.* New York: Norton, 1941.

Murphy, G. *Historical introduction to modern psychology.* New York: Harcourt, Brace, 1950.

Rousseau, J. J. *Émile; or, education.* New York: Dutton, 1911.

Thorpe, L. P. & Katz, B. *The psychology of abnormal behavior.* New York: Ronald, 1948.

Watson, R. I. *The clinical method in psychology.* New York: Harper, 1951.

Winkler, J. K. & Bromberg, W. *Mind explorers.* New York: Reynal & Hitchcock, 1939.

Zilboorg, G. & Henry, G. W. *A history of medical psychology.* New York: Norton, 1941.

Suggested Readings

These works are helpful to acquaint the reader with those periods not specifically covered in this book.

In order to obtain information about early attitudes toward the mentally ill and the development of psychiatry, see *A history of medical psychology,* by G. Zilboorg & G. W. Henry, New York: Norton, 1941.

An outstanding account of the growth of psychology in general is *A history of experimental psychology,* by E. G. Boring, New York: Appleton-Century-Crofts, 1950.

The mentally ill in America, by A. Deutsch, Garden City, N.Y.: Doubleday, 1937, is particularly valuable for its description of treatment and conditions in mental hospitals during colonial times and through the nineteenth century.

Of interest are Pinel's *A treatise on insanity* and Rush's *Medical inquiries and observations upon the diseases of the mind,* both available in paperback from Hofner Publishing Co. in New York; Rousseau's autobiography, *The confessions of Jean Jacques Rousseau,* in a Modern Library edition, No. 243; and Francis Tiffany's *Life of Dorothea Lynde Dix,* Boston: Houghton, Mifflin, 1892.

2

The Hopeful Psychologists

1890-1899

FOLLOWING ITS SUCCESS in the Franco-Prussian War of 1870, Germany was regarded as the most powerful nation on the Continent. Its status, while based on armed might, was enhanced by the achievements of its scientists and by its outstanding universities. These schools had a long and proud tradition of academic freedom and were further distinguished by their programs of advanced education leading to the Ph.D. degree.

In contrast, the American system of higher education was relatively new, and had begun only recently to offer graduate programs that led to the doctorate in philosophy. Up to the second half of the nineteenth century, this system had been composed mainly of colleges and universities affiliated, at least in some degree, with churches; a liberal arts education was emphasized, and little provision was made for professional degrees or scientific research. We may illustrate this state of affairs by noting that during the early years of the century it was possible to become a physician by simply entering a school for that purpose; accordingly, at that time, the bachelor's degree enjoyed greater prestige than the degree of M.D. because the former immediately denoted a liberal arts schooling while the latter did not. As for the Ph.D. degree, there was no American college which awarded it.

During the second half of the nineteenth century, a movement for academic freedom and reform bore fruit in the establishment of a number of secular colleges. Moreover, major efforts were being made to raise the status and quality of graduate and professional education. Yale, in 1861, was the first university in the United States to give a Ph.D. degree, conferring it upon three, undoubtedly proud, recipients; Harvard became second in 1872 when it announced that it would confer the Ph.D.; and Johns Hopkins, which opened in 1876 as a graduate school, was a leader in requiring its students to take courses in sciences and to conduct independent research. Therefore, although it was still necessary for many Americans to study in Europe if they sought advanced knowledge in their fields, a determined attempt was being made by American educators to emulate the German model and to institute research programs leading to the Ph.D.

This striving for academic excellence and recognition was a manifestation of the developing maturity of the United States. By 1890, the population of the country was 63 million and growing. The number of states in the Union had been increased in the period from 1889 to 1899 by the admission of Idaho, Montana, North Dakota, South Dakota, Utah, Washington, and Wyoming. Moreover, like the two leading nations of Europe, Great Britain and Germany, the United States was consolidating its position as an industrial power and continuing its scientific advances and social reforms.

Therefore, a feeling of self-awareness and a sense of national identity and purpose imbued the American people. They took pride in their numbers, their inventiveness, their national wealth, and the ability of their country to play a forceful role in world affairs. The Spanish-American War in 1898 was an expression of that awareness and of the vigor, boldness, and self-confidence of the American people. Ostensibly, the war was provoked by objections to the cruelties of the Spaniards in dealing with their Cuban subjects. At its conclusion, despite the altruistic nature of its intervention, the United States found itself in possession of Cuba, Puerto Rico, Guam, and the Philippine and Hawaiian Islands. Suddenly the United States had become a Caribbean power, a Pacific power, an Asiatic power, and a colonial power. Americans could no longer be ignored by other nations, though they could be considered brash and impudent.

American psychologists shared in the energy, enthusiasm, practicality, and optimism of their countrymen. The science of psychology they helped to form was infused with hope and an impatience to translate its knowledge into benefits to mankind. There was a hunger for recognition and status due largely to the very newness of psychology as an independent science and the consequent paucity of psychologists. Being one of a small group, each early psychologist was *ipso facto* a leader who was gambling on his ability to carve out a successful professional career in an untried field.

NORMAL PERSONALITY FUNCTIONING

An indication of the youthfulness of the science of psychology in 1892 may be gained from a survey of its basic treatises, for they were not text-books in the contemporary sense. Rest assured, our task is hardly overwhelming. In German, there would be Wundt's *Grundzüge der physiologischen Psychologie* (1873–1874); in English, there would be Ladd's *Elements of Physiological Psychology* (1887), and the delightful volumes by William James, *The Principles of Psychology* (1890). If given a choice, we would do well to select as a "must" for reading the text by James, the only one of the three to enjoy popularity in its time and a witty, brilliant, and highly stimulating work even today.

The author, William James (1842–1910), was the first-born of an erudite and intellectually provocative family. His grandfather, "Old Billy" James, came to the United States from Ireland in 1789. Through thrift, industry, and shrewdness, he amassed a fortune as a merchant and banker and gave his children a legacy of wealth and the problem of how to justify their living on it. His father, Henry, seemed to handle the problem by embracing socialistic ideas and the passion of the day for reform.

Through the James' household swirled a continuing parade of thinkers, and no thought, whether uttered by guests or family, eluded critical scrutiny. According to many of the biographers of James, an affectionate spirit pervaded these intellectual combats, rendering them psychologically harmless. Nevertheless, it is difficult to believe that being subjected to constant criticism could fail to elicit some feelings of inadequacy. While it is probable that many factors were involved in his troubles, certainly the subsequent history of William James indicates that he did not escape from the family arena unscarred.

At first the life of an artist beckoned to James. He was financially comfortable, and enjoyed the beer and the good comradeship of his fellow art students. However, he was displeased by his paintings and discouraged by his progress. So, at the age of about twenty, he decided to become a scientist. He enrolled in the Lawrence Scientific School at Harvard, studying chemistry under Charles W. Eliot and physiology under Jeffries Wyman. After two years he entered Harvard Medical School and seemed well on the way to accomplishment and stability. But prior to the completion of his studies, he began to experience feelings of despair, from which he sought to escape by joining an expedition to Brazil.

This expedition was organized under the leadership of the naturalist Louis Agassiz. Its purpose was to collect zoological specimens in the jungles of the Amazon, but James' interest in that was secondary, of course, to his interest in collecting himself. In 1865, they set sail. Accompanying the intrepid scientists was Bishop Alonzo Potter, who went along to insure that God would not be forgotten amid all the talk of theories of evolution. Once the expedition got down to work, Agassiz began to openly torture himself with the conflict between his religious and scientific principles. James, noting this, asserted he was only amused and denied any personal involvement in metaphysical problems. Quite the contrary, he claimed to be so impressed by the primitive simplicity and abundance of nature that "The idea of people . . . studying themselves into fevers, going mad about religion, philosophy, and such, seems almost incredible to me."

Evidently his trip to Brazil had been personally a success, and upon his return in 1866 James went back to medical school. He was able to remain for a year before once again being overcome by depression. Tormented by thoughts of suicide, he sought relief through another change of surroundings. The next year and a half were spent in Germany, supposedly to improve his understanding of the German language and to do advanced work in physiology. Little was accomplished either intellectually or emotionally. Hoping to pull himself out of his depression, he re-entered medical school and managed to obtain his degree in 1869. However he could not bring himself to practice as a physician.

The next three years found James a chronic invalid drenched in pessimism and gloom. His own intense sufferings during this period were to make him acutely sensitive and sympathetic to those who were mentally ill. As for himself, he proceeded in the only way he knew to cope with his depression: he read and read and read in the chance that somewhere there might be something that would help him alleviate his unhappiness. Then in 1870 he came across the writings of the French philosopher Charles Renouvier (1818–1903). Man, according to Renouvier, has liberty as his fundamental characteristic: what a man believes is what he *chooses* to believe; a person may alter his beliefs by an exercise of his will.

James regarded his encounter with the writings of Renouvier as a turning point in his life. He determined to believe in free will, and decided that henceforth he would make efforts to replace his depression with thoughts of becoming active, adventurous, and hopefully expectant. Apparently this was no easy process for it was not until two years later, in 1872, that he was appointed an instructor in physiology at Harvard; he had been torn between physiology and philosophy as his academic career but feelings of inadequacy led him toward the former since he felt it would be less demanding.

By 1875, James had established a "room for demonstrational experiments," a forerunner of Wundt's laboratory, and was made assistant professor of physiology. His teaching was vigorous and successful; he was wooing the future Mrs. James; he was writing; he was happy. In 1878, he married, and optimistically contracted to complete the writing of a book on psychology within two years. He underwent a not uncommon experience among authors; the two years stretched to twelve, and the writing of the free-flowing *Principles of Psychology* became a labor that tested James' determination to the fullest. For one special diversion he turned to psychic research, and at every opportunity engaged in reading.

His title was changed to Professor of Psychology in 1889. The following year the *Principles* was published. It won surprising, almost startling approval from the public, who rejoiced in its vividness and clarity. Fellow psychologists were not so impressed. Some felt it was too readable to be a scientific text. G. Stanley Hall, psychologist and president of Clark University, was critical because the *Principles* contained nothing about genetic psychology and, in general, had neglected the exposition of facts in favor of speculations. Wundt's appraisal was a kindly, back-handed compliment: "It is literature, it is beautiful, but it is not psychology."

James was hurt by these criticisms, but he had some strong opinions of his own, particularly since he believed that it was Wundt and his breed who by their narrow concept of psychology threatened to destroy it. He felt that their psychophysical, "microscopic" experimentation was cold, worthless, unfeeling, and worse, dull: "This method taxes patience to the utmost and could hardly have arisen in a country whose natives could be *bored.*"

For James, psychology was the "Science of Mental Life." With that definition there was no disagreement between James and the majority of other psychologists. However, there was a quick parting of the ways. James believed that a major characteristic of thought or consciousness was that it flowed in a continuing stream. Unlike the Wundtians who tried to study mental states and to break them down into elements, James asserted that by fragmenting and analyzing this stream, we lose sight of and do violence to its essential wholeness. In support of his assertion, he pointed out four characteristics of the stream of thought:

1. It is always changing. "No state once gone can recur and be identical with what it was before." By that James meant that the cumulative experiences of the person make unique and different what superficially appear to be identical situations. No thought, no state of consciousness, is exactly the same as any other. The second time we see a rose is not the same as the first or the third or the fourth. We see it with a new freshness or a new boredom, with memories of other roses on other days, with a new attention to detail or a new disinterest. Fundamentally, the fact that our brains constantly undergo modifications makes it physiologically impossible for one idea ever to be exactly the same as another.

2. It is personally owned. We recognize our thoughts to be *our* thoughts. We do not feel that what we are thinking has been put into our heads by someone or something else. They are our thoughts and we acknowledge them to be so. There is a feeling of personal familiarity and intimacy with our own ideas so that we do not confuse the thoughts of someone else with our own. Even when the thoughts of two people are highly similar, there is only a recognition of agreement and not a feeling of identity or a confusion that one person has somehow exchanged or transmitted his thoughts to another.

3. It is sensibly continuous. When we introspect, we can see that we experience our thoughts as a flow even though there may actually have occurred gaps in time or momentary interruptions. Upon awakening from sleep we quickly become aware of our identity and the flowing of our ideas. Shocks and interruptions, therefore, are not experienced as breaks in the stream but are themselves experienced as part of the stream. James illustrated this characteristic in this way: "The transition between the thought of one object and the thought of another is no more a break in the *thought* than a joint in a bamboo is a break in the wood. It is a part of the *consciousness* as much as the joint is a part of the *bamboo*."

4. It is selective and discriminating. Of all the objects before us we ignore most. We are interested in some parts and not others and because of our habits of attention we form our own individualized world. Our fundamental distinction, and one which is unique for each of us, is based on what is "me" and "not-me." From this distinction it is not normally possible for us to escape. As James put it: "No mind can take the same interest in his neighbor's *me* as in his own."

But of what is this *me* composed? James' answer was that it was the sum total of all that a person could call his own. Analyzing further, James stated that the *me* or Empirical Self was composed of three Selves: first, the Material Self, which consists of the person's body, clothing, family, home, and property. Second, the Social Self, which is the recognition we receive from others. James pointed out that we have different Social Selves (psychologists today might use the term *roles*) with different individuals and different groups of individuals, since with each set we must conform to different requirements of conduct: "We do not show ourselves to our children as to our club-companions, to our customers as to the laborers we employ, to our own masters and employers as to our intimate friends." Third, the Spiritual Self, which is the person's psychic faculties and dispositions, his conscience or morality, his will.

James went on to discuss conflict and rivalry between the Selves, but it was depicted as a gentlemanly, polite, rational conflict. The way he described it, a person simply could not be everything to all people or fulfill all his potentialities or interests. Instead he has to decide to be one thing or another and more or less to suppress the rest. If a man wished to be a lady-killer, he obviously could not be a saint and therefore, assuming he has been sensible about the matter, is not troubled by his lack of certain virtues. However, he *would* be troubled, his self-esteem would suffer, if his achievements do not measure up to his pretentions. To restore his self-esteem he might simply choose to win greater successes in the future or to abandon some of his pretentions. As far as James was concerned it is the giving up of pretentions that is often a boon for mankind and ordinarily a more practical course of action; he observed that often what people wish to be is unrealistic or foolishly based on vanity, and that they would be much happier if they could turn away from chasing these illusions. After all, had he not found happiness by lowering his aspirations and taking the glory road through physiology instead of philosophy? "Our self-feeling is in our power," he asserted, primarily because we can renounce our conceits, and so need not belittle ourselves for failing to live up to them.

Having discussed the *Me,* James turned to the I, or Ego. The Ego was considered by James to be the thinker or knower, and he tortured himself and the reader with his lengthy efforts to reason out what the Ego is. To be brief, James believed that what is involved in the Ego is the individual's sense of personal identity and continuity. He decided that this sense of identity is fundamentally rooted in the integrity of the person's body and how the body is regarded and treated by others. In the final analysis, he viewed the Ego as *a thought* which differed from moment to moment but which appropriated its preceding thought which had appropriated *its* preceding thought, and so on.

As we reflect upon the ideas of William James, we see early expressions of what were shortly to become areas of considerable interest in psychology: Gestalt psychology, the theory of self in relation to personality, role theory, ego psychology. We also note James' predilection to anchor psychology to biology and physiology rather than to philosophy, a position that should not surprise us since we know of James' early training as a physician and physiologist and his intention that the *Principles* be regarded as a scientific treatise.

Further, it is apparent that his emphasis is on adult functioning, with little attention paid to developmental changes. His approach was essentially descriptive. James started with a mind, to a large extent his mind, and proceeded to analyze it introspectively (in the popular, nontechnical sense of the term). In his own life, through what he believed was sheer will power, he had been able to free himself from severe feelings of depression and to move into highly productive activities. Thus James stressed in his psychology the importance of rational choice and volition, the freedom of a person to act and improve himself.

Nevertheless, James was aware of the unconscious, and devoted considerable space to its exposition. The term itself had been introduced recently by Pierre Janet, but mainly in the sense of "automatic"—to describe behavior, such as handwriting, that is produced without awareness by the individual of its content or the fact that he is performing the act. However, long before Janet, men were familiar with the concept and had realized that some psychological functioning is not conscious. Isaac, the Abbot of Stella, toward the end of the twelfth century pointed out that not all that a man knows remains always directly accessible to awareness. Spinoza, in the seventeenth century, argued that man's motives and emotions are often irrational and operate without his knowledge, leading to self-deception. Johann Herbart in the early nineteenth century conceived of ideas conflicting and competing with one another for a place in consciousness: those ideas that were inhibited, or passed below the threshold or *limen of consciousness,* were assumed to have a tendency to strive to come back. Schopenhauer, Leibnitz, and von Hartmann had also called attention to unconscious functioning. Yet in the 1890's the unconscious was still regarded as a somewhat speculative and enigmatic concept, and a process that was certainly less significant than consciousness.

Therefore we find James presenting the following evidence for recognizing the existence of the unconscious: the forgetting of dreams and momentary thoughts which must be stored somewhere in the mind since they often can be recalled; amnesia for events that occur in somnambulism; the ability of people to awaken themselves from sleep at a predetermined time; the demonstrations of posthypnotic suggestion and of suggestions carried out automatically among persons afflicted with hysteria.

Although these ideas of James represented an avant-garde position, we should note that he still held proudly to what we would consider to be some of the misconceptions of his time. The phrenology of Gall and Spurzheim, which was quite popular in the United States and which he conceded was unsatisfactory according to scientific standards, was nevertheless akin to physiognomy, which he believed did have empirical or clinical value: "A hook nose and a firm jaw are signs of practical energy. . . . Prominent eye is a sign of power over language and a bullneck is a sign of sensuality." And of course James is noted for his long list of instincts, which despite the incident in the Garden of Eden included even modesty, because he believed that man had more instincts than any other animal.

With publication of the *Principles* James had become one of the leaders of psychology. Yet now he showed signs of wishing to withdraw from the field. He claimed the subject no longer interested him and that the writing of the volumes had been an ordeal. His flowing, conversational style disguised the fact that ". . . (I) forge it all with blood and sweat, and groans and lamentations to heaven, and vows that I will never start to write anything again." Furthermore, he had been deeply wounded by the criticisms of his book and its "children of my brain," his ideas. Tolerance for the ideas of others was an outstanding characteristic of James, and he strongly believed that it was important for his colleagues to be more flexible and conciliatory, characteristics which he probably hoped they might well develop in their dealings with him.

In preparation for his own future, James was recommending the appointment at Harvard of Hugo Münsterberg (1836–1916), a young German experimental psychologist who had attracted his sympathetic attention. Münsterberg had conducted some original studies that had been criticized —all too severely in James' opinion—by Titchener and G. E. Müller. His plan was by means of some academic maneuvering to transfer his position as professor of psychology to Münsterberg and then obtain for himself a position in philosophy.

For financial reasons, James agreed to write *Psychology: Briefer Course,* an abridgement of the nearly 1,400 pages of the *Principles* to a more suitable length for use as a text. He found it a distasteful business and complained to his publisher, ". . . I think I have produced a tome of pedagogic classic which will enrich both you and me, if not the student's mind." The *Briefer Course* was published in 1892 and was an immediate success; that same year Münsterberg arrived at Harvard.

In 1897, James' title was changed to professor of philosophy. Despite this change in emphasis of his interests, his influence continued to be exerted on the field of psychology through all who read the *Principles* and were caught up by his vigor, expansiveness, optimism, and trenchant and engaging style.

DIAGNOSTIC TECHNIQUES

Although James had been disappointed by the psychology of the 1890's, evaluating it as not yet a science but only the hope of one, there were already some promising developments in the field. One of these, diagnostic techniques, can be introduced by that old story about the Frenchman who, hearing it said that there is little difference between a man and a woman, exclaimed, *"Vive la différence!"* Psychologists during the end of the nineteenth century were also interested in differences, specifically those differences that exist among individuals in their mental functioning.

As we might now expect, the problem was old but the scope and energy with which it was being attacked were new. Plato (427–347 B.C.) had recommended that tests of military aptitude be devised and administered to aid in the proper assignment of soldiers to tasks for which they were best suited. However, it was not until the beginning of the nineteenth century that scientists turned their attention to the serious study of the question of individual differences.

Strangely enough it was in astronomy that the first systematic measures of individual differences occurred. In 1816, Friedrich Bessel (1784–1846), the astronomer at Königsberg, read in the *Zeitschrift für Astronomie* that D.

Kinnebrook had been dismissed from his job at Greenwich observatory in England. The reason for his dismissal was that it had been Kinnebrook's misfortune to observe repeatedly the times of stellar transits almost a second later than his superior, Nevil Maskelyne, who was the Astronomer Royal. Rather than simply accept the opinion that Kinnebrook was incompetent, Bessel investigated and found large differences between persons in their observations of the times of stellar transits. Data were amassed and such characteristic differences as were found between two observers were recognized as due to a "personal equation" for each observer. Bessel's work stimulated the interest of other astronomers and led eventually to experimentation on reaction times in psychology.

The question of individual differences had more humanistic implications for Sir Francis Galton (1822–1911). He was interested in measuring the mental and physical characteristics of the average Englishman in order to improve the British race. A man of boundless energy, curiosity, and intellectual brilliance, Galton's wealth and social position would have permitted him to lead a life of aristocratic ease. However, his father, alert to the social changes threatening the upper classes of England, put his faith and that of his children in the future of science, while taking his money out of the family real estate and putting it to work in industry.

Galton's youth was very similar to that of William James. His home life provided intense intellectual stimulation; his medical education was also interrupted by foreign travel to alleviate feelings of fear and "boredom"; and his resumption of college was followed by periods of restlessness and depression. Unlike James, Galton never completed his medical education, but, being independently wealthy, he plunged into whatever interested him. He studied geography, anthropology, and meteorology, but these were no mere whims; in all these pursuits he was guided by a concern for practical applications of knowledge.

It was not until he was in his forties that Galton's interests in human evolution brought him into areas of research that would justify psychologists in claiming him for a colleague. He had collected a mass of assorted data on all the aristocrats, professional men, and university personnel he could corner as subjects. These data were analyzed statistically using the principles of probability and of the normal curve of distribution of individual differences; the former had been developed by Karl Gauss and Pierre Laplace, while the latter had been formulated by Lambert Quetelet in 1846. The results were published by Galton in 1869, in his book *Hereditary Genius: English Men of Science*. His conclusions were that bright parents tend to have bright children and that parents with good physiques pass on their good physiques to their offspring. Therefore, he suggested, a better race of human beings could be developed by carefully selecting those who are best fitted to receive an education and to become parents. Obviously, measurements and techniques for obtaining measurements were a pressing need in order to identify these individuals, and for this purpose Galton established an anthropometric laboratory at the Health Exhibition of the International Exhibition of 1884.

Galton had observed that idiots were less able than normals to discriminate differences between various weights and between various intensities of pain, heat, and cold. So, he reasoned, it should be possible to differentiate between persons of varying intelligence by using tests of sensory capacity. He also thought there might be significance in individual differences in height, both standing and sitting; weight; arm span; force of blow; breathing power; reaction time; color sense; visual and auditory acuity; and strength to pull a weight and squeeze a spring. For a slight and unprofitable threepenny fee, Galton would measure these variables and provide the person with a card containing his "test" results. When the Exhibition closed in 1885, Galton obtained permission to move his laboratory to a room in the Science Galleries of the South Kensington Museum.

Galton maintained this laboratory for about six years, and during its existence obtained measures from 9,337 persons, including 35 pairs of identical twins, 783 brothers, and 150 families. Not very much came of all these data, for before they were fully evaluated he became sidetracked by his new interest in fingerprints.

At first Galton hoped that fingerprints might be of great anthropological significance. He examined "large numbers" of persons of what were thought to be different races: Basques, East Indians, red Indians, Negroes, Jews, and Chinese. Also he examined fingerprints from groups of different interests and personalities: students of art, students of science, Quakers, distinguished persons, and idiots at Earlswood Asylum. In no group did he find any characteristic fingerprint pattern. Although disappointed, Galton did recognize the potential importance of fingerprints as a means of individual identification and succeeded in establishing three facts that commended them for use in criminal and other investigations. One, the fingerprint pattern remains constant throughout life, barring scarification. Two, the patterns exist in enormous variety. Three, they can be classified so that when submitted to an expert, it is possible to tell by reference whether a similar set has already been recorded.

Galton's versatility bore fruit in areas other than the use of whirls and loops in fingerprint identification. From his endless, energetic rushing from one interest to another came composite photography, systems for describing weather, the rudimentary form of what is now termed the correlation coefficient, the Galton whistle, the ticker tape, the questionnaire method, the discovery of eidetic imagery, the use of free association to demonstrate the significance of childhood memories upon adulthood, the development of percentile values, and perhaps his greatest contribution, the use of statistical methods in scientific investigation. "The greatest human being I have ever known," said James McKeen Cattell about Francis Galton.

James McKeen Cattell (1860–1944) graduated from Lafayette College in 1880. He was a brash, aggressive man who typified the European conception of the American. Armed with his B.S., he studied at Göttingen and Leipzig. He then returned to the United States for a year at Johns Hopkins, where he spent a semester as an inadvertent student of G. Stanley Hall. In 1883, Cattell made a triumphant return to Leipzig and virtually hired himself as Wundt's assistant. Seemingly cowed by Cattell's *ganz amerikanisch* behavior, Wundt allowed his assistant to do his doctoral dissertation on individual differences in reaction times.

After receiving his doctorate in 1886, Cattell taught for a year at the University of Pennsylvania, and spent part of the following year as a lecturer at Cambridge University. While at Cambridge, he met Galton and was immediately impressed. The similarity of their interests and views, not only with respect to individual differences but also on eugenics, drew Cattell to Galton. Perhaps, it was an instance of what Emerson had in mind when he wrote, "In every work of genius we recognize our own rejected thoughts. They come back to us with a certain alienated majesty."

Cattell returned to the University of Pennsylvania in 1888, and founded the third psychological laboratory in the United States. (The first, actually less a laboratory for research than a space to be used to demonstrate techniques and principles to students, was James' room at Harvard in 1875; the second laboratory was founded by Hall at Johns Hopkins in 1883.) Within a year, Cattell became the first professor of psychology at Pennsylvania.

In 1890, Cattell introduced the term "mental tests" in an article entitled "Mental Tests and Measurements." In that paper he insisted that psychology must rest on a foundation of measurement and experimentation. Through the use of mental tests, Cattell predicted, it would be possible to discover the constancy of mental processes, their interdependence, and their variation under different circumstances. He foresaw practical applications of the tests in the selection of people for training and as indicators of disease. However, his immediate concern was to propose a battery of ten tests which could be adopted and administered in a standardized manner so that the results from different investigators could be compared.

From a list of fifty tests Cattell nominated the following ten for approval: Dynamometer Pressure; Rate of Movement (speed to move an arm a specified distance); Sensation-areas (two-point discrimination); Least Noticeable Difference in Weight; Reaction-time for Sound; Time for Naming Colors; Bi-section of a 50cm. line; Judgment of Ten Seconds

Time; Number of Letters remembered on once Hearing. In a footnote to the article, he expressed the hope that Galton would approve of his suggestions.

Galton did not approve of them, and in an addendum to that same article criticized Cattell for neglecting to mention the importance of comparing the test results with an independent measure of the same variables. (Cattell had stressed reliability; Galton was correctly, though rather inappropriately, reminding him of test validity.) As if to add to his reservations, he proposed several new tests of his own for inclusion in the model battery. All of which must have been most distressing to Cattell, who was eager to obtain some agreement on this matter of standardization.

The need for agreement was felt to be urgent because it was clear that these tests could be put to immediate, practical use. One objective they could serve was in distinguishing between the psychotic and feeble-minded. The distinction between these two groups had been made by Jean Esquirol in 1838, but had only become significant after reformers had campaigned successfully to provide separate institutions for the mentally ill and retarded. It then became necessary to provide some objective means for the identification of the intellectually subnormal. A similar need was experienced in educational circles, where the selection of children for newly acquired special pedagogical programs and schools could not in good conscience be satisfactorily made on the basis of subjective impressions and appraisals.

As we know, there had been a number of attempts to devise tests that would discriminate between various levels of intelligence. But besides the efforts in this direction of Galton and Cattell there were those of A. Oehrn, a student of the psychiatrist Emil Kraepelin, who constructed a set of tests in 1889. There was also Joseph Jastrow's set of fifteen tests which he developed in 1890 and demonstrated at the Columbian Exposition in Chicago in 1893, and there was Münsterberg's set of fourteen tests for school children, in 1891. Unfortunately, whenever the matter of validity was considered, the picture became less encouraging. Franz Boas, at Clark University, in 1891 used simple sensory-motor tests with about 1500 school children. He checked for validity by comparing his findings with teachers' estimates of the children's "intellectual acuteness." His results were probably not very promising, since they were never fully published.

J. A. Gilbert, at Yale University, tested approximately 1200 school children in New Haven. On only two tests, rate of tapping and judgment of length of distances, were the children who were evaluated as "bright" by their teachers superior to their supposedly dull classmates. Evidently some of these simple sensory-motor tests distinguished between children who were quite different in intelligence, but were far from satisfactory in forming valid discriminations among children who were somewhere in between. An understandable lack of enthusiasm for mental testing was being generated; although the hope still prevailed that mental tests would eventually be devised that would meet the requirements of criterion predictability as well as reliability.

Fostering this hope were alternative suggestions that intelligence could be reliably and validly measured by tests of complex psychological processes. A quite neglected suggestion of this sort had at one time been made by Charles Bonnet in the eighteenth century. He proposed that minds could be ordered and measured on the basis of the number of correct conclusions that they are able to draw from the same principle. Hermann Ebbinghaus, who had a much greater influence on the course of psychology than Bonnet, thought that an important characteristic of intelligence is the ability to combine or organize words into a meaningful whole. In 1897 he reported promising results in differentiating between students who were grouped by scholastic standing into good, average, or poor; the technique he used that was most discriminating was a sentence "completion method," which he originated. This test required the child to complete sentences in a story by supplying missing words or syllables. Items similar in structure to those employed by Ebbinghaus are still found on intelligence scales and are looked upon with favor by many teachers when constructing final examinations.

Münsterberg, Kraepelin, and Alfred Binet and Victor Henri were also advocating tests of complex psychological functions, such as reading aloud, fatigability, and suggestability. Cattell, who had moved to Columbia University in 1891, was, of course, aware of these suggestions. Nevertheless at Columbia, he and Farrand persisted in making test measurements of simpler functions trusting that they might be able to find some significant relationship between their measures and grades of students in their freshman, sophomore, and senior years.

In 1896, Cattell and Livingston Farrand dismissed the suggestions of Münsterberg, Binet, and Henri on the grounds that with complex processes ". . . we find it difficult to measure definitely a definite thing." Instead, they seemed to favor more objective and easily measured functions, whether or not these functions had any demonstrable relation to what they were trying to measure. Mental testing in the United States of the 1890's was rapidly doing away with itself by its dogged insistence upon pursuing an illusion of scientific precision.

DIAGNOSTIC FORMULATIONS

From the middle of the nineteenth century, psychiatry was dominated by the schools of Germany and France. Generally, the French took the lead in the study of the neuroses, while the Germans were ahead in the classifi-

32 *Clinical Psychology*

cation of the psychoses. W. Griesinger (1817–1868), a leading German psychiatrist, insisted that mental diseases were diseases of the brain caused by physiological disturbances. Accordingly, in order for a diagnosis to be valid, the physiological cause of the disorder had to be specified. The fact that he was able to have such a profound influence upon his contemporaries was a reflection of a general reaction against romanticism and philosophical speculations in science, for the views of Griesinger persisted and reverberated after his death and helped turn Germany toward somatic and away from psychological explanations.

Considerable interest in psychiatry was manifested, therefore, in exogenous psychoses, or mental illness due to poisons or infections. Morphine addiction was known. Sergei Korsakov was studying the effects of alcoholism. Karl Wernicke was noting the characteristics of the aphasias. Richard Krafft-Ebing's experiments were demonstrating that paresis or general paralysis was caused by syphilis, which was particularly significant support for the position that psychological symptoms have an organic cause.

A vast amount of energy and ingenuity was being expended in devising labels and classification systems for psychiatric illnesses. Karl Kahlbaum wrote of neophrenias, enphrenias, paraphrenias, and dysphrenias. Heinrich Schüle distinguished allopathic and deuteropathic conditions, hereditary neuroses, and cerebropsychoses and cerebropsychopathies. Wernicke spoke of akinetic, hyperkinetic, and parakinetic motility, and also of allopsychosis, somatopsychosis, and autopsychosis. A major and all too easily attained goal for many psychiatrists was to invent their own new nomenclature. Somewhere behind the terminology stood the patient, but exactly where no one knew or apparently much cared.
no one knew or apparently much cared.

Emil Kraepelin (1855–1926) was probably the leading psychiatrist of this period. Though pleasant and warm personally, he remained professionally detached from his patients, whom he viewed as symptom complexes. He had studied for a time under Wundt (which makes clearer his interest in mental testing referred to in the preceding section) and used experimental techniques to investigate the effects of drugs, alcohol, and fatigue upon psychological functioning. His textbook on psychiatry was first published in 1883 and came to full flower with the fifth and sixth editions in 1896 and 1899.

Kraepelin divided mental diseases into those caused by external conditions (exogenous), which he considered curable, and those caused by inherent, constitutional factors (endogenous), which he regarded as incurable. His major assumption was that the outcome and course of mental disease was predetermined, that patients would recover or remain ill according to the natural law governing their particular condition. It was the natural law that he felt should be the object of psychiatric investigation, and not the idiosyncracies or personality of the individual patient. Perhaps an example will make this more clear. From the standpoint of knowledge today the disease syphilis usually exhibits the following course: a sore appears at the point of infection; two or four months later a copper-colored rash is evidenced; there is a symptom-free period of from ten to thirty years during which the spirochetes attack some organ of the body; and then symptoms reappear in the form of blindness, heart disorder, or mental illness (paresis). It was this kind of information that Kraepelin sought to obtain for each psychiatric disturbance.

Significantly, Kraepelin classified among the endogenous illnesses dementia praecox, a term introduced by B. A. Morel in 1860 to describe a form of mental and emotional deterioration that had its onset around the time of puberty. The meaning of the term was very different for Kraepelin than it had been for Morel. By "praecox" Kraepelin referred to early deterioration following the onset of the disease rather than its occurrence during an early period in the life span. Symptomatology consisted of hallucinations, delusions, incongruous emotions, and progressive deterioration in the presence of a relatively intact sensorium.

Hebephrenic and catatonic forms of dementia praecox were specified: the terms having been originated, respectively, by Evald Hecker in 1871 and Kahlbaum in 1874. Organic changes in the brain were viewed by Kraepelin as the cause of the disease; the illness itself was regarded as incurable. Paranoia was considered a distinct endogenous illness with its delusional system unshakable and permanent. Among the exogenous illnesses, manic-depressive psychosis and involutional melancholia were categorized as separate diseases with favorable prognoses.

The Kraepelinian system came under considerable attack, particularly since even Kraepelin admitted that 13 percent of the patients diagnosed as dementia praecox recovered without any apparent defects. Nevertheless, his classifications exerted a tremendous influence upon subsequent psychiatric nosologies and upon therapeutic attitudes—complacency toward manic-depressive psychoses, since the patients were expected to get well anyway, and futility and resignation toward dementia praecox, since deterioration of the patient was anticipated.

With regard to the neuroses, the prevalent attitude of physicians toward hysteria was that it was an illness peculiar to women and more than likely a devious method by which they sought to gain sympathetic attention. The reason for believing that this disorder was confined to women had a long and honorable tradition; Hippocrates (460–357 B.C.) had recognized hysteria as a disease entity and viewed it as caused by the uterus wandering about the female's body. It is a measure of the progress of medicine in this area that some 2400 years later, in 1882, Charcot attributed convulsions and iliac pain in hysterics to compression of an ovary.

Jean Martin Charcot (1825–1893), the brilliant French neurologist, is of course better known for his teaching at the Salpêtrière than for his ovarian hypothesis. Physicians flocked from all over Europe to see "The Master" in action at that first center of postgraduate psychiatric education. They were rarely disappointed, for Charcot was in his element when using a dramatic cast of hysterics to stage a production that was both instructive and startling. His aides would bring in carefully prepared hysterical patients who could fall into a deep hypnotic trance at his mere glance. Then Charcot would produce in these hypnotized patients the symptoms of hysteria—anaesthesias, falling fits, crying spells, glassy-eyed trances, and paralyses. The audience gave Charcot its rapt attention and Charcot gave his colleagues a new appreciation of, and respect for, this neurosis.

It was Charcot's belief that what Friedrich Anton Mesmer called animal magnetism, or what James Braid called hypnotism, was a condition peculiar to hysterics. After suffering some lapse in logic, he concluded that because he could produce all the symptoms of hysteria in hypnotized patients, only hysterics could be hypnotized and that hypnosis itself was a phenomenon of the disease. Therefore Charcot regarded hypnosis as *the* method of choice for investigating predispositions to hysterical disorders. One might say that Charcot's dictum would have been: No diagnosis of hysteria is possible unless the patient can be hypnotized, and then it is mandatory.

When investigating hypnosis, in short, Charcot thought that he was investigating hysteria. The three stages of hypnosis that he distinguished, lethargy (a drowsiness), catalepsy (loss of consciousness and muscular rigidity), and somnambulism (able to carry out complex commands with eyes open but in a sleeplike state), were regarded as fixed phases through which the patient had to pass. Coming to the right conclusion for the wrong reason, Charcot pointed out that since males could also be hypnotized, hysteria was not confined to women.

Charcot's ideas were subjected to censure from all sides. His more conservative colleagues scorned the notion that men could have hysteria, largely because the term had come from the Greek word for uterus and therefore men, obviously, are not equipped for the illness. More serious criticisms came from Nancy, in northeast France, where hypnosis and hysteria were also being studied by the physicians A. A. Liébeault (1823–1904) and his pupil Hippolyte Bernheim (1837–1919). They believed that hypnotism was not pathological but was induced by mental suggestions from the physician to his patient. In 1886, Bernheim hurled down a challenge at the Paris school of Charcot.

The phenomena observed at the Salpêtrière were artificial, Bernheim contended, the result of the hypnotizer's suggestions and were not in the nature of the disease. Moreover, he claimed that he had been able to produce hysterical symptoms by simply suggesting them to patients while they were in a waking state; further, that almost any person could be hypnotized; and that virtually everyone was, more or less, suggestible. It was Bernheim's conclusion that the symptoms of hysteria were largely attributable to the patient's suggestibility; the patients "create their symptoms at will." With the exception of this conclusion, it was, in a way, Bernheim's misfortune that he was demonstrably correct in his assertions. Being so quickly accepted he could not found a school of thought upon them.

Charcot was greatly disappointed to see the final performance of his career reviewed unfavorably. The methodical, autocratic, meticulous exhibitionist had enriched, and in the opinions of many had fathered, neurology with his astute observations on locomotor ataxia and multiple sclerosis. He had discovered an artery in the brain whose rupture could produce paralytic strokes. Now, it seemed to him, these years of his life devoted to hypnosis and hysteria would serve only as a comic reminder to posterity that even a person of his attainments could be wrong.

Charcot's successor at the Salpêtrière was his pupil Pierre Janet (1859–1947). It will be recalled that by 1890 some of Janet's work with hysterics had drawn the approving attention of William James. Janet also had rejected Charcot's idea that hypnosis was only to be found in hysterics. He discovered, through carefully re-examining the histories of his patients, that a large number had suffered some emotional shock preceding the onset of their illness. The memories of these shocks seemed to have been forgotten by the patients and must, he decided, have been pushed into the unconscious part of their minds. At this early stage of his career Janet concluded that the forgetting represented an abnormal and distinctive weakness in the personality of the hysteric, since the normal person was thought to have experiences much more fully integrated and accessible to consciousness.

According to Janet, then, the personality of the hysteric is a split personality. One portion of it operates automatically or unconsciously as a secondary personage which has invaded and taken over parts of the primary personality.

Similar ideas were published by Janet's compatriot Alfred Binet in 1890. Binet, too, thought that in hysterics there was a "double consciousness"—a second Ego which could apprehend impressions and excite ideas in the field of the main personality ". . . and the principal Ego of the 'subject' in no wise has consciousness of it." But he had conducted a study in which he had observed hysterical phenomena, particularly automatic movements, in his normal subjects. While the title of this article boldly proclaimed that normal people also have a double consciousness, Binet was cautious in the remainder of his report, stayed close to his own data, and only tentatively proposed extending the concept beyond hysterics.

By 1892, Janet was still arguing that hysteria was a splitting of the personality, but he had modified his terminology to bring the clinical and academic areas of psychology together with a unifying set of concepts: the splitting represented a concentration of the field of consciousness on one system of ideas and a retraction of consciousness from others. However, he did not modify his stand that hysteria was the inevitable manifestation and result of a hereditary handicap and of a kind of "degeneracy."

In the meantime, Bernheim continued to emphasize and expand upon his belief in the suggestibility of both normal and abnormal individuals. He believed that a broad range of behavior was due to suggestions and autosuggestions that might not be readily apparent to an observer or to the person performing the act. On the one hand, he felt that the label "hysteria" should be restricted to cases with convulsive symptoms; on the other hand, he conceived of "hysterogenous" tendencies in all of mankind. Broadly speaking, his second hand had more merit than his first. Bernheim's is the first known attempt to evolve a general understanding of human behavior and its motivation starting from the framework of the study of psychopathology.

In 1897, Bernheim presented a paper before the International Congress of Medicine in Moscow, in which he attacked the idea of free will in mental illness and crime. He argued that through a variety of obvious and subtle suggestions all of us at times engage in automatic acts, that is, acts without conscious origin or intent. Certainly the mentally ill appear to engage in activities that serve no reasonable purpose, but also, Bernheim contended, the behavior of criminals is not fully under their control. "Suggestion, that is the idea, no matter where it comes from, imposes itself on our brain and plays a role in almost all crimes." Therefore, he proposed a more humane, less punitive attitude in society's dealings with those who violate its laws, since it seemed clear to him that these men were no more responsible for their acts than is an avalanche crashing down a mountain side. Bernheim was thus the first physician to advance the concept of the "irresistible impulse" in criminal behavior. To date, it is a concept which still eludes popular understanding and incorporation in the majority of the world's penal codes.

It seems fair to say that Bernheim was not only ahead of his time, but in some respects ahead of our time as well. His beliefs are all the more remarkable when we consider that for the most part the field of psychopathology was just now being ordered and described. Yet that this was being accomplished in a scientific manner was itself alone a testimony to the progress that had been made in attitudes toward mental illness. In the vanguard of this field were those, such as Janet and Binet, who thought of at least one disorder, hysteria, in psychological terms, and who suggested that many of its symptoms are elicited by processes not in awareness or readily amenable to conscious control. A step or two beyond these gentlemen was Bernheim, who claimed that in all men, both normal and abnormal, there are, to some extent, suggestions that operate without conscious direction. However, with the death of Charcot in 1893, Janet dominated the area of psychopathology in France, although in relatively short order his formulations would be overshadowed by those of Freud.

TREATMENT FORMULATIONS

As would be expected from the concepts of mental illness held during this period, methods of treatment generally consisted of some physical procedure together with the use of suggestion. Psychiatric patients in mental hospitals received principally custodial care, while the treatment given neurotics varied considerably. Some physicians might recommend a pleasant vacation, some might suggest that the person simply try to forget his worries, while others might even advise that an operation was necessary.

Under these circumstances, any possible method of cure might be given serious consideration for a time. For example, "Chew each mouthful of food 300 times and you will be on the road to health and happiness." The proper mastication of foods until each bite was dissolved into a creamy pulp was advocated by Horace Fletcher (1849–1919), an American sociologist and nutritionist, as a means to prevent a variety of ills. While not enthusiastically endorsed by the medical profession, "Fletcherism" during the late nineteenth century was widely known and virtually a cult. "I tried it," William James remarked sadly, "but it nearly killed me."

Medically more respectable and as popular as "Fletcherism," were the ideas of S. Weir Mitchell (1829–1914). Mitchell, America's first neurologist, was the originator of the "rest cure." His treatment was not lacking in a *raison d'être*. During the eighteenth century John Brown had been a leading and influential exponent of the theory that irritability and exhaustion of the nervous system could lead to states of fatigue, weakness, and collapse. The theory seemed so plausible that a century later such terms as "neurasthenia" (introduced by Baird) and "psychasthenia" (introduced by Janet) were reverberations of Brown's hypotheses.

Mitchell's treatment was intended primarily for hysterics. He had observed that "nervous fatigue" was a prominent symptom among hysterics and that anemia was frequently found in these patients. "Let us bring in Dr. Diet and Dr. Quiet," he charmingly advised his colleagues. Through rest, good nutrition, encouragement, and understanding, the hysteric could be helped to return to a useful life; his book *Fat and Blood* indicated explicitly by its title what he considered to be their basic needs. The real significance of Mitchell's unique contributions to the treatment of the hysteric—patience, encouragement, and introducing a feeling of hope—were as little appreciated by him as they were by his brother neurologists.

Sending one's patients to a spa or on a long ocean voyage was definitely a relief, to the attending physician if to no one else. Charcot had even been known to send some of his hysterical patients to the shrine at Our Lady of Lourdes. At first sight this seemed rather puzzling, since it was no secret that Charcot had no great love of religion, and in fact disliked the Church. Moreover, he did not believe any miracle was likely to take place; the faith cures, he explained, were due to the latent hypnotic influence of the shrine acting on the hysterics. "What does it matter," Charcot would say when someone wondered if the Master might be thought a trifle hypocritical, "if the patient gets well?"

Other methods of treatment were less pleasant and more drastic. Acting on Charcot's thought that compression of an ovary produced iliac pain in hysterics, Péan surgically removed an ovary to cure hysteria. With less rationale but equal impetuousness, Bytford performed castrations on cases of hystero-epilepsy. Baker-Brown, of London, and Brawn, of Vienna, practiced the removal of the clitoris, and Friedrich, of Heidelberg, indulged in cauterization of the clitoris. It is to Charcot's credit that at no time did he approve of these somewhat sadistic medical excesses.

William James optimistically proposed that a cure of hysteria might be accomplished through hypnosis. By means of the hypnotic state he thought it possible for the physician to gain access to the secondary personage. James envisioned a kind of reasonable, man-to-man talk, with perhaps some additional strong speech by the hypnotist needed in more intransigent cases, that would induce the secondary personage to release control of the affected part of the body to the primary personality.

In 1891, Bernheim published his book *Hypnotismus, Suggestion, und Psychotherapie*. Bernheim followed the leads provided by Liébeault in recommending the use of hypnosis in treating hysterics. However, in contrast to the more commonly accepted recommendation, he advocated that hypnosis be employed, not to produce suggestions, but to remove the harmful effects of suggestions that had previously been unconsciously accepted by the patient. An interested visitor at the clinic of Liébeault and Bernheim in 1889 had been the Viennese neurologist Sigmund Freud.

Freud (1856–1939) had entered the University of Vienna in 1873 and received his M.D. degree in 1881. An outstanding, zealous student, he had come from a middle-class Jewish family, one in which from early childhood he had learned to anticipate and desire fame. "A man who has been the indisputable favorite of his mother keeps for life the feeling of a conquerer, that confidence of success that often induces real success." This expectation and need for recognition had frequently led him to feel overly enthusiastic about his ideas and to present them somewhat prematurely.

Through his discovery of a gold-chloride method for staining nervous tissue, Freud had made a definite contribution to neurology, but one which failed to lead to that full measure of success that he felt was destined to be his. In 1884, after finding that cocaine helped to alleviate his own periods of depression, he hastily assumed the drug would be an effective antidepressant for everyone and too eagerly advocated its use. The unfortunate consequences that soon followed did serious damage to the reputation that he wished to have as a prudent scientist. While the sad findings of research in cocaine habituation and intoxication were being discussed in Vienna during 1886, Freud was in Paris studying under Charcot. There, too, Freud was on the track of fame, his interest in hysteria having been stimulated by the experiences of his friend Josef Breuer.

Breuer (1842–1925) had the unenviable distinction of being a father figure to the man who was to discover the Oedipus complex. A successful and highly regarded neurologist, he had done significant research on the functions of the vagus nerve and the semicircular canals before going into private practice. Breuer met Freud in the late 1870's and aided him, both financially and through good counsel, in embarking on his professional career.

From 1880 to 1882 Breuer treated a young, attractive hysteric, Bertha Pappenheim (1859–1936), known in the literature as Fraulein Anna O. At one time or another this woman displayed almost all the symptoms associated with hysteria—anorexia (little appetite for food), paralyses, a severe cough (the symptom which first brought her to Breuer), double personality, and anesthesias. With this assortment of complaints and her engaging way with words, it is not too surprising that Breuer found himself becoming more and more preoccupied with her case (Today some might say that Breuer evidenced a countertransference.). Each evening she would talk over with him the events of the day. On one visit she related her memories concerning the first appearance of a symptom and, to Breuer's amazement, the symptom seemed to disappear. Miss Pappenheim felt there was value in this procedure and called it "the talking cure." Breuer also thought it valuable and called it "catharsis."

As Breuer's interest in this patient grew, he also began visiting her each morning to try treating her by using hypnotic techniques. By any standards this was an enormous amount of time to devote to one case, and Breuer's wife, who had at first found her husband's daily ministrations to Miss Pappenheim irksome, now became quite jealous. Therefore in the interests of preserving his marriage, Breuer felt compelled to abruptly terminate the treatment. When Breuer told his patient that their relationship was ended, her condition took a sudden turn for the worse. Breuer succeeded in relieving her immediate distress by employing hypnosis, and then fled with his wife to Venice for a vacation. Miss

Pappenheim, after several years of ups and downs, went to Germany and became the country's first social worker.

Breuer discussed the case of Bertha, or Anna O., with Freud, who, after overcoming his initial amusement at his friend's embarrassment, became deeply interested. Wishing to learn the latest thoughts about hysteria, Freud journeyed to Paris in 1885 to study at the clinic of Charcot. He was most impressed that a neurologist of Charcot's stature should devote himself to the study of the illness and thus lend it a semblance of medical respectability. Furthermore, Charcot's productions of hysterical symptoms through hypnosis indicated to Freud that, whatever the neurological basis of the disease, the symptoms themselves could be treated and alleviated by verbal means alone. Obviously Freud, unlike Bernheim, believed that hysteria was a definite illness; in support of this contention he pointed out that not all the symptoms could be epiphenomena caused solely by the hypnotist since hysterics everywhere presented similar syndromes.

Freud rushed back to Vienna to share all his newly gained impressions and ideas about neuroses with his colleagues. Having recently been burned in consequence of his enthusiasm for the use of cocaine, they gave him a chilly reception. The climate of the meeting was undoubtedly not helped by the sight of a young, ambitious Jew lecturing his elders. But Freud was not to be easily discouraged. He felt that he was on the trail of something momentous.

For a time he continued to treat his hysterical patients with the latest and most accepted methods, including electrotherapy (An electric shock, intended to be somewhat painful, was administered to that part of the body which the patient claimed was paralyzed or without feeling.), baths, massages, rest, and direct therapeutic suggestions while the patient was hypnotized. However, his dissatisfaction with these procedures mounted daily. Relative to his earlier enthusiasm, his disappointment with hypnosis was especially keen; not all his patients could be hypnotized and he found the whole business boring. In 1892, he began to use a "concentration" technique: the patient, while lying down, was directed and urged to recall all memories associated with a particular symptom. Gradually, Freud abandoned completely both hypnosis and the directing and prodding of the patient. At times he labeled this freer approach "Breuer's cathartic method," and at other times "psychical analysis."

Breuer and Freud published their *Studies in Hysteria* in 1895. As far as Breuer was concerned, their most important contribution in the book was the exposition of transference phenomena, that the patient could transfer into the relationship with the physician feelings and thoughts originally experienced in relation to someone else. Nevertheless, despite the significance which they attached to their work, this book was not favorably received in medical circles and Breuer became discouraged by his colleagues' criticisms. Furthermore, Breuer showed a reluctance to draw the same far-reaching implications that Freud was making on the basis of his investigations of his patients' sexual life. Breuer stated with mixed feelings of fear and admiration: "Freud's intellect is soaring at its highest. I gaze after him as a hen at a hawk."

By 1896, the relationship between the two men had definitely cooled. Freud was talking about *his* new technique "psychoanalysis," and about *his* new theory of hysteria. He rejected Janet's ideas about hysteria and announced that the cause of the illness was the memory of passive sexual experiences, traumatic seductions that had occurred before these patients were eight years old. Moreover, his investigations had revealed that in obsessional neuroses there were also prepubertal seductions, but, in contrast to those of hysterics, these patients had been actively aggressive and had found their sexual experiences pleasurable. These conclusions, Freud pointed out, were based on nineteen "fully analyzed" cases. He presented his findings before the Society of Psychiatry and Neurology in Vienna. The reaction of the group was, to say the least, icy. Krafft-Ebing commented that "It sounds like a scientific fairy tale."

Breuer, although trying to maintain their friendship, could not bring himself to accept Freud's conclusions. Such caution on his part about drawing the same implications from the data was justified. In fact, Freud was soon to learn for himself that he had been wrong in believing that the stories of seduction told him by his patients were actual incidents. Still, Freud remained confident that he had attained professional maturity and that he was correct. Therefore, he was displeased, not only by Breuer's lack of enthusiasm, but by his friend's good-natured reluctance to accept partial repayment of some old financial debts. Basically, Freud resented Breuer's paternalism, and by 1900 further contacts between the two men ended.

While Sigmund Freud was carrying on his twin search for understanding of neuroses and for personal recognition in Vienna, Lightner Witmer in the United States was introducing innovations into the area of remedial education. Witmer (1867–1956) had graduated from the University of Pennsylvania in 1888, and in his early career always seemed to find himself a step or two behind James McKeen Cattell. He had studied under Cattell as an assistant in psychology and followed his mentor's example by journeying to Leipzig to obtain his Ph.D. from Wundt. But where Cattell was forceful Witmer was pedantic, and therein lay a considerable individual difference.

Like Cattell, Witmer wished to do an "applied" dissertation, against the wishes of Wundt. Unlike Cattell, Witmer accepted Wundt's suggestion and wrote a thesis in aesthetics, including research upon the golden section. In 1892, he received his doctorate and returned to the University of Pennsylvania, where he took control of the psychological laboratory, since Cattell had just left to teach at Columbia. Four years later, in 1896, Witmer founded the first psychological clinic.

Witmer's clinic treated children, referred from the local school systems, whose problems were regarded as primarily learning difficulties of one kind or another. These included children whose behavior in the classroom was unruly and disruptive, and who today might be considered emotionally disturbed; such youngsters were described as having "moral defects." Each child was first examined by a physician and then received a mental examination (antropometric measures, eye tests, reaction time, etc.). Witmer placed considerable emphasis on the diagnosis. His concern was to determine whether the learning problem could be attributed to an arrest of cerebral development or to inadequate methods of education, and to delineate the "defect" precisely. Once an accurate diagnosis was made, treatment could be attempted. The treatment consisted of specific methods of retraining the child to alleviate his particular form of learning defect.

There are two stories as to how Witmer became interested in clinical work. Witmer himself claimed that he became involved in the area in 1889. He was teaching English at a prep school while pursuing his studies at the University of Pennsylvania. One of his students was a boy who was impeded in articulation and Witmer did what he could to help him. He believed that the cause of the speech problem was an injury to the head that the boy suffered when he was two years old. What bothered Witmer most was that the boy's talents had been wasted, perhaps needlessly, for years, simply because the condition had not been diagnosed earlier. It may have been contact with this particular case, along with his own personal bias, that led Witmer to stress the importance of prevention or early diagnosis rather than correction or treatment.

The other story, related by his friend Robert Brotemarkle, is that Witmer was challenged by a public school teacher, Margaret Maguire, to solve the problem of a "chronic bad speller." Witmer found that the child had a visual anomaly. By having him fitted with glasses and then tutored, he was able to effect improvement.

Both of these stories indicate Witmer's interest in being of help to the person and his utilization of whatever knowledge and skills were necessary to bring about optimum functioning. This was a far different role from the one which had been considered appropriate for psychologists. To be sure, individuals had been studied by psychologists before, but always with the aim of formulating scientific generalizations. Witmer's innovation as a psychologist was to suggest and practice the application of psychological techniques and principles in the diagnosis and treatment of individual cases. The treatment was pedagogical, in the tradition of Itard and his pupil Édouard Seguin (1812–1880), who had arrived in the United States in 1848 to carry on his work in the education or "treatment" of mental retardates. When we examine Witmer's theory and techniques, we find that at first he offered nothing original. His signal contribution was to suggest that psychologists take a new direction and discover new uses for already available methods.

PROFESSIONAL DEVELOPMENT

Although Witmer's suggestions were not to elicit any immediate enthusiasm from his colleagues, there were indications during this decade that the role of the psychologist was broadening. Around 1889, Edward Cowles, a former surgeon in the Union Army who had studied psychology at Johns Hopkins, was encouraging the practice of conjoint medicine at McLean Hospital in Waverly, Massachusetts. A laboratory in the hospital was set aside to be used for studies and experiments in physiological psychology; the purpose of this research was to determine the "exact nature and causes of departures from normal mental function." In 1893, August Hoch was selected by Cowles to be the hospital's psychologist and pathologist. Hoch had studied psychology with Wundt, Külpe, Marbe, and Kiesow, and was also a physician. Later he was to become professor of psychiatry at Cornell.

On July 8, 1892, a group of "rugged pioneers" in psychology met at Clark University at the invitation of G. Stanley Hall. There they founded the American Psychological Association. Seven men formed a Council, which was the governing body of the APA: Hall, G. S. Fullerton of the University of Pennsylvania, Joseph Jastrow of the University of Wisconsin, William James, G. T. Ladd of Yale, Cattell, and J. Mark Baldwin of the University of Toronto. The Council members, together with twenty-four others elected to membership, constituted the Association. Some of these original members were philosophers, educators, and physicians, and some were even psychologists. Today about a third of them would be unable to meet APA membership requirements.

The founder of the APA, Hall (1844–1924), was born and raised on a farm in Ashfield, Massachusetts. His parents, hardworking, devout, and puritanical, were mindful of education and placed great value on learning. They loved their son deeply but had little time or inclination to engage in open displays of their affection (Some years after the event Hall found out that his father had kept him from serving in the Union Army by bribing a physician to certify him ineligible for conscription.). At the age of sixteen Hall went away from home to teach in a country school. With the assistance of his mother and the reluctant consent of his father, he left that position for a year's study at a seminary in order to prepare himself for college. In 1863, he entered Williams College and graduated four years later in the bottom half of his class. Although rather skeptical of orthodox religious practices and convictions, from there he went to

Union Theological Seminary, where he studied for the ministry. Hall pursued his education with little zeal for he was still uncertain as to what it was he wished to do. For ten years he floundered, but was a far cry from being completely without purpose or direction.

By the age of twenty-seven, Hall had studied philosophy in Germany for two years, had been ordained, and had resigned from his first pastorate. Then came four years as Professor of Modern Languages and Literature at Antioch College, which were followed by two years as an English tutor at Harvard. But while at Harvard he studied psychology with William James, found this subject to his liking, and earned his doctorate in 1878. After that he spent two years studying under Wundt. So by the time of his second return to the United States from Germany, Hall had a clear idea of his goals and the area in which he wished to do research.

He decided to devote himself to the investigation of children's thoughts and beliefs, and to this end he devised interview procedures and questionnaires. One of the major findings from his study of Boston school children was that boys and girls are surprisingly ignorant about things which adults assume are known to everyone, e.g., only 10 percent of the youngsters knew where their ribs were located. Obviously, adults were giving children credit for knowledge which many of them did not possess, and Hall's research implied that educational practices might have to be altered if they were to make meaningful use of what they were being taught.

In 1881, Hall joined the faculty of Johns Hopkins University. There he established the second psychological laboratory in the United States, served for a time as lay superintendent of Bay View Hospital, and, in 1887, founded the *American Journal of Psychology*. Two years later he left for Clark University to become its first president. Unfortunately, a few months after assuming this position, Hall's wife and daughter were accidentally asphyxiated. As one might expect, this tragic event affected him profoundly, and it was only with considerable self-discipline that he managed to recover. Forthwith, he plunged himself into his work.

He founded the *Pedagogical Seminary* (later named the *Journal of Genetic Psychology*) in 1891. The following year he took steps that led to the founding of the American Psychological Association and became its first president. There were then only two American psychological journals and Hall was editor and founder of both. He taught psychology to psychiatrists at Worcester State Hospital until 1895, when one of his former students, Adolf Meyer, assumed this responsibility. Between 1894 and 1897, Hall and his co-workers published 194 articles on the thoughts and feelings of children. His book *The Contents of Children's Minds on Entering School* (1894) was the culmination of three years of study. It won almost instant world-wide acclaim from those who agreed that children were not "little men" and "little women." Although later the super-ficiality and flaws of his questionnaire method became apparent, Hall, vigorous, stimulating, and articulate, had achieved international recognition and had earned the distinction of being referred to as the "Father of Child Psychology."

Hall was followed in the presidency of the APA by G. T. Ladd (1842–1921), who had attained prominence through his text on physiological psychology. In his presidential address, delivered in New York in 1893, Ladd presented, essentially, a vision of the ever-increasing acceptance and prestige of psychology. He pointed out that while psychology was the youngest of the sciences, it had a particularly bright future. Its members were aggressive, enthusiastic, and hopeful. The implications of its researches were bound to arouse popular interest, and would soon begin to enrich many areas. Moreover, he predicted that the studies of Hall and Cattell would lead to improved methods of teaching, while "In the diagnosis and treatment of the insane, the incorrigible, the idiotic, etc., scientific psychology is surely destined to exert a growing influence."

Ladd was followed in the presidency by William James. The succeeding APA presidents were James McKeen Cattell, Fullerton, Baldwin, Münsterberg, and John Dewey. Although Germany was still the acknowledged world leader of psychology, the energetic and forward-looking Americans felt confident that that leadership would soon pass to them.

Despite the fact that Cattell had been unsuccessful in establishing a psychological service at Columbia in 1895, his presidential address delivered to the APA later that year spoke boldly as though the millennium had arrived. So much was being learned that Cattell believed that psychology was past the time of philosophical and speculative systems and was now advancing into scientific and practical usefulness: "While our confidence in the future of psychology rests on the knowledge of its intrinsic vitality, we are able for the convincing of others to offer the brute argument of material success."

The time certainly seemed to have come for action. At the APA meeting of 1895, J. Mark Baldwin proposed the formation of a committee to consider the feasibility of enlisting the cooperation of the various psychological laboratories in standardizing the collection of data obtained from mental and physical tests. This was a project dear to the heart of Cattell, who was appointed chairman of this committee, The Committee on Physical and Mental Tests.

Shortly thereafter, the Committee proposed a battery of tests to the APA membership: (1) Preliminary data, social and physical; (2) Physical measurements; (3) Keenness of vision, touch, and hearing; (4) Sensitivity to pain; (5) Reaction Time for sound; (6) Reaction Time with choice; (7) Perception of size; (8) Perception of time; (9) Memory type; (10) Imagery; (11) Fatigue; (12) Color vision; (13) Perception of pitch; (14)

Memory; (15) Apperception test of Ebbinghaus; (16) Perception of weight; (17) Dynanometer pressure of right and left hands; (18) Rate of movement; (19) Rapidity of movement; (20) Will power; (21) Voluntary attention; (22) Right and left movements; (23) Accuracy of arm; (24) Rate of discrimination and movement; and (25) Quickness of distinction and movement. It was hoped that this battery would be accepted by the membership and that it would be administered according to standardized procedures. Cattell estimated that under ordinary conditions it would take no more than an hour to give a subject all twenty-five tests.

The following year, 1896, James Sully organized a psychological laboratory for the study of difficult children in England, and Lightner Witmer appeared before the APA to describe his clinic at the University of Pennsylvania. Witmer felt that he was proposing something important, new, and exciting: a "clinical method" in psychology and a diagnostic method of teaching. He asserted that the psychological clinic, of which his was the first, is an institution for social and public service, for original research, and for the instruction of students in psychological orthogenics: a term coined by Witmer which includes the areas of vocational, educational, correctional, hygienic, industrial, and social guidance. His talk stimulated the elevation of some of his colleagues' eyebrows but little else.

The unresponsiveness of Witmer's audience seems to have been due to four reasons. For *one,* the majority of psychologists considered themselves scientists and probably did not regard the role described by Witmer as appropriate for them. *Two,* even if they had considered his suggestions admirable, few psychologists were prepared by training or experience to perform the functions he proposed. *Three,* they were not about to jeopardize their identification as scientists, which was tenuous enough in those early years, by plunging their profession into what they felt were premature applications. *Four,* aside from any prevalent skeptical and conservative attitude, Witmer had an unfortunate talent for antagonizing his colleagues.

To estrange himself was about the last thing Witmer sought to accomplish. Yet he had not endeared himself by his tendency to make overzealous criticisms or by the generally aggressive tone in which he delivered his remarks. For example, at the business meeting of the APA he pointed out that the Council was electing new members without adequately bringing them before the Association for approval. Witmer proposed a definite procedure: "all names (of prospective members) nominated by the Council, shall be presented to the Association at its opening meeting in written form or visibly displayed upon a blackboard, together with a statement of the contribution or contributions to psychology, . . . and that the final action upon such names shall be taken by the Association at the final business meeting." That Witmer was often correct (In 1897 definite procedures for nomination to membership were adopted consisting of formal nomination blanks and sponsorship by two members of the Association.) did not help him too much. Nor did it help when his friends argued that his aggression was directed at ideas rather than the people who espoused them; this was a subtle distinction often lost upon those whose ideas had been under attack.

However, Witmer was not the sort of person to give way easily to the opinions of others or to self-pity. Undaunted by the apathetic response to his talk at the APA Convention, he proceeded to expand and consolidate the services of his clinic. During the summer of 1897 he began to offer a four weeks course designed to demonstrate the clinical method in child psychology. There were case presentations, instruction in diagnostic techniques and pedagogical treatment, and convincing evidence of a growing interest in his work. Thus it might be said of Witmer that though he lost his battles he won his wars.

That same year, 1897, a psychologist, William O. Krohn (1868–1927), founded a laboratory for the study of the mentally ill at Eastern Hospital for the Insane in Kankakee, Illinois. Krohn had been a senior teaching fellow at Clark in 1892 and, like Witmer, was a charter member of the APA. After receiving his doctorate from Yale, he founded the psychological laboratory at the University of Illinois. Krohn quickly rose to the position of Head of the Department of Psychology and Pedagogy, but later entered Northwestern University Medical School, graduated in 1905, and ever after identified himself as a psychiatrist.

The field of psychology which Krohn left was still in an early stage of development, as is illustrated by Stella Sharp's presentation of an exhaustive and exhausting review of the area of mental tests in 1899. Her conclusion: "The tests employed, considered as a whole, cannot be said to yield decisive results for Individual Psychology if applied *once* only to individuals of *the same class.*" Some worthwhile information might be obtained, she suggested, if the tests were given in a series or, in other words, repeatedly administered to the same person. On second thought, she decided, considering the amount of work involved for the amount of information to be obtained, it really wasn't worth the trouble. She was encouraged, however, by the work of Binet and Henri, who were trying to construct tests to measure complex mental processes, and felt they were on the right track.

We can see then that in the absence of a consensus as to what psychology should do to study individuals, it was still largely up to each psychologist to decide in what direction he should expend his efforts and how he should proceed. Nevertheless, the treatment of persons with mental illnesses was not even remotely considered as one possible function of a psychologist. That was regarded as the province of medical practitioners, who in the first place were not scientists, and who in the second place were not doing too well at it. The "treatment" that Witmer discussed was essentially the tutoring of a child to eliminate, or at least lessen, his specific learning difficulties in the classroom . . . and even that was considered best left to professionals in other fields.

The tests that a psychologist wished to use, if he wished to use tests, and the way he wished to administer them were left to his discretion. The Committee on Physical and Mental Tests unhappily reported that the battery of tests they had proposed was not gaining any acceptance. After 1899 no further word was heard about the Committee, indicating that they had become otherwise engaged or had decided to abandon their designated task as hopeless.

Yet Witmer seemed to be just getting his second wind. He was talking about a new profession of clinical psychology which would be interested in the individual child. The clinical method, he claimed, was a protest against philosophical speculations and, more concretely, the direct application of results of laboratory experiments to children in the school setting. Each child was unique and had to be treated uniquely. While Witmer was not receiving enthusiastic support from his fellow psychologists, he was creating some stir among educators in Philadelphia and he was certain that in time his words would also be attended to elsewhere.

American psychology in the 1890's was thus a period of hope: collective hope in the future of the United States and the new science; individual hope in what might be achieved and gained. Few doubts were expressed by psychologists concerning the prospects of their profession, and there was ample reason to believe that the APA's increase in membership from thirty-one to almost a hundred was just one index of a growth that would continue.

References

Binet, A. & Féré, C. *Animal magnetism.* New York: Appleton, 1888.

Binet, A. Double consciousness in health. *Mind,* 1890, 15, 46–57.

Boring, E. G. *A history of experimental psychology.* New York: Appleton-Century-Crofts, 1950.

Brotemarkle, R. A. Clinical psychology. 1896–1946. *J. consult. Psychol.,* 1947, 11, 1–4.

Burns, E. M. *Western civilizations: their history & their culture.* New York: Norton, 1947.

Cattell, J. M. Mental tests and measurements. *Mind,* 1890, 15, 373–381.

Cattell, J. M. Address of the president before the American Psychological Association, 1895. *Psychol. Rev.,* 1896, 3, 134–148.

Dennis, W. & Boring, E. G. The founding of the APA. *Amer. Psychol.,* 1952, 7, 95–97.

Fernberger, S. W. The American Psychological Association: a historical summary, 1892–1930. *Psychol. Bull.,* 1932, 29, 1–89.

Hall, G. S. Laboratory of the McLean Hospital. *Amer. J. Insanity,* 1894, 51, 358–364.

Hall, G. S. *Life and confessions of a psychologist.* New York: Appleton, 1923.

James, W. *Principles of psychology.* New York: Holt, 1890.

James, W. The knowing of things together. *Psychol. Rev.,* 1895, 2, 105–124.

Jones, E. *The life and work of Sigmund Freud.* Vol. 1. New York: Basic Books, 1953.

Knight, Margaret. *William James.* London: Penguin Books, 1950.

Ladd, G. T. President's address before the New York meeting of the American Psychological Association. *Psychol. Rev.,* 1894, 1, 1–21.

Mensh, I. N. An historical footnote. *Amer. Psychologist,* 1960, 15, 221–222.

Meyer, A. August Hoch, M.D. *Arch. Neurol. Psychiat.,* 1919, 2, 573–576.

Meyer, A. G. Stanley Hall, Ph.D., LL.D. *Amer. J. Psychiat.,* 1924–25, 81, 151–153.

Murphy, G. *Historical introduction to modern psychology.* New York: Harcourt, Brace, 1950.

Peterson, J. *Early conceptions and tests of intelligence.* Yonkers, N.Y.: World, 1925.

Ramul, K. The problem of measurement in the psychology of the eighteenth century. *Amer. Psychologist,* 1960, 15, 256–265.

Rosenblum, Eve. Le développement de la pedagogie curative: aperçu historique. *Enfance,* 1961, 2, 165–178.

Shaffer, G. W. & Lazarus, R. S. *Fundamental concepts in clinical psychology.* New York: McGraw-Hill, 1952.

Shakow, D. Clinical psychology: an evaluation. In L. G. Lowrey & Victoria Sloane (Eds.) *Orthopsychiatry 1923–1948: retrospect and prospect.* Amer. Orthopsychiat. Assoc., 1948.

Sharp, Stella E. Individual psychology: a study in psychological method. *Amer. J. Psychol.,* 1899, 10, 329–391.

Stafford-Clark, D. *Psychiatry to-day.* London: Penguin Books, 1952.

Wallin, J. E. W. William O. Krohn: early psychological practitioner. *Amer. Psychologist,* 1961, 16, 259.

Watson, R. I. *The clinical method in psychology.* New York: Harper, 1951.

Watson, R. I. A brief history of clinical psychology. *Psychol. Bull.,* 1953, 50, 321–346.

Watson, R. I. Lightner Witmer: 1867–1956. *Amer. J. Psychol.,* 1956, 69, 680–682.

Winkler, J. K. & Bromberg, W. *Mind explorers*. New York: Reynal & Hitchcock, 1939.

Witmer, L. Clinical psychology. *Psychol. Clinic,* 1907, 1, 1–9.

Zilboorg, G. & Henry, G. W. *A history of medical psychology*. New York: Norton, 1941.

3

Early Triumphs

1900-1909

STRIDING ACROSS THE BEGINNING YEARS of the twentieth century was a man who was the embodiment of rugged individualism and direct action, President Theodore Roosevelt. Round about him were the people of the United States, who in this decade absorbed 8,202,388 immigrants into the melting pots and sweat shops of their cities, cheered their President's fight against monopolies and the exploitation of natural resources, and swelled with pride in their country's "Big Stick" foreign policy and the digging of the Panama Canal.

By and large, it was still a time of peace. Of course there had been a war between Russia and Japan and there were squabblings in South Africa, Morocco, and China. But for the most part, peace prevailed and industrialization, despite some setbacks, advanced. The push for social reforms and respect for the dignity of the individual continued, so that by 1909 only Russia was governed by an absolute monarch and even there Tsar Nicholas II was obliged to make concessions to the peasants and the proletariat.

New discoveries in science seemed to conflict relentlessly, not only with traditional thinking, but also with theories in science itself. In 1901, the Dutch botanist Hugo DeVries published his data on mutations, indicating a mechanism for introducing sudden and radical innovations in the process of evolution. The Japanese-American scientist Jokichi Takamine inspired research on the endocrine glands when he succeeded in isolating adrenalin and demonstrated its importance in regulating heart action. Ernest Rutherford and Frederick Soddy concluded that X-rays, light, electricity, and all other forms of energy were essentially the same, and Albert Einstein began a revolution in physics and astronomy with his theories of relativity.

Paradoxically, man's very progress in understanding himself and his world was construed by some as divesting man of his distinctiveness in nature, and hence his immortality and *raison d'être*. In such an apparently mechanistic universe, new urgency was given to that old search for a meaning for life, but the metaphysical solutions proposed were rather grim.

The Nihilists argued that people should believe in nothing which rested on faith, and the scientist and philosopher Ernest Haeckel (1834–1919), an avowed materialist, tended to agree. He claimed the mind of man was as much a product of evolution as was his body, and differed only in its complexity from the minds of lower organisms. Further, he could see no fundamental difference between living and nonliving matter, except that the former was more complicated. The essayist Walter Pater believed that man, as the helpless victim of fate, deserved compensation for living, which could be found in judicious aesthetic and sensuous enjoyments. In contrast, the author Anatole France seemed to think that the best one could hope to get from life was an occasional laugh at one's own expense; thus he advocated the cultivation of a taste for irony and placid despair.

More optimistic views were expressed in literature by men such as George Bernard Shaw, H. G. Wells, and Frank Norris. Their writings conveyed a spirit of confidence and hope that, despite weaknesses and errors, man was about to thrive upon the great benefits from science and education and would awaken to the need to rectify prevailing social injustices.

William James, publicly, had long since ceased to give himself over to despair, fatalism, and a world view based on mechanistic determinism. The universe that he championed was not closed, mechanistic, and determined. Such a world would have no place for individuality and free will. Instead, he argued for a changing, expanding world, one in which a man might feel free to alter his role and shape his future. He found himself influenced by and in agreement with the French philosopher

Henri Bergson, who stated: "Life is a flux, reality can only be known by living it. . . . The experiences of life are outside of logic."

The consequences of these beliefs, according to James, were *better* than the consequences of a belief in a closed universe. Instead of being resigned to his fate, man could exercise initiative and do something about his problems. To critics who questioned the truth of his assertions, James responded by questioning the concept of absolute truth.

In a world always changing, James contended, our basic attitude in judging the value of an idea or the truth of a belief should rest in the practical consequences that result from its acceptance. Rather than question whether a general notion is true, he claimed we should ask: "What sensible difference to anyone will its truth make? . . . What experiences will be different from those which would obtain if the belief were false? What, in short, is the truth's cash value in experiential terms?"

More specifically, to those who wondered about the existence of God, James pragmatically posed two questions: What would be the consequences after death if one had believed in God and He did not exist? What would be the consequences if one had not believed in God and He did exist?

To his energetic countrymen who were impatient to assert their significance James' philosophy, pragmatism, made sense. It was a philosophy that urged men to test out their ideas in real experiences rather than by logic. It counseled them to stop worrying about problems incapable of solution and to address themselves to tasks that would reward the investment of their time and effort.

John Dewey also embraced pragmatism, and in the spirit of Rousseau, as well as of James, encouraged teachers to be flexible in their techniques and to break away from rigid pedagogical methods. In Italy, the philosopher Giovanni Papini enthusiastically came to James' support; that country had been particularly impressed by James and psychology since the appearance of Guilio Ferrari's Italian translation of the *Principles*. In England, H. G. Wells allied himself with the pragmatic point of view.

Now at last James appeared to have some admissible justification for his receptivity to all ideas. His tolerance, his kind acceptance of the views of others had already engendered warm respect, though in some quarters accompanied by considerable dismay, among psychologists. A noted leader of the new science, he had claimed that the supposedly supernatural and the exploits of mediums were proper areas for scientific study. Among large segments of the population a synonym for "psychologist" was fast becoming "spook-chaser." Sadly, Joseph Jastrow took note of this trend in his APA Presidential Address of 1900, and warned of the damage being done to the public image of psychology.

In 1901–1902, James published his Gifford Lectures on *The Varieties of Religious Experience*. Essentially, James was attempting to incorporate all of man's experiences within the scope of psychology. Explicitly, he contended that the mystic and ascetic could not be explained merely by attributing some form of psychopathology to them. A neurotic temperament might well furnish the chief condition for a person's receptivity to so-called divine inspiration, but, in and of itself, he did not think this could result in a full understanding of the religious individual. James suggested that psychologists concern themselves with what there was in religion that was of value to man. It was his belief that deep religious feelings were not always explicable as fanaticism, but that at times they were a sign of the steady growth of the personality into a wider self, a maturing and flowering of the whole person, a broadening and deepening and fullness of experience that might be cultivated profitably by each one of us.

To psychologists who had troubles enough in their attempts to define themselves to the public and to university administrations, James' intellectual catholicism was probably something less than a blessing. Their hope was to achieve independence from departments of philosophy and to occupy a respected place among the sciences. James, with his armchair speculations going off in every direction, was certainly not helping to clarify the boundaries of their discipline, nor did his methodology bear much resemblance to the scientific model. Lightner Witmer was one of his leading critics, but then Witmer not only attacked James' laxity as a scientist but virtually all the psychologists at Harvard, with President Eliot thrown in for good measure.

Although James may have been wounded by these criticisms, he did not alter his position, and remained accessible to ideas and those who wished to avail themselves of him. Generously he gave of his time and willingly lent his considerable prestige to worthy causes. It was even possible for an unknown former mental patient, by the name of Clifford Whittingham Beers, to gain an audience with the leading psychologist of the day.

Clifford Beers (1876–1943), a graduate of Yale, had suffered a "mental breakdown" at the age of twenty-four, which he believed was caused by excessive worry about becoming an epileptic. One of his older brothers had suffered from epilepsy, and Beers became increasingly convinced that he would eventually have the same disorder. Rather than face life afflicted, he attempted suicide by throwing himself out of a fourth-story window; fortunately he landed on soft earth. For a year he languished in depression, and was then committed to the Hartford Retreat.

In 1902, his depression lifted and was replaced by feelings of exultation. Apparently in a manic phase, he decided that he would describe his experiences in the mental hospital and embark on a crusade for reforms. His literary output, comprising an account of the abuses and cruelties he had met with, together with his own feelings and those of his fellow patients, was turned out at a maximum rate of twelve feet of manila wrapping paper an hour.

An assistant physician resented Beers' journalistic interviewing of patients and retaliated by confiscating his writing materials. A vendetta followed which culminated in Beers spending twenty-one nights in a strait jacket in a padded cell.

Within a few months Beers was transferred to the Connecticut State Hospital at Middletown, and approximately a year later was released: "I left the state hospital in September, 1903, firmly determined to write a book about my experiences and to organize a movement that would help do away with existing evils in the care of the mentally ill and, whenever possible, to prevent mental illness itself."

Beers wisely recognized that if his book were to be taken seriously he first had to prove to himself and others that he was sane. He took a position in business, married, and, encouraged by friends and his wife, wrote his autobiography, *A Mind That Found Itself*. A studied and successful attempt was made to avoid those emotional excesses and redundancies as had marred previous writings of this sort and had led to their dismissal as the ravings of persons still disturbed.

Bearing a rough draft of his manuscript, he called upon William James in 1906. James read the work, was favorably impressed, and sent a letter to Beers indicating his approval. That letter served as part of the Introduction to the book when it was published in 1908. An endorsement by James carried such significance that persons of importance soon rallied to Beers' support. Among them was the leading psychiatrist in the United States, Adolf Meyer.

The relationship between Meyer and Beers had its beginnings in 1906 shortly after the visit with James. It was a mutually beneficial one in which each man was able to satisfy some of the needs of the other. Meyer wrote of his encounter with Beers: "I have had an unusual experience in finding in him a man not only without a chip on his shoulder, but one with a sound and worthy conviction that something must be done to meet one of the most difficult, but also lamentably neglected problems of sociological improvement. . . . It looks as if we had at last what we need: a man for a cause."

Meyer suggested the name of the movement be called "mental hygiene." This suggestion was adopted, and in May of 1908, Beers founded, in Connecticut, the first mental hygiene society. There was, of course, suspicion and hesitancy about endowing the society with public financial support, but the times certainly seemed generally propitious. Government agencies at federal, state, and local levels were pushing for prevention of diseases, such as hookworm, tuberculosis, pellegra, and anemia. It seemed reasonable to expect that mental disease could also get its share of the community funds available for remedial and preventive efforts.

Dr. William H. Welch, an eminent pathologist at Johns Hopkins, joined the movement, and notified Beers of an encouraging development:

Henry Phipps, a philanthropist, had read Beer's book, and this had influenced him considerably in endowing the school's Psychiatric Clinic; perhaps, within the near future, Phipps could be counted upon to make a sizable contribution to the cause. Thus the founding of the National Committee for Mental Hygiene, in 1909, despite its empty treasury, was fraught with hope.

While the stage was being set for an organized, massive attempt to educate the public on the subject of mental illness and health, an English physician was ripping into the "conspiracy of silence" that surrounded sex as an appropriate topic for scientific investigation. Henry Havelock Ellis (1859–1939) had published in 1898 the first of seven volumes of his *Studies in the Psychology of Sex* (1898–1928). For the most part, Ellis presented a biological, anthropological approach to his subject, describing the various manifestations and forms of sexual activity. It was no accident that the only sexual practice denied an adequate exposition in his works was happy conjugal love.

Ellis was the only son of an English merchant sea captain. During his father's long absences from home, Ellis grew "unusually" fond of his mother, and became painfully lonely and shy. For escape he turned to voluminous reading, a continuing practice that later caused him to be acclaimed "the best read man in the world."

At the age of sixteen, he abruptly broke away from home and left for Australia. Like most adolescent males, Ellis felt keenly his amorous interests in women, but unlike most of his peers, seemed unable in any way to declare his feelings. Then he claimed he underwent a mystical experience, which did not make it any easier for him to express love and desire, but mercifully left him content not to do so.

Ellis decided to devote his life to the study of sex and to write about it in the manner of natural history. To achieve this end, he returned to England to become a physician, and succeeded in obtaining his M.D. from St. Thomas' Hospital in 1889. However, he did not practice medicine, but turned quickly to literary and scientific work. Almost immediately, his writings on sex created a sensation in Europe and the United States.

It was Ellis who introduced the terms "autoeroticism" and "narcissistic" to refer to love or affection directed by the person toward himself. These terms were later incorporated into psychoanalytic theory: a fate probably pleasing to Ellis who had been among the first to comment favorably upon the writings of Freud.

NORMAL PERSONALITY FUNCTIONING

Just before the beginning of the year 1900, Freud's *The Interpretation of Dreams* was published. It received generally unfavorable reviews from those who bothered to comment upon it, and sold only 351 copies during its first three years of life. Yet Freud regarded this book as probably his best and most important work.

Following the death of his father in 1896, Freud had begun his self-analysis. Guiding him was the assumption of psychic determinism: man's thoughts and behaviors are not accidental or freely willed, but are products of natural laws. This assumption had been promoted by his teachers Brücke and Meynert, who had in turn been influenced by Herbart, a philosopher-psychologist, who protested, in 1824, against "this false doctrine of free will." For Freud the implication of psychic determinism was that any thought or act, regardless of how trivial, might with scrutiny and analysis reveal causes or motives of which the person was not aware. It followed, then, that dreams, so often reported by his patients, and noted by Freud himself in his own analysis, might prove a particularly rich source for the understanding of unconscious processes. His ideas developed quite rapidly from this conclusion.

Freud's investigations into the meaning of dreams had led him to conceive of three kinds of mental functioning which differed in the ease with which their contents could be known by the person. Unconsciousness consists of those ideas and perceptions which are ordinarily inaccessible to awareness but which can become known if considerable effort is directed to their discovery, e.g., forgotten events during the first five years of life. Preconsciousness consists of those ideas which are not known at the moment but which are accessible to awareness if an effort is made to recall them, e.g., the names of some of your teachers in grade school. Consciousness consists of the feelings, sensations, and thoughts which are in immediate awareness, e.g., the sight of this page and, hopefully, the meaning of these words.

In his formulation, Freud thought of unconscious ideas as governed by the primary process, i.e., an unlearned type of functioning in which ideas continuously press for immediate, unrestrained expression in perceptions or actions, regardless of the duration of their exclusion from awareness or of how inappropriate they might be currently. Conscious ideas, in contrast, are thought to be governed normally by the secondary process, i.e., an acquired or learned type of functioning in which the ideas or impulses are delayed in their expression with due regard given to the existing circumstances or situation. Functioning as a filter between consciousness and unconsciousness are preconscious processes which repress or exclude from awareness ideas which would be too painful or distressing if known, but which allow some ideas access to awareness in a distorted, disguised, or tolerable form of expression.

The unconscious ideas seemed to Freud to be mainly sexual wishes. More precisely, they appeared to be the person's incestuous wishes toward the parent of the other sex, and aggressive, hostile wishes toward the parent of the same sex; Freud was reminded by them of the legend of Oedipus. (Oedipus, a king of Thebes, who, according to Greek myth, without realizing the consanguineous relationships, killed his father and married his mother.)

At first Freud could not believe that oedipal impulses could originate in preschool age children; he decided that these wishes came about when a child is between eight and twelve years old, but they are later thought by him to represent events of his earlier childhood. This conception of incestuous desires replaced Freud's previous formulations about actual seductions occuring in the early years of his patients' lives. In either case, a Freudian childhood was far from idyllic and certainly seemed to be an exciting, important, and sometimes momentous period.

During sleep the inhibiting, perceiving, rational thought processes of the individual, which Freud called the ego, are relatively quiescent. Therefore, it seemed reasonable to Freud that the relative force with which unconscious ideas press for expression in perceptions or motor acts is greater while the person sleeps than when he is awake. In order to preserve sleep, a compromise is effected: the unconscious ideas are expressed, at least imaginarily, though even in this form they are disguised and distorted, i.e., as a dream. Among the distortions and disguises in the dream are the following: two or more unconscious ideas might be represented by a single detail (condensation; for example, a ring belonging to the person's father might stand for the oedipal wishes); the emphasis might shift from what is significant to what is insignificant (displacement); an image might represent something else (symbolization, e.g., water might refer to birth). Freud called the mental processes which produced these distortions the censor. It seemed to him clear that, in essence, dreams are fulfillments of unconscious wishes, and that the major wish of the dream is to maintain sleep.

Although most of Freud's Viennese colleagues remained coldly unimpressed by his ideas, a small group of physicians began meeting with him to learn and discuss them. These weekly sessions began in 1902, and among the original members at the gatherings was Alfred Adler. Still, Freud had hoped for a more enthusiastic and widespread reception. The recognition he anticipated seemed so slow in coming that he felt that it would not be until after his death that his views would be appreciated. However, good news came in 1904. Eugen Bleuler, professor of psychiatry in Zurich, wrote that he and his staff were very much interested in psychoanalysis. Furthermore, one of his staff, Carl Jung, by using tests of free association, had experimentally demonstrated one of Freud's contentions: that emotions interfere with recall. Freud, of course, was delighted.

Although Freud's books, *Psychopathology of Everyday Life* (1904), *Jokes and Their Connection with the Unconscious* (1905), and *Three Essays on the Theory of Sexuality* (1905), were far from what would be considered best-sellers, more and more people seemed to be waiting and willing to listen to his latest ideas. Their attentiveness was somewhat taxed by his unending expansions, revisions, and extensions of the theory. A vast terminology was developing in which the use of old words frequently seemed to outrun and betray their earlier definitions. Meanwhile, new concepts were being introduced rapidly, and the theory was leaping from its origins in what Freud had discovered about the neuroses to permeate virtually every facet of human life.

Freud argued quite convincingly that unconscious processes interfere with, and are a part of, the ordinary functioning of "normal" people. He illustrated his thesis by discovering unconscious reasons for a variety of commonplace occurrences: the forgetting of names and numbers, slips of the tongue, mistakes in reading and writing, and a generous sampling of so-called accidents (spilling liquids, breaking glassware) which have been the grief (and apparently the pleasure) of almost everyone. But what was even more startling was his extension of sexual behavior to infancy.

Freud now believed he had found evidence that heterosexual behavior does not emerge with relative suddenness at puberty, but instead evolves or develops over the years from birth. Unlike the other instincts of man (the ego instincts, which have to do with self-preservation, e.g., hunger, thirst), the sexual instincts do not require almost immediate gratification, but can be postponed indefinitely and satisfied in a variety of forms: masturbation, fetishism, homosexuality, heterosexual intercourse, etc. Moreover, those forms regarded as deviant in adulthood are often found normally during the early course of the individual's life. It was the delineation of this progression from infantile sexuality to mature heterosexual behavior that was Freud's most controversial and distinctive contribution.

The process of human development was seen by Freud as involving changes connected with the most sensitive areas of the body, those most suitable for providing sexual gratifications. These changes were conceptualized as expressions of a sexual force or energy, called the libido, which not only motivates the individual, but which also determines the vividness and intensity of the mental representations (the sensations, thoughts, and perceptions) of the sexual instincts. The distribution of libido about the body was not viewed as uniform or haphazard. On the contrary, the investment of libido, in this case the acuteness and pleasurableness with which bodily stimulations are experienced, appears to shift from one specific portion of the anatomy to another in an orderly and predictable manner.

A very early phase of sexual development is the oral stage, during which the person derives erotic gratification primarily from stimulation of his lips and mouth in feeding. Then follows the anal-sadistic stage, when sexual pleasure is derived mainly from stimulation of the bowels in the act of retaining and expelling feces. If the person is overly gratified during this stage, he might evidence a cluster of characteristics which Freud called the anal character: excessive neatness or orderliness, thrift or miserliness, and obstinacy.

A phallic stage comes next, when the principal organ for sexual gratification is the penis or the clitoris. Since Freud had recently participated in the analysis of a five-year-old boy who evidenced fears of being castrated and wishes associated with what was now being called the Oedipus complex (the case of little Hans), it was decided that the incestuous desires of children first develop during the phallic stage, i.e., when they are about three to four years old.

From about the age of four to eleven there is apparently a time of relative stabilization in psychosexual development, an interval which Freud named the latency period. After latency comes adolescence, which seems to be less complicated for males than for females, although troublesome for both sexes. Boys continue to experience the penis as the primary zone of erotic gratification; however, girls are expected to shift from the clitoris to the vagina as the area giving the greatest sexual pleasure, a change which Freud believed was not accomplished too readily. Freud supposed that because of this complication, women are in general more prone to sexual conflicts and neuroses than men.

Freud took particular pains to emphasize two points about his theory. *One,* although conceding that he had accumulated his evidence from neurotic patients in Vienna, he nevertheless regarded his exposition as universally applicable and descriptive of normal psychosexual development. *Two,* despite the orderly changes in the salience of the principal sexual organs and zones, components of preceding stages normally continue to find a function in adult life, as for example, the mouth continues to serve as a source of pleasure in eating, drinking, and kissing.

This theory propounded by Freud was surely remarkable, and by 1908 there were enough people sufficiently interested in psychoanalysis to warrant convening an international meeting in Salzburg. Forty-two persons attended, including A. A. Brill, Alfred Adler, Paul Federn, Otto Rank, Wilhelm Stekel, Ernest Jones, Karl Abraham, Sandor Ferenczi, E. Bleuler, Edouard Claparède, Max Eitington, and Carl Jung. The convention was truly unique: Freud's talk lasted for four hours, and when he indicated they might adjourn for lunch, his eager audience prevailed upon him to continue for an hour more.

G. Stanley Hall was familiar with the news from Europe about Freud's theory and was favorably impressed. This was significant approval, coming as it did from a prominent educator and psychologist, especially since the luster of Hall's reputation had been recently enhanced by the publication of his monumental work, *Adolescence* (1904). However, Hall's approval was based mainly on seeing in psychoanalysis a corroboration of the importance of the study of childhood, and not so much on an agreement with its specific doctrines and details. Still, Hall regarded the theory as of sufficient consequence to begin, in 1908, to give courses on the new Freudian psychology. That same year, Brill began his analytic practice in New York City.

Nevertheless, to Ernest Jones, there seemed to be ample cause for gnashing of teeth and lamentations over the deplorable neglect of psychoanalysis in English speaking countries. But in fairness to the professionals of the United States and Great Britain, it should be pointed out that nothing that Freud had written had as yet been translated into English.

The first article on psychoanalysis published by a United States psychologist appeared in 1909. Its author, W. D. Scott, concluded: "The thesis here defended is that the psychoanalytic method is nothing more than an unusually skillful application of the method of suggestion and that it offers no proof for the existence of subconscious complexes of suppressed emotional ideas." Fortunately, those Americans who could not read German could soon begin to judge for themselves. Brill's English translation of Freud's and Breuer's papers on hysteria was published in 1909, and that same year Hall invited Freud, Jung, and Ferenczi to come to Clark University to participate in the festivities celebrating the twentieth anniversary of the school.

Interpreting dreams en route, Freud arrived in Worcester to deliver a series of lectures that were to win him several new adherents. James J. Putnam, professor of neurology at Harvard, was one of those most strongly affected by Freud's maturity and humility, by the freely given acknowledgments to the contributions of Breuer, and by Jung's enthusiasm and vigor. Although he had had some reservations about psychoanalysis, Putnam stated with deep feeling: "But I have learned to believe fully in the theory and in the value of their methods of analysis and of treatment, and I am the more ready to accept their views for having made the personal acquaintance of (Freud, Jung, and Ferenczi) . . . and for having found them so kindly, unassuming, tolerant, and sincere." Putnam was not alone in his praise. At the conclusion of Freud's talks, William James parted from him with the words: "The future of psychology belongs to your work."

Just the year before, in 1908, James had characteristically gone out of his way to give encouragement to a psychologist who was finding it difficult to be personally accepted, but who was having better luck with his ideas. That psychologist was William McDougall (1871–1938).

McDougall had been born in England, and was fond of attributing to his Saxon and Nordic heritage "the fact that I have never fitted neatly into any social group." A self-diagnosed domineering and precocious child, he matured into a self-consciously arrogant adult: a flaw which he frequently deplored, and which he never felt he successfully concealed.

He entered the University of Manchester at fifteen, Cambridge at nineteen, and lost his faith in God at twenty when his mother died of cancer.

By the age of twenty-eight, McDougall had become a neurologist. However, he was bored by the practice of neurology because of its emphasis on diagnosis, and turned for stimulation to anthropology. He went on an expedition to the Torres Straits in 1899, and from there to Borneo, and unquestionably showed promise of being an outstanding anthropologist. But then, he also became bored by anthropology, and so decided upon a career in psychology. While he had many subsequent regrets about that choice, boredom was never one of them.

To implement his decision, he studied briefly with G. E. Müller at Göttingen. Then, in 1900, he accepted a faculty position at University College, London. During the following years, he helped found the British Psychological Society (twelve members strong) and the *British Journal of Psychology*. In 1904, he accepted a chair in Mental Philosophy at Oxford, and in 1907 (according to McDougall) or 1908 (according to almost everyone else), he had published the book that established his professional reputation, *Introduction to Social Psychology*.

McDougall defined psychology as a positive science of conduct or behavior. Aside from his obvious intent to broaden the scope of psychology from the study of consciousness to the study of the behavior of all living organisms, McDougall wanted to get away from a rational, intellectual concept of motivation. To do this, he argued that the motivation for all human activity could be traced to some innate disposition, which he unfortunately chose to call by the term "instinct."

Perhaps by virtue of his predilection for heredity, then, McDougall saw the human being born with a certain small number of fundamental instincts. These instincts were thought to be composed of three integrated processes: *one,* a predisposition to perceive significant stimuli, e.g., increased sensitivity to cues of food when hungry, leading to; *two,* an emotional impulse, or response, which is the "core" of the instinct, and which leads to; *three,* a predisposition to make certain movements or overt approach responses in the direction of the goal. This third component clearly indicates that McDougall saw purpose in behavior as an essential characteristic.

The first and third processes of the instinct are related to environmental stimulation, and thus involve learning. McDougall's compounding of hereditary and acquired characteristics was fundamental to his position and led into some unique features of his theory. Beginning with twelve primary instincts, he pointed out that each of them becomes modified by learning since new and different stimuli become capable of arousing them, and since their movements or responses to the goal become altered. For example, our tastes in food change, and many people acquire a revulsion for pap and a fondness for beer; moreover, our eating responses are (we trust) guided by rules of etiquette, some recognition of the principles of a balanced diet, and often by the prescriptions of religious ceremony. Thus McDougall was trying to emphasize that instincts are seldom, if ever, observed in forms not modified by learning and experiences.

Further, two or more instincts frequently become fused or attached to a single object. When that happened, one could speak of a sentiment. In the case of a sentiment of a love of food, the instincts of hunger and a seeking of new tastes (curiosity) might be said to have combined into an epitome of a gluttonous person. McDougall thought that most behaviors of adults are motivated by sentiments, and since sentiments are largely composed of instincts, and instincts have emotions at their cores, human conduct is driven, in essence, not by reason but by mixed feelings of loves and hates.

Social behavior could then be viewed and evaluated in terms of its meeting and satisfying certain basic needs. But McDougall wanted it to be understood that he believed interpersonal activities were in the main directly motivated by sentiments, not by instincts. Although his explanations are neatly circular, it is instructive to sample them. Man originally joins with others into groups because of the instinct "to seek company," but other instincts eventually become associated with the social grouping. The sentiment of patriotism is partially explained by the following instincts: the instinct of domination is aroused when the person desires that his group control other groups; the person's acquisitive instinct is expressed in wanting to get things for his group; when his leader speaks, the person's instinct to submit is stimulated, and he accepts the suggestions of authority. However, the ideal person, in McDougall's opinion, appears capable of controlling the expression of his instincts and of maintaining his ideas in the face of pressures to conform; such an individual is no longer submissive to the praise or blame of his group, and is sufficiently integrated to have adopted his own moral code which he regards as superior to any the group might attempt to impose upon him.

McDougall's theoretical formulations were helping to bring a new field—social psychology—into being. Although not all psychologists applauded or agreed with his conceptualizations, they heartily welcomed the new area, and promptly added courses in social psychology to the curricula of their departments.

It is interesting, and possibly a function of the *Zeitgeist,* that while neither Freud nor McDougall was aware of the work of the other, there are obvious similarities in their formulations. Both emphasized instinctual strivings, the significance of emotions in human behavior, and the minimal role played by rational considerations in much of man's conduct. Man to them both is a creature often driven to do things by forces which he does not fully comprehend or control. Their view of human behavior is in opposition to the concept of man as unique in nature, freely choosing between good and evil, and usually capable of sensibly deciding his fate. But does man have to be regarded as one way or the other? Some psychologists certainly believed that a reconciliation is possible between a deterministic and a willing, elective conception of human activities. William Stern (1871–1938) was one of them.

Born and raised in Berlin, the only and lonely child of a merchant, Stern graduated from the University of Berlin in 1892. The deaths of his father, in 1890, and his mother, in 1896, left him feeling more isolated than ever. He turned to find his personal salvation in "the philosophical discipline of psychology." "I have never . . . become 'scientificated'," Stern claimed proudly many years later. Others agreed with his self-appraisal, though they did not consider it a compliment as he did.

Stern began teaching philosophy, psychology, and pedagogy at Breslau in 1897. By 1901, he felt that the key to resolving the conflict between science and the need to experience a meaning for existence is somehow connected with the concept of the *person*. Stern's views on the subject were stated at length in three volumes under the general title *Person und Sache,* the first of which was published in 1906.

If one wishes to study the human being part by part, analyzing the workings of internal organs or examining the functionings of specific and limited physiological processes, then, Stern believed, the person could and should be viewed mechanistically. However, if one wishes to study the whole human being as a functioning entity, since the person has purposes, his behavior can be understood only with knowledge of these goals and values. As Stern put it, the person is "a unique and self-sufficient *unitas multiplex,* whose activity as a purposive function is directed toward self-preservation and self-development."

By *unitas multiplex,* Stern meant the person's multiplicity of traits, drives, and abilities organized and converging into a unitary developing personality. This personality is stimulated, and also inhibited, by environmental influences, and strives to maintain equilibrium between tensions arising from within and those of his external environment. Since Stern believed a philosophical orientation is necessary to comprehend the person's system of values, he did not think that psychology alone would ever fully understand the unitary person . . . such an understanding requires the cooperation of both philosophy and psychology. What psychology can hope to accomplish within the twentieth century, Stern suggested, is the determination of the psychological differences which exist between one unique individual and another.

DIAGNOSTIC TECHNIQUES

Of course Stern was not alone in his view that individual differences are a worthy field for investigation. In 1896, Binet and Henri put the matter this way: "General psychology studies the general properties of psychical processes, those, therefore, which are common to all individuals. Individual psychology, on the contrary, studies those psychical processes which vary from one individual to another; it seeks to determine the variable qualities, and the extent and manner of their variation according to the individual."

Alfred Binet (1857–1911), whom we met in the previous chapter, had originally decided upon a career in law, and obtained his degree in that subject from the Lycée Saint-Louis in 1878. However, an interest in research and the influence of Charcot led him to switch to the study, but not the profession, of medicine. Beginning around 1880, Binet decided to investigate psychological problems; at first, he delved into abstruse philosophical questions and theory building, though at the same time giving some attention to thinking, hypnosis, and hysteria. Later his apparent repudiation of this phase of his professional development seemed so complete that he was criticized for a lack of theoretical perspective in his work. This criticism was not justified, for at the time of his death, Binet was attempting to make clear the place of his efforts within the framework of a theory he was trying to develop.

One product of his early investigations was *La magnetisme animal* (1886), written with C. Féré. During their studies of hypnosis they observed that some patients were actively participating and expending effort to overcome inhibitory suggestions, while other patients were passive and inclined to be resistant; they recommended that a distinction be made between the hypnotic states of these patients, referring to the former as active and the latter as passive.

In 1889, with Henri Beaunis, Binet founded the first laboratory of physiological psychology in France, at the Sorbonne. The following year he obtained a degree in the natural sciences, and began studying the development of behavior in his two daughters. He noted the differences between them in their learning to walk. One would hold onto a post and look for another to go to before venturing forth, while the other child walked boldly into an empty room undeterred by the possibility that she might fall. These personality differences were particularly fascinating to him, although he was uncertain as to how to deal with them systematically. Over the course of time, Binet also made records of his daughters' skills in recognizing objects in pictures, and in giving definitions.

Binet earned his doctorate in science in 1894 (His thesis had to do with the insect nervous system.), and when his colleague Beaunis retired in 1895, he took over direction of the laboratory. That same year the two men had founded the first French journal of psychology, *L'année psychologique,* with Beaunis as editor. It was this publication that served as the major vehicle for the dissemination of Binet's research on intelligence.

Binet was convinced that in order to study individual differences, it was necessary to sample the most intellectual and complex processes so that the spread of scores would be broad: "the more complex and the higher a process, the more it varies according to the individual: sensations vary from individual to individual but less than memory." Therefore, he recommended the construction of psychological tests which sampled judgment, memory, and imagination (Binet even proposed that imagination might be assessed through the use of ink blots.).

The basic concept for individual psychology, Binet asserted, is the norm with the deviations from it. But he believed that ascertaining these norms is only a beginning. He wanted to know additionally what the relations between the various mental processes are, so that he could predict the degree of development of one process from knowledge of another. Mental tests, he thought, should also yield information about qualitative differences, as well as quantitative differences, for, as he might have said, a child not only has a smaller memory than an adult but a different memory.

In 1896, Binet and Henri described a series of tests to measure attention, comprehension, memory, imagery, aesthetic appreciation, moral sentiments, sustained effort in muscular tasks, motor skill, imagination, and visual space judgment. As we have already seen, some American psychologists were enthusiastic about this work, but Cattell was not one of them. With the resignation of Beaunis as editor in 1897, Binet assumed that post on *L'année psychologique* and pressed on with his research into intelligence and its components.

In the years that followed, Binet continued to emphasize the importance of qualitative variables, and particularly the influence of personality on intellectual functioning. His studies made it clear that psychological measurement was not absolute but ordinal: "But we cannot know, with respect to memory, if the difference between the memory of five figures and the memory of seven figures is or is not equal to the difference between the memory of seven figures and the memory of eight figures. We do not know, moreover, what the value of this difference is. We do not measure, we classify."

Binet returned briefly to the problem of suggestibility, and found through experimentation with children that it decreased with increasing age. Nevertheless, he found enough suggestibility in adults to feel justified in cautioning his colleagues to guard against subtly indicating to their experimental subjects how they might expect them to respond. Also, he thought it wise to warn lawyers about the influence they might exert upon the testimonies of their witnesses by the way in which they formed their questions. Such, in brief, were Binet's ideas at the beginning of the twentieth century.

Stella Sharp's unfavorable evaluation of the Cattell variety of mental test was reinforced in 1901 by Clark Wissler's report of the results of this type of testing at Columbia and Bernard. Wissler's findings were: (a) the scores obtained from various laboratory mental tests correlated only slightly with each other; (b) the same was true of the intercorrelations between physical tests and mental tests; and (c) correlations were low between mental tests and college grades. For example, the correlation of reaction time with class standing was —.02, while the correlation between the grades in gym and class standing was +.53. Clearly, something was amiss. The mental tests as then devised in the United States had little demonstrable validity or usefulness . . . at least for making predictions within a relatively homogeneous college population.

Meanwhile back in France, Binet was still observing his daughters with scientific detachment. Perhaps, he thought, one might be able to determine personality types by using mental tests. He had the two girls write down a list of twenty words. By analyzing the lists, he decided that Marguerite was a practical girl whose concern was with concrete objects in the external world. Armande, on the other hand, seemed to be turned inward and had little interest in the world about her. Momentous findings to someone else, perhaps, but not to a man who was reluctant to venture far from his immediate data. Binet dismissed the whole thing as an exercise in labeling rather than explaining, as "a literary game rather than science."

Then, in 1904, the Minister of Public instruction in Paris appointed a commission to investigate what steps were needed to insure that defective children received the benefits of an education. Special classes were to be formed, but before a child could be removed from ordinary schooling and admitted to these classes, an examination had to be conducted to certify that the child could not profit from regular classroom instruction. Obviously, subjective examination procedures were inadequate since authorities disagreed among themselves in diagnoses and in the meanings of the terms used to designate the intellectually subnormal. In the hope that they might provide an objective basis for distinguishing the "degrees of inferior mentality," Alfred Binet and Théodore Simon (1873–1961), medical chief of the Insane Asylum of La Seine Inférieure, were consulted.

The first outcome of this consultation was the 1905 Binet-Simon Scale. This scale was composed of thirty items arranged in order of increasing difficulty. Its score was simply the number of items passed. Binet claimed only that the scale provided a crude means of differentiation, e.g., an ordinary five-year-old did not get beyond question fourteen. A trifle more distressing even than its crudeness was the inconsistency between the content of the scale and Binet and Simon's definition of intelligence. Although claiming that the fundamental faculty of intelligence is sound judgment, they were forced to admit that many of the thirty items did not test judgment.

However, they went on refining their work, and the result was the more sophisticated 1908 Binet-Simon Scale. In it were fifty-nine tests grouped at age levels from three to thirteen years according to the percentage of children of a particular age who passed a given item. This percentage varied anywhere from 67 to 75. If a higher percentage passed the item, it was thought to be too easy for that age level; if a lower percentage passed the item, it was thought to be too difficult for that age. Binet and Simon did not know it, nor did hardly anyone else for that matter, but a pediatrician, S. E. Chaille, had constructed a series of tests for infants extending up to three years and had arranged them in order of age usually passed. Chaille's scale had been published in the *New Orleans Medical and Surgical Journal* in 1887.

In their 1908 revision, Binet and Simon introduced the mental age as a score for their scale. Binet recognized that in so doing they might be exchanging one evil for another: the demon of subjectivity was being replaced by an illusion of objectivity. He had no such illusion, however: "It is not, in spite of appearances, an automatic method . . . an interpretation is necessary . . . all scientific procedure is but an instrument which requires the direction of an intelligent hand." The scale, he warned, did not measure intelligence alone, but intelligence and also the knowledges gained from school and from the environment in general. He stressed the importance of qualitative variables: the persistence and attention of the child while taking the test as an influence on the score that would be obtained. In short, Binet had many reservations about the Binet-Simon Scale.

Credit for introducing the Binet-Simon Scale into the United States is usually accorded to Henry H. Goddard (1866–1957). Goddard had been one of G. Stanley Hall's students. During these early years of the twentieth century he was working as director of the Research Laboratory at the Institute for Backward Children at Vineland, New Jersey. (Incidentally, it was Goddard who coined the term "moron" to designate the highest grade of feeble-mindedness.)

While visiting Brussels in 1908, Goddard heard about the Binet-Simon Scale. At first he was somewhat skeptical of its value, but decided to give it a try among the children at Vineland. He was pleased to find that the scale did seem able to make discriminations, and so began to work on a revision that would make it suitable for general use in the United States. Even while Goddard tackled that problem, the scale was gaining acceptance. In 1909, the city of Rochester, New York, which had organized special classes for subnormal children in 1906, appointed a Binet examiner into their school system.

When due consideration is given to the criteria that authorities were forced to rely upon up to that time, the eager welcome to the Binet-Simon Scale does not appear excessive. Some physicians had struggled bravely to implement Pinel's dictum for differentiating between the idiot and the imbecile, to the effect that the former's attention is "fugitive," while the latter's attention is "fleeting." Some frankly acknowledged that their judgments were uncertain. Dr. Walter Fernald, head of the Massachusetts School for the Feebleminded, regretted that the best that he had been able to do for the classification of children was to depend on observations of their posture and motor coordination when they stepped from the vehicle that brought them to his institution. Of course, others insisted they could tell more about a child from the feelings they had about him or the twinkle, or lack of it, in his eye than could ever be learned from mental testing; but these voices were drowned in the chorus of approval. In Belgium, Germany, Italy, England, and the United States, great interest in Binet's work was aroused. Here at last seemed to be an objective means of classification and a convenient device upon which could be placed the greater part of the responsibility for making decisions.

During this period the testing of personality was not completely neglected. Some psychologists were impressed by developments in Zurich. Two psychiatrists, Eugen Bleuler (1857–1939) and Carl Gustav Jung (1875–1961), who were introduced earlier in connection with their interest in psychoanalysis, had been trying to discover a person's complexes (unconscious interrelated ideas capable of arousing strong feelings) by using free association techniques.

Jung, the younger and more inventive of the pair, had been born in Switzerland, the only son of a Protestant clergyman. His family had a rich religious tradition, as well as interests in medicine. An integration of these divergent backgrounds was formally incorporated by Jung in his thesis for the M.D. degree in 1902: "On the Psychology and Pathology of So-called Occult Phenomena." The thesis concerned Jung's observations of the trance states of a young medium. It appeared to him that during the trances a more comprehensive, promising personality was attempting to break through from unconsciousness into consciousness—a somewhat optimistic interpretation and a recurrent theme in Jung's writings. After receiving his degree, Jung studied briefly under Janet in Paris, and then returned to Zurich to work under Bleuler. Very soon thereafter they began their experimentation with the free-association method.

Galton had originated free association techniques in 1879, and quickly recognized that what was significant about them was that they had been misnamed: tell a person he is free to say the first word he thinks of after hearing "table," and very likely he will say "chair." A person's associations are not really free, Galton found, but determined by his experiences and thus usually restricted to only a very small number of words.

In 1889, Münsterberg had thought that a free association test might be useful to detect lying and criminal guilt. The only trouble was that innocent people seemed to get about as upset as guilty ones, while some guilty people did not seem to get upset at all. Nevertheless, Münsterberg had faith in the potential of the technique, and in a subsequent series of popular magazine articles predicted its eventual use in aid of the long arm of the law. Jung, of course, had in mind a different purpose for the test, although he did use it on one occasion to investigate a theft at a hospital. His major interest, however, was in seeing if the technique could be developed into a sensitive instrument for the detection of complexes, or conflicts and problems about which the individual was not aware.

Jung thought that hallucinations, delusions, and the other symptoms of dementia praecox are due to the activities of a complex, whose dynamic force comes from the strong emotions associated with it. He speculated that these emotions disturbed the individual's ideational processes, and might even engender a toxin or metabolic anomaly that irreparably injured the brain and in this manner produced a mental illness, or psychosis. This was a startling hypothesis for it asserted that a psychic disorder could produce an organic disorder.

He prepared a list of one hundred words, e.g., "sick," "pride," "angry," "sad," and noted carefully the behavior of the person when he tried to respond freely with another word. Usually Jung used simply a stopwatch to measure the interval between the presentation of the word and the response, but at times he also employed a pneumograph to measure breathing rate and a psychogalvanometer to measure changes in electrical conductivity in the palm of the hand produced by sweating (the psychogalvanic reflex or response).

It seemed to Jung, in 1905, that blocking, unusual responses, and a delay of over two seconds in responding were indications that some unconscious complex had been touched upon. As a result of his experimentation, Jung became convinced that the dissociated ideas of the complex were charged with emotions, and that the mechanisms which kept them isolated from awareness were the same as those described by Freud in hysterics. The symptoms of dementia praecox could thus be viewed as having, in a sense, a purpose, and the verbalizations of these patients, far from being mad ramblings without meaning, might be analyzed, interpreted, and understood. Jung reported on his work at the Clark University anniversary celebration to an enthralled audience, many of whom hailed his free-association technique as a potentially significant tool for research and diagnosis.

DIAGNOSTIC FORMULATIONS

The development of diagnostic instruments appeared to make it imperative to explain what it was that these tests were supposed to measure. In particular, the concept of intelligence seemed to have been hazy and was now in urgent need of clarification. Many people had explained intelligence in terms of the so-called "faculties," "powers" of the mind (such as perception, judgment, and moral taste) which were supposed to be relatively independent. If a person showed good judgment, his faculty for judgment was said to be well developed. Similarly, if a person seemed to remember things well, it was because his faculty for memory was well developed. While faculty psychology of this sort had the obvious virtues of simplicity and versatility, it became quite clear that its use was circular and not very enlightening.

Charles Spearman (1863–1945) was among the first to offer an explanation of intelligence based on some empirical evidence. Early in his career Spearman served in the British armed forces. By 1897, he considered that his military years had been frittered away, and he turned to the serious study of psychology. His Ph.D., with a thesis on space perception, was earned under Wundt, whom he admired greatly as a scientist and as a person. Although in later years he despaired of ever reading all that should be read in psychology, he felt confident that he knew as much about the subject as most psychologists did.

The work of Galton inspired Spearman in 1901 to try to find out if intellectual abilities are related to each other, and also what their relationship might be to the capacity for making discriminations. He employed the school grades of children in various subjects for his measures of intellectual abilities, and tested their sensory discrimination by sounding musical chords. From an examination of his data, it seemed there was a considerable relationship between the different mental abilities, but Spearman realized that he had no way of numerically determining how close the relationships were. After investing a great deal of time and energy in devising the kind of statistical measure we now know as the correlation coefficient, he discovered that he had overlooked two things already in the literature. The same work had already been done by Galton, and coefficients of correlation had already been used to analyze data by Cattell.

Nevertheless, Spearman did notice that Cattell's results were the opposite of his own. Therefore, he concluded there must have been something wrong in Cattell's study. This led Spearman to the concept of attenuation: correlation coefficients are spuriously decreased in value because of random errors of measurement, as when they are computed from measures that are not perfectly reliable. He invented a statistical procedure to correct for attenuation, and when this was applied to Cattell's data, was pleasantly surprised to find that the conflict between the two sets of results had been resolved in his favor.

In 1904, Spearman brought forth from the fruits of his correlated labors the concept of general intelligence or *g*. The intercorrelations between the various measures of intellectual activity, considered negligible by many psychologists, indicated to Spearman that: "all branches of intellectual activity have in common one fundamental function (or group of functions), whereas the remaining or specific elements of the activity seem in every case to be wholly different from that in all the others." Thus Spearman believed that he had objectively determined the existence of a general intellectual ability which is expressed in all functioning. (Perhaps, he suggested modestly, this is the ability to discover relations.) Spearman now felt that all that remained to be done in this area was to convince other psychologists to come around to accepting the fact that he was right.

Signs arose, however, that the rush to embrace Spearman's formulation would not be too pressing. Edward Lee Thorndike (1874–1949) and Robert S. Woodworth (1869–1962) had published a paper in 1901 on transfer of training that seemed to indicate the existence of specific abilities in intelligence. Essentially, they had attempted to discover whether or not there is any foundation for the belief that by learning one subject, a person could more easily learn some other subject, e.g., whether by learning Latin one could facilitate learning in the sciences. Their experiments convinced them that improvement in one area rarely brought about equivalent improvement in another area. Furthermore, the improvement that did occur seemed to be attributable not to the strengthening of some broad mental or intellectual faculty but to the presence of identical elements involved in the performances of the tasks.

The interpretation offered by Spearman for his results appeared to contradict the interpretation offered by Thorndike and Woodworth for their findings. This contradiction was more apparent than real, but it persisted and was intensified by implicit demands for capitulation by one position to the other. Of all the major participants in this dispute, Thorndike seemed to relish it least, and probably entertained the hope that such barren arguments would be put aside and everyone would go back to the work of being psychologists engaged in profitable research, rather than polemists.

Edward Thorndike had graduated from Wesleyan before going to Harvard for advanced studies in 1895. He was attracted there, and to psychology, by having read and enjoyed James' *Principles*. (In fact, Thorndike had enjoyed the books so much that he later voluntarily bought both volumes.) Originally, he had hoped to work with children as subjects, but was refused permission to do so, and therefore studied chickens instead. This did not end his troubles. The psychology department refused to give his chickens any space, and his landlady prudishly objected to their presence in her house. It remained for kindly William James to save the day once again by allowing Thorndike to use the cellar of his home for a chicken coop. Thorndike was able to emerge from that cellar when Cattell offered him a fellowship at Columbia and a room in an attic for his chicks.

At that time many people believed animals were accustomed to thinking in the same way that people did, but just not as well. Thorndike's thesis, in 1898, demonstrated that animals learn by a trial-and-success method rather than by thinking their problems through to a solution the way humans supposedly do. Not only his results but his use of animals for psychological experimentation were favorably received. Although Thorndike's experiments led him to believe that learning occurred when a pleasurable or satisfying effect followed an activity, he felt that his own behavior was determined by a sense of duty: "I did in those early years and have done since what the occasion seemed to demand."

Such was not the case with Thorndike's colleague at Columbia, Robert Woodworth, who professed to take great delight in all his activities. He loved science and the out-of-doors, and during his childhood wondered whether he should become an astronomer or a farmer. His parents would have preferred that he enter the ministry. Nevertheless, they did not interfere with his plans when he finally decided upon a career in teaching.

After graduating from Amherst in 1891, Woodworth taught mathematics for four years. Then he decided to enter Harvard and begin the serious study of psychology (A momentary pause to note that one of his fellow graduate students was Thorndike.). While at Harvard, Woodworth conducted some studies on dreams. He found that very often the content of the dream involved bringing to imagined completion an activity that had been interrupted during the day. Then he went to Columbia and received his Ph.D. under Cattell in 1899. For a while he taught physiology in the hospitals in New York City. Evidently Woodworth's interest in that subject was more than passing for he spent the academic year of 1902–03 as C. S. Sherrington's assistant in Liverpool learning more about the physiological functioning of the brain. In the autumn of 1903 he returned to Columbia with the rank of instructor. By that time Thorndike was a full professor; Woodworth became one too in 1909.

Glancing at the status of the concept of intelligence toward the close of the decade, we might describe the situation as follows. There were disagreements among psychologists about its definition, but no one seemed really to care too much about that. Spearman had advanced some ideas about its structure, and he cared very much indeed. Some psychologists, including Binet, thought that the intelligence of the feeble-minded was qualitatively different from that of normals. However, a study by Norsworthy in 1906 favored the view of quantitative differences, a continuum of intelligence from the lowest to the highest. Woodworth suggested that there was no such thing as intelligence, and all that the others were

actually talking about was an evaluation of the way an organism be-
haved—intelligently or not so intelligently. Finally, whatever intelligence
might or might not be, there was a growing demand made upon psychologists to devise instruments to measure it.

In contrast to the mild state of confusion in the area of intelligence, at
the beginning of the twentieth century diagnostic or descriptive psychiatry
was enjoying professional status and respectability. In 1903, Janet described the syndrome of psychasthenia, which had as its major symptom
pathological feelings of inadequacy. Then, in 1906, August von Wasser-
mann discovered a specific test for the presence of syphilitic antibodies.
Research soon demonstrated that over 90 percent of the cases of general
paresis gave a positive reaction to this test. A diagnosis of paresis was thus
greatly facilitated, and the theory of the syphilitic origin of the disease
was supported. In 1906, A. Alzheimer reported the first case of an illness
which was soon to bear his name: a precocious senile psychosis occurring
as early as thirty years of age, with a rapid course culminating in severe
dementia and deterioration of the brain. These diagnostic advances and
the Kraeplinean classification of diseases, which was a help in making
the bewildering variety of disturbed behaviors seem more comprehensible
and which was an aid in reporting and in hospital organization, gave a
scientific air to psychiatry that was most gratifying to its practitioners.

Yet, in the main, descriptive psychiatry shed little light on the problems of human personality which lay at the core of its specialty. Nor
did its professionals seem too likely to do so for two reasons: one, in
their concern for objectivity and for maintaining the appearance of being
scientific, they had turned their backs on the actual thoughts and feelings
of their patients; two, they were hesitant to accept the assumption and
implications of mental illness as a continuation of the individual's
psychological development. Accordingly, they were reluctant to grant
that by the study of the person's early life, information could be gained
about the genesis of a disturbance shown in adulthood. Furthermore,
they were unwilling to concede that by the study of psychiatric disturbances, information could be gained about mental health and normal
psychological development. They perceived the actions of the mentally
ill as distinct from those who were not ill, and they had resolved the
mind-body dualism by ignoring the mind.

On the fringes of descriptive psychiatry was Freud, still carrying on
and incurring the disapproval, and sometimes distaste, of many of his
colleagues. Freud had not discarded the mind. Instead, he regarded
mental processes as though they were *there,* as quasi-physical and thus
obedient to natural laws.

Freud was still talking about hysteria. He claimed that the symptoms
of the illness were "conversions" of unconscious fantasies that gratified
sexual wishes. Later, he emphasized that the symptoms represented com-

promises between the expressive sexual forces and the repressive non-sexual forces. His psychoanalytic work with hysterics showed that these patients had amnesia for their important complexes. In contrast, patients with obsessional neuroses were aware of their complexes but did not seem to experience the feelings associated with them.

Obsessional neurotics, Freud observed, also failed to make connections between thoughts that one would reasonably think should be related or integrated. For example, a man might say in one sentence that his parents were cruel disciplinarians, and in the next sentence complain that he could not understand why he should dislike his father and mother. It appeared to Freud that the two major symptoms of obsessional neurotics were doubting and a sense of compulsion. He explained the doubting as an expressing of deeply conflicted feelings of love and hate. He explained the compulsion, or necessity to perform a certain act, as an overcompensation for the doubting. What he considered as also noteworthy about these patients is their belief that if they thought something, it would have an effect or come true; Freud termed this belief "the omnipotence of thought." While the followers of Freud dined happily on his insights, interpretations, and terminology, some psychiatrists and psychologists found the opinions of Adolf Meyer more easily digested.

Adolf Meyer (1866–1950) was born in Niederwenigen, near Zurich. He believed that witnessing the sufferings of his mother enduring long periods of melancholia was responsible for his entry into medicine and the dedication of his life to the alleviation of psychiatric disorders. After receiving his M.D., he traveled to Vienna, Paris, London, Berlin, and Edinburgh for graduate study in pathology, neurology, and psychiatry. In 1892, he came to the United States as a fellow in neurology at the University of Chicago, and then was employed as a pathologist at the Illinois Eastern Hospital for the Insane before leaving, in 1895, for a similar position at Worcester Insane Hospital. During his seven years at Worcester, Meyer became acquainted with G. Stanley Hall and other psychologists in eastern Massachusetts.

The Cartesian dualism that prevailed, and dominated the thinking of scientists, was a prime source of irritation to Meyer. On the one hand the majority of psychologists were claiming that their sole interest was in the mental life of the person. On the other hand there were psychiatrists asserting that their only interest was in the physical or organic condition of their patient. It seemed to Meyer that this dichotomization of the individual was leading into two dead ends: many psychologists were minimizing and ignoring the individual's biological functioning; many psychiatrists were minimizing and ignoring the individual's personal life and his feelings and beliefs.

Meyer proposed a synthesis in place of the mind-body dualism, which first began to attract attention in 1897. He pointed out that man is a mental and physical unit or whole. Think for a moment, he urged his colleagues, that the organism developes from a one-celled egg, and throughout its life continues to grow and function as an integrated unit. Therefore, what is called mental illness should not be regarded as distinct physical *or* mental pathology, but as a maladjustment of an entire person. Meyer contended that frequently a psychiatric disturbance is an expression of unhealthy living, of an individual's habitual and progressive adaptations, ineffective though they might seem, to his environment. People are sensitive beings who have to be understood in all phases of their activities and in their past and current adjustments. To gain this understanding, Meyer advised psychiatrists to obtain developmental histories of their patients and to study their life situations thoroughly.

Meyer soon had the opportunity to translate his ideas into practices. From 1902 until 1910, he served as pathologist and director of the New York Psychiatric Institute. Out of his convictions evolved the "psychiatric interview": a probing of the details of personality development in order to discover the reasons for a particular individual's disturbance. As a means of complementing the psychiatric interview, Meyer began, in 1904, to send his wife, staff physicians, and medical students into the homes of his patients so that a more complete life history could be obtained and so that relatives could be interviewed, evaluated, and become involved in whatever form of treatment was instituted. These practices marked the beginnings of psychiatric social work, and established closer ties between psychiatry and the social sciences. Nevertheless, the contrast between the mental and the physical aspects of functioning persisted in discussions within the sciences, and Meyer continued to hammer away that what we mean by the mind "is a sufficiently organized living being in action; and not a peculiar form of mind-stuff."

The conceptions in psychiatry then current as to the causes of criminal behavior illustrate the emphasis placed on organic etiology. Juvenile delinquency was attributed to such conditions as bad heredity, enlarged tonsils, inflamed adenoids, uncorrected refractive errors, impacted teeth, cigarette smoking, intracranial pressure, systematic absorption of toxins from focal infections, phimosis (need for circumcision), and feeblemindedness. Regardless of what the cause of delinquency might be, there certainly seemed to be delinquents in abundance, and by 1908 a systematic attack on the problem was not only contemplated, but about to be brought into action.

In that year a prominent social worker, Julia Lathrop, Allen Burns, and William Healy met at Hull House in Chicago to consider what new approaches to juvenile delinquency might be of help. They were especially troubled by the practice of the judiciary in imposing penalties on children and formulating their judgments with nothing more than a physical examination of the youth to guide them in reaching their decisions. Surely something more was needed in order to make a wise disposition with such great consequences for the child, his family, and ultimately society at large. As a first step, they decided to initiate a program of research to determine why children become delinquent.

Visits by Healy to the clinics of Witmer and Goddard, and some suggestions from Thorndike, William James, Meyer, and James R. Angell helped in formulating the organization of the program. The plan was to have interviews with each child's relatives to evaluate the possible influence of heredity, obtain a developmental history, and secure a picture of family interrelationships and personalities. His school would be asked to provide material on his educational and classroom adjustments, and the child himself would be given mental tests and interviewed. Financial support for the venture was pledged for five years by a philanthropist Mrs. W. F. Dummer. Judge Pinckney of the Juvenile Court in Chicago promised to cooperate as fully as possible with the group, and all that remained was to select someone to direct the project. Influenced by the favorable recommendation of William James, Julia Lathrop invited William Healy to consider the position as director, and he accepted it.

William Healy (1869–1963) had been born in England, but he received his A.B. in 1899 from Harvard and his M.D. in 1900 from Rush Medical College. He served as assistant physician at the Wisconsin State Hospital, and then took the position of associate professor of nervous and mental diseases at the Chicago Polyclinic in 1903. During the academic year of 1906–07, Healy took a leave of absence for postgraduate training in neurology and psychiatry in Vienna, Berlin, and London.

Healy's work had been based upon two major assumptions: one, he was disinclined to accept the theory that criminal behavior was inherited; two, he assumed that serious antisocial acts indicated the presence of some psychopathology in the offender. In view of the second assumption, the clinic was named The Juvenile Psychopathic Institute. It opened in 1909 in three rooms on the ground floor of the Detention Home. The staff consisted of Healy, a psychologist Grace M. Fernald (1879–1950), and a secretary.

Healy's first case of delinquency was a girl who falsely accused others of committing sexual offenses. After interviewing her it seemed to Healy that the child, far from being a born delinquent, was suffering from hysteria. Further study indicated that the girl's unconscious feelings of guilt had been aroused when she attended a revival meeting, and that this incident had stimulated her to make the false accusations. Healy's studies of other delinquents did not lend much evidence to support the concept of criminal atavism or degeneracy, which had been proposed by the Italian psychiatrist Cesare Lombroso. Supposedly, the presence of three stigmata (unusual marking or conformation of the body) would indicate a degenerate, but very few delinquents had as many as three, although Healy did find a successful and widely respected businessman in Chicago who had five.

Thus The Juvenile Psychopathic Institute, considered by many to have been the first child guidance clinic, was off to a promising beginning. It was blessed with a psychiatric and dynamic orientation. In the east, was the psychological clinic of Witmer, thirteen years older but unwilling to draw the same far-reaching implications from the concept of unconscious motivation.

TREATMENT FORMULATIONS

The situation in psychiatry, as far as the treatment of patients was concerned, had made little discernible progress. In the more "modern" mental hospitals, mechanical restraints had either been abandoned completely or replaced by the use of drugs. However, emetics, douches, baths, static electricity, salves, and ointments were still employed in treatments, and a comfortable hospital environment was still regarded as about the best one could do or hope for. The disenchantment and feeling of futility experienced by many psychiatrists when they surveyed their limited therapeutic armaments caused some to give serious attention to those who spoke convincingly of the effects of ideas upon bodily functioning.

Freud was attracting both medical and nonmedical interest in his psychoanalytic theory and techniques. He had abandoned hypnosis with the assertion that its use deprived the analyst of the opportunity to come to grips with the patient's resistances. This deprivation, he believed, eventuated in an incomplete analysis and only transitory improvement. The mitigation or elimination of symptoms, which heretofore had not been considered a modest goal of treatment, was thus de-emphasized by Freud and made secondary to the resolution of unconscious conflicts. Moreover, since it is expected that the patient will resist bringing these conflicts into awareness and dealing with them reasonably, the duration of treatment in most cases was thought to be unavoidably long. Freud did not suppose that there were any therapeutic shortcuts to the unconscious, but he did recommend exploration by three lengthy roads: (1) the interpretation of dreams, (2) of "accidents" and word slips, and (3) of thoughts in free association. By traveling these paths, he believed it would be possible to bring unconscious ideas and impulses into awareness. But was this desirable? Some people wondered whether the patient might not become confused and even dangerous once his sexual conflicts and urges were out in the open. Freud did not think so. On the contrary, he contended that making the unconscious material accessible to rational scrutiny brought it under better control than had existed before.

Another development in psychoanalytic treatment was the growing distance placed by the analyst between himself and his patient. On the analyst's part, the relationship was becoming more formal and less personally revealing than it had been. Freud had stopped his custom of inviting his patients to have dinner with him and his family, and while refreshments might still be served during the session, he attempted to keep the whole relationship on a professional basis.

Jung noted that Freud appeared more concerned with his status even in their relationship to each other. He reported that during their trip to the United States, Freud had dampened their game of interpreting one another's dreams by asking Jung at one point not to press him for free associations. When Jung wondered why, Freud responded, "But I cannot risk my authority." This remark shocked Jung, and he traced the origins of his serious doubts about psychoanalysis to this incident. Regardless of how much credence one wishes to give to Jung's anecdote, his dismay upon discovering that Freud had human weaknesses is a not uncommon sequence of events in a teacher-pupil relationship. Perhaps the incident illustrates the foibles of both men. At any rate, it makes more meaningful this thought of Dubois: "I know of no idea more fertile in happy suggestion than that which consists in taking people as they are, and admitting at the time one observes them that they are never otherwise than what they can be."

Paul Dubois (1848–1918), professor of neuropathology at the University of Bern, was another psychiatrist who argued vigorously against the materialistic bias adopted by most of his professional colleagues. In his book *The Psychic Treatment of Mental Diseases*, Dubois contended that to help neurotics, psychiatrists should spend less time prescribing rest cures and bromides and more time in talking with their patients. He suggested the goal of treatment was "to make the patient *master of himself*," and in general, he believed that the key to human happiness was self-control, in the interests of leading a truly moral life. The best way to achieve that goal of self-mastery was by education, a rational appeal to the intellect.

Dubois' rational approach consisted of enlightening the patient about the false premises and injurious habits out of which his symptoms developed and upon which they depended. Together, he and his patient would discuss the nature of his difficulties and complaints. Then Dubois would, through reasonableness, encouragement, and moralizing, try to get the person to exercise control over his symptoms so that they would be less debilitating. But probably of greatest significance in Dubois' success as a therapist was his respect for his patients, his boundless optimism in their ability to get well, and his infectious self-confidence: "Let one display the legend 'Master of myself!' and patients will follow it to victory."

A kindred spirit of Dubois was William James, whose primary interest was in making life better not just for neurotics but for everybody. James felt a major trouble with Americans was their inability to relax. They also seemed too troubled by little things and too worried about big ones. To free their minds of petty matters so that they would be able to grapple with complex problems, James advised them to acquire useful habits; a man should make his nervous system his ally instead of his enemy. The procedure he recommended for forming habits was as follows: resolutely to start a new, beneficial habit; allow no exceptions to it until it is rooted firmly *in* the nervous system; put it into action at every opportunity; and try never to permit an exception, for one must remember, "Every smallest stroke of virtue or of vice leaves its never so little scar."

There were other bits of good counsel. For composure in the face of adversity, James urged his fellow Americans to "unclamp" their intellectual machinery, decide upon a course of action, and then stop worrying. For those who are afraid, he prescribed: "To feel brave, act as if you were brave, use all your will to that end, and a courage-fit will very likely replace the fit of fear."

James himself bravely followed his own advice. At the time, James was quite sick, and the feelings of depression which had troubled him earlier in life had returned, though in milder, more fleeting forms. He traveled to Europe in hope of finding health at various spas, and while there, he lectured in Rome, at Oxford, and at Edinburgh. His welcome, particularly in Italy, was enthusiastic and warm. In person, as on paper, James was charming, witty, stimulating, and kind.

Though Witmer disagreed with James on a number of issues, he shared with him a similar concern for the prevention of psychological disturbances. However, at first Witmer addressed himself specifically to the problem of mental retardation among children rather than emotional distress. Still, his conception of mental retardation was so broad that it encompassed disturbances not ordinarily considered to be in that category. To the extent that any child is developing at less than his fullest capacity, to that extent, asserted Witmer, the child is retarded.

Within Witmer's frame of reference, a retarded child might be even one of outstanding ability who is doing just passing work in school, and he placed the responsibility for such a child's lack of achievement upon the school. Nor did Witmer feel that educators were justified in shirking their obligation to teach by claiming a child was feebleminded or not educable. He contended the issue was not so simple, the diagnostic techniques were not so valid, while the consequences of such a course of action for the child were so great that every effort must be made to insure that the child is not being deprived of an education unnecessarily or unjustly. He emphasized that some children, for a variety of reasons, appear intellectually retarded, and insisted that only after a persistent attempt at training and mental stimulation, could one hope to make a legitimate diagnosis of feeblemindedness. Witmer recognized that this would be a time-consuming and expensive process, but judged it mandatory and emphatically worthwhile in view of what is at stake for the child.

Referring to the material, social, and intellectual deprivations existing where children grow up in slums, Witmer exhorted, "The problem calls for preventive social action. . . . We should offer the slum parent something better than a choice between race suicide and child murder." This awareness of a need for reform within society in order to prevent cases of "retardation" led Witmer to broaden considerably what he felt should be the concern of clinical psychology, and to coin a term for this new area—"orthogenics": "While orthogenics concerns itself primarily with the causes and treatment of retardation and deviation, it is by definition the science of normal development, and comprehends within its scope all the conditions which facilitate, conserve, or obstruct the normal development of mind and body."

A similar breadth of conception was evidenced by Morton Prince (1854–1929). After receiving his M.D. from Harvard in 1879, Prince engaged in private practice in Boston. From 1902, he served as a professor of neurology at Tufts Medical College, and in 1906 founded the *Journal of Abnormal Psychology,* of which he became editor.

Prince attracted the attention of psychologists with his studies of dissociated or multiple personalities, a disorder which he thought was a type of hysteria. He also aroused interest with his attempt to introduce the term "co-consciousness." Prince felt a need to distinguish unconscious processes governed by areas in the cerebral cortex from unconscious processes governed by areas in the spinal cord and noncortical areas of the brain. He suggested that the latter processes were really properly called unconscious. However, he believed ideas dependent upon cortical functioning existed in some state of active consciousness because they could be recalled, and so should more precisely be called co-conscious instead of unconscious. Few of his colleagues shared this need for precision and Prince did not consider the issue important enough to raise a fuss. He was firmer in his convictions about psychotherapy.

It seemed to Prince that the same principles which govern learning in general could be discerned in pathological behavior. He explained his thesis in this way. Normally, the process of learning involves integrating and relating ideas. When this association between ideas is useful, we do not become concerned about it. But when the association between ideas is harmful to the individual, we refer to it as a complex. In essence the processes are similar, except that in the functional illnesses the processes had been perverted by trauma or inappropriate learning. Psychoneuroses, for example, can best be viewed as perversions of memory or "association neuroses," since neurotics have difficulty in recalling the past.

"Theoretically," Prince claimed, "it would follow what can be done by education can be undone by the same method, and in practice we find this to be true." He noted that psychotherapeutic techniques appear to employ ordinary learning principles to re-educate the person and effect his adjustment to his environment. Old complexes "are modified by being interwoven with new ones, and new systems of ideas or complexes are artfully created and substituted for the old." In the final analysis, Prince concluded, all psychotherapies are only different forms of education.

Prince's conclusion undoubtedly startled his fellow members of the medical profession, for he implied that others who were not physicians might be qualified to treat functional diseases. Equally disconcerting were public indications that the area of psychiatry did not fall neatly and exclusively within the medical-somatic domain. In 1907, Auguste Forel reported success in curing alcoholics by converting them to religion, and in Boston there were signs that a Pandora's box of nonmedical practitioners of psychotherapy was being opened. Under the guidance of Reverend Elwood Worcester, groups of patients with nervous disorders were being given "moral" treatment.

Elwood Worcester (1863–1940) had graduated from Columbia in 1886, studied under Wundt, and received his Ph.D. from Leipzig in 1889. From 1890 to 1896, he taught philosophy and psychology, and served as chaplain, at Lehigh University. He assumed the rectory of Saint Stephen's Church in Philadelphia in 1896. While in Philadelphia, Worcester received his doctorate in divinity from the University of Pennsylvania, and formed a friendship with S. Weir Mitchell. In 1904, he became rector of the Emmanuel Church in Boston.

Shortly after his arrival in Boston, an internist, Joseph H. Pratt (1872–1942), approached Worcester with requests for the use of his church's facilities and for funds in order to test his idea that it would be possible to treat indigent tubercular patients without removing them to an institution. What Pratt wished to do was to teach them to follow a strict routine of rest, fresh air, and proper diet. In order to save time, he proposed to gather his patients into groups so that they could learn and discuss the reasons for his hygienic methods. Pratt hoped such classes could be held in a room in the church. Worcester, going farther, wondered if the patients might not have souls as well as lungs in need of saving. The two men decided to work together.

A class began in 1905 with the Reverend Dr. Worcester opening each meeting with prayers and giving spiritual counsel to the patients. This "class," conducted by Pratt and Worcester, is regarded as a precursor of what we now know as group therapy. The next year Worcester and his associate, Reverend Samuel McComb, started health classes of their own "among the nervously and morally diseased." Physicians were invited to speak on topics such as worry, anger, and suggestion, but a major purpose of the group meetings was to treat the afflicted through religion, prayer, and inculcation of faith in God. For Worcester had aims that extended beyond his "classes" in Boston. He hoped to achieve a revival of faith healing, not only within the clergy, but within medicine. He had a vision of mental health clinics attached to churches where psychiatrists and ministers would work hand in hand to cure the sick. He saw the lustre of religion, which had been dimmed by the ascendence of science, re-stored by the cooperation of religion with science.

Soon the health classes attracted enough attention and enthusiasm to be christened the Emmanuel Health Movement. Soon, too, the medical societies erupted in a storm of indignation protesting the usurption of the physician's role in treating disease. And before long the effects of profes-sional opposition and the discouragements of adherents who were unable to achieve their founders' therapeutic successes led to the Movement's demise.

Psychologists were little, if any, involved in this clash between med-icine and one of their former colleagues on the issue of who was entitled to treat the mentally ill. The issue at the time seemed to be no issue at all as far as they were concerned: treatment of disease fell within the province of medicine, and that was that. However, this attitude did not exclude the possibility of psychologists and psychiatrists working to-gether within the same area. Psychologists could be very useful, and per-haps no psychologist better exemplified for physicians the kind of usefulness they envisioned as ideal than Shepherd Ivory Franz (1874–1933).

Following his graduation from Columbia in 1899 with a doctoral thesis under Cattell on visual afterimages, Franz spent the next seven years teaching physiology in the Medical Schools of Harvard and Dart-mouth. He was also psychologist at McLean Hospital, and founded its psychological laboratory. His research on touch and cortical localizations endeared him most to his fellow psychologists.

It was Franz, around 1900, who introduced a novel method for de-termining cortical functions. First, an animal was trained to perform a task, and then a certain area of the cortex was extirpated. Following the animal's recovery from the surgery, its performance on the task was re-evaluated to see what role, if any, had been played by the removed portion of the brain. Almost everyone believed that when an area of the cortex was destroyed a permanent loss of its functions resulted. If the functions later recovered they inferred that the area had not been completely destroyed. But Franz proved by his research that it was possible for other cortical areas to assume the functions of those that had been removed.

In 1905, Franz began applying his research findings to patients with brain damage. He initiated a training program for aphasics to help them

overcome their speech handicaps. His successes with these patients immediately demonstrated to physicians that there was hope for the rehabilitation of individuals who had suffered cortical lesions.

The following year Franz left McLean to assume the positions of
psychologist at the government Hospital for the Insane in Washington,
D.C., and professor of physiology and professor of psychology at George
Washington University. In 1907, he introduced the practice at the
Hospital of administering Cattell-type mental examinations routinely.
His contributions were considered of such merit that in 1908 he was
elected an honorary member of the American Medico-Psychological Association, later called the American Psychiatric Association. Franz was a
tough-minded, organically oriented, brilliant, no-nonsense researcher—
just the kind of psychologist whom any doctor might have ordered.

PROFESSIONAL DEVELOPMENT

From 1900 to 1909, the presidents of the APA were, in order, Jastrow,
Royce, Sanford, Bryan, James, Calkins, Angell, Marshall, Stratton, and
Judd. Jastrow, we may recall, was troubled about the public image of
psychology. A facile writer and an entertaining though somewhat ram-
bling speaker, he was particularly interested in acquainting a wide audience with the new science.

Jastrow graduated from the University of Pennsylvania in 1882, and
obtained his doctorate from Johns Hopkins in 1886 with the thesis "Perception of Space by Disparate Senses." University positions in psychology
were then few, so Jastrow was forced to remain at Hopkins as a "fellow-
by-courtesy." He managed to supplement his income by writing popular
articles for magazines until, in 1888, he received an appointment at the
University of Wisconsin.

The Chicago World's Fair of 1893 found Jastrow on hand at the
psychology booth explaining apparatus and testing the sensory capacities
and mental powers of adventurous spectators. In 1894, for some unde-
termined reason, he began to experience periods of depression. He sought
out William James in the hope of getting some helpful advice, but at the
time James also was depressed and so Jastrow returned to Wisconsin
with the consolation that at least he was not suffering alone. Despite his
episodes of "prostration and exhaustion," Jastrow led a very active life.
Not only did he manage to fulfill his professional responsibilities, but he
continued to promote the public's familiarity with psychology through
lectures and books.

There was still considerable debate among psychologists as to what it
was Jastrow was attempting to popularize. Much discussion centered
around what the content of psychology should be, and Jastrow, for one,
thought he knew. In his presidential address of 1909, he urged his col-

leagues to become involved in the applications of their science: "Psychology and life are closely related; and we do not fulfill our whole function if we leave uninterpreted for practical and public benefit the mental nature of man."

A closely allied point of view was expressed by Stern, in 1900, in his book *Über Psychologie der individuellen Differenzen*. He attempted to outline a new discipline, differential psychology, which he believed should be given the status of an independent scientific area. Differential psychology, as he conceived it, would focus upon the individual person, would attempt to understand him and to discover by measurements how he differed from other persons. He hailed the topic of individuality as "the problem of the twentieth century."

In a similar though quite different vein, Mary Whiton Calkins (1863–1930), originator of the method of paired associates for the study of memory, was pushing to define psychology as the science of self.

Although Calkins had studied at Smith and at Clark, her life seemed to begin for her in 1890 when she became a student of James and Münsterberg at Harvard. She left Harvard to take charge of the psychological laboratory at Wellesley, and in 1900 began strongly advocating a psychology of the self. To illustrate how Calkins proposed to interpret all mental processes in terms of a self, we may note her distinction between perception and imagination: in perception the person is aware of sharing a similar experience with a number of other selves; in imagination the person is aware that his experience is private and unique. She contrasted her position with an atomistic point of view in psychology, the latter being concerned with the contents of consciousness and identified with Wundt and Titchener. The self-psychologists, or Calkins at any rate, were also concerned with the contents of consciousness but as experiences of some self. She allowed that there was room in psychology for both points of view.

In her APA presidential address in 1905, Calkins argued that the self was not a metaphysical concept but a fact of experience. While she never defined the self, she did describe its characteristics: (1) persistence or stability of identity—"The same 'I' must exist if there is to be consciousness 'in the same way' or 'of the same object'."; (2) uniqueness; (3) complexity; (4) relations to, or awareness of, objects in the environment by observing, manipulating, and emotionally responding to them.

Calkins' self seemed to exist without a body, and her critics wondered if this were an oversight on her part. Not so, Calkins explained, to give the self a body would endanger the identity of psychologists, perhaps turn them into biologists, and so lose an important though as yet undeveloped science. In 1909, to highlight her position, she abandoned her previously expressed tolerance of an atomistic view and came out for "a single-track self-psychology." Though most psychologists of her day were in favor of allowing her to travel her track alone, recent developments in the psychology of personality have in part supported her stand.

During this period considerable interest was being aroused in functional psychology, especially at the University of Chicago, where John Dewey and James R. Angell (1869–1949) were its champions. Both of these men had been influenced by James. They defined psychology as the study of consciousness but recommended approaching the subject from a different perspective. Their position was clearly stated in Angell's APA presidential address of 1906.

According to Angell, functional psychology aimed to portray the operations of consciousness as organic adaptations to a social and physical environment, in contrast with the structural approach (the atomistic approach), which attempted to analyze consciousness and describe its contents. It followed that the functionalist was interested in the evolutionary purpose, or usefulness, of mental activity, the significance of the relationship between mind and body, and the conditions under which an activity occurred and was elicited.

Moreover, Angell asserted, the functionalist did not shrink from biology, but was "cheek by jowl with the general biologist." Having placed psychologists in that intimate but rather uncomfortable position, Angell went on to describe an executive function of consciousness which both prescribed and inhibited behavior, selecting out from the environment only certain aspects to which it attended: "The functionalist's most intimate persuasion leads him to regard consciousness as primarily and intrinsically a control phenomenon."

Many psychologists found the functional position congenial since they had been functioning as functionalists in everything but name. If psychology had to be divided into structuralist and functionalist camps, then all applied psychologists would have been swept into the latter. But matters did not rest there. In 1907, Witmer complicated the issue by describing yet another approach which he called clinical psychology.

Witmer used the term "clinical" to refer to a method of teaching and research and not merely as the adjectival form of the noun clinic, a place where persons are examined. The clinical method consisted of a gathering of instructors, students, and those needing help for the purpose of studying, doing research into, and treating mental abilities and defects. Although the clinical psychologist's major purpose would be to examine the person with the goal of prescribing beneficial measures for his development, Witmer emphasized two points: one, as a teacher, the clinician was to conduct demonstrations in the presence of students so that they would be instructed in the science and the art of psychology; two, as a scientist, the clinician was to regard each case as in part a research experiment in which the effects of his procedures and recommendations were to be discovered.

Further, though Witmer recognized that clinical psychology was something of an encroachment upon other professions, he dismissed the matter this way: "While the field of clinical psychology is to some extent occupied by the physician, especially by the psychiatrist, and while I expect to rely in a great measure upon the educator and social worker for the more important contributions to this branch of psychology, it is nevertheless true that none of these has quite the training necessary for this kind of work. For that matter, neither has the psychologist, unless he has acquired this training from other sources than the usual course of instruction in psychology."

Witmer had, of course, been continuing his work at his clinic at the University of Pennsylvania, and by 1900 was seeing about three children a day. For some of the cases, he called S. Weir Mitchell into neurological consultation. However the ultimate responsibility for the case and the prescription of pedagogical treatment rested with the precise and erudite Witmer.

Witmer succeeded in persuading the administration of the university to begin to offer formal training in clinical psychology, and its catalogue of 1904–05 announced that students in this area could take courses for credit in psychiatry and neuropathology in the Medical School. By 1907, Witmer had been able to raise sufficient funds to establish a hospital school for the training of retardates as an adjunct of his clinic, and to found a professional journal, *The Psychological Clinic,* of which he became editor. Regular and continuing Summer School courses were offered in child psychology, educational psychology, and the functioning of his clinic; an undergraduate course was offered in abnormal psychology. The following academic year, 1908–09, five clinical psychology courses were offered in the Graduate School: three on developmental psychology, one on abnormal psychology, and one on mental and physical defects in school children.

Not the least of Witmer's interests at this time was in promoting his term "orthogenics" and in encouraging psychologists to do work in the area it defined. Issues of *The Psychological Clinic* prominently displayed the term's definition, and the journal itself was subtitled *A Journal of Orthogenics.* However, this was another of Witmer's losing battles. "Clinical psychology" was the more congenial and generally accepted of the two terms, probably because psychologists did not relish the possibility of being known as "orthogenicists." Nevertheless, Witmer was successful in the more important aspect of his campaign, that of encouraging his colleagues to become involved in correcting aspects of the social system that produced harmful psychological consequences.

From its opening in 1896 to 1909, Witmer's clinic evaluated 459 children, and the University of Pennsylvania recognized its value by increasing its financial support. The staff consisted of Witmer as director, an assistant director, five trained Ph.D.'s as examiners, one social worker, three assistant social workers, and a recorder. By then their clinic was no longer alone.

In addition to Healy's clinic, which we noted earlier, there was the Iowa Psychological Clinic, founded in 1908 by Carl Seashore and R. L. Sylvester. Seashore (1866–1949) was an optimistic, self-satisfied individual: "I have been a lucky man—lucky in the place and race of my nativity, in the 'choice' of my parents, in my education, in my jobs, in my travels, in my marriage and children, in success and recognition beyond my fondest dreams."

He had sung his undergraduate way through Gustavus Adolphus College, in the glee club, as a member of quartets, and as a choir director. In 1895, Seashore received his doctorate from Yale, and in 1897, after two years of postdoctoral studies, accepted the position of assistant professor of philosophy at the University of Iowa. Seashore endeared himself to the university administration by his willingness to undertake assignments even before having any idea as to how he could fulfill them. The following example will suffice.

Around 1900, the University of Iowa inadvertently found itself with more applicants for entrance than it could possibly handle. Seashore obligingly volunteered to accept the responsibility for solving this problem. He began giving a test devised by Thorndike as a qualifying entrance examination for incoming freshmen. As a screening device, the test owed much of its success to the fact that a sizeable proportion of the applicants timidly withdrew rather than take it. Seashore had saved the day, and encouraged by his victory began constructing his own aptitude and achievement tests.

In 1908, Seashore was appointed dean of the Graduate College. The clinic he helped found that year was patterned after Witmer's. While the major emphasis was on research, the clinic did offer some services in remedying speech and reading disabilities and mental defects. Perhaps the case most fondly recalled by Seashore was that of a girl who needed help because she flatted in her singing.

The following year, 1909, Clark University also established a psychological clinic. Furthermore, courses in clinical psychology were introduced at the University of Minnesota and the University of Washington, and both schools subsequently established clinics.

Obviously, aside from Healy's clinic, which was affiliated with the court but which did accept some graduate students for training, there was a growing number of psychological clinics located in academic settings. Their orientation, and that of their clientèle, was based on the assumption that psychologists did not deal with, nor were they dealing with, people who were mentally ill, but with persons who had learning difficulties. Even in nonacademic settings, psychologists, by virtue of their scientific and scholastic background, were engaged to fill positions that involved research, mental testing, and pedagogy, not treatment.

Only a very few psychologists worked outside of universities. Among this hardy group were the following: R. T. Wylie, who in 1898 began research and psychological testing at the state institution for the retarded in Faribault, Minnesota; Goddard, who became director of research at Vineland in 1906, and who began offering the first psychological internships two years later; Edmund Huey, who was appointed in 1909 to a position in the State Institution for the Feeble-Minded in Lincoln, Illinois; and F. Lyman Wells, who succeeded Franz at McLean Hospital.

Much to everyone's pleasure, psychology was continuing to expand in the United States and Europe. In 1901, Edouard Claparède helped found the Swiss journal *Archives de Psychologie,* and in 1903 Guilio Ferrari founded the Italian journal *Revista di Psicologia.* Cattell predicted that someday there would be a profession of applied psychology, and the Fifth International Congress of Psychology, which met in Rome, was pronounced by one and all a great success. The outstanding attractions at the Congress were a paper delivered by James and a presentation of data and results with the Binet-Simon Scale.

In 1906, standards for election to membership in the APA were tightened: a prospective member had to have psychology as his profession and give evidence of research accomplishment; philosophers, educators, and those who merely held assistantships were no longer accepted as members. It was also proposed, but not agreed upon, that continued membership in the Association should be contingent on continued scientific contributions. An APA committee, composed of Angell, Judd, Pillsbury, Seashore, and Woodworth, was formed to develop a series of improved group and individual tests that would have practical applications.

Yet all this occurred early in the development of the profession. The APA dues had been reduced in 1904 to $1.00 a year, and the membership by 1910 numbered only 222. Psychology was still largely a hope and a promise. Its devotees struggled for emancipation from departments of philosophy, and yet found themselves faced with rejection by the established natural sciences. For the most part, psychologists had no secure place within universities. Unsure of their own professional identities and even of the identity of their science, striving for recognition, and widely regarded by the academic world as troublesome upstarts who did not meet accepted standards for status as an independent, scientific field, psychologists still dreamed of a bright future.

"Psychology will one day, in all probability, have a dominant place among the sciences, instead of its present somewhat humble rank," said Stratton wistfully encouraging his colleagues in his APA presidential address of 1908. And a similar sentiment was expressed by Judd in his presidential address of 1909: "Psychology will boldly assert its right to

90 *Clinical Psychology*

exist as the science which deals in a broad way with the evolutionary processes by which consciousness arose and through which the trend of life has been changed from organic adaptation to intelligent conquest."

Some psychologists—to borrow a phrase from James—probably had a "courage-fit" from Judd's words, others no doubt mumbled and grumbled their disagreement with his definition of their science, but most of them assuredly experienced to some extent the feeling of exhilaration and defiant pride that comes with pioneering in a new field.

References

44444Angell, J. R. The province of functional psychology. *Psychol. Rev.*, 1907, 14, 61–91.

Beers, C. W. *A mind that found itself.* New York: Longmans Green, 1908.

Binet, A. & Henri, V. La psychologie individuelle. *L'année Psychol.*, 1896, 2, 411–465.

Binet, A. & Simon, T. Upon the necessity of establishing a scientific diagnosis of inferior states of intelligence. The development of the Binet-Simon Scale. In Judy F. Rosenblith & W. Allinsmith (Eds.) *The causes of behavior: readings in child development and educational psychology.* Boston: Allyn & Bacon, 1962.

Boring, E. G. *A history of experimental psychology.* New York: Appleton-Century-Crofts, 1950.

Burns, E. M. *Western civilizations: their history & their culture.* New York: Norton, 1947.

Calder-Marshall, A. Ellis, Havelock. In L. Shores (Ed.) *Collier's Encyclopedia.* Vol. 9, New York: Crowell-Collier, 1962.

Calkins, Mary W. Autobiography. In C. Murchison (Ed.) *A history of psychology in autobiography.* Worcester, Mass.: Clark U. Press, 1930.

Cattell, J. M. Retrospect: psychology as a profession. *J. consult. Psychol.*, 1937, 1, 1–3; 1946, 10, 289–291.

Dubois, P. *The psychic treatment of mental disorders.* New York: Funk & Wagnalls, 1908.

Fernberger, S. W. History of the psychological clinic. In R. A. Brotemarkle (Ed.) *Clinical psychology: studies in honor of Lightner Witmer.* Philadelphia: U. Pennsylvania Press, 1931.

Fernberger, S. W. The American Psychological Association: a historical summary, 1892–1930. *Psychol. Bull.*, 1932, 29, 1–89.

Fernberger, S. W. Shepherd Ivory Franz: 1874–1933. *Psychol. Bull.*, 1933, 30, 741–742.

Ferrari, G. C. Autobiography. In C. Murchison (Ed.) *A history of psychology in autobiography.* Vol. II. Worcester, Mass.: Clark U. Press, 1932.

Forel, A. *Collected papers*. Baltimore: Phipps Psychiatric Clinic, 1907.

Franz, S. I. The present status of psychology in medical education and practice. *J. Amer. Med. Assoc.,* 1912, 58, 909–911.

Freeman, F. S. *Theory and practice of psychological testing.* New York: Holt, 1950.

Freud, S. *The basic writings of Sigmund Freud.* A. A. Brill (Ed.) New York: Modern Library, 1938.

Freud, S. Analysis of a phobia in a five-year-old boy. In *Collected papers.* Vol. III. New York: Basic Books, 1959.

Healy, W. & Bronner, Augusta F. The child guidance clinic: birth and growth of an idea. In L. G. Lowrey & Victoria Sloane (Eds.) *Orthopsychiatry 1923– 1948: retrospect and prospect.* New York: Amer. Orthopsychiat. Assoc., 1948.

Jastrow, J. Some currents and undercurrents in psychology. *Psychol. Rev.,* 1901, 8, 1–26.

Jastrow, J. Autobiography. In C. Murchison (Ed.) *A history of psychology in autobiography.* Vol. I. Worcester, Mass.: Clark U. Press, 1930.

Jones, E. *The life and work of Sigmund Freud.* Vols. I & II. New York: Basic Books, 1953, 1955.

Judd, C. H. Evolution and consciousness. *Psychol. Rev.,* 1910, 17, 77–97.

Jung, C. G. The psychology of dementia praecox. *Nerv. Ment. Disease Monograph Series,* 1936, No. 3.

Jung, C. G. Memories, dreams, reflections. New York: Pantheon, 1963.

Kiernan, J. G. Limitations of the Emmanuel Movement. *Amer. J. clin. Med.,* 1909, 16, 1088–1090.

Knight, Margaret. *William James.* London: Penguin Books, 1950.

McDougall, W. *Introduction to social psychology.* London: Methuen & Co., 1908.

McDougall, W. Autobiography. In C. Murchison (Ed.) *A history of psychology in autobiography.* Vol. I. Worcester, Mass.: Clark U. Press, 1930.

Murphy, G. *Historical introduction to modern psychology.* New York: Harcourt, Brace, 1950.

Norsworthy, Naomi. The psychology of mentally defective children. *Arch. Psychol. N.Y.,* 1906, No. 1.

Obituary. Alfred Binet. *Amer. J. Psychol.,* 1912, 23, 140–141.

Pratt, J. H. The home sanitarium treatment of consumption. *Johns Hopkins Hosp. Bull.,* 1906, 17, 140–144.

Prince, M. Hysteria from the point of view of dissociated personality. *J. abnorm. Psychol.,* 1906–07, 1, 170–187.

Prince, M. The unconscious. *J. abnorm. Psychol.,* 1908–09, 3, 261–297.

Prince, M. The psychological principles and field of psychotherapy. *J. abnorm. Psychol.,* 1909–10, 4, 72–98.

Putnam, J. J. Personal impressions of Sigmund Freud and his work, with special reference to his recent lectures at Clark University. *J. abnorm. Psychol.,* 1909–10, 4, 293–310, 372–379.

Scott, W. D. An interpretation of the psychoanalytic method in psychotherapy with a report of a case so treated. *J. abnorm. Psychol.,* 1908–09, 3, 371–377.

Seashore, C. Autobiography. In C. Murchison (Ed.) *A history of psychology in autobiography.* Vol. I. Worcester, Mass.: Clark U. Press, 1930.

Shaffer, G. W. & Lazarus, R. S. *Fundamental concepts in clinical psychology.* New York: McGraw-Hill, 1952.

Shakow, D. One hundred years of American psychiatry: a special review. *Psychol. Bull.,* 1945, 42, 423–432.

Spearman, C. General intelligence, objectively determined and measured. *Amer. J. Psychol.,* 1904, 15, 201–293.

Spearman, C. Autobiography. In C. Murchison (Ed.) *A history of psychology in autobiography.* Vol. I. Worcester, Mass.: Clark U. Press, 1930.

Speer, G. S. A survey of psychologists in Illinois. *Amer. Psychol.,* 1950, 5, 424–426.

Stern, W. Autobiography. In C. Murchison (Ed.) *A history of psychology in autobiography.* Vol. I. Worcester, Mass.: Clark U. Press, 1930.

Stratton, G. M. Toward the correction of some rival methods in psychology. *Psychol. Rev.,* 1909, 16, 67–83.

Symonds, P. M. *Diagnosing personality and conduct.* New York: Century, 1931.

Thorndike, E. L. Autobiography. In C. Murchison (Ed.) *A history of psychology in autobiography.* Vol. III. Worcester, Mass.: Clark U. Press, 1936.

Varnon, Edith J. The development of Alfred Binet's psychology. *Psychol. Monogr.,* 1935, 46, Whole no. 207.

Watson, R. I. A brief history of clinical psychology. *Psychol. Bull.,* 1953, 50, 321–346.

Winkler, J. K. & Bromberg, W. *Mind explorers.* New York: Reynal & Hitchcock, 1939.

Wissler, C. Correlation of mental and physical tests. *Psychol. Monogr.,* 1901, No. 16.

Witmer, L. Clinical psychology. *Psychol. Clinic,* 1907, 1, 1–9.

Witmer, L. Retrospect and prospect: an editorial. *Psychol. Clinic,* 1908–09, 2, 1–4.

Witmer, L. The treatment and cure of a case of mental and moral deficiency. *Psychol. Clinic,* 1908–09, 2, 153–179.

Witmer, L. The restoration of children of the slums. *Psychol. Clinic,* 1909–10, 3, 266–280.

Witmer, L. Psychological diagnosis and the psychonomic orientation of analytic science. *Psychol. Clinic,* 1925, 16, 1–18.

Woodworth, R. S. Autobiography. In C. Murchison (Ed.) *A history of psychology in autobiography.* Vol. II. Worcester, Mass.: Clark U. Press, 1932.

Woodworth, R. S. *Contemporary schools of psychology*. New York: Ronald, 1948.

Young, K. The history of mental testing. *Ped. Sem.*, 1924, 31, 1–48.

Zilboorg, G. & Henry, G. W. *A history of medical psychology*. New York: Norton, 1941.

4

Psychologists Go To War

1910-1919

THE BEGINNING OF THIS TURBULENT DECADE found intellectuals in almost all fields of human expression affirming their faith in science and looking forward to continued advances for mankind. Any feelings of pessimism and futility that may have persisted as a legacy from the past soon receded in the warm glow of immediate change and exciting prospects. There was a break with tradition in art, where futurism departed from former aesthetic ideals and called for the depiction of machines and scientific achievements. Similarly, functional or modern architecture stressed the beauty to be found in simplicity in design and in the imaginative use of the newest materials provided by technology. The new realists of philosophy, while acknowledging that there was little comfort and probably some error in the truths provided by science, nonetheless believed them to be the best available guide for ordering one's life. Accordingly, they advised man to accept his existence without fear and to grace his years with dignity by actively dealing with his environment and benefiting his fellow man.

Encouragingly, the benefits did continue to come from what was called the "White Magic," science. Airplanes, motion pictures, and automobiles were but three inventions that were rapidly losing their novelty and becoming an integral part of Western life. And there were discoveries whose full implications are still being pursued: the importance of the pituitary gland in the control of human growth, the necessity of vitamins for a proper diet and the prevention of illness, and the finding that electrical charges are a fundamental constituent of matter.

An important by-product of this progress was that those Americans who had directly or indirectly profited from the achievements of science made generous contributions of large sums of money among various educational causes. Henry Phipps gave $50,000 to the mental-hygiene movement, thus putting it on its feet financially. Andrew Carnegie gave $10,000,000 for pensions to college teachers, $10,000,000 to advance the cause of peace, and $135,000,000 to promote human knowledge and understanding. Rockefeller gave over $165,000,000 to further the noble aims of humanity.

As we might have predicted from our contacts with the movements for reform, not everyone received these philanthropic acts gratefully. Some, Cattell for one, saw something other than hard work and thrift in the fact that one man was able to accumulate over $300,000,000 within his lifetime. Cattell was particularly indignant about the discrepancy between the incomes of those who produced ideas, specifically college professors, and those who simply marketed and made use of those ideas, specifically corporation executives. He made a strong argument, not only for increases in faculty salaries, but also for faculties being given greater responsibilities in the administration of their respective schools.

In 1910, Cattell attacked the Carnegie Foundation for the Advancement of Teaching as subversive of academic freedom. Since President Butler of Columbia University was a trustee of the Foundation, a clash between the two men was virtually inevitable. Each invited the other to resign from Columbia, but neither did so. Instead, their conflict smoldered with occasional outbursts by Cattell and others, including Jastrow, against the domination of faculties by university administrations.

Elsewhere, two years of minor wars in the Balkans finally erupted, in 1914, into one that was world-wide. By 1916, Serbia, Russia, France, Great Britain, Montenegro, Japan, Italy, and Rumania were allied against Austria, Germany, Turkey, and Bulgaria. Each side was convinced of its own virtue and attempted to justify and make reasonable its actions. However, feelings within the United States tended from the outset to be more sympathetic to the French and British cause and grew increasingly hostile to that of the Germans.

In 1917, with a mingled feeling of relief, determination, and considerable enthusiasm, the United States declared war against Germany in order to "make the world safe for democracy" and, ultimately, to end all wars among nations. Naturally, in the emotional excesses of the period the loyalty of Americans of German descent or of those who had studied in Germany became suspect. Among those caught up by the misguided patriotism of the moment was Cattell.

Although his son McKeen was in France with the first group of volunteers, and although Cattell was participating in the war effort by organizing committees of scientists for the National Research Council, he found himself brought into federal court. Cattell's "crime" had been to speak out in favor of exempting conscientious objectors from combat (Under the Espionage Act of 1917 and the Sedition Act of 1918, federal authorities arrested over 1500 persons; these laws were in part so vague that they provided penalties for discouraging recruiting and "disloyal and abusive" language about the government.). The trustees of Columbia judged Cattell with greater speed and harshness than the judiciary and summarily dismissed him, minus accrued pension and salary, on the grounds of treason, sedition, and opposition to the laws of the United States. However, Cattell was not to be disposed of so easily. For five years he fought in the courts to regain his pension, and won. That made his war with Columbia four years longer, but more profitable in outcome, than the one his country had waged.

Meanwhile sweeping changes had been taking place within the social structure of the United States. Women were assuming a new status and demanding the rights to vote and be treated as equals. They wore lipstick and rouge—a practice previously considered "immoral." And in the words of H. L. Mencken: "The veriest schoolgirl of today knows as much as the midwife of 1885, and spends a good deal more time discharging and disseminating her information."

Similar pressures for reform and just treatment were exerted by labor, which was intensifying its expressions of dissatisfaction with being dependent upon the generosity of employers (Textile workers in Massachusetts were given a pay of $10 for a 54-hour week, which even at that time was not enough to insure survival.). Demands were pressed to have management respect its rights to organize and bargain as equals for an equitable wage.

Disturbed by these signs of internal agitation and unrest, many people looked for their causes in influences from outside the country and seemed to feel that the best course was a revival of isolationism. It appeared as if they hoped to restore their previous feelings of security by a fervent holding to those ideals and spiritual values that seemed to them to have made the United States unique and great. A Red Scare, a fear of Communist subversion, swept through the country in 1919. Before it ended, almost six hundred aliens were deported, and a man who killed an immigrant for yelling, "To hell with the U.S.," was acquitted by a jury of his peers in two minutes.

By 1920, women had the right to vote, and an experiment was about to begin in the legislation of morals. The United States was to prohibit itself from indulging in alcoholic beverages. With the death of Demon Rum, the evangelist Billy Sunday, eloquently expressing a popular belief, predicted a beautiful future: "The slums soon will be only a memory. We will turn our prisons into factories and our jails into storehouses and corncribs. Men will walk upright now, women will smile, and the children will laugh. Hell will be forever for rent."

NORMAL PERSONALITY FUNCTIONING

The fast tempo of the times was reflected in the elaborations taking place within psychology. Perhaps in part because Ernest Jones became assistant editor in 1910, few issues of the *Journal of Abnormal Psychology* failed to mention the latest developments in psychoanalytic circles. Generally, even the critical articles were favorable in their conclusions, and the critics themselves were censured if their published comments indicated an uncalled for emotional reaction against the theory. "He who cannot endure the truth should keep away from science," admonished Bleuler.

The critics seemed to agree that what irritated them most was the tendency of psychoanalysts to generalize and rush with haste into dubious applications of analytic ideas. More specifically, even Bleuler was annoyed by the "pathographies," or the psychoanalyses of persons long dead that were appearing frequently in the literature. Nor could he see why the contents of the unconscious had to consist only of wishes, and not fears as well. Woodworth pointed out quite plausibly that any train of association, if pursued long enough, would lead to a complex. Therefore he questioned the validity of the analytic interpretations and found too many of them that seemed, frankly, far-fetched. He also rejected the assertion that successful therapeutic outcomes indicated the rectitude of the theory since other forms of treatment based on different theories claimed to produce equally effective results.

Moreover, while none of the critics denied that sexual motivation is important, all wondered why Sigmund Freud insisted it is so very important. Bleuler could not see any sexual origins in a person's devotion to religion, or appreciation of aesthetics, or desire to obtain knowledge. Nor did he feel that every neurosis had some sexual cause. Instead, he suggested as an alternative that it might be possible for the person to have a nonsexual predisposition which renders him vulnerable to sexual

disturbances later in his life, and these later disorders in sexual functioning might eventually find expression in the form of a neurosis.

Yet when all was said and done, Bleuler concluded that psychoanalytic
theory was essentially correct. He noted quite reasonably: "That in the
minor work of the whole school many details are problematical, too
hastily generalized, or directly untrue, should not appear strange. It
would be curious if in this freshly explored field, and in the endless complications of the mind false conclusions were not reached as well as in
every other sphere."

Janet also ended his appraisal of psychoanalysis in what was intended
to be complimentary fashion: "Later on we shall forget the excessive
generalizations and adventurous symbolisms, which at present seem to
characterize these studies and to separate them from other scientific
works, and only one thing will be remembered, namely, that psychoanalysis has rendered great service to psychological analysis."

Certainly psychologists were receptive to the psychoanalytic concepts of
the defenses and unconscious motivation. Neither required allegiance to
any particular theory, and both were readily inferred from overt behavior, once a person had knowledge of them and was sensitive to their
manifestations. Binet had been traveling in this direction, and shortly
before his death in 1911, gave a hint of the framework in which his
formulations would have been cast: "Against this theory (of rational
thought) stands the new one, a theory of action, according to which
mental life is not at all a rational life, but a chaos of shadow crossed by
flashes, something strange, and especially discontinuous, which appeared
continuous and rational only because after the event it was described in a
language which brings order and clarity everywhere."

Another illustration of the favor with which the concept of the unconscious was regarded may be found in an article by Ogden in 1911. Ogden
suggested that the reason some psychological laboratories were unable to
find imageless thoughts was because the unconscious attitudes of the experimenter were being communicated without his awareness to his subjects, thus biasing their reports.

What did bother psychologists, however, was the Freudian insistence
upon the saturation of the unconscious with sexual content. While non-
analysts such as Borris Sidis spoke disparagingly of "Freudian twaddle,"
a similar discontent bloomed and flowered deep in the garden of psychoanalysis itself. In 1909, Jung wrote to Freud recommending a more
discreet approach to the "unsavory topic" of sex: "Both with the students
and with patients I get on further by not making the theme of sexuality
prominent." But Freud would tolerate no compromise on this issue,
arguing that to minimize the pervasiveness of sexual motivation would
render psychoanalysis sterile and impotent. His firm stand was perceived
by some of his dissident followers as a personal rejection and also as a

welcome signal of their maturity because they had dared to openly challenge him.

A series of ruptures began around 1911. First, Alfred Adler left the Vienna Psychoanalytic Society to form his own group, the Society for Individual Psychology. Wilhelm Stekel departed for greener pastures of his own in 1912. Neither of these losses distressed Freud personally. Adler was viewed as a morose and cantankerous fellow who never did quite fit in with the group, while the depth of Stekel's devotion to science was questioned. There were still 106 members of the International Psychoanalytic Association, with Jung serving as president, and Brill had just founded a Psychoanalytic Society in New York. Things were really going much better than Freud had ever expected. His only worry was over the use his critics could make of the defections to discredit analytic theory. To prevent recurrences, he suggested that an analyst should be "fully analyzed" lest: "He will easily yield to the temptation of projecting as a scientific theory of general applicability some of the peculiarities of his own personality which he has dimly perceived."

Then in 1913 Jung, the heir-apparent of the psychoanalytic movement, broke with Freud. Now this was a distressing blow that Freud had tried to prevent. Some solace was provided by Jones' suggestion that a secret inner committee of trustworthy analysts be formed. They would be dedicated to insuring the development of Freud's theory and therapeutic techniques. The Committee, as it was unimaginatively called, was composed of Freud, Jones, Otto Rank, Sandor Ferenczi, Hanns Sachs, and Karl Abraham. The following year, 1914, Jung resigned his presidency of the International Psychoanalytic Association and severed his formal ties with psychoanalysis.

Freud was deeply concerned, and tried to explain to the world what had happened by setting down a history of the psychoanalytic movement. Above all, he wished it to be known that it was his ideas that were in danger of being distorted and appropriated. With genuine feelings but questionable assumptions, he repudiated his former "modesty" and rescinded much of the credit he had once accorded Breuer for helping develop psychoanalysis: "I have never heard that Breuer's great share in psychoanalysis has earned him a corresponding measure of criticism and abuse and as it is long ago since I recognized that to stir up contradiction and arouse bitterness is the inevitable fate of psychoanalysis I conclude that I must be the real originator of all that is particularly characteristic in it."

Because of the growing popularity of psychoanalysis with its attendant abuses, Freud's efforts during this period were directed largely at illustrating and putting into print techniques and principles for interpretation and therapy. The outbreak of World War I and his concern for the safety of his sons who were serving in the Austrian army were said to have contributed to a relatively sharp drop in his fundamental discoveries. Nevertheless, by ordinary standards Freud was still exceptionally productive, and he continued to shape elaborations, extensions, and modifications of psychoanalytic theory.

It seemed to Freud that unconscious mental processes consist of wishes which have been aroused by instinctual excitation. These wishes exist not in verbalized form but as images and sensations. This partially explains why it is so difficult to communicate the contents of unconsciousness to others. Only as the wishes proceed into preconsciousness and consciousness do they become accessible to verbal concepts and labeling operations.

Within unconsciousness all is absolute and there is no conception of time. The wish for something to happen is equivalent to its actual occurrence, and wishes of long ago that have been repressed are still experienced as current feelings and attitudes.

Repression, itself, was differentiated into two forms. Primary repression refers to the process involved when the mental representation of an instinct is kept from awareness. Secondary repression refers to the process of keeping ideas from awareness that are connected or associated with the primary repressed material. For example, a person represses not only a wish that is incestuous (primary repression) but also thoughts that might remind him of the wish (secondary repression). In distinguishing both of these processes, Freud devoted considerable attention to the problem of what happens to the charges of energy with which all ideas and sensations are supposedly invested. He envisioned a highly mobile psychic system always in flux in which there are attractions and repulsions and removals of energy preconsciously.

Governing the unconscious is the pleasure principle: to seek gratification of the repressed wishes and to avoid the unpleasure caused by denying them expression in overt behavior. Governing the functioning in consciousness is the reality principle: a recognition of, and adjustment to, the demands of the environment so that instinctual impulses can be gratified without bringing the individual into interpersonal conflict or pain.

To sharpen and implement the task of taking reality into account involves the development of perception, memory, attention, judgment, thought, and a capacity to delay gratification. Freud's formulation of the role of conscious functioning, or the ego, as mediating between the demands of instinctual strivings and environmental restrictions thus furnishes a bridge for psychoanalysis to cross over and encompass virtually all areas of psychology.

However, Freud did not see ego functioning as exclusively conscious. The ego processes involve many that operate preconsciously or unconsciously to defend the person from awareness of his instinctual impulses, and at times to allow them disguised gratification. These defenses include: repression; projection, or attributing one's own feelings and thoughts to others; turning against the self (rather than expressing the impulse toward the person who aroused it); and reversal into the opposite, e.g., changing unconscious love into conscious hate for someone.

By 1914, Freud had ventured into anthropology, and saw in the reported taboos and rituals of primitive peoples defenses similar to those observed in patients suffering from obsessional neuroses. He also thought he recognized another "institution," or related group of mental functions, similar to the conscience. This institution comes about during the individual's growth when he acquires from the teachings and criticisms of parents and others a set of standards and ideals by which he seeks to guide his behavior. Freud called this system of values the ego-ideal. He suggested that with its formation not only are new demands imposed on the ego to measure up to certain standards, but also feelings of self-approval or narcissistic gratifications are experienced when the person succeeds in acting in accordance with these ideals. Therefore, the function of the conscience is to evaluate critically the individual's behavior in terms of his particular ego-ideal and to see to it that rewards and punishments of self-satisfaction and condemnation are provided.

In 1919, the Committee completed its membership by adding Max Eitington. In the meantime Carl Jung, whose defection had been a prime reason for the Committee's formation, had been developing and expressing his own theoretical formulations. Intellectually, Jung explained his break with the psychoanalytic movement on the ground that Freud "identified his method with his sex theory which I deemed to be inadmissable." In keeping with his expressed dissatisfaction, Jung had redefined libido to mean a general psychic energy, rather than an energy that was specifically sexual.

Jung envisioned libido, under normal circumstances, as rhythmically flowing back and forth. This forward and backward libidinal flow represents, respectively, progressive adaptation by the individual to his external environment and regressive adaptation to his inner needs. A blockage in either direction, or a failing on the part of the person to attend to and satisfy either environmental or internal demands, is indicative of a psychological disturbance.

In understanding the causes of these dammed disturbances, Jung emphasized the importance of the present. We are dealing, he argued, with a person who has withdrawn libido or interest from his current surroundings. For us to probe, then, into the patient's past searching for a cause in his childhood will only serve to comply with his desire to refrain from coming to grips with his present difficulties. The questions that concern us, therefore, are related to the current obstacles which the person cannot overcome, the tasks and duties of the present that the person is seeking to avoid. Within this framework, dreams and fantasies of the individual may be regarded as compensations for his unfulfilled adaptations to reality. Jung thus questioned not only the psychoanalytic emphasis upon sexuality, but its focus upon the past. However, his most startling innovation was the concept of a collective unconscious.

Jung called the relatively long-recognized and much-discussed unconscious processes of the individual, those stressed by the Freudians, the personal unconscious. The collective unconscious refers to those mental processes operating within the person's awareness which are a product, not of his particular development, but of the development of the human race. Over countless years, Jung explained, man's brain has been shaped and influenced and conditioned by the past history of mankind. The supposed result of this racial development is that each person has inherited unconscious sets or tendencies to experience and understand certain persons and events in a universal way. Jung called these "pre-existent forms of apprehension" *archetypes*. The archetypes are illustrated by man's unlearned inclination to react to birth and to such things as death, the rising and setting of the sun, the earth and the sea, with certain characteristic feelings and perceptions.

Primordial images, later also termed archetypes by Jung, are said to exist in the collective unconscious. These images of power, of the sun, of the hero, of the earth mother find expression in myths, folklore, dreams, religions, and mental disorders. Since the archetypes help determine our perception of the world, it is upon the inherited foundation of the collective unconscious that the entire structure of personality is thought to be erected.

The collective and personal unconscious are viewed by Jung as repositories of wisdom from the racial and individual past. Thus by dipping into his unconscious with understanding, man can gain knowledge that will help him to overcome his present frustrations. Dreams, in this context, are seen as helpful guides in the solution of life's problems. For man, according to Jung, is constantly striving to progress to a more complete stage of development in which all his functions and processes may be acknowledged, integrated, and expressed. Pointing the way for him to travel are symbols from his unconscious, indicating those aspects of his personality which he has repressed and ignored and which thus represent profitable lines of future growth.

Few psychologists have begrudged Jung his optimistic orientation; more have found it difficult to agree with his contention that human behavior is determined not only by the past but, teleologically, by man's supposed aims and aspirations for completion and fulfillment; most, being good Darwinians, have rejected his concept of a collective unconscious with its Lamarckian flavored inheritance of acquired characteristics, which in this case are thoughts. It is this very collective unconscious that inspired Solomon, a reviewer of Jung's book *Psychology of the Unconscious*, to write:

"Jung has presented us, in all sincerity and with the full force of his personality and the very fire of his soul, with a system of ideas than which, spite the many truths included, the undersigned can conceive of none that is a greater menace to mankind and modern civilization." Most psychologists did not share Solomon's alarm, in part because a large majority of them had not felt close enough to this area to feel obliged to read Jung's book.

In general, it seems fair to say that the chief significance to their contemporaries of the theoretical writings of those who had broken with Freud was the fact that a crumbling within psychoanalysis was occurring. Here were criticisms of Freud's theories with consequences in real life. Many psychologists who followed these developments with interest, and a touch of satisfaction, believed that further breaks with Freud would take place. Within a few years, they predicted, the young renegades would modify psychoanalysis to take into account the criticisms that had been made, justly—in their opinion—of it. There no longer seemed to be too much point in excitedly attacking a theory already showing signs of moving toward moderation, or perhaps disintegration.

Nevertheless, nothing originating within the United States, or anywhere else for that matter, rivaled psychoanalytic theory and its derivatives in scope, depth, and comprehensiveness—and despite the personal disagreements, psychoanalysis was still building. American formulations, by comparison, seemed pale, plodding, and fragmentary, restrained and cautious, and lacking dramatic fire and sweep. The emotions of American psychologists appeared to be channeled, for the most part, into heated discussions about definitions of their science and its course.

Woodworth made an effort to achieve peace among the structuralists, functionalists, behaviorists, analysts, self-psychologists, and anyone else interested by proposing dynamic psychology for everyone's approval. The phrase "dynamic psychology" had been in circulation for a number of years. F. L. Wells and J. H. McCurdy had used it in writing on wishes, conflicts, emotions, tendencies, and inhibitions. T. V. Moore applied it in a restricted sense to imply emotion and conation. R. Dodge had in mind mainly physiological processes and functioning, and therefore, when he suggested, in 1913, that cortical operations could be measured "psychodynamically," he proposed to do so by recording pulse and respiration rates.

It was not until 1918 that anyone seriously advocated dynamic psychology as a rubric embracing all the various schools of psychological thought. That someone was, of course, Woodworth in his book, entitled appropriately, *Dynamic Psychology*. Wishing to make dynamic psychology inclusive of all topics and aims, Woodworth did not really help his cause by implementing it through stretching the term to include both the "workings of the mind" and the workings of the whole organism.

Few psychologists cared for his vague definition. What aroused more interest in the book than its attempt to achieve a compromise was that it contained a challenge to McDougall's views about the source energies, or motivation, for all behavior as being derived from instincts. Woodworth preferred to speak in terms of "mechanisms" and "drives." A mechanism, he thought, is a course of behavior that brings about an adjustment, while: "The drive is a mechanism already aroused and thus in a position to furnish stimulation to other mechanisms. Any mechanism might be a drive."

"Any mechanism might be a drive." Therefore, what had been a means to an end might also become an end in itself. For example, a person might have hunted to obtain food, but later continues the activity of hunting because he finds it interesting in and of itself, even when food is no longer desired or obtained. For an activity "To be interesting," Woodworth added, "the process must present some difficulty and yet some prospect of a successful issue." It seemed reasonable to Woodworth, as it might to any man who enjoyed being with people and roaming the out-of-doors, that instincts did not have to be invoked to explain behaviors such as sports and social activities, since they were so intrinsically stimulating and pleasurable.

The immediate response to Woodworth's book was not gratifying with regard to his professed aim of unifying psychology. Although Woodworth was to serve increasingly as a symbol and rallying point for a middle-of-the-road position in psychology, the next ten years were distinguished more by contentious theoretical schools and systems than by harmonious relationships. There was no noticeable rush among psychologists to leap aboard the dynamic bandwagon, and even those who might have been expected to be sympathetic seemed only to have been antagonized. Probably the most personally injured reaction was evidenced in the pages of *The Psychological Clinic*. Its review of *Dynamic Psychology* noted that clinical psychology had not been specifically included nor its areas of interest adequately covered. The book was dismissed contemptuously as " 'brass instrument psychology,' with the instruments cunningly concealed from the public."

However, it should be pointed out that this disputation was not, in and of itself, detrimental to psychology, nor did it really involve the majority of psychologists, who simply took what they considered worthwhile from each position. Furthermore, such differences would be expected in any area subject to interpretation and accessible by many avenues and levels of approach. Thus the proliferation of points of view, while disconcerting, may be seen as a manifestation of healthy growth. Here, amid all the charges and countercharges, were also constructive criticisms for broadening psychology. When these criticisms were heard, when the various "schools" of psychology felt their positions were secure and established, then there would be present those conditions suitable for integration.

DIAGNOSTIC TECHNIQUES

Clearly dominating the field of testing during this period was the Binet-Simon Scale with its revisions and derivatives. At the beginning of the decade a prominent Italian physician Sante de Sanctis was using mental tests of his own making to evaluate intellectual deficiency in the feebleminded, while Goddard was pursuing investigations with the Binet-Simon Scale that would shortly convince him of its great value.

In 1911, Goddard published his revision of the 1908 Binet. Some items were shifted about and new ones were introduced; his scale gained quick and wide acceptance. Also a revision by O. Bobertag appeared in Germany, and Binet presented another revision of his own.

Many criticisms had been directed at the Binet-Simon Scale, although almost everyone liked the idea of grouping items according to the age at which most children passed them. The comments of two critics may serve to typify the remarks of many. Ayres was dissatisfied because the Scale was too heavily weighted with tests involving verbalizations and the child's acquisition of knowledge. For example, the child might be asked to give the date, identify coins, write a sentence, and read a passage. Such tests did not seem to him to be a measure of judgment, which is how Binet and Simon defined intelligence, nor did they seem to be the right kind to evaluate a child's inherited intellectual ability, which is what most psychologists of that day strived to assess.

Moreover, Terman's use of the Scale convinced him that it was too easy at the younger age levels and too difficult at the upper ages. He recommended a radical reclassification of items. He also thought it would be more judicious to express the score in terms of "test age" rather than "mental age." As a further safeguard against making too much of the score and misjudging native ability, Terman recommended that each child should be rated as to his or her physiological age and then a comparison made between the two age levels, intellectual and physiological. Yet these criticisms did not obscure the enormous value of the Scale. Terman expressed the confidence of a large number of his fellow psychologists when he concluded: "I believe that it is possible for the psychologist to submit, after a forty-five minute diagnostication, a more reliable and more enlightening estimate of the child's intelligence than most teachers can offer after a year of daily contact in the classroom."

After it had taken some of these recommendations into account, Binet's 1911 Scale extended from three years to an adult level, but with gaps at eleven, thirteen, and fourteen years. The score was still expressed in terms of mental age and was interpreted as follows: if a child's mental age equalled his chronological age, he was considered "regular" (average) in intelligence; if his mental age was higher, he was "advanced"; if his mental age was lower, he was "retarded."

Further, Binet continued to emphasize the importance of the qualitative aspects of performance. He suggested a possible means for differentiating among the total group of retardates by observing the highest medium through which a child is able to maintain social relations. Idiots can do no more than communicate by gestures; imbeciles are able to maintain contact with others by speech; morons can learn to relate to people through writing.

Following Binet's death, Henri Piéron succeeded to the position of Director of the Laboratory of Physiological Psychology at the Sorbonne. Victor Henri, Binet's earlier collaborator had switched his interests from experimental psychology to physical chemistry and then to theoretical physics. Simon, however, continued his work in the field of mental retardation, cherishing the memories of his encounter with brilliance.

Nevertheless, despite the improvements that had been effected, a general feeling of annoyance with the Binet-Simon Scale persisted. This irritation was that as the child grew, his intelligence score expressed as mental age also grew, assuming a normal course of development. There was thus no way of knowing from the child's mental age alone how intelligent he was in relation to his peers. It was also thought to be confusing to have mental age increase, since few psychologists then believed it possible for intelligence to increase. A solution that would simplify things and indicate how bright a particular child is was proposed by Stern in 1912 for those able to read him in German, or in 1914 for those forced to wait for an English translation of his book. Stern suggested dividing the child's mental age by his chronological age. He called the result of this mathematical computation a "mental quotient." If the child is of normal intelligence, his mental quotient is 1.00; quotients above or below 1.00 indicate, respectively, superior or retarded intelligence. It follows that since mental and chronological ages should increase concurrently, the mental quotient would presumably furnish a relatively stable index of intelligence throughout childhood. This seemed to be a happy and simple solution to the problem.

At least two more revisions of the Binet were published in 1912: one by Kuhlmann and one by Terman and Childs. Meanwhile back at the Psychological Clinic of the University of Pennsylvania, Witmer, never one to be swayed by a crowd, was hard at work with his colleagues on standardizing and obtaining norms for performances on certain tasks. R. H. Sylvester standardized the Seguin Form Board in 1913, but it proved too large and cumbersome to use comfortably with children. Witmer suggested adding another block, and making the whole thing smaller, more attractive, and easier to handle. The result, the Witmer Form Board, was standardized in 1916 by H. H. Young. Two years later, in 1918, the Witmer Cylinders were standardized by F. C. Paschal and Gladys G. Ide. This was a circular board with holes of varying diameters and heights into which appropriate cylinders could be fitted.

The Knox Cubes Test, an instrument used to assess the intelligence of illiterate immigrants at Ellis Island, appeared in 1914; the person was required to tap cubes in a specified order. That same year Healy published his Picture Completion Test; a picture with parts removed, so that the person tested had to select from an assortment of pieces those that seemed most appropriate and was required to insert them in their proper positions. Another version of this test was introduced in 1917 and was used by psychological examiners in the Army during World War I.

Yerkes, J. W. Bridges, and R. S. Hardwick came out with their revision of the Binet in 1915. Robert Yerkes (1876–1956) received his Ph.D. from Harvard in 1901, and from 1913 was employed halftime as a psychologist at the Boston Psychopathic Hospital. The major innovation introduced by his test was the use of a point scale: items were grouped according to the processes they were supposedly measuring, e.g., memory, motor coordination, and were arranged in order of increasing difficulty. Each item carried a certain number of points credit. The person's score was divided by the average score of other individuals of the same age yielding a Coefficient of Intellectual Ability (CIA), which was thus an index similar to Stern's mental quotient. However, despite its merits, Yerkes' scale was soon overshadowed by Terman's revision of 1916.

Lewis M. Terman (1877–1956), who lived his early years as a farmboy in Indiana, recalled fondly that his childhood friends included a veritable collection of cases in abnormal psychology: a seriously disturbed youngster, a pathological liar, a crippled boy prone to stealing and temper tantrums, and a fellow who was a "lightning calculator." In 1892, Terman entered Central Normal College in Danville, Indiana, and by the age of twenty-one had earned three academic degrees from that institution, which unfortunately at that time carried little weight beyond the village limits. He became principal of a local high school, married, and became a father.

Yet Terman's ambition was to teach psychology and for that he needed a degree from a recognized school. So in 1901 he borrowed $1200 and enrolled at Indiana University. Within two years he had his A.B. and M.A. Borrowing another $1200, he accepted a fellowship at Clark in 1903. What impressed him most about the psychology department at Clark was the freedom it gave students. To register, the graduate student simply told his name and the courses he wanted to Hall's secretary. Of all the courses, Terman thought Hall's Monday evening seminar was the best.

Each seminar consisted of two students reporting on their work. Following their presentations, Hall would comment generously, express some doubts, and then allow his victims to be attacked by the group. Terman's reaction: "I always went home dazed and intoxicated, lying awake for hours rehearsing the clever things I should have said and did not. If there is any pedagogical device better adjusted to put a man on his mettle than a seminar thus conducted, I do not know what it is. To know that his contribution would be subjected to merciless criticism from every angle was enough to arouse even a naturally indolent person to Herculean effort."

Terman's childhood interests persisted and found expression in study of the retarded and gifted. He received his doctorate in 1905 with a thesis on mental tests. Because he had suffered a pulmonary hemorrhage and had been advised to live in a warm climate, Terman accepted the position of principal in a high school in San Bernardino, California. The next year he became professor of child study and pedagogy at Los Angeles State Normal School, and from there went on to become professor of education at Stanford.

Around 1910, Terman was introduced to the Binet-Simon Scale by a colleague, E. B. Huey, who had worked with Adolf Meyer at Johns Hopkins. Terman set himself the task of improving the scale and making it suitable for American children. Apparently, he regarded himself as a quiet individual who could make up for a lack of intellectual brilliance by careful, well-designed research. We know for certain that Terman considered himself an introvert, and that he was repelled by the self-confidence of Spearman and Thorndike and the "looseness" of Hall's studies with the questionnaire method.

Terman's revision, The Stanford Revision of the Binet-Simon Scale, was standardized on 2100 children and 180 adults. It covered an age range from three years to a "superior adult" level, but there were no tests for eleven years. The score was expressed as a Mental Age, and this could be converted into an Intelligence Quotient or IQ; the latter score was simply Stern's mental quotient multiplied by 100 to eliminate the decimal point.

From the distribution of IQ's obtained with the scale, Terman suggested a classification scheme: IQ's from 90 to 109 indicate average intelligence; an IQ below 70 indicates definite feeblemindedness; an IQ above 140 indicates genius. Much to Terman's pleasure and surprise, The Stanford Revision soon became the most widely used individual scale of intelligence in the United States. In its reliability and validity it was a definite improvement over the Binet. Nevertheless, many of the criticisms directed at the Binet could be leveled at Terman's revision with equal justification.

There was still an overemphasis on verbal skills so that the measures obtained on the foreign-born and those handicapped in expressing themselves linguistically were spuriously low. Each individual task set by the test was so brief that it was difficult to evaluate an individual's persistence (This was a criticism that was hard to avoid, since the brevity of items was deliberate and was intended to help maintain a child's interest.). Without an eleven year level, the scale was really only satisfactory through ten years, for it was problematical as to what interpretation to give to the results if a person passed all the items at ten years and/or failed all the items at twelve.

Furthermore, there was still the question of what significance, if any, was to be attached to the "spread of scores" or "range of irregularity" or "scatter," i.e., that test performance when the successes of the person were distributed over several age levels. Some psychologists thought scatter was specific to defectives, and indicated an unequal development of abilities among retardates. However, John E. W. Wallin (b. 1876) found that normals had about as much scatter as the retarded, which seemed quickly to explode that hypothesis. He did note greater scatter among epileptics and the insane, but judiciously advised further investigations before accepting the validity of his observations.

In 1916, Augusta Bronner (b. 1881) described some additional variables that had to be considered in evaluating an individual's test performance. Taking her lead from Thorndike's comment "It is a general law of behavior that the response to any external situation is dependent upon the condition of the man as well as upon the nature of the situation," she argued that certain test-taking attitudes could adversely affect scores. Her experiences while testing delinquents at Healy's clinic made her sensitive to factors such as deliberate deception, recalcitrancy, sportiveness, general depression, anger, resentfulness, fear, shyness, embarrassment due to onlookers, homesickness, nervous excitement, feelings of shame, and lack of confidence. Naturally, when a child adopts such "attitudes" as these his level of performance is often lowered. Yet all too frequently these variables had not been taken into account when it would have been pertinent to have done so.

In the following year, 1917, Bronner pointed out that a child might have special disabilities which could lead to an invalid estimate of his intelligence. Since at that time it was thought that children who could not read were probably retarded, she particularly stressed the possibility of special reading handicaps in children of average intellectual ability. The findings of Bridges and Coler of a high correlation between the intelligence of children and their fathers' occupational status raised another question. Is such a correlation due to heredity or environment? Although no conclusive answer was immediately available, the host of considerations bombarding the IQ score made it apparent to clinicians that the administration and interpretation of an intelligence test could not wisely be entrusted to the inexperienced and untrained.

To aid in solving the problem of estimating the intelligence of children who were deaf, who were handicapped in their reading, or who were impaired in speaking English because they were immigrants or the children of immigrants, psychologists began combining several performance tests into what they hoped would be, with much work, a valid scale. Among the first of these performance scales was one constructed by Healy and Grace Fernald. However the Pintner-Paterson Scale of 1917 was the earliest of this group to be standardized and to enjoy a measure of continued popularity. This scale was composed of fifteen tests, which included various form boards, Healy's Picture Completion Test, and the Knox Cubes. Unfortunately, as was the case with other performance tests, the scores on the Pintner-Paterson were not found to correlate too highly with the scores obtained on verbal scales, such as the Binet.

With the entry of the United States into the World War, Robert Yerkes, who had just been elected president of the APA, became chairman of a committee of five experimental psychologists working within the Medical Department of the Army. Their task was to devise methods of classifying men according to their abilities. Arthur S. Otis, who had been working on a group intelligence test, assisted the committee in developing an appropriate scale (The members of the committee, which had its number increased from five to seven, were Yerkes, W. V. Bingham, Goddard, T. H. Haines, Terman, G. M. Whipple, and F. L. Wells.). The products of their work included: a group intelligence test known as the Army Alpha, which was a verbal scale that sampled such abilities as following direction, solving problems in arithmetic, supplying synonyms and antonyms, and displaying practical judgment; another group intelligence test, known as the Army Beta, which was nonverbal; and the Personal Data Sheet, a neurotic inventory designed by Robert Woodworth that contained such questions as, "Do you feel sad or low-spirited most of the time? Did you ever walk in your sleep?"

A school of military psychology was established at the Medical Officer's Training Camp, Fort Oglethorpe, Georgia, to provide instruction for the psychologists who were going to be testers in the Army. One of the "recruits" was the experimentalist Edwin G. Boring, who later served as Chief Psychological Examiner at Camp Upton, Long Island. Boring found the experience refreshing and broadening: "I learned about testing and about theory of probabilities, and I discovered also that the mental testers among the psychologists were, like the experimentalists, honest, sincere, intelligent, eighty-hour-a-week psychologists."

During the War, 1,726,000 men were tested in groups and 83,000 were examined individually. Over 500,000 were found to be illiterate; about 8,000 were recommended for discharge on the basis of low intelligence; approximately 20,000 were put in special battalions for observation and further training or to work on intellectually nondemanding tasks. About

3 percent of the nation's young males were found to have an MA below ten years, and the average MA of the American soldier was found to be only 13.5 years. Wide publicity was given these findings and the country was shocked. The United States seemed to be a nation of childish mentality!

Some psychologists unfortunately managed to get swept along in the stream of unwarranted inferrences from the results of mental testing and found themselves out on a limb. Edgar Doll argued that since the average MA of recruits was 13.5 years, mental growth in the average person probably stopped at thirteen years. However, other psychologists took a look at the same statistics and saw little to justify coming to such a conclusion. Yerkes and C. S. Yoakum pointed out that the tests sampled a limited range of abilities, and therefore a person might score low on them yet be able to perform some other skill in superior fashion. F. N. Freeman made a similar point, contending that the tests failed to adequately sample abilities ordinarily found in adults. Though the reservations of Yerkes, Yoakum, and Freeman were well-taken, the public tended to share the gloomy appraisal of H. L. Mencken that a new breed of man was being spawned in the Western Hemisphere—"Boobus Americanus."

In 1919, the APA committee on mental tests which had been organized in 1906 peacefully passed away. Each member of the committee had succeeded in developing tests to suit his own interests: in 1911, Woodworth and Wells produced their Association Tests; Pillsbury worked on the determination of the auditory limen; Judd devised tests of motor processes; Angell pursued research on ideational types; and Seashore contributed to the growth of special aptitude testing by his efforts to discover musical talent through measures of rhythm, pitch discrimination, and memory for tones.

Turning quickly from tests of intelligence to survey the techniques intended to diagnose psychiatric disturbances, we find Kent and Rosanoff hoping to detect insanity by noting the number of atypical free associations produced in responding to a list of one hundred words. First, they had to find out what were the typical responses. They did that by administering the list to a thousand "normal" persons, and then carefully tabulated the results. Their next step was to administer the list to 250 insane patients. They found that patients diagnosed as having dementia praecox produced many atypical responses, but those diagnosed as paranoiac and epileptic did not. Their findings were published in 1910, and they considered the free-association technique promising.

In 1912, Grace Fernald came out with a set of character tests purporting to measure moral consciousness. A little later, in 1913, Rosanoff and Rosanoff published their research on the free associations of children. It had been noted earlier that youngsters frequently gave idiosyncratic responses to the words, and they wondered at what age children started to give associations similar to those of adults. Testing three hundred children of varying ages, they found that by age eleven there was a considerable decrease in the frequency of doubtful and individual responses.

Woodworth's Psychoneurotic Inventory of 1917, labelled the Personal Data Sheet to appear innocuous to those taking it, was the first questionnaire designed to detect and measure abnormal behavior. It was intended as a rough screening device and as such it served its purpose.

Clearly, there were few techniques designed for the evaluation of personality disturbances or functioning. This paucity may be attributed, in part, to the newness of the field of mental testing in general and, in part, to the much greater involvement of psychologists in what they considered were pedagogical and educational rather than emotional problems. Of course, psychologists were quite successful in devising valid techniques for educational purpose, and by this time they could point with defensible pride to a variety of instruments for the measurement of intelligence. Unfortunately, in the heady warmth of public recognition, some of them lost sight of the limitations of their tests and took the scores they obtained at face value. Their error was made the more poignant by its having been forewarned by Binet. The movement, however, was forward, in terms of an increasing number and diversity of tests, in terms of greater efforts in delineating the host of variables that might affect results, and in terms of laying a firm foundation of healthy skepticism about the adequacy of the tools he employs, a skepticism which every practitioner should keep alive.

DIAGNOSTIC FORMULATIONS

The ideas of Alfred Adler were receiving considerable attention from psychologists and psychiatrists. What appealed to members of both groups was Adler's minimization of sexuality. Further, his emphasis upon organic problems giving rise to feelings of inadequacy and distress made his theory especially palatable to the medical profession.

Adler (1870–1937), the son of a grain merchant in Vienna, was fond of recalling two events from early in his childhood. At the age of four, when he overheard a physician telling his parents that he was in danger of dying from pneumonia, he resolved to recover from his illness and devote his life to the profession of medicine. The other memory was that at the age of ten, when he was failing in mathematics, he learned that his teacher had advised his father to apprentice him to a cobbler, since to continue his schooling would be a waste of time. In consequence, he resolved to apply himself to his studies and actually became the best student of mathematics in his class.

Adler received his M.D. from the University of Vienna Medical School in 1895. Perhaps, if Adler acted in keeping with his own theories, he began by specializing in ophthalmology because of the fact that his own vision was impaired. However, he soon turned to general medicine and also became involved with Freud. Their friendly relationship formally ended in 1911, but Adler claimed he had never agreed that neuroses originated from early sexual trauma. Starting in about 1907 Adler had begun to express his own views on the genesis of neurotic behavior.

At first Adler emphasized aggression as a more important drive than sex. Aggression seemed to be transformed or expressed in a variety of forms, including competition; less obviously altruism, when aggression was reversed in overt behavior; and anxiety, when it was turned upon the self. However, Adler soon abandoned the centrality of the concept of aggression, replacing it with the "will to power." He regarded the will to power as a masculine characteristic, while in contrast, he viewed "weakness" as typically feminine. By 1911, Adler's theory went somewhat as follows:

Neuroses have their origin in a child's feelings of weakness and inferiority. These feelings are based upon an inferior organ, really any part of the body, that has not developed or does not function properly. The child becomes aware of his defect and therefore feels inadequate. There are several ways in which he may handle his inferiority feelings. One, he can experience a need for and demand support and affection from his parents or other adults. This may prove to be a useful resolution since it at least helps the child's social development. Another outcome may be the acquisition of "attitudes" that compensate for the feelings of inadequacy, such as indulging in fantasy or often being disobedient. The child may also attempt to overcompensate for the inferior organ by striving to excel in just those functions which are defective, e.g., a boy with weak legs forces himself to exercise and eventually becomes a runner in track. However, a form of overcompensation frequently found among neurotics is the "masculine protest," an intensification on the part of the individual to surpass his father in every respect, to become stronger than his father, to outdo and even to dominate him.

Although Adler did not deny the importance of sex, it is obvious from the account thus far that he considered it of minor significance. The symptoms of neurotics were, for him, not compromises between impulses and their repressing forces but attempts to deny feelings of inadequacy and protests against parents and others.

Following his break with Freud and the formation of his own school of Individual Psychology, Adler continued to revise and extend his theory. By 1920, he no longer believed that there actually had to be a defective organ for a neurosis to occur. Instead, he emphasized the individual's subjective feelings of inferiority or incompleteness as the great driving force.

The philosopher Hans Vaihinger had claimed that all persons were guided in their behavior by fictions or beliefs that tended to grow into dogmas. Adler was impressed by Vaihinger's ideas and utilized them in his theoretical system. He asserted that the neurotic person, more intensely and rigidly than the normal, clings to some guiding fiction or ideal and attempts to make it into a reality: "This formula, 'I want to be a real man,' is the guiding fiction . . . in every neurosis, where it demands realization to a higher degree than in the normal psyche."

If we could discover the unique fiction or goal of the person, Adler believed we would be in a good position to predict his behavior. Among neurotics the general goal is to be big, to be powerful, to enhance one's self-esteem. It does not matter that the individual may be in reality physically big or actually in a position of power, since we are dealing with his subjective evaluations and feelings. To safeguard his self-esteem, the neurotic may depreciate others or things in his environment, he may blame people for his own failures, or he may reproach himself and in so doing maintain the fiction that he can achieve his goal. Regardless of his specific tactics, his general aim is to feel secure in his strength. Yet in this process the neurotic becomes farther removed from reality and less able to adjust to the demands of his society and fellow man. Adler was thus led to the formulation that mental disease is the resultant of feelings of inferiority and external demands imposed upon the individual to live sociably within his culture.

An article about Adler's theory appeared in the United States in 1915, and two years later the psychiatrist William Alanson White commented favorably upon his concepts. Soon psychologists and psychiatrists everywhere were talking about feelings of inferiority and compensations. Even G. Stanley Hall announced that he endorsed the Adlerian position over that of psychoanalysis. Freud, though hurt by Hall's statement, was not visibly impressed by Individual Psychology, which he regarded as being in essence an ego psychology and so too one-sided and neglectful of instinctual forces. Still, Freud's ideas were also changing.

By 1913, Freud had interpreted obsessional neuroses as fixations or regressions to the anal-sadistic stage of development. He thought neuroses in general came about when sexual impulses have to be restrained beyond the capacity of the ego to handle them. Freud modified this formulation when he learned of combat neuroses.

Shortly after the onset of the World War it was observed that soldiers developed neurotic symptoms. At first, psychiatrists thought the explosions of shells produced minute cortical lesions and that this damage to the brain in turn produced the disorder. Hence, they called this disturbance shell shock. But soon it was noted, at least in the Canadian Army, that the neurotic symptoms followed a pattern according to the rank of the soldier: officers seemed to suffer mainly anxiety states, while enlisted personnel usually evidenced symptoms of hysteria. This observation seemed to rule out an organic explanation, unless one could demonstrate how the same exploding shells produced discriminatory lesions among commissioned and noncommissioned officers. At any rate, a Canadian psychiatrist Schwab claimed that the war neuroses were a personal response of the individual to trauma, and that this response represented a compromise between the soldier's wish to preserve himself and his sense of obligation to his comrades and country.

Freud offered a similar explanation in terms of intrapsychic conflict within the ego. This conflict was experienced as a struggle between two ego ideals: the soldier's desire to preserve and enhance himself versus his sense of duty, loyalty, and honor. The ego, weakened by this internal narcissistic warfare, might easily become overwhelmed by threatening external stimulation, and thus a regression and a neurosis would be caused. Significantly, Freud explained the genesis of war neuroses, not by repressed sexuality, but by a clash between opposing value systems existing within a single hypothetical structure of the mind, the ego.

If we look at this issue more broadly, we see that shell shock produced by brain damage versus war neuroses produced by internal conflict was but one example in the repeated clash between two points of view within both psychiatry and psychology: hereditary and organic as opposed to environmental and psychological explanations of etiology. Any territory not demonstrably staked out by those favoring an organic view was quickly claimed by the other side. For example, Edith Spaulding, a psychologist working with Healy, stated, in 1913, that the studies conducted at the Juvenile Psychopathic Clinic and elsewhere had failed to demonstrate any conclusive proof that criminalism was hereditary. Ergo, environmental factors had to be considered responsible for criminal behavior. Whatever one may think about the truth of this conclusion, the logic by which it was derived is certainly faulty. Yet it is also true that, unlike genetic variables, psychological and environmental factors are not hard to find, and so directing one's efforts in their direction can be a more immediately rewarding and profitable enterprise, as well as perhaps ultimately the truly correct one.

Thus there began a deluge of information about neighborhoods, living conditions, companions of delinquents, and school adjustments or maladjustments and their effects on crime. Yet there still seemed to be few data about the effects of emotional interrelationships within the child's family.

In 1917, Healy hit upon the idea of asking the delinquent to tell his "Own Story" about his feelings and attitudes toward his parents and others. From these interviews, Healy concluded that delinquents are emotionally disturbed and in need of some sort of treatment. More specifically, it seemed to him that there is always some unconscious experience involved in bringing about the delinquency, though there are invariably a number of other factors, such as poor parental relationships, which have to be present to account fully for the behavior. Much interest was aroused in Healy's findings and in his novel technique of asking the child to tell him how he felt.

In 1911, Freud held that a factor in criminality is an unconscious sense of guilt. The criminal breaks the law in order to provoke society into punishing him, thereby alleviating his guilt feelings. Thus aggression directed outward against society can at times be viewed as basically a form of aggression directed against oneself. By the same token, aggression directed against one's own person can be viewed as aggression directed against someone else. Citing the extreme case of suicide, Freud commented: "Perhaps no one can find the psychical energy to kill himself unless in the first place he is thereby killing at the same time someone with whom he has identified himself."

In the same year, 1911, Freud interpreted the delusions of paranoia as denials of repressed homosexuality through the use of projection. Instead of experiencing the thought that he loves another man, the paranoiac denies it and claims he hates him; then, finding his hatred intolerable, he projects it and so believes the man hates him. Therefore, delusions (The foregoing passage discussed the development of the delusion of persecution.) may be considered more or less successful attempts at resolving a conflict. Freud arrived at these views on the basis of studying the diary of a man named Daniel Schreber, who suffered from paranoid schizophrenia.

Such psychological explanations as were proposed by Freud, Adler, Healy, and others were novel ideas. They were at considerable variance from the organic explanations for crime and mental illness which were predominantly held within their professions and which were widely accepted by the public. It was generally believed that the criminal, the epileptic, the defective, and the insane genetically transmitted their disturbances to their offspring. Here were new views challenging those beliefs and directing attention from inborn characteristics toward the problems and conflicts with which all individuals contend in their everyday lives.

Occupying a slightly middle-of-the-road position was the work of Bleuler (1857–1930), who published in 1911 his monograph *Dementia praecox, oder die Gruppe der Schizophrenien*. Bleuler argued that dementia praecox is not a disease entity, is not invariably incurable, nor does it always progress to dementia. Instead, he suggested, there is a group of diseases, which he named "schizophrenia."

The major symptom of schizophrenia is a splitting of various mental processes or a disorder in the train of associations. Thus these patients are more or less incoherent and illogical in their thinking and speech. His description of the course of the disease was quite different from

Kraepelin's description of the course of dementia praecox: "This disease (schizophrenia) may come to a standstill at any stage, and many of its symptoms may clear up very much, or altogether, but if it progresses it leads to a dementia or definite character." Furthermore, Bleuler believed a large number of cases of schizophrenia are latent. Such schizophrenics are never hospitalized because their behavior, while odd, is not severely symptomatic.

Among the symptoms of schizophrenia described and named by Bleuler are two that soon passed into common terminology: ambivalence and autism. Ambivalence refers to having simultaneously two opposite feelings toward the same person, usually both love and hate. Autism is a turning away from reality, a living in fantasy in which the person's wishes and fears seem real to him; while to others, his thinking appears illogical, symbolic, and not bound to the facts of the outer world. Bleuler considered autistic thinking not only a schizophrenic phenomenon but also claimed it appeared among children and among adults when they are swayed by their emotions.

Although Bleuler thought schizophrenia was curable, and although he offered psychogenic, often Freudian, interpretations of its symptoms, he believed it probable that the disease process itself is organic in origin, perhaps caused by some toxin in the body. It should be noted that there is no incompatibility between an organic cause of a disease and its alleviation. Thus the supposedly incurable illness described by Kraepelin, dementia praecox, had in the space of a few years started on its path toward becoming a group of reactions which may be ameliorated.

During this period Kraepelin was far from idle and participated in bringing about some of the changes taking place within psychiatry. While he continued, understandably enough, to use much of his own terminology, he joined with Bleuler in broadening the conception of psychosis. In 1913, Kraepelin described constitutional personality types who evidence to a lesser degree symptoms displayed by the mentally ill. There is the autistic personality, characterized primarily by relatively little interest in his external environment and by a preoccupation with his own thoughts and fantasies. He regarded this predisposition to autistic behavior as the constitutional basis for dementia praecox. Further, Kraepelin believed that there are distinguishable subtypes of the autistic personality which are similar to the subtypes of the psychosis, though of course the symptoms are not as extreme. He also described the cyclothymic personality, which exhibits in milder forms the behaviors that distinguish manic-depressive psychoses. Here, too, Kraepelin differentiated subtypes: manic, depressive, irrascible, and emotionally unstable.

The year 1913 seemed to be a busy one for personality types. It was also then that Jung introduced his dichotomy of introvert and extravert. Jung explained that the major distinction between the two types lies in the direction of their psychic energy. Introverts direct their psychic energy centripetally, i.e., away from the environment and toward the self; and hence they seldom express their feelings overtly. Patients with dementia praecox seemed to Jung to have personalities of the introvert type. Extraverts direct their psychic energy centrifugally, i.e., toward the environment and away from the self; and hence they tend to express their feelings overtly and in an exaggerated manner. Patients with hysteria, Jung thought, have personalities of the extravert type.

Freud also spoke of the constitutional factors that were involved in the genesis of neuroses and psychoses. But having little more to say on the subject other than that such factors were a part of their etiology, he pushed on with his psychoanalytic interpretations. Perhaps it was a matter of emphasis rather than a choice between mutually exclusive alternatives, though at the time many people acted as if they felt that if an illness had an organic cause, psychological variables were excluded and vice versa. Yet no one could deny that certain mental diseases were organic in origin, and with the advance of science it was only reasonable to expect discoveries of bodily causes for additional psychiatric disturbances. It seemed to follow that with the finding of such a definite, tangible cause, all that was needed to be said was said, and it remained only to find a remedy for the illness.

The organic position thus appeared to be the position of strength. This position was buttressed in 1913 when Hideyo Noguchi and J. W. Moore conclusively demonstrated the presence of the spirochete, *treponema palidum,* in paretic brains. General paresis was caused by syphilis and that was that.

Among the minority of psychiatrists stressing psychological variables was Adolf Meyer. In 1910, he became professor of psychiatry at Johns Hopkins, and in 1913, also director of the Phipps Clinic. Through his training of psychiatrists, Meyer was able to impress his viewpoint upon a considerable portion of the profession. What he wished his students to realize was: "Mental activity is really best understood . . . as the adaptation and adjustment of the individual as a whole."

Meyer called his approach "psychobiology." The individual is to be understood as a functioning whole whose organic, sociological, and psychological aspects are all to be considered. Yet often no somatic disorder can be found and the evidence for physical variables at work in the genesis of a psychiatric disturbance is equivocal. In such cases, Meyer urged his students to use such facts as are immediately available—the patient's behavioral life history and his present condition. Through studying the past lives of his patients, Meyer found that these individuals had been reacting ineffectively to their problems over long periods of time. Their faulty reactions had become habitual ways of responding to stresses leading to: (1) more severely maladaptive patterns of behavior;

(2) greater inability to cope with life; and (3) further difficulties in achieving any constructive adjustments. Meyer concluded that many psychiatric disturbances should be regarded not as diseases but as psychopathological reactions, as disturbances in learning to adjust satisfactorily to the demands of living. He believed the symptoms of neuroses and dementia praecox could be interpreted as inappropriate reactions of the whole organism.

Meyer's position appealed to many psychiatrists and psychologists because of its simplicity and reasonableness. Moreover, Meyer was respected as an erudite man of good will. His approach stressed the longitudinal study of the individual's reactions as he faced the need to make all kinds of adjustments. Such an approach could readily be incorporated into almost any other psychological formulation. Thus his views aroused little opposition or conflict within the field, and so were destined to lose their distinctive association with their original proponent.

Turning our attention to the concept of intelligence, we find the persistence and amplification of disagreements of the previous decade and considerable support for a one-sided view of intelligence as determined by heredity. In 1912, Stern defined intelligence as a general mental adaptability to new problems and conditions of life. A few years later, in 1915, Witmer proposed a similar definition: "the ability of the individual to solve what for him is a new problem."

Witmer stressed the importance of the problem being *new* for intelligence to be measured. Therefore he believed that retesting a person with the same scale plainly ruled out the possibility of obtaining a valid estimate of intelligence, and recommended to psychologists that they devise scales which could grade the person's resourcefulness and creativity. It also seemed obvious to Witmer that intelligence scales were not measuring intelligence. What they were measuring was a level of performance. He had no objections to psychologists doing that so long as they were clear about what they were doing.

Witmer considered that an individual's performance level is his average way of performing certain tasks, and he pointed out a variety of different perspectives from which this level could be evaluated: by age scales such as the Binet; by education scales which measure academic achievement; by a species scale, which would rank man, along with other species or organisms, in the performance of a task; by civilization scales; masculinity scales; femininity scales; insanity scales; and deficiency scales. Since Witmer was convinced that each type of scale measured a different kind and quality of performance, he warned: "The performance of the feebleminded are (sic) qualitatively and quantitatively different from the performance of normal children. Each child, normal or feebleminded, can be assigned a level on both the age scale and the deficiency scale. The deficiency scale cannot be superimposed on the age scale to make a single scale." Actually what Witmer meant in that last statement is not "cannot" but "should not," and since he had neither of these scales to offer, practical considerations overruled what attention might have been paid to his injunction.

To a number of psychologists, the devising of a hotch-potch of scales to evaluate intelligence was not such a bad idea and really made some sense. The leading member of this group was Charles Spearman, who was still talking about his two-factor theory: "all the intellective activity of any person depends in some degree on one and the same general fund of mental energy" plus "his specific capacity for that particular kind of performance."

Opposing Spearman's position was a group of psychologists whose reluctant champion was Thorndike: "Are not our minds made up of an enormous number of highly specialized capacities to operate with particular kinds of problems? Do we have a mind with a capital M that can operate with any kind of material, and on any kind of problem, or are we a bundle of specialized capacities to do particular things?" Quite obviously, Thorndike's questions were rhetorical.

Spearman could not for the life of him understand why it was so difficult for his colleagues to see that he was right. Patiently, he would reanalyze and correct their data. With great forbearance, he would answer their criticisms in the hope of resolving "a disquieting scientific discord into firm harmony," or, in other words, so that their findings would agree with his findings.

One critic of Spearman who was not easily dismissed was Godfrey Thomson (1881–1955). Born in England, Thomson had graduated from Armstrong College (now King's College, University of London) in 1903, and had received his doctorate in physics and mathematics at Strasburg in 1906. He had returned to Armstrong College to fulfill the obligations of a scholarship, and there taught educational psychology. His interests centered on statistics as they related to psychological problems, and particularly on factor analysis. In 1916, Thomson found that by throwing dice randomly he could make a set of artificial test scores which, when analyzed according to Spearman's procedure, yielded a general factor.

After three more years of investigating the problem, Thomson concluded, in 1919, that the reason a general factor was found was because the sampling errors in coefficients of correlation were themselves correlated. The general factor was produced, he claimed, by the random interplay of small independent factors, such as test-taking attitudes and the effect of previous testings. There was thus no general intellective factor.

Spearman was stunned, though only momentarily. Soon he was as confident as ever of the rightness of his original position. Meanwhile, although psychologists disagreed about the definition and structure of intelligence, they and their tests were being used more and more in measuring intellectual functioning and in diagnosing feeblemindedness.

In 1900, the British Royal Commission had defined mental deficiency as social incompetence due to mental incompetence resulting from arrested development of a constitutional, chiefly hereditary, origin. Despite the fact that almost all authorities agreed that social incompetence was an essential characteristic in the concept of mental deficiency, after intelligence tests with some validity had been devised, the temptation became great to diagnose feeblemindedness solely on the basis of the test scores. The American Association for Study of the Feeble-Minded, in 1910, recommended that the diagnosis be established by criteria other than tests, but that after the diagnosis had been made, retardates could be classified on the basis of their Binet mental ages. In practice, however, the idea of social incompetence tended to be neglected and mental age became the major criterion for making the diagnosis. An MA of twelve years in adults was generally accepted as the lower limit of normal intelligence, and in 1916 people began following Terman's suggestion: "All who test below 70 IQ by the Stanford Revision of the Binet-Simon Scale should be considered feebleminded."

At this time the preponderant view was that intelligence and scores on intelligence scales were a function almost exclusively of heredity. Therefore when studies consistently found the average MA of Negroes to be two years lower than that of whites, it was generally believed the Negro race was of inferior intelligence.

Strong support for the hereditary position came from the work of Goddard in his study of a family he called the Kallikaks. Goddard's findings described the offspring of a man of normal intelligence who at about the time of the American Revolution first mated with an unknown defective girl, and then later married a girl of normal intelligence. A defective, illegitimate son of the first union had 480 known descendents; of this lineage, 143 were judged to have had some heredity defect such as low intelligence or criminality. From the second union, 486 descendents were traced, all considered normal. These results, published in 1912, aroused much discussion and brought Goddard some degree of fame.

He followed with another study, in 1914, based on the case histories of 327 families of inmates at the Vineland Training School. The records seemed to Goddard to indicate that when both parents were defective, all the children were defective; when one parent was defective, half the children were defective; when both parents were normal but a close relative was defective, a fourth of the children were defective. Goddard concluded that feeblemindedness was inherited as a simple recessive Mendelian unit-character.

Armed with these data and the means by which feeblemindedness could be diagnosed, Goddard and others vigorously urged the adoption of eugenic measures, e.g., sterilization and segregation of the defective. It was now possible, they believed, to realize Galton's hope of improving the genetic stock of mankind, to sharply reduce the incidence of mental deficiency.

Of course, the actions of legislators are not always motivated solely by idealistic considerations. Many, at this time no doubt, took into account the possibility that sterilization might reduce the costs of welfare programs since, not only mental deficiency, but insanity, criminality, and epilepsy were thought to be genetically determined. The first state to enact a sterilization law was Indiana in 1907, and by 1919 Alabama, California, Connecticut, Kansas, Nebraska, New Hampshire, New York, North Dakota, South Dakota, and Wisconsin had similar legislation. However, perhaps because of the doubts raised about the inclusion of the criminal and the insane, qualms were experienced about enforcing these laws, and, with the exception of California, sterilization operations were seldom performed. Yet despite the reluctance to enforce sterilization laws, their enactment was to continue through the next decade and into the early thirties.

TREATMENT FORMULATIONS

For the majority of patients hospitalized with mental illnesses the treatment was essentially the same as it had been in previous years: more or less adequate, or sometimes very inadequate, custodial care. However, a virtual revolution took place in the therapy of paresis.

Around 1910, arsphenamine (Salvarsan), an organic compound containing arsenic first used by Paul Ehrlich in antiluetic therapy, began to be employed in arresting the course of paresis. The serum was either injected into the cerebrospinal fluid or was introduced via a trephined opening in the skull. While reports were favorable, the results still left much to be desired.

A breakthrough came in 1917 when Julius Wagner-Jauregg (1857–1940), an Austrian psychiatrist, innoculated nine paretic patients with tertian malaria. His rationale was based on an old observation by physicians that the progress of a serious illness could sometimes be favorably influenced by introducing another, less dangerous, disease. Hippocrates, for example, had commented: "persons attacked with convulsions, they cease if a quartan (an intermittent fever which recurs every fourth day) supervene." In 1887, Wagner-Jauregg had proposed malarial infections for paretics, but had decided to experiment first with tuberculin injections and typhus. Using malaria, six of the nine patients benefited, and within a short time the induction of fevers became the treatment for arresting the course of syphilis. To many physicians, all of this demonstrated again that once the physical basis of an illness was known, the means for its amelioration soon followed. Encouraged, they pushed on in their search for organic causes of functional or psychological diseases.

Boris Sidis (1867–1923), an American psychologist and psychiatrist, thought he had the answer to the cause of mental illness. Before going into his discovery, we should note that Sidis had done some well-received work on hypnotism. In 1898, he had named and described the hypnoidal state, a condition in which the subject, after attending to a monotonous stimulus, appears to hover between wakefulness and sleep in a relaxed condition characterized by diminished pulse rate, deep and slow respiration, heightened suggestibility, and recall of previously inaccessible memories.

Now Sidis noticed that all his patients either explicitly claimed to be afraid of something or else evidenced behavior indicative of fear. In one of those lapses of logical and sound judgment that sometimes strike down even the best of men, Sidis concluded that the cause of all psychopathic diseases must be the fear instinct.

While Sidis' etiological explanation was not generally accepted, some psychiatrists regarded his techniques of treatment with favor. What Sidis would often do was induce his patients to experience the hypnoidal state. During that state, the person often gained some relief from his fears, tensions, and worries. Essentially, it was a supervised period of relaxation, and virtually all his patients found it acceptable, including those who could not be hypnotized. Sidis thought of the hypnoidal state as an aid to therapy, but some of his colleagues regarded it as a therapy in and of itself.

Early in this decade the foundation upon which James rested his notions about mental health was attacked by Thorndike. It may be recalled that James advised people to think themselves brave so that they might conquer their fears. This bit of advice was derived from the widely accepted concept of ideomotor action: the idea of a particular form of behavior inherently tends to produce in some degree its corresponding action or movement. Thorndike not too graciously dismissed ideomotor action as sheer rubbish. He argued that it was analogous to the beliefs of primitive men in the magical powers of their thoughts to produce effects. Since few psychologists relished the notion that there is any similarity between their thinking processes and those of the natives of the South Seas, a dark cloud passed over the concept of ideomotor activity and its derivatives.

However mental health is something everyone favors. Its principles are phrased in such inoffensive generalities—for example, many persons are hindered in achieving a happy life by being too sensitive, overly ambitious, and excessively depreciatory of themselves—that hardly anyone can disagree with them. Yet they have had profound implications. "What unfavorable environment causes," F. L. Wells asserted, "correct external influences can prevent," as he urged psychologists and psychiatrists to join forces in educating the mentally ill to face their problems squarely and in a socially approved manner.

The principles of mental health, as both implicitly and explicitly applied to the prevention and cure of mental illness, were easily extended to encompass relatively mild problems of adjustment which heretofore had not been thought of as psychiatric disturbances. They thus broadened the scope of psychiatry. Further, they seemed to endow psychiatrists and psychologists with the power of solving these problems. There was little questioning of any of these assumptions, although some psychologists and psychiatrists felt a trifle uneasy about finding themselves in the same strange territory.

Freud was not specifically worried about the assimilation of relatively normal behavior to the domain of psychiatry, but he was concerned about the abuse of psychoanalytic treatment by the untrained. He accordingly addressed himself to two problems: the techniques for implementing psychoanalysis and considerations as to when this treatment should be advised. Freud warned against the fanatical desire to see everyone undergo analysis. Well-meaning, but misguided, people were recommending his treatment for all persons because they naively believed that analysis, if it could not help, at least would not harm. On the contrary, Freud cautioned, some patients would be harmed if deprived of the benefits received from their illnesses. He urged his colleagues to evaluate the total situation of each prospective patient, to carefully consider what effects an improvement in the individual would have upon his way of life and upon the reactions of others to him, and to weigh the cost of treatment against any advantages that might be gained before prescribing psychoanalysis. It seemed to Freud that there was room enough in the world for some neuroses.

As far as psychoanalytic techniques were concerned, he advised that analysts should be passive in their sessions and should avoid pushing their patients for material. What an analyst is supposed to do is always to keep in touch with the person's current thoughts and feelings, and not allow his scientific interests to be expressed in any show of enthusiasm about the interpretation of any dream. Otherwise, Freud warned, the patient may show his resistance by overwhelming the analyst with dreams, or by bringing no dreams at all into the hour.

Freud advised against taking notes or using notes because he believed those procedures would interfere with the receptive and spontaneous attitude which he felt the analyst should possess. He counseled the analyst to exercise care in keeping his personal feelings in the background, while at the same time remaining alert to recognize and understand any emotions aroused in him by his patient. Those feelings experienced by the analyst toward his patient, the problem of counter-transference, constitute yet another reason why all those employing Freudian procedures are encouraged to themselves experience a thorough and constant self-analysis. Freud cautioned that all positive feelings are derived from sexual sources since "Originally it was only sexual objects that we knew," and therefore they tend to be to some extent irrational and unconsciously determined. Still another problem for the analyst to guard against is that when unconscious impulses emerge, there may be an attempt by the patient to put them into action or act them out.

All these issues and matters, Freud recognized, make the task of the analyst far from an easy one. Still there is one saving admonition which he announced in 1913: the analysis should proceed with the patient lying down and the analyst seated out of the patient's line of vision. A major reason for this tactic, Freud stated honestly, is that he himself simply could not tolerate patients looking him in the face all day.

The ink had hardly dried on Freud's writings when an article appeared by Smith Elly Jelliffe, a neurologist in New York, giving his views on the subject of transference. In Jelliffe's opinion the concept needed broadening and revision. He contended that a transference relationship occurs immediately in the physician-patient relationship by virtue of the status accorded the healer within our culture: "The physician, viewed as a functional unit in society, represents for the individuals in that society, that portion of themselves given over to the protection of their bodies from the forces of disease." Therefore transference feelings do not develop during the course of the analysis, but are there at the very beginning, and from that first session have to be dealt with and understood. Similarly, the analyst may experience countertransference feelings in his first encounter with his patient. If the analyst cannot control his countertransference, Jelliffe recommended a transference of a different sort: the patient should be transferred to a different analyst.

Ideas about the significance of the doctor-patient relationship were beginning to be expressed by men of differing orientations and to appear in a variety of professional areas. William McDougall was one of these men. He touched upon its importance incidentally, since it came to his attention during that interlude of his life occupied by the War. In one of those classic boners of military organization, McDougall had served for almost a year as an ambulance driver before it was recognized that he was a neurologist. He was then quickly promoted to the rank of major in the Royal Army Medical Corps and placed in charge of treating "nervous" soldiers. Although McDougall employed several techniques, including hypnosis, it was his impression that "sympathetic rapport . . . a very natural and simple human relation" was of greatest importance in benefiting his patients. At the war's end McDougall journeyed to Switzerland for a didactic analysis by Jung, and through 1919 continued practicing psychotherapy at the out-patient department at Oxford City Hospital.

Guilio Ferrari (1869–?1933), an Italian psychiatrist who had studied with Binet, was another person who commented upon the therapeutic significance of his relationship with his patients. In 1910, Ferrari was in charge of running an institution for forty children in Bologna. Half the children were mentally retarded and half were termed "morally insane," or what we might call "delinquent." He noticed that by placing the two groups together, the delinquents soon came to understand that they, as well as the retarded children, were regarded as abnormal. A great improvement in their behavior occurred, which Ferrari attributed both to their recognition of their need for change and to the manner in which he handled them. At all times he expressed confidence in their ability to better their conduct, was sincere, impartial, and honest in his dealings with them, and related to the children, not as inferiors, but as individuals who merited his respect.

A somewhat different perspective, and one which suggests that the therapist should be guided in the course of his treatment by his patient, was furnished by Édouard Claparède (1873–1940). A Swiss psychiatrist who also included Alfred Binet among his friends, Claparède was interested in psychotherapy and the education of the retarded. Respect for the individual's uniqueness and potentialities for growth found expression in his concept of "the school made to measure," i.e., a school whose programs were adjusted to the differences of its children. In 1912, he founded the Jean-Jacques Rousseau Institute, where he was able to translate his attitudes into action. Claparède urged teachers to learn from their pupils what should be taught. Instead of being a teacher who routinely and mechanically tries to instruct her charges, she was told to encourage the children to engage in play situations where their need to be mentally active would naturally arise. By this means a child's interest in a subject could be expressed "spontaneously," and his active participation in the learning process could be gained. Claparède's ideas were thus similar to what John Dewey thought of as progressive education, and both men received international attention and support.

Claparède had been a student at the Salpêtrière under the neurologist Joseph Déjerine (1849–1917). In 1913, Déjerine's book *Psychoneurosis and Psychotherapy* appeared in the United States. Déjerine, like many others, believed that neuroses were caused by emotional trauma. In order to be cured, a neurotic has to be freed from his harmful feelings through cathartic expression of them. Yet the means by which Déjerine brought about improvements seemed to lie more in the exhortative, trusting relationship between himself and his patients than in his exhaustive questionings about their emotional problems. Déjerine would urge them to get well. He would untiringly point out that there was no reason why they should not get well. Above all, he would remind them that he, Déjerine, was confident that they would get well, so how could they who trusted in his judgment have any doubt of their eventual cure. Apparently many of his patients agreed with him.

Perhaps the most explicit statement made during this period about the therapist-patient relationship came from Alfred Adler: "The actual change in the nature of the patient can only be his own doing. I have found it most profitable to sit ostentatiously with my hands in my lap, fully convinced that no matter what I might be able to say on the point, the patient can learn nothing from me that he, as the sufferer, does not understand better, once he has recognized his life-line."

Adler saw the patient's understanding evolving in a process of free and supposedly friendly conversation with his therapist. From the very beginning of treatment, the initiative and responsibility for cure rests with the patient. The job of the therapist is to be a co-worker in comprehending the person's style of life, to communicate his understanding of it, and to point to its manifestations repeatedly in all the neurotic's thoughts and feelings.

Adler was convinced that the neurotic has a strong tendency to depreciate his physician in an effort to establish his superiority over him, and that this tendency is evidenced in all significant relationships and so might well be apparent from the very beginning of treatment: "I expect from the patient again and again the same attitude which he has shown in accordance with his life-plan toward the persons of his former environment, and still earlier toward his family."

As Adler envisioned it, the office of the therapist becomes a battleground where two people are locked in struggle. On one side is the patient, waiting to get well, yet persisting in a pattern of behavior in which mutually satisfying relationships are sacrificed for an illusion of superiority. On the other side is the therapist, wanting to be of help, hoping to assist the person to assume responsibility, and aware that any failure to recognize and come to grips with any show of hostility will only serve to perpetuate the neurosis.

Briefly, then, there were some who saw the doctor-patient relationship as therapeutic in itself (McDougall, Ferrari); while some viewed it mainly as a means toward achieving catharsis (Déjerine), an integrated awareness of unconscious thoughts (Freud), or a recognition of characteristic ways of interacting with others (Adler). All these objectives in turn were regarded as therapeutic. The relationship was promoted by social expectations (Jelliffe) and distorted by unconscious strivings and attitudes (Freud, Adler). Within this relationship, the therapist was supposed to be relatively passive (Freud, Adler), active (Déjerine), or naturally friendly (McDougall, Ferrari). The patient, not the disease or the therapist, was being held increasingly responsible for the outcome of the therapeutic venture—perhaps because it was perceived, although no one as yet seemed to acknowledge it, that regardless of the treatment employed, some patients improved and others did not.

PROFESSIONAL DEVELOPMENT

Two mutually supportive developments characterized these years: one, a reorientation within psychology, called behaviorism, swept through the field as a powerful protest against the past; and two, a small, but growing, number of psychologists, who also were waging a fight against tradition, tried to involve their colleagues in applications of their science to practical problems and to gain recognition for their existence as a profession.

The shortage of trained psychologists to administer and interpret intelligence scales was a source of dismay to the few clinical psychologists available. In contrast to the swiftly rising demand for their services, there was the slow, dragging response of the universities, which seemed disinclined to set up graduate programs in this field.

The APA showed little concern for the professional problems of its members. Its pristine purpose was to advance psychology as a science, an objective favored by its membership, and to which the large majority of psychologists saw no reason to add other goals. As late as 1917 Cattell noted that of the 307 members of the APA, only 16 were primarily engaged in nonacademic positions in which they were applying psychology. In 1918, just 15 of the approximately 375 APA members listed clinical psychology as a research interest.

Yet the demand for testing, particularly from school systems, was immediate and pressing. Teachers and principals, unable to wait, often resentful of the threat to their status by psychologists, but for the most part naive about testing, assumed the functions of psychological examiners. In one school system almost half the children tested by one teacher were classified as feebleminded, an incident which, though extreme, was not unique.

J. E. W. Wallin (b. 1876) attempted to alleviate the problem by organizing a program in which teachers would be taught how to administer the Binet-Simon Scale. That was at the Training School at Vineland in 1910. Then there was, of course, the Psychological Clinic at the University of Pennsylvania, which offered the following: a special class in the study of "backward" children, initiated in the summer of 1911; by 1913, a total of fourteen courses related in some way to clinical psychology; a biweekly clinic conducted by Edwin B. Twitmyer in the diagnosis and correction of speech defects, set up in 1914; and, in 1919, a course in remedial teaching taught by a person who held the position of Clinic Teacher.

Beginning in 1914 the School of Education at the University of Pittsburgh offered summer courses in the study of mentally retarded children, and in 1915 the first Department of Applied Psychology was established at Carnegie Institute of Technology with Walter Van Dyke Bingham as its chairman.

Bingham (1880–1952), who was born in Iowa, had special interests in persons and vocational counseling: "I have preferred to give a hand to the promising rather than to the third rate." After his undergraduate work at the University of Kansas and Beloit, he taught for four years. In 1905, he entered the University of Chicago, and in 1908 received his Ph.D. From 1908 until 1910, he was an instructor at Columbia working with Thorndike, and from 1910 until he went to Carnegie he was at Dartmouth.

The Department of Applied Psychology was particularly involved in the study of aptitudes, vocational counseling, the measurement of interests, and research in salesmanship. Walter Dill Scott (1869–1955) was appointed in 1916 as professor of applied psychology, thus becoming the first of his kind in the United States, though just barely nosing out James P. Porter (1873–1956), whose position was given the same title at Clark that same year. During the War, Bingham and Scott contributed their services in work on the problems of classification of military personnel and the selection of officers.

Throughout this decade the number of psychological clinics increased. We shall list those in operation in 1914 in order to give some idea of their distribution throughout the United States. By then there were nineteen of them in universities, colleges, and medical schools. In addition to the clinics already mentioned, there was a psychological clinic at Woman's Medical College in Philadelphia established in 1910, Seashore's clinic at the University of Iowa, Gesell's clinic at Yale (1911), Wallin's clinic at the University of Pittsburgh (1912), a Bureau of Social Hygiene to study the causes and treatment of delinquency in women at Bedford Reformatory for Women (1912), and clinics at or in New York Post-Graduate Medical School and Hospital (1912), Hospital of the City of New York (1912), Boston Psychopathic Hospital (1912), State University of Iowa (1913), Albany (1913), Tulane (1913), Rutgers (1914), Cornell (1914), Trenton (1914), Philadelphia (1914), Los Angeles (1914), and Oakland (1914). An important function of these clinics was training would-be clinical psychologists. Among the institutions offering internships in clinical psychology were the Boston Psychopathic Hospital, McLean Hospital, Western State Penitentiary in Pennsylvania, New York Institute for Child Guidance, and the Psychopathic Hospital at the University of Iowa. There may not have been many clinical psychologists, but they were turning up everywhere.

In 1910, a psychologist, P. F. Lange, was appointed to the staff of the Iowa State Institution for the Feebleminded, and London, England, engaged its first school psychologist, Cyril Burt, for halftime work in 1912. Shortly before the War, Burt was joined by a social worker and a medical assistant. By that happy circumstance the first child guidance clinic in England was formed. In 1919, Alfred Adler organized the first child guidance clinic in Vienna.

Back in the United States, Healy's clinic was attracting the attention of a number of judges. They came, were impressed by what they saw and heard, and helped set up similar diagnostic services in their own courts. Among the distinguished visitors were Judges Frater of Seattle, Waite of Minneapolis, Hoffman of Cincinnati, and Baker of Boston. During the summers of 1912 and 1913, Healy taught a course at Harvard describing his work. In 1913, Augusta Bronner, who had trained at Teacher's College, Columbia University, under Thorndike joined Healy's staff in Chicago. The following year, 1914, Cook County assumed financial responsibility for support of the clinic.

A book by Healy, *The Individual Delinquent: A Textbook of Diagnosis and Prognosis,* appeared in 1915. It offered descriptive case presentations and an exposition of the new field of mental testing. Its major contention was that the procedures, then current, for handling delinquents were ineffective; that the majority of delinquents, despite the measures taken by courts and reform schools on their behalf, did not become useful citizens and tended to continue to violate the law. Healy argued that what these children needed was treatment which would attempt to eliminate the emotional disturbances at the root of their delinquencies, and he strongly advocated that steps be taken to insure that such treatment was provided. Healy's book caused some alarm and provoked some action. Of most importance, it was eminently successful in influencing legal authorities and others to discard organic and hereditary concepts of etiology in favor of environmental and psychological explanations.

Healy was lured to Boston in 1917 to organize the Judge Baker Foundation, and with him went Augusta Bronner. Among the inducements which prompted them to move were the treatment services which would be available to their patients in the Boston area, the promises of cooperation by a variety of agencies, and the assurance of financial support for ten years. The work of the Foundation consisted mainly of diagnostic evaluations made for the local courts. Treatment of the delinquents was provided by their probation officers.

In spite of the paucity of clinical psychologists, their number was sufficient so that by 1913 the field attracted the attention of critics. The major criticisms were that: there was an overemphasis on mental tests; the work was too exclusively diagnostic; it had little practical value because it was so largely confined to retardates for whom virtually nothing could be done; it was based on the wrong kind of psychology and should incorporate some psychoanalytic concepts; and finally it might

be best to abandon the field of mental retardation to the medical profession, and allow physicians to face its frustrations all by themselves.
There was not too much to say in rebuttal, other than to plead that
clinical psychology was still young and developing, and that it wished
to build upon as solid a scientific foundation as possible . . . which was
what Rene Sylvester said in 1913.

However, to some critics it appeared that the field of clinical psychology was growing too rapidly. New terms were being introduced into
the literature at a gallop, and, in the opinion of Shepherd Ivory Franz,
they were being used vaguely and inconsistently. Franz was particularly
alarmed by all the "new psychologies"; by which he meant abnormal
psychology, clinical psychology, medical psychology, psycho-clinical psychology, psycho-pathology, and pathopsychology. In 1912, he advised
his colleagues to curb their urge to go in for linguistic innovation, and
suggested a division of labor: "when an investigator is concerned chiefly
with the general course of a disease and its treatment his interests are
in psychiatry, but when his chief concern is the investigation of the
development or interrelations of mental symptoms his interests are in
psychology." How Franz proposed to distinguish between the "general
course of a disease" and the "development or interrelations of mental
symptoms" he did not specify.

In 1915, the APA took official note of the abuses occurring in diagnostic testing by adopting a resolution proposed by Guy M. Whipple: "That
this Association discourages the use of mental tests by those unqualified."
Not too happily at first, the APA was being forced to become involved
in the practical applications of the science and the professional problems
of its members. To avoid such involvements would have required unusual
agility, for the status of clinical psychologists was being legally acknowledged by some states.

In 1916, Wallin, who at that time was working in St. Louis, was asked
to serve as chairman of a committee on defective children for the Missouri
Children's Code Commission. One of his recommendations, later enacted
into law, was that a child could not be assigned to a school for the
mentally defective unless he had been examined individually by the use
of standardized tests of intelligence. Around 1917, the Illinois legislature
ennacted a law allowing a psychologist to serve as one of the two members of a commission of experts certifying persons for commitment to
institutions for the retarded. The two members of the first commission
were Healy and Bronner.

Reaction from the medical profession to this threat to their authority
came swiftly. A letter from the New York Psychiatrical Society to the
APA was dispatched in 1917. These psychiatrists deplored what they
hoped was not a trend, and officially registered their disapproval of
psychologists being regarded as experts. Moreover, they objected to the

activities of psychologists in problems of diagnosis, social management, and the institutional "disposal" of patients who evidence abnormal mental conditions. The grounds for their objections were simple: these were medical problems and so only physicians were competent to deal with them.

Franz, who was Scientific Director at St. Elizabeth's Hospital and who had been awarded an honorary M.D. degree in recognition of his outstanding medical contributions from George Washington University in 1915, became angry. He denounced the contention that psychiatrists, ipso facto, were experts while psychologists, ipso facto, were not, and observed: "If some states have decided to utilize psychologists as experts regarding the normality or abnormality of the mental states of individuals, it is conceivable that it was done because previous medical expert testimony was not satisfactory."

Tempers were rising everywhere in 1917. The APA appointed a committee to consider what qualifications were necessary to become a psychological examiner, or "expert," a move that did not especially please anyone. At the APA convention, a group of rather dissatisfied clinicians got together and decided that their interests would best be served by forming an organization of their own. Wallin, who claimed he had been working on just such a project since 1911, met with Leta Hollingworth, Francis Maxfield, James Miner, David Mitchell, Rudolf Pintner, and Clara Schmitt. Then and there, December 28, 1917, at Carnegie Institute of Technology, they founded the American Association of Clinical Psychologists. Among the other early members of the A.A.C.P. were Augusta Bronner, Grace Fernald, Healy, Kuhlmann, Terman, Wells, Whipple, and Yerkes. Actually, there were only early members of this organization because the A.A.C.P. voted to dissolve itself in 1919.

Two major factors accounted for its short life: first, after the War, psychologists expressed opposition to the formation of splinter groups from the APA, which would have fragmented their strength; second, the APA agreed to provide a voice for clinicians within the Association and to involve itself more whole-heartedly in professional matters. An APA committee was appointed to consider methods for certifying members as Consulting Psychologists, and the rebels were welcomed back into the fold as the Clinical Section. Chairing the last meeting of the A.A.C.P. was Arnold Gesell (Wallin could not attend the convention.). Thus on December 31, 1919, the first section or division of the APA, the Clinical Section, came into being.

Not only clinicians, but the entire field of psychology was gaining in prestige and recognition. By 1913, there were sixteen psychological journals in the United States, a quite impressive gain of fourteen journals in twenty-two years. Yet it seemed to a number of young psychologists that the growth of their science was being impeded by the persistence of an "Old Guard" who were bogged down in philosophical speculations. With mounting restlessness, they felt that something had to be done. That *something* took place in 1913 when John Broadus Watson energetically repudiated the attachment of psychology to philosophy.

Watson (1878–1958) was born and grew up in South Carolina, where he was fondly remembered by his teachers as "an indolent, argumentative boy, impatient of discipline, and content if he barely passed his studies." His youth was distinguished by two arrests: one for fighting, and the other for shooting off firearms within the town limits. At the age of sixteen he entered Furman University, and it is somewhat of an understatement to remark that he was not exactly a scholar. Lonely and irritable, he resented college seeing it as an impractical, frustrating prolongation of infancy. In 1900, after receiving his A.M., Watson entered the University of Chicago. There, in a citadel of philosophers, he sulked and fumed about his inability to grasp philosophy. For the life of him, he could not understand what in blazes George Mead and John Dewey were talking about.

In the Fall of 1902 Watson suffered from severe insomnia and feelings of anxiety. He managed to recover after several weeks, and received his Ph.D. in 1903. That same year he married and continued on at the University of Chicago as a member of the faculty. He turned to experimentation with animals because he felt uncomfortable and awkward with people and hated to give them directions. In 1908, he went to Johns Hopkins as a professor, and in 1913 published his manifesto, "Psychology as the Behaviorist Views It."

Watson proclaimed that psychology "is a purely objective experimental branch of natural science. Its theoretical goal is the prediction and control of *behavior*." He argued that since there was no dividing line between man and other animals, by studying the behavior of animals, psychologists could understand, at least in principle, the behavior of people. He contended that all that psychology had to concern itself with were stimuli and responses: given the stimuli, to discover the responses; given the responses, to discover the stimuli.

In the new psychology proposed by Watson, the method of introspection (which he termed "verbal report") would be minimal and was thought to be best avoided. Functional and structural psychologies were deemed unsatisfactory because they dealt with consciousness. Such subjects as mind-body conjectures and other philosophic puzzles were regarded as better entrusted to philosophers than psychologists. Psychology, in short, was to change radically from the study of consciousness to the study of behavior. However, Watson did not mean by "behavior" only simple activities remotely related to the complexities of human life. What he had in mind was very different from that. He urged his colleagues to integrate their findings with the problems of living and to use their understanding to deal with matters of practical consequence, e.g., the psychology of advertising and of testing, areas of knowledge which he believed would make contributions to a "true," worthwhile science.

Angell thought that, in general, Watson was on the right track, although he did think his program a little too sweeping in what it would discard. But Watson's attack had hit bluntly at the heart of an issue, and did not intend to compromise. Those psychologists who had more or less clearly shared his discontent rallied vigorously to his support. Many psychologists feared their science would be split into warring factions.

A reconciliation was attempted by Warren (1867–1934) in his APA presidential address of 1913. Warren noted, "The mind-body relation is the Wandering Jew of science," and then proceeded to put it at rest. He advocated a double-aspect conception of mind-body: there was only one single process observable in two ways; the neural changes were simply the external appearance of mental changes. Having settled the issue to his satisfaction, Warren sought to resolve all differences by this new view of the mind-body problem. On the one hand, he asserted, "The hope of psychology . . . seems to lie in the study of behavior." On the other hand, he defined psychology as "the science of individual experience." Then quickly, he redefined psychology as: "the science of the individual organism or consciousness, as related to its environment."

But Warren's attempt to combine the new and old psychologies was doomed to failure. The movement of behaviorism was young and successful, and far from modifying its position, it became even more extreme. In 1915, Watson, now President of the APA, announced that all forms of behavior should be analyzed in terms of the conditioned reflexes espoused by the neurologist V. M. Bekhterev. His supporters cheered his stand.

The enthusiasm for behaviorism was promoted by some simple facts. Society, men and women in general, took no interest in psychology as a source of information about mind-body theories, and they seemed to have little patience with such speculations and enigmas. Instead, the public was interested in the practical applications of knowledge; in testing, diagnosing mental deficiency, identifying talent and skills, and similar enterprises. Moreover, the public was willing to give recognition, status, prestige, and financial support to those who were responsive to its needs. By attempting to serve the public, by striving to gain information that could be used, psychology could advance both as a science and as a profession.

In 1916, Carl Seashore was invited to help in the organization of the National Research Council. Although at first psychology had not been formally represented in the Council, at the close of the War a Division of Psychology and Anthropology was permanently installed with an alternating chairman and vice-chairman from the two sciences.

The development of clinical psychology was fostered by concomitant growths in related areas. In 1917, Smith College started its School for Social Work. That same year a physician, Clarence M. Hincks of Toronto, after visiting Clifford Beers, founded the National Committee for Mental Hygiene of Canada. Meanwhile, the National Committee for Mental Hygiene in the United States was prospering under its medical director, Thomas W. Salmon. Following the War, Salmon was influential in persuading politicians to appropriate funds for the establishment of veterans' hospitals. At the same time, in order to bolster his arguments for greater financial assistance in the field of mental health, Salmon was mustering all available resources to gather data on the extent of mental illness throughout the country and the number and condition of the facilities for treatment. Under his direction, the National Committee was preparing to embark on a massive campaign of public education concerning mental hygiene.

The significance of such innovations and changes as these was noted in Scott's APA presidential address in 1919. Noteworthy in itself is the simple fact that Scott, an industrial psychologist, had been elected president of the Association. Although most of his remarks were restricted to the profession of personnel administration, the general tenor of his address had broader ramifications. Scott observed that the concept that "all men are created equal" had been replaced by a psychology of individual differences, which recognized the inequalities between men. From this new foundation, merit not seniority, mental age not chronological age, fitness for a task rather than merely being available to perform it, were now the crucial factors in assigning men to useful functions in society. The task and the worker were no longer seen in isolation, but as a unity, a biological kind of relationship, a developing, living, whole situation in which emotions, impulses, habits, and sentiments are of importance.

Society needed to fit the right man in the right job, but Scott believed that society, the man, and the job would all benefit by appropriate matchings. Through vocational guidance, the analyses of jobs and the measurements of talents and skills, much better results could be achieved. A man and his work were to become a productive complex, with the man profiting from his labor, not only materially, but intellectually and emotionally.

Thus by 1919 psychology had attained some status as a science and a profession: the former promoting the latter, and the latter promoting the former. As Yerkes put it: "Largely because of the way in which it responded to the practical demands and the opportunities of the military emergency, psychology today occupies a place among the natural sciences which is newly achieved, eminently desirable, and highly gratifying to the profession."

References

Adler, Alexandra. Adler, Alfred. *Collier's Encyclopedia.* Vol. 1. New York: Crowell-Collier, 1962.

Adler, A. Individual-psychological treatment of neuroses. In *The practice and theory of individual psychology.* New York: Harcourt, Brace, & Co., 1927.

Ansbacher, H. L. & Ansbacher, Rowena R. *The individual psychology of Alfred Adler.* New York: Basic Books, 1956.

Arieti, S. *Interpretation of schizophrenia.* New York: Brunner, 1955.

Ayres, L. P. The Binet-Simon measuring scale for intelligence: some criticisms and suggestions. *Psychol. Clinic,* 1911–12, 5, 187–196.

Bingham, W. V. D. Autobiography. In E. G. Boring, *et al.* (Eds.) *A history of psychology in autobiography.* Vol IV. Worcester, Mass.: Clark U. Press, 1952.

Bleuler, E. *Dementia praecox or the group of schizophrenias.* New York: International Univ. Press, 1950.

Bridges, J. W. & Coler, Lillian E. The relation of intelligence to social status. *Psychol. Rev.,* 1917, 24, 1–31.

Bronner, Augusta, F. Attitude as it affects performance of tests. *Psychol. Rev.,* 1916, 23, 303–331.

Burt, C. Autobiography. In E. G. Boring, *et. al.* (Eds.) *A history of psychology in autobiography.* Vol. IV. Worcester, Mass.: Clark U. Press, 1952.

Claparède, E. Autobiography. In C. Murchison (Ed.) *A history of psychology in autobiography.* Vol. I. Worcester, Mass.: Clark U. Press, 1930.

Dejerine, J. & Garkler, E. *Psychoneurosis and psychotherapy.* Philadelphia: Lippincott, 1913.

Dodge, R. Mental work. A study in psychodynamics. *Psychol. Rev.,* 1913, 20, 1–42.

Durant, W. *The story of philosophy.* Garden City: Garden City Publishing Co., 1926.

Fernberger, S. W. History of the psychological clinic. In R. A. Brotemarkle (Ed.) *Clinical psychology: studies in honor of Lightner Witmer.* Philadelphia: U. Pennsylvania Press, 1931.

Fernberger, S. W. The American Psychological Association: a historical summary, 1892–1930. *Psychol. Bull.,* 1932, 29, 1–89.

Fernberger, S. W. The scientific interests and scientific publications of the members of the American Psychological Association. *Psychol. Bull.,* 1938, 35, 261–281.

Ferrari, G. C. Autobiography. In C. Murchison (Ed.) *A history of psychology in autobiography.* Vol. II. Worcester, Mass.: Clark U. Press, 1932.

Fordham, Frieda. *An introduction to Jung's psychology.* London: Penguin Books, 1953.

Franz, S. I. Experimental psychopathology. *Psychol. Bull.,* 1912, 9, 145–154.

Franz, S. I. Psychology and psychiatry. *Psychol. Bull.,* 1917, 14, 226–227.

Freeman, F. N. Mental tests. *Psychol. Bull.,* 1920, 17, 353–362.

Freud, S. The origin and development of psychoanalysis. *Amer. j. Psychol.,* 1910, 21, 181–218.

Freud, S. On narcissism: an introduction. In *Sigmund Freud: Collected papers.* Vol. 4. New York: Basic Books, 1959.

Goddard, H. H. *The Kallikak family.* New York: Macmillan, 1912.

Goddard, H. H. *Feeblemindedness, its causes and consequences.* New York: Macmillan, 1914.

Hall, C. S. & Lindzey, G. *Theories of personality.* New York: Wiley, 1957.

Healy, W. A pictorial completion test. *Psychol. Rev.,* 1914, 21, 189–203.

Healy, W. & Bronner, Augusta F. The child guidance clinic: birth and growth of an idea. In L. G. Lowrey & Victoria Sloane (Eds.) *Orthopsychiatry 1923–1948: retrospect and prospect.* New York: Amer. Orthopsychiat. Assoc., 1948.

Janet, P. Psychoanalysis. *J. abnorm. Psychol.,* 1914–15, 9, 1–35, 153–187.

Jelliffe, S. E. Some notes on "transference." *J. abnorm. Psychol.,* 1913–14, 8, 302–309.

Jones, E. Book review: *Die Psychoanalyse Freuds. Verteidigung und kritische Bemerkungen.* By E. Bleuler. *J. abnorm. Psychol.,* 1911–12, 6, 465–470.

Jones, E. *The life and work of Sigmund Freud.* Vol. II. New York: Basic Books, 1955.

Jung, C. G. *Psychology of the unconscious.* New York: Moffat, Yard, 1916.

Jung, C. G. A contribution to the study of psychological types. In *Collected papers on analytical psychology.* London: Bailiere, Tindall, & Cox, 1920.

Kent, G. H. & Rosanoff, A. J. A study of association in insanity. *Amer. j. Insanity,* 1910, 67, 37–96, 317–390.

Kraepelin, E. *Dementia praecox and paraphrenia.* Edinburgh: E. & S. Livingston, 1919.

McDougall, W. Autobiography. In C. Murchison (Ed.) *A history of psychology in autobiography.* Vol. I. Worcester, Mass.: Clark U. Press, 1930.

Meyer, A., Jelliffe, S. E., & Hoch, A. *Dementia praecox: a monograph.* Boston: Gorham Press, 1911.

Murphy, G. Robert Sessions Woodworth 1869–1962. *Amer. Psychol.,* 1963, 18, 131–133.

New York Psychiatrical Society. Activities of clinical psychologists. *Psychol. Bull.,* 1917, 14, 224–225.

Ogden, R. M. The unconscious bias of laboratories. *Psychol. Bull.,* 1911, 8, 330–331.

Pintner, R. & Paterson, D. G. *A scale of performance tests.* New York: Appleton, 1917.

Porter, F. Difficulties in the interpretation of mental tests—types and examples. *Psychol. Clinic,* 1915–16, 9, 140–158, 167–180.

Rosanoff, Isabel R. & Rosanoff, A. J. A study of association in children. *Psychol. Rev.,* 1913, 20, 43–89.

Schwab, S. I. The mechanism of the war neuroses. *J. abnorm. Psychol.,* 1919–20, 14, 1–8.

Scott, W. D. Changes in some of our conceptions and practices of personnel. *Psychol. Rev.,* 1920, 27, 81–94.

Sidis, B. Fear, anxiety, and psychopathic maladies. *J. abnorm. Psychol.,* 1911–12, 6, 107–125.

Solomon, M. Book review. *Psychology of the unconscious.* By C. G. Jung, *J. abnorm. Psychol.,* 1916–17, 11, 277–279.

Stern, W. *The psychological methods of testing intelligence.* Baltimore: Warwick & York, 1914.

Sylvester, R. H. Clinical psychology adversely criticized. *Psychol. Clinic,* 1913–14, 7, 182–188.

Tanner, A. Adler's theory of *Mindeswertigkeit. Ped. Sem.,* 1915, 22, 204–217.

Terman, L. M. The Binet-Simon Scale for measuring intelligence. *Psychol. Clinic,* 1911–12, 5, 199–206.

Terman, L. M. *The measurement of intelligence.* Boston: Houghton Mifflin, 1916.

Terman, L. M. Autobiography. In C. Murchison (Ed.) *A history of psychology in autobiography.* Vol. II. Worcester, Mass.: Clark U. Press, 1932.

Thomson, G. H. A hierarchy without a general factor. *Brit. j. Psychol.,* 1916, 8, 271–281.

Thomson, G. H. The proof or disproof of the existence of general ability. *Brit. j. Psychol.,* 1919, 9, 321–336.

Thomson, G. H. Autobiography. In E. G. Boring, *et. al.* (Eds.) *A history of psychology in autobiography.* Vol. IV. Worcester, Mass.: Clark U. Press, 1952.

Thorndike, E. L. Ideo-motor action. *Psychol. Rev.,* 1913, 20, 91–106.

Varnon, Edith J. Alfred Binet's concept of intelligence. *Psychol. Rev.,* 1936, 43, 32–58.

Wallin, J. E. W. *The mental health of the school child.* New Haven: Yale U. Press, 1914.

Wallin, J. E. W. Re-averments respecting psycho-clinical norms and scales of development. *Psychol. Clinic,* 1913–14, 7, 89–96.

Wallin, J. E. W. The phenomenon of scattering in the Binet-Simon Scale. *Psychol. Clinic,* 1917–18, 11, 179–195.

Wallin, J. E. W. A study of the industrial record of children assigned to public school classes for mental defectives, and legislation in the interest of defectives. *J. abnorm. soc. Psychol.,* 1922–23, 17, 120–131.

Wallin, J. E. W. A note on the origin of the APA clinical section. *Amer. Psychol.,* 1961, 16, 256–258.

Walsh, J. J. *Psychotherapy*. New York: Appleton, 1913.

Warren, H. C. The mental and the physical. *Psychol. Rev.,* 1914, 21, 79–100.

Watson, J. B. Psychology as the behaviorist views it. *Psychol. Rev.,* 1913, 20, 158–179.

Watson, J. B. The place of the conditioned-reflex in psychology. *Psychol. Rev.,* 1916, 23, 89–116.

Watson, J. B. Autobiography. In C. Murchison (Ed.) *A history of psychology in autobiography*. Vol. III. Worcester, Mass.: Clark U. Press, 1936.

Watson, R. I. A brief history of clinical psychology. *Psychol. Bull.,* 1953, 50, 321–346.

Wells, F. L. The systematic observation of the personality in its relation to the hygiene of mind. *Psychol. Rev.,* 1914, 21, 295–333.

White, W. A. The Adlerian concept of the neuroses. *J. abnorm. Psychol.,* 1917–18, 12, 168–173.

Witmer, L. On the relation of intelligence to efficiency. *Psychol. Clinic,* 1915, 9, 61–86.

Woodworth, R. S. *Personal Data Sheet*. Chicago: C. H. Stoelting, 1917.

Woodworth, R. S. Some criticisms of the Freudian psychology. *J. abnorm. Psychol.,* 1917–18, 12, 174–194.

Woodworth, R. S. Autobiography. In C. Murchison (Ed.) *A history of psychology in autobiography*. Vol. II. Worcester, Mass.: Clark U. Press, 1932.

Yerkes, R. M., Bridges, J. W., & Hardwick, R. S. *A point scale for measuring mental ability*. Baltimore: Warwick & York, 1915.

Yerkes, R. M. Report of the psychology committee of the National Research Council. *Psychol. Rev.,* 1919, 26, 83–149.

Yoakum, C. S. & Yerkes, R. M. *Army mental tests*. New York: Holt, 1920.

Zilboorg, G. & Henry, G. W. *A history of medical psychology*. New York: Norton, 1941.

5

School Rivalry

1920-1929

WITHIN THE UNITED STATES the decade of the twenties was a continuation of the unsettled social conditions that seemed so distressing to so many Americans shortly after the First World War. Relentlessly, but very often justly, the trade union movement pressed its demands for its rights to organize and bargain for higher wages and benefits from management. Women, now armed with enfranchisement, sought opportunities and prerogatives equal to those of men. A new generation of Americans struggled to free themselves from the cultures of their parents, seeking assimilation in the evolving culture of the United States. Codes of conduct were challenged and a new morality was being discussed, one based on greater individual freedom, especially in acceptance of sex. Unquestionably the social sciences were promoted by, and played some role in promoting, this examination of traditional values and attitudes.

At the same time, of course, there were bound to be resistances and disillusionments. A great disappointment was that the prohibition of alcoholic beverages produced few of the advantages predicted for it. In fact, far from converting the country into a paradise of sobriety, prohibition had spawned a flagrant flouting of the law by ordinarily sober, law-abiding citizens. The feelings of turmoil and the reactions to it were epitomized in President Harding's wish to return the nation to normalcy and the recommendation of his successor to "Keep Cool with Coolidge."

On the other side of the Atlantic, there was similar unrest, and without the compensation of the material prosperity enjoyed by the United States. The League of Nations strived to maintain peace in spite of its inability to deal effectively with growing international friction and resentments. Many of these resentments had been intensified by the War. In particular, the German people, embittered by the terms of the Treaty of Versailles and periodically impoverished by inflation, brooded about vengeance and the restoration of honor. But their anger and dissatisfaction were shared by other nations in Europe. In Soviet Russia the Bolsheviks were using their power to carve out a monolithic Communist state. In Italy the Fascists, under their leader Benito Mussolini, were urging their countrymen to accept discipline, hard work, and sacrifice for the glory of their homeland. In all areas intellectuals were driven to the disturbing conclusion that democracy seemed to have little appeal when it appeared to be exchanged for national strength and purpose.

Ironically, the twenties came to a close with the United States reeling from the impact of a serious financial crisis ushered in by the New York Stock Market "crash" in 1929. A period of world-wide economic depression ensued.

Yet through it all, science had progressed, and literature and art, if they were not unanimously regarded as having advanced or improved, did at least change. Frederick Banting developed insulin for use in the treatment of diabetes, and Sir Alexander Fleming discovered penicillin. The medical world was excited by the discovery of filterable viruses and ascribed to them responsibility for the causation of yellow fever and infantile paralysis. It was not too far-fetched to suppose that they, or something similar but still unknown, might be involved in the causation of mental illness. In 1927, Werner Heisenberg proposed his principle of uncertainty or indeterminacy, which states that in the sub-atomic world the more accurately one measures the velocity of a particle, the less accurately one can specify its position. A profound implication of Heisenberg's principle is that it assigns limits to man's knowledge since it predicts that no scientist will ever determine the exact position and velocity of a particle at the same instant.

The most widely-read writers of the day, influenced by realism and troubled by a feeling of pessimism and futility, included Erich Remarque, Sinclair Lewis, Ernest Hemingway, William Faulkner, F. Scott Fitzgerald, André Malraux, and Eugene O'Neill. A new literary trend, influenced in some measure by psychoanalysis, appeared and was notably illustrated by the stream-of-consciousness writing of James Joyce, who attempted to portray the functioning of the human mind in all its symbolism and complexity. Also influenced by psychoanalysis was a new form of painting, surrealism, which tried to depict the psychic condition of man in dream-like canvases. People read the words and stared at the paintings and wondered why the artists seemed so troubled. Meanwhile, the godfather of them all, Sigmund Freud, was having troubles of his own.

NORMAL PERSONALITY FUNCTIONING

Freud continued to encounter resistance within medical circles, particularly in Austria and Germany, but as it did not greatly trouble him, it need not trouble us. The general trend was for recognition and honors to keep coming Freud's way. Unfortunately, though, he shared the financial fate of his countrymen and saw his savings erased by inflation. As far as Freud was concerned, there was little pleasure in being a distinguished and honored pauper. Moreover, even his analytic colleagues had not greeted the ideas expressed in his latest work, *Beyond the Pleasure Principle,* with much enthusiasm.

For several years, Freud claimed, he had been pondering his new formulations. The experiences of the War had been decisive and had convinced him of their validity. Just as Schopenhauer had proclaimed, "death is the goal of life," Freud now asserted that the basic aim of the instincts was to regress to a preceding state, which ultimately would be nonexistence.

Once again he pictured two opposing sets of instincts: the Life Instincts, which strive to perpetuate and preserve life; the Death Instincts, which strive toward self-destruction. The Life Instincts, Eros, are manifested in binding, integrating, and uniting activities. The Death Instincts, later to be called Thanatos, are manifested in differentiating, disintegrating, and separating activities. A new principle, the repetition compulsion is thought to govern them both—a tendency to repeat experiences in thought and/or action in order to attain a feeling of mastery over them. Of course this tendency to repetition may also be viewed as an effort to regain a previous state of affairs. Freud modestly explained, "It would be counter to the conservative nature of instinct if the goal of life were a state never hitherto reached." If the final goal of life is death, aggression, even in its most violent manifestation, war, can be interpreted, paradoxically, as a defensive maneuver to preserve one's own life by displacing the destructive tendencies against oneself toward other people, while at the same time courting annihilation.

Many analysts found it difficult to accept these ideas, and Jones came to suspect that perhaps they represented Freud's desire not for death but for reunion with his mother. However, McDougall greeted them warmly, even though he did not agree with them. What he welcomed, because it coincided with his own beliefs, was Freud's dethronement of the pleasure principle. It seemed to him that he and Freud agreed that instinctive urges operate independently of pleasure and pain. So McDougall hailed the latest developments from Vienna as "a great advance."

Early in 1923, cancer was detected in Freud's jaw and palate. Thus began a series of operations which succeeded in their major purpose, that of preserving Freud's life, but which required that he suffer serious disability. The effects of surgery made it necessary that Freud wear a prosthesis, which proved to be irritating and painful. Furthermore, his speech was made nasal and thick, and his hearing was impaired. His life became one of daily torment, alleviated to some extent by the ministrations of his daughter, Anna, and by the courage and heroism which he showed in continuing his work.

Possibly he was cheered by the favorable reaction of his colleagues to his book *The Ego and the Id* (1923). Freud had described three major groups of psychological functions and named them the Id, Ego, and Super-Ego. The Id refers to the undifferentiated energy and unconscious instinctual impulses present from birth which press for immediate expression. The Ego, he supposed, originally derived its energy from the Id. It was now thought to involve both conscious, perceptual, cognitive, and motor processes and unconscious mechanisms for keeping impulses and thoughts from awareness. The Super-Ego, a newly distinguished "structure," included, in part, his older concept of the ego-ideal. Largely unconscious in its functioning, the Super-Ego is derived from the child's identification with what he perceives to be the demands, prohibitions, and commandments of his parents, especially during the time the Oedipus complex is being resolved. Conscience and the ego-ideal are regarded as derivatives of the Super-Ego, and thus these functions involve punishment by feelings of guilt for "misbehavior" and rewards of self-approval for "correct" action.

During this period Freud was distressed once again by the defection of one of his inner circle of analysts. The incident "began" with the members of the Committee being upset by the presumptuousness of their associate, Otto Rank, who had the temerity to publish a book without consulting them. Though Rank dedicated his work to Freud, his views, as they saw them, conflicted with the tenets of psychoanalysis.

The instigator of their concern and alarm, Otto Rank (1884–1939), had been born in Vienna as Otto Rosenfeld. His youth was miserable. The son of a poor and alcoholic father, he suffered from rheumatism, had few friends, and fed himself mostly on a diet of books and a bountiful contempt for people in general: "If anything could drive me to suicide, it would be the stupidity and commonness of mankind."

After graduating from a trade school, he worked in a machine shop. At nights he tried to be a writer of poetry and literature, but his wretchedness often led him to spend his evenings wrestling with a temptation to kill himself. Then he came across *The Interpretation of Dreams.* Inspired by his reading of Freud's work, he wrote a manuscript (published in English in 1932 with the title *Art and Artist*) using psychoanalytic principles to explain artistic productions. He showed this manuscript to Adler, and around 1906 Adler introduced him to Freud. Impressed, Freud generously helped Rosenfeld to enter the University of Vienna and obtain a formal education.

Rosenfeld legally adopted his pen name, Rank, in 1909, and in 1912 received his Ph.D. with a psychoanalytic interpretation of the saga of Lohengrin as his thesis. During the War he served as the editor of an army newspaper in Poland. He married and upon returning to Vienna seemed to those who had known him from the old days to have become more self-assertive and self-confident. The following year, 1920, he began to practice psychoanalysis.

In his book *The Trauma of Birth,* Rank proposed that the transition from the security of the womb to the painful stimulations of the postnatal environment is experienced by the infant with tremendous fear or anxiety. This primal anxiety is repressed, but throughout life the individual reacts with fear to subsequent separations and strives to reinstate the bliss he experienced in the womb. Despite such strivings for maternal comfort and protection, the person's feelings are conflicted. Though unconsciously desiring to return to the safety within his mother's body, he is at the same time frightened and angered by such a possibility because of the terror which originally followed his presence there, i.e., the birth trauma.

Rank's formulations thus put great emphasis upon the issue of separation as a universal dilemma of major significance. In line with his views, he advocated the setting of a termination date early in an analysis so that the conflict over the separation could be speedily faced and treated.

Freud did not object to Rank's experimentation with techniques, and was undecided whether acceptance of the birth trauma concept necessitated a professional separation. Others of the group, however, were more critical, and Rank left for New York in a huff. Anna Freud then took his place on the Committee.

Considering the fact that in those days Rank had to travel by ship and train, there followed an extraordinary and pathetic sequence of journeys. Within the year Rank was back in Vienna begging Freud's forgiveness and attributing his ideas to an unresolved neurosis on his part or to manic-depressive psychosis or anything other than his genuine convictions. Soon he was off again to New York, back in Vienna, off to Paris, back to New York, back to Vienna and a final break with Freud, then off to Paris again, then to Philadelphia, back to Paris, and then back and forth between Paris and the School of Social Work in Philadelphia. It was certainly most fortunate for Rank's livelihood that he had hit upon the desirability of setting a time limit on a course of therapy.

Meanwhile, in 1925, the old ex-friend and collaborator of Sigmund Freud, Josef Breuer, died. A few years before his death, Breuer wrote an autobiography of some twenty pages of which only one paragraph dealt with his relationship with Freud and psychoanalysis. He realistically appraised his contribution to science and spoke proudly and caressingly of the benefits he had received from life: "It (*Studies on Hysteria*) is the seed from which psychoanalysis was developed by Freud. . . . (that I have been) completely happy in my home; that my beloved wife has given me five sturdy, fine children; and that none has ever caused me serious sorrow—then I may well consider myself a fortunate man."

Karl Abraham also died in 1925, and the position he had occupied on the Committee was allowed to go unfilled. The following year Freud was interviewed on the occasion of his seventieth birthday. Despite his physical suffering and his theory of death instincts, Freud proclaimed: "Seventy years have taught me to accept life with a cheerful humility . . . I still prefer existence to extinction."

It was also at about this time that Freud promulgated his views on anxiety. Like Rank, he traced the first experiencing of anxiety to birth. Unlike Rank, he did not attribute anxiety to separation but to the overwhelming feeling of stimulation from the infant's receptors, which at this early stage of development the child cannot handle or comprehend. Later, as he grows older, whenever impulses or thoughts threaten to be overwhelming, anxiety is re-experienced and serves as a signal of danger. This signal anxiety operates unconsciously to set off processes, ascribed to the ego, which protect or defend the person from the excitation by keeping it from awareness or by so distorting it that it becomes tolerable.

In 1927, the Committee was dissolved, and Freud published *The Future of an Illusion*. This book attempts to explain the bases for man's religious beliefs, and its title may suffice to allow the reader to predict the reaction it received, at least in certain quarters.

Elsewhere in Vienna, Alfred Adler had done very well without psychoanalysis and had a science of his own, which he called Individual Psychology: "The science of Individual Psychology developed out of the effort to understand that mysterious creative power of life which expresses itself in the desire to develop, to strive, to achieve, and even to compensate for defects in one direction by striving for success in another."

Adler saw people confronted by three major problems that have to be solved in living: one, finding a suitable vocation; two, maintaining satis-

fying social relationships; and three, experiencing satisfying sexual relationships. Actually, the resolution of all these problems requires what
Adler called "social feeling" or "social interest." Social feeling is an innate potential, which to be actualized requires learning by the child, as
well as conscious attempts to develop it by those responsible for the
child's training. Although Adler never precisely defined social interest,
he described it as something very much like empathy: "To see with the
eyes of another, to hear with the ears of another, to feel with the heart
of another." However, this empathic effort, to qualify as social interest,
has to have as its ultimate goal the creation of a harmonious, ideal community of all mankind.

Not surprisingly, some self-interest is served by social interest: "The
only salvation from the continuously driving inferiority feeling is the
knowledge and the feeling of being valuable which originates from the
contribution to the common welfare." In other words, the person can
only find his path to psychic health and contentment, not through self-
scrutiny and understanding alone, but through being of some use to his
society. "A man of genius," according to Adler, "is primarily a man of
supreme social usefulness."

The individual's goal in life is, therefore, of tremendous significance to
him. All people, Adler now thought, inevitably have some feelings of
inferiority. These feelings are unavoidable because children are naturally weak and dependent in relation to adults. The important thing is
how the person intends to go about alleviating these feelings. Is the goal
he sets for himself to dominate others or to be of service to them? Will he
receive the training and guidance that enables him to choose a constructive rather than a destructive style of life? Adler felt it was impossible
to overestimate the importance of this unconscious choice. Not only does
the person's final goal influence his current behavior and what he intends
to do in the future, but it affects his perception of events, gives meaning
to his existence, and allows him to transcend the difficulties of the
moment by contemplating future successes. Such are the ramifications of
the individual's goal as Adler saw them toward the close of the twenties.

Earlier in the decade there had been quite a furor in the United States
about whether behavior is or is not fundamentally goal-directed. Heading
the negative position was John B. Watson, who had come upon some
hard times but was rising above them.

During World War I, Watson had antagonized his superior officers by
going out of military channels to express publicly his opinion of the "rotation test," (a neurological test which seeks to detect disturbances in the ves-
tibular apparatus) as it was being used in the selection of pilots. He
thought it worthless. His disregard of the chain of command was to be rewarded by transferring him from the United States to the discipline and

dangers of the front lines in Europe. Fortunately, the armistice enabled Watson's return to the temporary safety of Johns Hopkins. There he conducted some research studies of infant behavior, which we shall discuss shortly. In 1920, Watson was divorced, and soon thereafter married his co-worker in the research just mentioned. A divorce involving a socially prominent wife, two children, and a professor at Johns Hopkins who almost immediately took another bride was a great scandal in Baltimore in 1920, and resulted in Watson being quickly relieved of his position.

For several days after his dismissal, Watson fought against giving way to feelings of depression. All academic positions seemed closed to him, and he was at a loss to decide what he might be able to do. His friends suggested that he try his hand in the field of advertising, though it would require him to be willing to start from the bottom. So start at the bottom he did. To gain familiarity with people as the salesman sees them, Watson spent some time going from door to door selling coffee and asking the occupants what brand of boots they wore. In the summer of 1921 he worked as a clerk in Macy's Department Store.

Evidently he proved quite successful in this new field, for by 1924 Watson had risen to the position of vice-president of a large advertising agency. His abiding interest, however, was psychology. Through books, magazine articles, and lectures at Clark University and the New School of Social Research, he was able to continue to give expression to his thoughts and opinions.

Watson believed that heredity is of negligible significance in the development of the person. Environment and training were practically everything. He was fond of challenging: "Give me a dozen healthy infants, well-formed, and my own specified world to bring them up in and I'll guarantee to take any one at random and train him to become any type of specialist I might select." One of the major regrets of Watson's life was that no one ever gave him the babies to be used in the research he proposed. Perhaps, all things considered, it was just as well.

According to Watson, all that man inherits are certain kinds of structure which force him to respond to stimuli from birth in certain ways. Just as a boomerang returns to its thrower because of the way it has been shaped, so men respond to forces because of the manner in which they are formed and connected, or joined internally by bone, muscle, and nerve tissue. All behaviors are products of learning and structure. Therefore Watson saw no need in psychology for such terms as instincts, capacities, talents, temperaments, traits; personality is just a "sum of activities . . . the end product of our habit systems."

On the basis of his studies of infants being raised in Harriet Lane Hospital, Watson concluded that unlearned behavior consists only of a few simple motor responses, such as sneezing, crying, grasping, and three emotional reactions: love, elicited by stroking or gentle stimulation of the skin; rage, elicited by physical restraints; and fear, elicited by loud noises and loss of support. More complex responses and reactions to more complex patterns of stimuli are acquired, or learned, through conditioning.

Watson did not hesitate to generalize from his data and go far beyond them. He strongly believed that child training is important and blamed most of the troubles in the world on incompetent rearing. Particularly distressing to him were manifestations of excessive parental love. He was convinced that too much affection causes children to become dependent and emotionally unstable. His advice to parents was to pay less attention to their offspring and to spend less time in pampering them. They were further instructed to give their child a rap across the fingers firmly, though gently, whenever he was caught doing something wrong. Failure to heed his advice might produce the most dire of all consequences, a child who had grown up to be a "lounge lizard."

Little tolerance was shown by Watson for anyone who disagreed with him. As far as he was concerned, only three kinds of people did not share his way of thinking: first, those who were unable to accept the facts; second, those who liked to think heredity was important so they could feel superior to other people; and third, those who wished to avoid feeling responsible for the training of their children. What Watson may have lacked in sophistication, he more than made up in zeal.

Eloquently opposing Watson was McDougall, who was appointed professor of psychology at Harvard in 1920. His description of Watson may serve to illustrate the high level of verbal aggression attained in this period: "Thus, by repudiating one half of the methods of psychology and resolutely shutting his eyes to three quarters of its problems, he laid down the program of Behaviorism and rallied to its standard all those who have a natural distaste for difficult problems and a preference for short, easy, and fictitious solutions."

McDougall argued that behavior is basically purposive. He insisted it could not be understood only as responses to stimuli. In bolstering his argument he left no appeal unturned. He appealed to reason by showing that behaviorists were forced to assume that their animal subjects were trying to reach some goal in order to make their findings meaningful. Even a behaviorist, Tolman, he noted, now recognized purposiveness in the activities of organisms. He appealed to common sense by pointing out that it is impossible to know what a machine is until it is known what the machine was designed to do. Who among those hearing these words, he questioned, does not feel he has been working toward a desired goal. His appeal went so far as to take a pragmatic turn when he pointed to the profit to be gained if people were seen as capable of striving "with some success to improve themselves and the conditions of their life in this strange world."

Yet McDougall was fighting a defensive war, and his appeals did not touch many psychological heads or hearts. Most psychologists mistrusted the concept of instincts, or anything that smacked of innate restrictions on what a person could be taught to do. Instincts implied purposive behavior, and the two terms were closely identified with one another, particularly in the person of McDougall. Besides, purposiveness reminded many psychologists of teleology, and teleology was associated with an unsophisticated science which claimed current behavior was determined by what might take place in the future rather than by what had taken place in the past. Therefore when the behaviorists had thrown out the concept of instincts, they also threw out purposiveness, and the behaviorists, though they certainly did not constitute the majority of psychologists, clearly dominated psychological thinking in the United States.

McDougall recognized that instincts were taboo in psychology, and so he tried to save his theory by making some revisions and repudiating the term. He said that by an instinct all that he now meant was an innate impulse or disposition. These impulses were no longer thought to be inherently bound to any specific motor mechanism, but could be expressed by means of a variety of neuromuscular connections. At the "core" of the instinct is a "capacity for desiring" the end result of the behavior, or a striving to attain that particular goal. To illustrate the distinction between the instinct and its associated behavior, McDougall asked that we imagine an elderly man whose "sexual fire" (sex instinct) has died out. Now this gentleman, for old times' sake, might repeat his youthful courting behavior with women. But obviously, his attitudes and feelings toward women would not be the same as when he was young, and despite his manifestation of the same overt wooing behavior, his actions would strike others as a sad mockery of his former self.

At any rate, McDougall regretted that he had ever used the term instinct. He now preferred the word "horme" (a Greek word that means "animal impulse," and one that had achieved scientific respectability in the word "hormone"). Consequently, the point of view championed by McDougall came to be called "hormic psychology."

During the early twenties McDougall had been most interested in the sentiments. He speculated that character or personality is really made up of a system of sentiments, and specified the following among them: love, hatred, contempt, respect, friendship, morality, and self-regard. Human development, he reasoned, seems to progress from: (a) strong impulses toward some vague goal; to (b) instinctive strivings that are regulated by social approval; and then to the most advanced stage (c) the labors of an integrated individual to realize his ideals of character and conduct whether or not they meet with the approval of his group.

While McDougall saw autonomy as the highest stage of development, he expressed his personal dilemma by making self-regard the most important of the sentiments. And self-regard, he decided, is derived from the opinions and reactions of others to the person as he struggles to effect a compromise between gaining their favor through acquiescence and giving expression to his own demands and ideas: "the word 'I' or 'me' grows richer in meaning, as he builds up a system of beliefs about his own nature, a system of beliefs which is rooted in, because in the main sprung from, the two great conative dispositions of self-assertion and submission."

It was McDougall's tragedy to be unable to resolve to his own satisfaction the conflict he experienced between arrogantly espousing unpopular ideas and winning the friendship of his colleagues. In the psychology of the United States, where human "instincts" had become an anachronism, McDougall published lists of them; where environment was almost everything and heredity was being discounted in favor of learning, McDougall persisted in speculating that the Nordic race, of which he considered himself a member, was superior to all others; where Darwin's theory of evolution reigned supreme, McDougall thought it possible to inherit acquired characteristics; where psychologists expressed interest only in the objective and observable, McDougall expressed interest in research in fields that many people thought of as supernatural. Each of his ideas would have been sufficient to alienate a goodly portion of psychologists; all of them together took care of alienating just about everyone.

Yet McDougall was not trying to be negativistic or cantankerous. He was for the most part sincerely trying to be a scientist by questioning and subjecting to experimental research the conclusions which he felt many other had simply assumed to be correct.

Although the majority of psychologists argued against instincts, especially human instincts, there were some, like Tolman, who thought a precise definition might be enough to salvage the concept. His "precise" definition of instinct was: an innate connection of specific driving adjustments to specific stimulating conditions which tends to release particular sets of random acts until some one act occurs which provides a stimulating condition which innately relaxes the driving adjustment itself. Other psychologists took a different tack.

Knight Dunlap was against instincts but felt that McDougall was really talking about emotions. It didn't really matter what McDougall was talking about because Dunlap felt the term he should have used was "desire." In his APA presidential address of 1922, Dunlap "rashly" offered a tentative list of nine desires: alimentary, excretory, rest, activity, shelter, amatory, parental, pre-eminence, and conformity. He thought the last four should be of major importance to psychologists.

Woodworth was not very happy that people were not too interested in his dynamic psychology. He was also not very happy that so many of them were interested in behaviorism. It seemed to Woodworth that there was more to behavior than simple stimuli and simple responses. After all, the organism is not at rest when the stimulus is presented but is engaged in some form of activity. The stimulus, therefore, is evaluated by the organism in the context of its on-going behavior, and its response is determined not only by the stimulus but by its pre-existing actions.

Furthermore, while Woodworth shared in the dissatisfaction with the concept of instinct, he thought psychology could tolerate a concept such as "need": "what we call 'need' is a prepotent activity, i.e., an activity not readily deflected moving forward without responding to stimuli disconnected with itself. What we see is an activity going forward in a definite direction and rendering the organism unresponsive to certain stimuli while unusually responsive to others."

Morton Prince did not care for instincts and neither did Floyd Allport. The latter talked instead about "prepotent reflexes," while the former saw the human personality as the sum total of traits and neurograms. The traits of the individual could be either innate or acquired behavioral tendencies. Neurograms were traits that had become organized systems of neural dispositions. There was no discernible enthusiasm to embrace the term "neurogram," but Gordon Allport, for one, believed the trait concept had value and a large number of other psychologists shared his point of view.

Allport thought of a trait as a characteristic form of behavior that is more generalized than a reflex or simple habit. It can be viewed as an adjustive tendency of the individual, particularly in his relations with his social environment. Sample traits are extroversion, introversion, ascendence, submission, and self-seeking.

Unfortunately, some psychologists described people by stringing together a list of their traits. For example, one psychologist depicted the personality of a delinquent girl as follows: "This girl is of the overactive type, intelligent, ego-centric, introspective, seclusive, excitable, and rather inclined to be depressed. She is impulsive, opinionated, sensitive, and easily offended." Allport was firmly against this practice of trait cataloguing. He insisted that to picture an individual's personality adequately, the psychologist has to know and demonstrate how the person's traits combine and interact.

So we see that even if instincts had fallen into disrepute, man was given at least hormes, desires, needs, prepotent reflexes, traits, and neurograms to help him make his way in the world.

Toward the close of the decade considerable interest and discussion centered around the work of the Gestalt school and the challenges it offered to behaviorism and, to a lesser extent, the work of Jean Piaget. Let us look at Piaget's work first.

Jean Piaget (b. 1896) was born and raised in Switzerland. While an undergraduate in college he became interested in philosophy and zoölogy, and then earned his Ph.D. at the University of Neuchâtel in 1918 with an investigation of the distribution of molluscs in the Valasian Alps. At about that time Piaget had reached the conclusion that life could be best understood in terms of stages of development or "structures-of-the-whole" (*structure d'ensemble,* which in his theoretical formulations refers to inferred and relatively stable qualities of intellectual functioning that seem to characterize behavior at a given period in the sequence of growth). His attention then turned to psychology. After studying in Zurich by reading Freud and attending lectures by Jung, he went to Paris and for two years worked with Simon. While there he began wondering about the wrong answers that children gave on reasoning tests and decided to investigate them. In 1921, he went to Geneva to work with Claparède at the J. J. Rousseau Institute. Five years later Piaget became professor of philosophy at his alma mater; three years after that he became professor of psychology at the University of Geneva.

Piaget's book *The Language and Thought of the Child* was published in 1923, with an English translation in 1926. On the basis of talking with and listening to the verbalizations of children who were between two and eleven years of age, Piaget found what seemed to be two different kinds of speech. The first, egocentric speech, had self-expression and self-stimulation as its intent. It was characterized by the child's lack of concern as to whether or not people had attended to his language or what their point of view might be. It was manifested when the child talked to himself, parroted speech, and simply when he expressed his own thoughts without waiting or listening to hear what anyone else might have to say about them. The second kind of speech, socialized speech, had as its intent communication with someone, and the speaker evidenced consideration for the reactions and points of view of his listener. Piaget liked to think that socialized speech was characteristic of adults.

Consequently, Piaget found that as children grew, their speech became less egocentric and more socialized. By citing ages and the percentages of the kinds of speech found at each age level, he stimulated many psychologists to repeat his work, many of whom got somewhat different results. But his more abstract findings seemed to hold firm. At a time when psychology needed the reminding, Piaget's work illustrated that careful observations of children in natural settings might shed light on human functioning.

Turning to the Gestalt school of psychology, which was beginning to cause all kinds of excitement about configurations and organizations in perception, we take note of the work of Lewin as the Gestaltist most relevant to us.

Kurt Lewin (1890–1947) was born in Prussia and attended the Universities of Freiberg, Munich, and Berlin. He received his Ph.D. in 1914 and spent the next four years in the German army. Lewin then returned to the University of Berlin as instructor and research assistant in the Psychological Institute. In 1926, he was appointed professor of philosophy and psychology. His close associates at the University were Max Wertheimer and Wolfgang Köhler, both leaders in the Gestalt school.

Like other Gestalt psychologists, Lewin disputed virtually every tenet of behaviorism. The behaviorists, he claimed, tend to ignore individual variations from the average; extreme cases are usually attributed to chance fluctuations and may even justifiably be eliminated so as not to distort the data. For Lewin, the individual case is lawful and may be sufficient to support or refute a hypothesis. Behaviorists argue that psychologists should deal only with what may be observed. Lewin argued that observable behavior or appearances, phenotypes, can be produced by a variety of underlying causes, genotypes, and that psychologists have to be concerned with the interactions of both. Behaviorists claim that the stimulus elicits a response. Lewin claimed that the external stimulus influences, directs, and regulates a response which is produced by a tension within the individual striving toward discharge.

According to Lewin, an individual's behavior is a function both of his tension and of his immediate perceptions of himself and his environment. The person's activities tend toward the restoration of equilibrium, or the release and satisfaction of his tensions. In seeking to obtain this restoration, his environment can be perceived as having attractions and repulsions, goals and barriers to the goals. These formulations of Lewin led to some novel experiments.

Psychologists were surprised by the reports from his laboratory of the Zeigarnik effect. Bluma Zeigarnik had found that people seem better able to recall those tasks in which they are interrupted than those they have completed. Supposedly, the tension to attain the goal persists in the case of interrupted tasks, causing better recall of them. Clearly, the behaviorism of Watson could not have predicted that. And does not this failing of behaviorism, it was argued, indict the entire position of the school, while indicating the correctness and fruitfulness of the Gestalt approach? Well, the issue is not really so stark, though the proponents of one position or the other often made it seem that way. Each school had focused on different aspects and problems of behavior. The emphasis of behaviorism was on conditioning and overt behavior. The emphasis of the Gestalt school was on perception and experiencing. Both schools, and in fact all the schools of psychology, share the aim of trying to understand people, and the confirmed findings of each obviously require integration within the science as a whole.

DIAGNOSTIC TECHNIQUES

Psychologists not only continued to devise and revise tests for the measurement of intelligence, but they also turned their attention to the assessment of other facets of personality. Interests and aptitudes, traits and emotions were challenging the ingenuity of the psychometrician.

Far and away the most widely used of the individually administered scales, Terman's Stanford Revision of the Binet-Simon retained its popularity. But there were revisions of previous revisions of the Binet-Simon by Kuhlmann (1922) and Yerkes (1923), and also a brand new revision by Herring (1922).

There were more group administered scales of mental ability: the Otis Classification Test, Forms A and B (1923), which measured achievement as well as "mental alertness"; Dearborn Group Tests (1922); the Institute of Educational Research Intelligence Scale CAVD (1925), developed under Thorndike's direction; the Miller Analogies Test (1926); Kuhlmann-Anderson Intelligence Tests (1927); the Terman Group Test of Mental Ability (1920); and the Northumberland Mental Test (1920), later called the Moray House Tests (1925), which enjoyed popularity in England and were developed by Godfrey Thomson.

To round out this capsule picture of mental tests, there were also: Ferguson Form Boards (1920); The Assembly Test of General Mechanical Ability, the first test designed to measure the ability of children and adults to assemble the parts of mechanical devices, devised by J. L. Stenquist (1923); Florence Goodenough's Draw a Man Test (1926), in which a measure of a child's intellectual level is obtained from scoring his drawing of a man for completeness, accuracy, and motor coordination; and the Porteus Maze Tests, first developed by Porteus in Australia around 1913, improved by him throughout the years, including those after he took over from Goddard as director of research at Vineland in 1919.

Still there was a degree of dissatisfaction with most of these tests and an awareness that much more needed to be done. Three problems were immediately recognized: one, the lack of a suitable individually administered scale of intelligence for adults; two, the need for a suitable individually administered scale of intelligence for infants; and three, a clarification of both the concepts underlying tests in general—test theory— and concepts such as intelligence, personality, and interests. Since most clinical psychologists were involved with schools and children's agencies, virtually nothing was accomplished in producing an adult scale. The need for an infant scale was, however, urgent, particularly for use in adoption agencies and child care institutions. Some help in filling this need was provided in 1925 by Arnold Gesell's book *The Mental Growth of the Pre-School Child.*

Gesell (1880–1961) had prepared himself for his area of interest with admirable dedication. He was raised in Wisconsin, growing-up, he claimed, with a love of nature, orderliness, and serenity. In 1899, he graduated from Stevens Point Normal School. For the next two years he taught a variety of subjects in a high school, and even served as the football coach. Then he spent two years at the University of Wisconsin, worked for a year as a high school principal, and went to Clark University. In 1906, Gesell received his Ph.D. from Clark with a thesis under Hall on a genetic study of jealousy.

After receiving his doctorate, Gesell went to work with Terman at the Los Angeles State Normal School. Because he was interested in the study of child development he visited Witmer's clinic and Vineland. Gesell felt, however, that in order to pursue his interests properly, he needed a more complete understanding of human functioning and illness. Therefore he decided to obtain a medical education. In 1911, he became assistant professor of education at Yale, began the Yale Clinic of Child Development, and entered Yale University Medical School. Gesell received his M.D. in 1915, became a full professor at Yale, and also worked as a school psychologist for the State Board of Education of Connecticut, helping in the identification of retarded children and the formation of special classes and programs. We may recall, as he himself proudly did, that in 1918 he was a charter member of the American Association of Clinical Psychologists.

Gesell pioneered in the use of cinematography and cinemanalysis for the study of infant behavior. From 1924, with the help of grants, he began amassing a Photographic Research Library devoted to films of child development. On the basis of his observations, Gesell presented in his aforementioned book and in a subsequent publication *Infancy and Human Growth* (1929) 195 items which could be used to evaluate the progress of children between the ages of three and thirty months, with still other items chosen to be diagnostic up to an age of sixty months. These items were presented in the form of developmental schedules that described typical behaviors found at certain chronological ages. There were four broad categories of items: motor; adaptive, e.g., picking up objects, conjugate movement of eyes; language; and personal-social, e.g., ability to feed self, bowel and bladder control.

While psychologists were happy to have Gesell's developmental schedules, they recognized a number of weaknesses in them. Obviously, not all four categories were represented at each level. However, it did not seem likely that this weakness could have been overcome in view of the fact that children develop, rather than spring forth with demonstrable skills in every area. Criticisms were also directed at the large number of personal-social items, these being largely dependent on parental training; also at the items involving gross motor control, such as sitting and walking, which do not seem to be directly related to intellectual functioning; at the standardization sample; and at the lack of precise directions for administering and scoring the items. All in all, the Gesell developmental schedules were not perfect, but they were unique, and psychologists and parents busied themselves seeing whether children were doing what the schedules said they should be doing.

As a little sidelight, in 1927 Dorothy Hallowell published an article on her research in testing preschool children. Her standardization sample consisted of 657 urban boys and girls, ranging in age from one year to three years eleven months, of whom 15 percent were Negro and 85 percent were white. She used Wallin Peg Boards, formboards, color cubes, and digit memory span as tasks, and obtained promising results, though very little attention was given to her work.

During the twenties, then, there were all kinds of intelligence tests, more or less suitable for persons of every age. By the public and by members of other professions, the clinical psychologist was identified as primarily an intelligence tester or psychometrician. Usually he was caricatured as being of a rather stuffy scientific sort because he was always dressing up his reports with statistical terms—correlations, averages, standard deviations, and the like—that caused social workers and psychiatrists some uneasiness. His obsessions were with percise numerical results laced with qualifiers (usually necessary, we might add) and with the administration of tests according to exact procedures.

Not all clinicians fitted their prevailing stereotype and, of course, none was exactly flattered by it. Some of them, F. L. Wells for example, tried to stress that when they went about their job they did so with human feelings and a certain amount of judicious flexibility: "The function of psychometrics is not the accomplishment of a ritual, but the understanding of the patient. The ceremony of mental tests is valuable so far as it serves to reach this end. Ability to do this (modify testing procedures) intelligently is what distinguishes the psychologist, properly so called, from the 'mental tester.'" Nevertheless, clinical psychologists, psychometricians, or mental testers did not enjoy too much prestige, and being alert, intelligent, sensitive people, they were aware of this fact and naturally not very happy about it.

While there were other tests available, they were not used as frequently as the intellectual tests nor were they as closely associated with the function of the clinician. Interest and aptitude tests were primarily thought of in connection with the work of vocational guidance counselors and industrial psychologists, who were themselves quite a busy group.

In 1921, Stenquist published his Mechanical Aptitude Test; in 1922, Freyd introduced his Occupational Interest Blank; and in 1927, Strong came out with his Vocational Interest Blank. Seashore's tests of musical aptitude had become well known and were of sufficient worth to move George Eastman, benefactor of the Eastman School of Music, to say: "You (Seashore) have saved us vast sums of money and undoubtedly you have prevented much human suffering by the introduction of this procedure."

As a matter of fact there were enough aptitude tests around so that by

1928 C. L. Hull could write a book on aptitude testing. Hull is better known for his work in learning theory than for his excursion into testing, and he and his students will be encountered frequently in the chapters that follow.

Hull (1884–1952) grew up on a farm in Michigan and worked his way through Alma Academy. His plan was to become a mining engineer, but an attack of polio left him paralyzed in one leg and caused him to abandon that ambition. He spent two years convalescing and teaching in a junior high school. During that period he became interested in psychology. Hull went to the University of Michigan and then on to graduate work at the University of Wisconsin. He received his Ph.D. in 1918, remaining on the faculty at Wisconsin thereafter for the next ten years. His opinion of Joseph Jastrow was of a kindly, literate man, who could lecture beautifully and long, and yet say almost nothing of importance.

Hull wrote his book *Aptitude Testing* because he was supposed to teach a course on the subject and wanted to learn something about the field before his class began. In the process of writing about these tests, he became so discouraged about their future that after his book was published he would have nothing more to do with the area, and left it completely. His interests next became focused almost exclusively on hypnosis.

He and his students published a number of studies on hypnotic phenomena, and in 1929 Hull described his postural sway technique for evaluating the suggestibility of a subject (by measuring how far the person swayed after being given suggestions that he was losing his balance). While his research in this area was in progress, Hull was invited to join the faculty at Yale University. He arrived in 1929, almost immediately encountered strong opposition from the "medical authorities" to any experimentation by a psychologist involving hypnotic techniques, and was forced to abandon his research in this area. This setback in his career was only temporary and actually proved somewhat of a blessing for it ennabled Hull to devote himself to learning theory sooner than he had intended. We may also note that despite Hull's guardedly pessimistic prognosis the field of aptitude testing continued to develop and to find usefulness.

Psychologists were trying to construct measures of personality or character or temperament, in addition to interest and aptitude tests. The Allport brothers, Floyd and Gordon, suggested having the person's traits rated by associates and preparing a profile graph. They were willing to concede there were some flaws in rating scales. For example, Thorndike had recently demonstrated the existence of a "halo effect" in making ratings, i.e., a tendency to rate a person high or low on all scales rather than score each characteristic independently. Moreover, Hollingworth had cautioned that self-ratings are difficult to interpret because people tend to overestimate the socially desirable qualities they possess and to underestimate themselves on those qualities which are not socially desirable. Nevertheless, Gordon Allport thought rating scales would just have to be used because no other objective method for evaluating personality was in sight. Well, help of all kinds was on the way.

In 1921, Voelker pointed out that it might be valuable to observe a person's behavior on a specified battery of performance tests as a method for assessing his personality. This simple idea had been used in a group-administered test, the Pressy X-O, and in an individually-administered test, the Downey Will-Temperament Tests.

The Pressy X-O tests consisted of lists of words. The person was supposed to cross out certain words according to specified directions: those that he felt had unpleasant meanings; the word that he most closely associated with a given key word; the words that referred to things he worried about; the words which, in his opinion, stood for moral wrongs. This test first appeared in 1921, but it was soon put out in a new form because school teachers had objected to the sexual words it contained. In both forms the Pressy X-O Test was found to be low in reliability and low in validity. Even worse, no one knew what sense to make of its scores once they had been obtained.

The Downey Will-Temperament Tests made their appearance in 1919 and touched off a flurry of research. June Downey (1875–1932) was trying to measure impulsivity, forcefulness, decisiveness, persistence, attentiveness to details, and, of course, their opposites. She attempted to do all this by timing how long it took a child to write "United States of America" at his normal speed, then as fast as possible, then as different as possible from his usual handwriting, and finally as slowly as possible without ceasing to move the pencil. There were eight other tasks, most of them involving handwriting, their aim being to sample the child's reactions to the contradictions and frustrations imposed on him by the psychologist.

Studies indicated that the Downey had some validity in differentiating between groups of delinquents and nondelinquents, and between Indians and whites, but that it was of little value in understanding an individual. The intercorrelations among its tests, even those supposedly measuring the same thing were low, and the results of some thirty-five pieces of research uniformly agreed that the test was, at best, of questionable validity. Regretfully, it was concluded that the Downey Tests, "the most carefully standardized and most highly elaborated personality test which has yet been devised," was not suitable for widespread or routine use in the schools.

The free association method was still regarded as promising, although even thirty years after its introduction very little had been learned from its use or accomplished by it. Mateer had suggested that ten "individual" reactions to a list of one hundred words should be considered indicative of "psychopathy." But the large amount of overlapping between groups of normals and psychotic patients argued emphatically against the free association technique as a single instrument for diagnosing mental illness.

Woodworth's Psychoneurotic Inventory or Personal Data Sheet was the forerunner of a number of similar questionnaires. Ellen Mathews had 75 items for children twelve years old and up. There was the Woodworth-Cady revision of the Personal Data Sheet, with 85 instead of 116 questions. Laird's Personal Inventory had 75 items for college students, with a breakdown of the results into Schizoid, Neurasthenoid (hypochondriasis, fatigue), Hysteroid (convulsions, amnesia), and Psychasthenoid (obsessions, fears). Symond's Adjustment Questionnaire aimed to discover how well a person was getting along in school, at home, and with his peers. There was also the Woodworth-House Mental Hygiene Inventory, and Thurstone produced a Personality Schedule of 223 items, e.g., "Are your feelings easily hurt?"

In 1924, L. R. Marston introduced some tests for introversion-extraversion, which included a list of twenty items by which children as young as two years of age could be classified depending upon the answers given by their parents. However, enthusiasm for these tests waned as their findings showed that most people occupied some middle range, and rated themselves as somewhat extraverted, but more introverted than their friends rated them.

Although admittedly it was not very practical for individual diagnosis, Harthshorne and May's use of real-life situations for the study of cheating, lying, suggestibility, and persistence among school children aroused interest. What they did was place the children in situations where they could be dishonest without realizing that Harthshorne and May had devised a way of knowing just how dishonest they had been. They found that a child's honesty depended upon the social circumstances, just as did the honesty of the experimenters from psychology.

Some work was done on graphology, notably by Robert Saudek (1881–1935). Perhaps unfortunately, psychologists, especially those in the United States, were reluctant to investigate handwriting analysis seriously, probably because it was a technique that had been and would doubtless continue to be readily exploited by persons outside the profession.

Meanwhile Witmer was suggesting a very different approach to diagnosis. In 1924, Witmer, E. B. Twitmyer, and Henry E. Starr established a Psychobiochemical Laboratory and Clinic, associated with and under the control of the Psychological Clinic. At the same time the Department of Psychology at the University of Pennsylvania began offering a graduate course in "Metabolism and Behavior." Characteristically, Witmer invented a new term to cover the new aspect of clinical psychology he had in mind: psychobiochemistry—the science of relations between metabolism and behavior.

Feeling very enthusiastic about this latest direction in his work, Witmer, in a talk before the Section on Clinical Psychology of the APA, stated: ". . . would you dedicate yourselves to original research in the field of science most likely to be distinguished above all others for discoveries of importance during the latter half of this century, make ready, then, in the laboratory of physiological chemistry for work in clinical psychology and diagnostic orthogenics."

Some psychologists had been making ready. They were trying to get a measure of emotions, and perhaps a method which would differentiate between groups of psychiatric patients, by determining the acidity and alkalinity of saliva and the creatine concentration of urine. Some were using pneumographs (to measure respiration rate), sphygmographs (to measure pulse rate), sphygmomanometers (to measure blood pressure), plethysmographs (to measure blood volume changes in a part of the body), and galvanometers (to measure the electrical resistance of some area of the body). A lot of research was conducted with galvonometers in studies of the psychogalvanic reflex, i.e., a drop in the electrical resistance of the skin supposedly due to emotional activity.

Such studies had a kind of theoretical foundation in the James-Lange theory of emotions: to the effect that the individual's experiencing of an emotion is actually his experiencing of the organic and physiological changes which follow his perception of some event. The James-Lange formulation was very popular among psychologists despite some inadequacies discovered in it. For one thing, around 1900, Sherrington had found in experiments with dogs that when the viscera were separated from the central nervous system by cutting the motor nerves leading to them, the animals still exhibited "emotional" behavior. For another, it had been found that the same visceral changes occurred in different emotional states. A third difficulty was that visceral changes took place too slowly to correspond to the speed of changes in experienced emotions. A fourth difficulty was that when visceral changes were artificially produced, emotions were not experienced.

In 1929, W. B. Cannon proposed a theory of emotions which he hoped would take all the difficulties into account. He suggested that emotions were mental processes connected with activity in the thalamus that adds a feeling tone to sensations. Regardless of whether or not Cannon was correct, the evidence made it clear that physiological changes alone are not a direct index of emotions.

A further note of caution was provided by Landis, who admonished psychologists to bear in mind several pertinent variables in evaluating their research on the psychogalvanic reflex. Not only emotions but changes in temperature, the pH of blood, and any variable that influences sweat secretion can affect the reflex. After reviewing the literature, Landis concluded that the psychogalvanic reflex had no more significance for indicating emotions than changes in blood pressure, the pupillary reflex or the knee jerk.

Thus by the close of the twenties psychologists were finding that the measurement of physiological variables was not the simple, uncomplicated, valid indicator of a person's emotions that they had hoped it would be.

Unknown to almost all psychologists in the United States and to most psychologists elsewhere, a Swiss psychiatrist Hermann Rorschach had been approaching the diagnosis of personality by using ink blots. As early as 1857, ink blots had been employed for scientific studies of imagination. Among these earlier, pre-Rorschach investigators were Kerner, Binet and Henri, Dearborn, Sharp, Kirkpatrick, Whipple, Pyle, Rybakof, Bartlett, and Parsons. Not one of these investigators entered into this area of research with the complexity and breadth of conceptualization dared by Rorschach, nor were they prepared to see, as Rorschach did, that this method might reveal the intellectual and emotional functioning of a person.

Hermann Rorschach (1884–1922) was born in Zurich, the son of an art teacher in the public schools. He was one of the oldest of three children. His mother died when he was twelve and his father died when he was eighteen. During his school years he was an excellent, but not memorable, student, and was nicknamed *Klex,* which means "ink blot" or "painter," probably indicating that his classmates' predicted that he would follow in his father's profession.

Although Rorschach did consider becoming an artist, he decided in favor of medicine. In keeping with the Swiss custom of studying at various universities, he attended, from 1904 to 1909, Neuchâtel, Zurich, Berlin, and Bern. While in Zurich he had been, of course, exposed to the ideas of Bleuler, Jung, and Freud.

From 1909 to 1913, Rorschach worked as a resident in psychiatry at an asylum in Münsterlingen; he had received his M.D. in 1912 from the University of Zurich with a dissertation under Bleuler, "On Reflex-hallucinations and Kindred Manifestations." During this same period he carried out some studies with ink blots but published none of them and abandoned this area of interest to concentrate on psychoanalysis.

In 1913, he went to work in Russia, his wife's native country, but returned to Switzerland after several months to take a position at a mental hospital in Waldau. In 1915, he became associate director of the asylum in Herisau, and in 1917 and 1919, he became the father of first a daughter and then a son. His interests were still focused on psychoanalysis until in 1917 he came across the dissertation of a Polish student Szymon Hens, who had studied medicine in Zurich.

Hens had devised an ink blot test of eight cards which he administered to 1000 children, 100 normal adults, and 100 psychotics. His intention had been to study fantasy, and, in keeping with what had been done previously, he restricted his analysis to the content of the responses. Again, as was customary, Hens concluded his dissertation with an exhortation that further research in this area was needed and went on to raise several questions: What does it mean when some people use all the blot for their interpretations while others use only parts? Would colored blots give different results from those obtained with black and white blots? Could this method be used to diagnose psychosis?

After reading Hens' dissertation Rorschach plunged with all the energy at his command into the creation of an inkblot test and the development of its rationale.

He came across the writings of a Norwegian philosopher J. Mourly Vold (1850–1907) and from him borrowed two ideas: kinesthetic imagery is stimulated by restrictions of muscular activity and is inhibited by the movements of muscles; kinesthetic perceptions form the most important part of the material of dreams. Rorschach used Mourly Vold's ideas to assert that the inhibition of impulses tends to stimulate the production of fantasy, the content of which is determined by dynamic variables such as complexes and repressions.

Rorschach applied the term "introversives" to those persons who tend to inhibit their movements or impulses and who turn inward upon themselves for understanding and creativeness. Such persons are expected to perceive movement (M) in inkblots. They are characterized by a more individualized and imaginative intelligence, stable emotional responsiveness, more inner life with less adaptability to their external world, more intensive than extensive rapport, and controlled but awkward and clumsy motility.

Rorschach applied the term "extratensives" to those persons who tend to express their movements or impulses and who thus interact with the environment and direct themselves outward. Such persons are expected to use color (C) in their perceptions because they tend to express emotions and many people associate colors with feelings. They are characterized by a stereotyped or imitative and conforming intelligence, labile emotional reactions, more outward life with greater adaptability to their external world, more extensive than intensive rapport, and a restless but skilled and adroit motility.

Rorschach's conceptualization owes much to Jung's introvert-extravert typology. However, Rorschach's formulation differs from Jung's in that introversives and extratensives are not thought to represent constitutional types but two modes of psychological functioning which are not mutually exclusive. People are more or less introversive and extratensive, and both functions are considered necessary for optimal development and performance. Therefore, in each person both modes of functioning coexist in some proportion and to some extent, ranging from individual cases where both are highly developed, the "dilatated" person, to cases where both are minimally in evidence, the "coartated" person, with all transitions between these extremes possible in both dimensions. An index of the individual's introversive-extratensive balance can be found, Rorschach believed, by the relationship between the number of movement to color responses elicited by a standard set of inkblots. He called this balance the *Erlebnistypus.*

Although he did not treat it very elaborately, Rorschach also attributed importance to Jung's distinction between internal or semantic associations and external or verbal associations. Semantic associations are inferred from delays in responding. It is supposed that the person is producing associations but is not expressing them; this is thought characteristic of introverts. External associations are immediate verbalizations and are regarded as characteristic of extraverts. In his Association Test procedure, Jung noted semantic associations on the left side of the page and external associations on the right. A similar framework was followed by Rorschach in recording material elicited by ink blots.

In 1918, Rorschach began experimenting with fifteen ink blots, using his patients as subjects. At the same time he worked feverishly on the preparation of his book, the *Psychodiagnostik,* so rapidly in fact as to impair the clarity of the text. He sent the fifteen ink blots and the manuscript to seven publishers; all rejected it. Finally, in 1920 it was accepted by a publisher, but only on condition that ten cards rather than fifteen would be published.

The book appeared in 1921, though with several unsolicited contributions made by the printer. The cards had been reduced in size and their colors had been altered. Furthermore, though Rorschach's original cards had uniformly black areas, the printer in reproducing them introduced a variety of shadings so that forms could be perceived within them. Far from being upset, Rorschach was delighted with the possibilities which the shadings of the blots might afford.

Rorschach discussed his test before the Swiss Psychiatric Society and the Swiss Psychoanalytic Society but aroused little interest in his work. His book was a complete failure and most of its copies remained undisturbed in the basement of the publishing house. Some of his colleagues were impressed by Rorschach's "blind diagnoses," i.e., his diagnosis of a patient solely on the basis of responses to the blots, but they were not sufficiently enthused to care to learn how he did it.

Emil Oberholzer, who had worked with Rorschach, taught the test to an American psychiatrist studying in Switzerland, David Levy. In 1921, Levy returned to the United States bringing a set of the blots with him. That same year the test was described to the German Society of Experimental Psychology as of possible use in vocational counseling. Immediately William Stern denounced it as faulty, arbitrary, artificial, and incapable, as was any test, of understanding the human personality. That seemed to finish it, and on April 2, 1922, Hermann Rorschach died.

The year after Rorschach's death Ludwig Binswanger commented somewhat critically but also favorably on the *Psychodiagnostik*. However, perhaps because Rorschach lacked the prestige associated with a university affiliation, his test was not taken seriously. In 1927 David Levy was working as chief of staff at the Institute for Child Guidance in New York City. While there he taught the test to a psychology trainee, Samuel J. Beck, who decided to use it as the subject of his dissertation. At about the same time Manfred Bleuler, a psychiatrist, introduced the technique at the Boston Psychopathic Hospital. Seven years after Rorschach's death his ink blots were being used occasionally in a few psychiatric installations, while a number of psychologists were agonizing about their difficulties in devising a test for the evaluation of personality functioning. Fortunately, unlike Evangeline and Gabriel, there was soon to be a meeting.

DIAGNOSTIC FORMULATIONS

More or less polite controversy about the concept of intelligence continued among psychologists. At issue were its definition, its structure, and the question of its origin, whether due primarily to inheritance or environment. Aside from disagreements on these points, all agreed that intelligence was clearly understood.

To the growing number of definitions of intelligence were added Terman's, the ability to carry on abstract thinking, and Edwards', the capacity for versatility or variability of response. T. L. Kelley believed there were three independent kinds or traits of intelligence: verbal; quantitative, as evidenced in mathematics; and spatial, as evidenced in performances on such things as form boards. In view of their independence, Kelley argued against the practice of adding up the scores of all the items on a scale to come up with one final score, as in an intelligence quotient. Thorndike also believed that there were three kinds of intelligence, but his were abstract, social, and mechanical or motor. Respectively, they were evidenced by the person's ability to deal with symbols, people, and objects. It seemed to him that psychologists had been mostly interested in abstract intelligence and were still neglecting the other two.

Spearman, of course, still held to his view of a general factor of intelligence, *g*. Thorndike claimed his results agreed with Thomson's in pointing to several factors in intelligence. Cyril Burt agreed with Karl Pearson that there were special factors and also agreed with Spearman that there was a general factor. In the meantime, Spearman was wondering whether he really disagreed with any of these colleagues or whether he was just acting out of "a streak of perversity and negativism." He concluded that he was sincere, and decided to issue "a friendly challenge" to Thorndike to get together with him in designing a crucial study that would show Spearman was right. As far as is known, Thorndike made no published or publishable reply.

By 1927, Spearman had no less than four general factors in intelligence: *g*, the ability to educe relations and correlates; *c*, the degree of "inertia" in shifting from one task to another; *w*, the degree of determination or persistence evidenced in pursuing a task; and oscillation, the ease with which a person recuperates after expending effort. It also seemed clear to him, as well as to Thorndike, and to all other interested parties that when there are a number of correlated variables, these variables can always be factored into either a general factor and specific factors or into a number of independent factors. The two systems of Spearman and Thorndike, then, are really interchangeable, and whether evidence was found to support the position of one or the other depended upon the method of factor analysis employed. Naturally, Spearman was delighted by this clarification since he believed that it meant that everyone had come around to his point of view.

Thorndike seemed to have grown weary of the whole dispute: "The great merit of the Binet Test is that it is a graded scale for intellectual difficulty, and it is only weakened by being interpreted loosely as a measure of some mysterious essence called intelligence which grows in man." His weariness was shared by Wallin, who contended that clinical psychologists did not care about definitions of intelligence or whether Spearman or Thorndike was right. However, if someone did want a definition of intelligence, Wallin thought of it as a complex of cognitive activities that are interrelated and interdependent because of a similarity of processes and the integrative activity of the neural mechanism, and that these activities are initiated, modified, and directed by nonintellective factors of an affective and conative nature, and that they are manifested in their highest operations as successful adjustments to novel situations and to solutions of difficult problems. Who could say what a clinical psychologist might have contributed if one of them had become interested in the problem?

Having vented his dissatisfactions, Wallin forcefully concluded: "There is no more important lesson for the practitioner to learn than that existing psychological and psychiatric measures . . . are far from perfect, that they are affected by the personality characteristics of the examiner and by the influences of the physical and social environment as well as by native endowment . . . and that improvement in scientific testing techniques and ability analysis waits upon the solution of fundamental theoretical questions in psychology."

Wallin's somewhat oblique attempt at clarifying issues did not receive the notice accorded the frontal assaults launched by Thurstone.

L. L. Thurstone (1887–1955) had been at first mainly interested in mathematics, and had obtained his undergraduate degree in electrical and mechanical engineering from Cornell. For two years, 1912 to 1914, he taught engineering at the University of Minnesota and while there became increasingly interested in psychology. In 1914, he began his graduate work at the University of Chicago, and the following year accepted a faculty position at Carnegie Institute of Technology under Bingham. He received his Ph.D. from Chicago in 1917. Seven years later Thurstone married and returned to the University of Chicago to teach statistics and the theory of mental tests.

In 1926, Thurstone attacked and mildly damaged the concept of mental age by demonstrating its illogicality when applied to adults. At the root of the difficulty was the fact that scores on a particular test did not continue to increase with increasing age. Therefore, if mental age were defined as that chronological age for which a certain test performance is average, there would be several mental ages for the same score. On the other hand, if mental age were defined as the average chronological age of people who made a certain test score, the mental ages for older children would be grossly inflated. This problem could be easily resolved, Thurstone suggested, by using percentile standings of the individual with reference to his age group as the test score. Thurstone's suggestion had merit, but other psychologists believed teachers understood mental ages and would be confused by percentiles, and so they did little to implement his idea.

A fundamental question raised and partially answered during this period was whether or not the intelligence quotient remained constant for a specific individual from year to year. This was a different problem than the statistical constancy of the IQ, i.e., arranging the test items so that the average MA equaled the average CA which would then equal an IQ of 100. It would be possible to have statistical consistancy though not individual constancy if, for example, dull children grew duller and bright children grew brighter.

William Stern, in 1925, was pleased to report that a number of studies had indicated his IQ was a relatively stable index. To be sure, he conceded, variations of five IQ points on retesting were common, but differences much greater than that were seldom found. Knowing this, any large discrepancy between one test performance and another would merit exploration.

Stern was less happy with his colleague Bobertag's revision of the Binet but was delighted with the job Terman had done. However, he went on to caution his American friends against believing that the IQ represented the total mental status of the person. An IQ, he believed, represents only the individual's level of mental alertness and not his personality. Therefore, an IQ makes possible negative predictions of high probability (predicting what the person cannot do) but is less significant in making positive predictions (predicting what the person will do). Stern suggested that the reason for lower positive predictability is that in such predictions personality traits, e.g., creativity, persistence, etc., are involved.

Three years before, in 1922, another psychologist had said, "No one has ever devised an intelligence test that tests intelligence and nothing else." That psychologist was Witmer. Three years later he wrote: "The unit of observation is a performance, but the unit of consideration is personality, defined by the perfectability of behavior, which is measured or estimated in the units of progress which men make toward the perfection they prefer."

Witmer's years of research in clinical psychology had led him to a discovery: man is constantly striving toward the perfection of all his behavior. He was convinced this significant discovery had been made possible only because he had studied man to understand man and had not tried to understand man through the study of other animals, as some of his misguided colleagues (no names mentioned) seemed to be doing. Moreover, he urged psychologists to focus on those characteristics of man which distinguish him from other animals—his ethics, his moral codes, his cultures, his pursuit of what seems good and perfect—rather than concentrating on those resemblances between him and other organisms. But Witmer was plainly tired of urging and bitterly disappointed by his lack of recognition: "I have received from my professional contemporaries that most sincere tribute—imitation, often enough without acknowledgment."

The impression that intelligence and personality are not distinct functions was shared by persons other than Witmer. For one example, three of the four general factors in intelligence described by Spearman could be considered personality characteristics, and, for another example, there were the thoughts of Guy G. Fernald. In 1920, Fernald, a physician, argued that intelligence and character are blended. Not only that, he considered it reasonable to think that culture can affect intellectual functioning by emphasizing and minimizing the development of certain skills. Personality, as Fernald conceived it, is inclusive of intelligence. Therefore, tests and studies of intelligence will furnish information about personality, but tests and studies of personality will not necessarily furnish information about intelligence since they might not sample that area.

Now thus far in this section we have discussed some of the ideas current in the twenties about intelligence. Next we shall direct our attention to some of the major research findings of this decade.

Mental tests were increasingly being used not only as instruments of diagnosis, but as tools for conducting experimental research. Terman, in his presidential address before the APA in 1924, emphasized the valuable contributions that were being made and that could be made in the future to the science of psychology by the use of mental tests. In particular, they were thought useful in solving problems such as the measurement of individual and race differences; the structure and interrelation of mental traits; the evaluation of intellectual growth; the limits of educability; and the understanding of genius, mental deficiency, and insanity. Let us see how much.

Catherine Cox assembled all the information that she could obtain about the childhood of three hundred persons of outstanding accomplishment. On the basis of these biographical sketches, four psychologists who were expert in the field of child psychology and intelligence testing estimated what the IQ's of these men would have been had they been tested in childhood. Although their estimates for some of these acknowledged geniuses varied considerably, the IQ's were almost without exception very high. This study demonstrated that adults of high accomplishment had been highly accomplished children. Its conclusion was that, in general, geniuses come from the ranks of gifted boys and girls.

The accolade of genius was bestowed liberally at this time by Terman and his colleagues on anyone with an IQ of 140 or more earned on the Stanford Revision of the Binet. Terman had in mind an ambitious, unprecedented, longitudinal study of "genius in the making." As the first phase of this study, approximately one thousand school children in California with IQs above 140 were identified and evaluated. These evaluations were to be repeated over the years, but even the first results were exciting. In contrast to the stereotype of the highly intelligent child being weak, thin, short, sickly, and bespectacled, Terman found him to be taller, healthier, heavier, and better adjusted socially than the average of his peers. He planned, so far as possible, to chronicle in subsequent studies the achievements and adjustments of these gifted children as they progressed into adulthood.

Incidentally, by the middle of the twenties, Terman, in referring to highly intelligent children, was using the term "gifted" more and the term "genius" less. "Gifted" had been suggested by Leta Hollingworth, who was following the recommendation of Whipple, that "gifted" instead of "genius" be used in referring to unusually bright children, since a genius properly is a person who has made an outstanding contribution to the enrichment of the culture. "It is only when a man's life is recognized by others as having significance for them that we call him a genius." (Alfred Adler)

A possible fly in the Terman group's ointment was pointed out by Witty and Lehman. These devil's advocates called attention to previously obtained evidence that not all gifted children become gifted adults. One plausible and even probable reason for this lack of adult achievement is a lack of drive. Possibly this lack of drive might be interpreted in terms of not experiencing a need to compensate for feelings of inadequacy. Now if Terman's children were as well adjusted as he claimed, they wondered if it would not be likely to find that these children would progress through adulthood without becoming geniuses or making any outstanding record of accomplishment. Of course only in time would it be possible to provide an answer to the question they raised, but to anticipate a little, their fears for the worst were not realized.

Another topic of considerable interest in this area is the issue of the extent to which human behavior is innate *versus* the extent to which it is acquired. In the controversy about intelligence, this question of nature *versus* nurture, or heredity *versus* environment has been particularly vexing. At one extreme were those who held that intellectual ability is almost entirely inherited; therefore certain races and ethnic groups cannot be expected to achieve the highest cultural levels because of their inherent limitations. At the other extreme were those who believed that intellectual ability is almost completely acquired, and therefore, healthy children of different races raised under identical environmental conditions could be expected to function identically in school.

Most psychologists were less extreme than either of these positions and simply emphasized one of the major variables over the other. For example, Goddard, Gesell, and Terman stressed the significance of heredity over environment, while Thorndike and Witmer stressed the significance of environment over heredity. One of the great changes of the twenties was that within the span of a few years a large number of psychologists shifted from a nature to a nurture emphasis and denied racial and ethnic inherent inequalities.

As late as 1925, T. R. Garth could survey the literature on racial psychology and note: "the thing most predominant is a characteristic state of mind . . . and that is a belief in racial differences in mental traits." On the basis of his review, Garth concluded that the white race is probably superior to all others. And most psychologists interested in the problem probably would have agreed with him. Almost every study pointed in the direction of inherited racial differences probably because everyone had it in mind that because intelligence tests are supposed to measure inherited intelligence, that is what they do measure. Accordingly, Brigham concluded, after finding the scores of foreign-born recruits were lower on the Army Alpha among those who had more recently arrived in the United States, that more recent immigrants were less intelligent than the earlier ones.

The nature camp of intelligence was shaken by several lines of converging evidence. From the land of animal studies Carmichael reported the sexual behavior of castrates and the inept pecking of chicks which had been deprived temporarily of visual stimulation indicated: "the development of the behavior mechanism is not alone dependent upon heredity or environment, but that it is the result of the *interdependent* action of both of these factors."

Moreover, Thorndike warned that in determining whether one race was superior to another it was more important to consider the ranges of intellectual functioning than the averages. He pointed out that in certain studies comparing Negroes with whites, the upper limits of the Negro scores exceeded the white average score. With such results and in view of the environmental handicaps confronting Negroes, he found it difficult to assert the superiority of one race over the other.

Within the next few years Brigham rescinded his earlier conclusion about immigrants. If his colleagues were to avoid similar errors in the future, he warned, when they are comparing groups on intelligence tests, they should exercise care to insure that the individuals in both groups have had equal educational opportunities.

In a later review of racial studies (1930), Garth concluded: "It would appear that it (the hypothesis of intellectual differences between races) is no nearer being established than it was five years ago. In fact many psychologists seem practically ready for another, the hypothesis of racial equality." Therefore within a period of five years there was an almost complete reversal in the interpretation of the results of racial studies, the outcome of which was that the influence of environment, rather than heredity, was stressed.

The last finding to be noted involving intelligence tests was provided by Mary Wentworth. She had administered the Stanford Revision to two hundred patients diagnosed as dementia praecox. Impressed by the successes of some patients on adult items and their failures on less difficult questions, Wentworth suggested the psychosis should be regarded as a volitional and affective disorder rather than one in which an intellectual defect is primary.

Wentworth's suggestion is significant in that it serves to illustrate again a tendency of this period toward the use of emotional and interpersonal variables as explanations for illnesses previously thought to be organic or inherited disorders. Cyril Burt, after studying comparable groups of delinquents and nondelinquents, concluded that heredity is of trifling importance in the genesis of criminal behavior: "It is clear that the commonest and the most disastrous conditions are those that center about the family life." Davies thought the symptoms of withdrawal and oversensitivity in dementia praecox could be attributed to the patient's wounded self-feeling. Therefore, what the patient needs are experiences to reinstate positive self-feelings, assistance in maintaining contact with the environment, and exposure to new situations which could arouse the emotions and be integrated (both in the sense of having feelings that are appropriate to the situation and in the sense that the experience is retained and recalled).

Thus we can see that the nature-nurture controversy in respect to intelligence was paralleled by organic versus nonorganic etiologies offered in explanation of abnormalities of behavior. In this area as well, hereditary and constitutional factors were relegated to roles of minor significance in comparison with the importance assigned to interpersonal and environmental variables. Here too behaviorism made a contribution.

After the war Watson reported a study he and Rosalie Raynor had conducted at Johns Hopkins. They took Albert, the eleven-months-old son of one of the wet nurses in the Harriet Lane Hospital, and conditioned him to fear a white rat by pairing the presentation of the rodent with a loud noise. Not only did Albert become conditioned to fear the rat but the fear response generalized to rabbits, dogs, and other furry objects. Obviously, Watson had demonstrated that some fears could be acquired and illustrated a procedure by which fear responses could be produced. Unfortunately for Albert, he was adopted and moved out of Baltimore before it was possible to complete the extinguishing of his conditioned fear reaction.

The effects of learning and of adverse relationships within the family had also begun to occupy the attention of Adler. While he still thought it possible that some feelings of inferiority are caused by being born with inferior organs, he was now stressing their development in unfavorable home environments. A child who is pampered or rejected, whose parents emphasize his weakness and dependency and make unreasonable demands upon him, is likely to suffer from feelings of inadequacy regardless of the health of his body. By decompensating, i.e., developing neurotic symptoms, the child attempts to enlist the sympathy of his parents, to impose an authority of his own over them, and to insure that this pitiable exploitative relationship is perpetuated.

The effects of interpersonal variables upon hypnosis were also becoming prominent, and study of them was radically changing the concept of hypnosis as simply a special condition of the person. The four major symptoms of the hypnotic trance were thought to be: (1) loss of initiative; (2) loss of memory; (3) increased suggestibility; and (4) rapport, or a state of dependence between the subject and operator. After reviewing the literature, Young dismissed the view that the subject is a helpless automaton controlled by a strong-willed operator: "It is nearer the truth to regard the operator as allowing himself to play a part, and by no means an indispensible one, in a drama constructed and acted in the depths of the subject's mind." According to Young's formulation of the hypnotic process, the subject unconsciously hypnotizes himself, but in order that this may take place it is essential that he believe in the power of the operator and be willing to cooperate with him in the unconscious act of submission involved in hypnosis.

Similarly, Gordon Allport thought that interpersonal factors are of major significance in explaining the process whereby one person obtains a clear understanding or grasp of the personality of another. He suggested that this is accomplished by a process called empathy, a term introduced by T. Lipps in 1907. Although empathy was not precisely defined, its meaning was made clear. Allport regarded it as a sympathetic apprehension or comprehension of the feelings and beliefs of another person, and taking empathy in this sense Allport believed people are limited in their capacity to employ it: "the extent of our understanding of another is rigidly determined by our own attitudes and habits. . . . A thoroughly intimate appreciation of personality is a difficult accomplishment. Few people have such an appreciation for even one personality, and no one has it for an unlimited number."

Human understanding, hypnosis, psychological disturbances, and intellectual functioning were not the only areas enlightened by the use of interpersonal, emotional, environmental, often unconsciously operative variables. They were frequently applied in generating dramatic but credible explanations for behaviors previously dismissed as unimportant. For example, Lehman and Witty found that Negro children who were educationally retarded in comparison to whites played school much more than did the white children; they interpreted this finding to mean that the Negro children used their play of school to compensate for their lack of achievement and intellectual prestige in reality. The point to be noted is that these concepts were no longer confined to the adherents of a particular theory but were being expressed by psychologists of varying persuasions, or of no persuasion in particular, and thus were being assimilated to psychology.

Meanwhile, a prime mover in fostering knowledge of these influences on behavior, Freud, continued the task of extending psychoanalytic concepts in the understanding of pathology. He viewed psychoneuroses as conflicts between ego and id, depressions and melancholias as conflicts between ego and super-ego, psychoses as conflicts between ego and the outer world or reality. To speak more specifically of the neuroses, he saw repression as the central defense mechanism in hysteria, while reaction formation (displaying in behavior the opposite of a strong unconscious impulse), isolation (an impulse or wish is recognized, although it is not understood in what way it might relate to one's own behavior; put differently, thoughts and feelings that might be reasonably connected or associated are not), and undoing (an activity is carried out in the magical hope that it will cancel out a previous action about which the person feels some guilt) were the characteristic defenses of obsessive-compulsive disorders.

Freud still acknowledged the importance of constitutional variables in the etiology of these disturbances, but discussed them so little that the tendency of psychoanalysts was to pay them only lip service. Instead, analysts riveted the attention of psychologists on unconscious conflict, defenses, and early childhood determinants of adult behavior. This was done so successfully and became so pervasive that anyone who indicated the significance of current conflicts did so with the conviction that he was making a novel contribution to science. To illustrate, in 1923 Rivers pointed out the importance of problems in the present: "recent conflicts are far more influential in the production of both dreams and psychoneuroses than is now usually supposed."

It should be stressed that these widespread shifts in emphasis were not initiated by any conclusive research or positive results from experimentation that would fully justify them. In other words, there was no evidence that demonstrated environment was more significant than heredity in intelligence or psychopathology. Rather a basic change had occurred in the interpretation of findings and observations. To a large extent this change was brought about by a greater understanding of research methodology and diagnostic techniques and by a wish to examine new, more hopeful alternatives than those of the past. For, viewed practically, the focus on acquired, environmental explanations had the effect of infusing the field with fecundity and optimism, since genetic factors were considered virtually immutable.

Arrayed against these formulations were those that emphasized constitutional differences between persons. Here we find the typologies, and even here we shall find an exception . . . a typology that is acquired. However, let us first consider those systems which held to the rule.

The most popular typology was Jung's extravert-introvert. We recall that this pair of terms represented essentially innate differences in attitudes: the extravert turning toward his external environment; the introvert turning inward upon himself. While psychologists were busy investigating this dichotomy, Jung was studying the Pueblo Indians and the natives of Africa and India to see if there were similarities between the contents of the unconscious in Western man and primitive myths, cults, and rituals. Basically, he was searching for universal symbols and archetypes.

Jung saw his two major types of persons as capable of relating to their world by four major functions which were antagonistically paired. As we list them the first of each alternative indicates the form of the function if extraverted; the second alternative indicates the form of the function if introverted: thinking or understanding *versus* feeling or valuing; external or internal perception *versus* intuitive prediction (sensing what an object or person will be or has been) or unconsciously perceiving. Accordingly, Jung envisioned an extravert *or* introvert relating to his environment by thinking *or* feeling, by perception *or* intuition. Furthermore, those personality characteristics and functions which are not overt are considered suppressed. Within the unconscious they supposedly continue to strive for expression and, being denied accessibility to awareness, they are compensated for by the formation of symbols. At any rate, psychologists focused their attention upon extraverts and introverts, and when they found it well-nigh impossible to isolate pure types of either, they lost much of their enthusiasm for Jung's dichotomy and its elaboration.

Another major typology, based on body build, was first proposed by the psychiatrist Ernst Kretschmer (1888–1964) in 1921. First, the tall and thin *asthenic,* with a schizophrenic temperament. Second, the muscular *athletic,* a variant of the asthenic, and also, though to a lesser degree, prone to exhibit schizophrenic characteristics. Third, the pudgy *pyknic,* with large body cavities, who tends to be cyclothymic. Fourth and finally, there is the *dysplastic* type evidencing deviant physical features due in the main to endocrine disturbances. The schizophrenic temperament is quiet, reserved, and unsociable; the cyclothymic, moody, emotional, genial, and cheerful. Kretschmer reported relationships between the asthenic type and schizophrenia and between the pyknic type and manic-depressive psychosis.

Psychologists, however, noted that in Kretschmer's sample the schizophrenics were younger than the manic-depressive patients and thus less apt to have suffered the "middle-aged spread" associated with chronological maturity. Also, psychologists were less fortunate than Kretschmer in being able to locate pure types, and so might be forgiven for not sharing in his excitement.

A similar fate awaited the typology of S. Naccarati and H. E. Garrett. They described microsplanchnics, who are long and thin with small trunks in comparison to their limbs and who expend their energies. At the other end of their continuum were the macrosplanchnics, who are stout or fat with large trunks in comparison to their limbs and who conserve their energies. Midway along the continuum were normo-splanchnics. Naccarati and Garrett derived, by complex maneuvers, a Morphologic Index as their measure. But neither they nor other investigators found too much relationship between the Index and scores on Woodworth Personal Data Sheets, Pressy X-O tests, or anything else.

L. Berman offered a typology based on the glands: thyroid, pituitary, and gonadocentric personalities. At about the same time, A. Rosanoff (1878–1943), a psychiatrist, presented a system based on psychiatric disorders. Rosanoff defined personality as inborn capacities, traits, and tendencies. He thought certain abnormal constitutions were hereditarily transmitted as Mendelian recessives and these provided the foundation for specific mental illnesses. He saw the antisocial personality as the constitutional basis for hysteria and criminality; the cyclothymic personality for manic-depressive psychosis; the autistic personality for schizophrenia; the epileptic personality for epilepsy (This is a personality characterized by fussiness, irritability, fault-finding, and brief periods of elation and ecstasy). From the beginning, Rosanoff stated that there is no sharp demarcation between the "normal" personality type and its pathological manifestation, and furthermore that in normality mixed types are the rule. Still the similarities between the descriptions of cyclothymic personality and extraversion and between autistic personality and introversion caused many psychologists to believe the results of studies of Rosanoff's typology would yield familiar fruit. Nevertheless, some psychologists became interested in his concept of an epileptic personality and undertook considerable research on the topic.

As we pause to survey the scene, what is most worthy of attention is the growing awareness of psychologists of the complexity of their subject matter. In every area, problems and concepts turned out to be no longer simple, even on the surface. And where new formulations or techniques might have been accepted uncritically, they were now met by an attitude of skepticism. A ceaseless questioning was in progress in which ideas were challenged and then the challengers were challenged. But in these disputes the weapons were more and more not polemics but facts, the results of adequately controlled experiments and penetrating analyses.

The last typology we shall consider is explicitly without a constitutional reference, and therefore something of an exception: types of men based on their acquired value systems. This typology was introduced by Eduard Spranger (b. 1882) around 1928. Spranger believed that behavior can be understood or experienced as meaningful only in relation to what he called value systems, which provide unity and consistency in an individual's life. He described six ideal types or value orientations, and made no value judgments about whether one type is to be regarded as any better than another. Spranger recognized also that ordinarily a person will express a preference for two or more different value systems. Briefly, in ideal or pure form Spranger's types were: the aesthetic type, valuing beauty, form, and harmony; the economic type, valuing practicality and usefulness; the political type, valuing power and leadership; the religious type, valuing mysticism and the experiencing of oneness with God and the universe; the social type, valuing the love and approval of others; and the theoretical type, valuing truth and the ordering of knowledge. Gordon Allport, for one, was favorably impressed by this formulation.

Let us now turn to the work of Shepherd Ivory Franz, which was creating a feeling of hope about a field that had been regarded as unpromising for psychologists. In his presidential address before the APA in 1921, Franz reported that organic problems can be circumvented and, to some extent, remedied. His studies and those of others had indicated a general dependence of mental states upon states of the brain, but not, as had been believed, a specific dependence of particular functions upon the integrity of definite cerebral areas. He reiterated his findings that although cerebral damage may temporarily affect psychological functioning, the disturbance need not be permanent. Franz therefore urged his colleagues to participate more in the diagnosis of central nervous system pathology: "Some neurologists have waked up to an appreciation of the necessity for finer examinations and for greater analyses along psychological lines, and it is to be hoped that psychologists will not hold themselves aloof from this field." However, Franz's enthusiasm was based less on his diagnostic successes than on the encouraging experiences he had in treating these patients. It is to his thoughts about treatment that we shall now direct our attention.

TREATMENT FORMULATIONS

Franz demonstrated that retraining and re-education are useful procedures in helping patients to regain habits and functions lost through brain damage. Thus in large part through his efforts rehabilitation came to be seen as a feasible goal. He also believed these procedures valuable as occupational therapy with motivated psychotics in inculcating social skills and activities. But regardless of whether they are brain-damaged or psychotic patients, Franz considered the patient's motivation and his relationship with his therapist as supremely important. It is essential, he insisted, that the patient recognize his abnormality, evidence a desire to get well, and possess confidence in himself and his therapist. The techniques alone cannot provide success.

It should be emphasized that Franz and the vast majority of psychologists thought of their approach to helping persons as a form of education. (In 1924, Franz left Washington to assume the positions of Lecturer at the University of California and Chief of the Psychological and *Educational* Clinic of the Children's Hospital in Hollywood.) They did not think of themselves as being involved in treatment, a function which, as Seashore put it, was entrusted only to "duly qualified psychiatrists." Clinical psychologists, for the most part, thought of themselves as more or less working with principles of learning to ameliorate undesirable habit patterns. They attempted to correct reading and speech defects, and at first saw these problems arising from organic causes or from some flaw in the educational process. Thus Twitmyer in discussing the etiology of speech disorders mentioned deafness, amentia, brain injury, anatomical or functional anomalies of speech organs, and negativism. Similarly, David Mitchell described the role of the clinical psychologist in private practice as follows: "His study includes a consideration of the situation which must be set and the stimuli which must be used in order that desirable habits be strengthened and unfortunate ones modified or eliminated."

Clinicians, therefore, perceived themselves as dealing with educational, not psychiatric problems. But this distinction was growing increasingly difficult to maintain.

On the one hand, some psychologists saw that learning principles could be usefully applied to modify behaviors which were strikingly similar to psychiatric disturbances. Watson, for example, reported investigations of the effectiveness of various conditioning techniques in the reduction of children's fears. The method of disuse was not very effective (attempting to weaken the stimulus-response association with the passage of time by avoiding its exercise), nor was verbal organization (talking about the feared object), nor were frequent and repeated presentations of the feared object, nor were social factors (observing other children playing with the noxious stimulus). What seemed to be most effective was unconditioning or reconditioning, as illustrated by the case of Peter in a study reported by Mary C. Jones. Three-year-old Peter had been afraid of rabbits and other furry things. By pairing the presentation of a caged rabbit while he was eating lunch and daily bringing the animal closer and closer, Peter seemed to lose his fear of it and of other furry things as well. It appeared to Watson that many psychiatric disturbances could be explained without recourse to unconscious complexes, wishes, and the like. Instead, they could be understood in terms of conditioning, and ameliorated by the application of conditioning techniques.

On the other hand, some psychiatrists saw neurotic disorders as problems in re-education. Austen Riggs (1876–1940) reported success in treating neurotics by removing them from their stressful environments to the more insulated regimen and safety of his sanitorium. There the patient was told he was in need of re-education, which he was definitely going to obtain from his physician and other members of the staff. Demands upon him to exercise initiative and make decisions were immediately minimized. His life at the sanitorium was orderly and quietly regimented. It was from this very routine that he was to learn to do things just because they had to be done. In the course of daily interviews with his therapist, he was given assigned readings to inspire and discipline him. He heard lectures and participated in group discussions in the psychology of adjustment. He participated in activities that emphasized the importance of cooperation in social living, and by attending these activities, he gave order to his life. All these things, Riggs claimed, produced improvement in his patients, and without delving into any unconscious goings on.

Thus among both psychologists and psychiatrists there were those who advocated considering what had been thought to be mental illnesses as problems in learning and adjustment. From some points of view this rapprochement was regarded as an exciting advance, while from another vantage it was seen as having the unfortunate consequence of tending to befog the boundaries between the two fields. What made the subject of professional identities a sensitive matter of great significance was the challenge it posed to the assertion that the practice of psychotherapy is the exclusive province of medicine. Within the ranks of psychiatrists a small but influential group raised objections to this traditional claim . . . and in so doing served to soften further the points of contrast between their field and clinical psychology.

Freud did not regard a medical degree as necessary to practice psychoanalysis and could point to Hanns Sachs, his daughter Anna, and perhaps even Otto Rank as successful nonmedically trained analysts. Nor did Alfred Adler believe that only physicians should undertake treatment. On the contrary, he made a clear distinction between patients who were children and those who were adults: "Children who are lacking in a social feeling and therefore in courage and self-confidence must be changed by their teachers. Adults who develop neurosis must have their courage increased by psychotherapists."

To implement this view, Adler, in 1922, began conducting clinics where problem children and their parents were interviewed. These interviews were conducted before an audience of teachers as a way of helping to train them in understanding and dealing with these disturbances. Shortly after Adler began this work he reached the conclusion that the presence of the audience, in and of itself, had therapeutic value. He thought this procedure made it immediately evident to the child that his problem was of concern to the community and that it proved to him that people in general wished to be of help. (Incidentally, Rudolf Dreikurs, a psychiatrist who was one of Adler's pupils, introduced this method of family counseling to the United States in 1928. Subsequently, he extended it by arranging to see his alcoholic patients in groups.)

Well, is mental illness really an illness? Should physicians alone be deemed competent to treat neurotics and psychotics? Will such patients get well no matter who does what for them? Adler thought a sizeable percentage of them would. He saw the therapist taking on the functions of a mother, giving the patient the experience of feeling himself close to an utterly trustworthy person and thereby having his social interest strengthened and broadened. Through simple, direct, inoffensive explanations of the patient's behavior which he could immediately acknowledge and experience as his own, Adler saw the therapist building up the neurotic's independence and courage. Yet he believed that despite all that his theory and techniques might add, fully half his patients were already on the road to recovery simply by virtue of their wish to get well. Nor did he consider that such a proportion among his cases was unique: "It is this 50 percent of 'cures' that enables all schools of psychiatry to live."

As if to demonstrate anew that both psychologists and psychiatrists had cause to wonder, the phenomenon of Émile Coué burst forth in the

United States in 1923. Coué (1857–1926), a former French chemist, had studied hypnotism and the power of autosuggestion. His theory was that imagination, when engaged in conflict with the will, is of superior strength and will triumph. Therefore, all one has to do to achieve peace of mind and mental health is to invoke vividly enough the imagination that one is well. Coué believed that the means by which this happiness can be attained is by repeating each day: "Day by day in every way I am getting better and better."

Having reputedly achieved great success in Europe, Coué was greeted in the United States as a virtual Messiah. People flocked to hear him deliver his gospels and his formula in person. They jammed Coué Institutes in order to make certain that they had the words right. So simple and emphatic was Coué's prescription that, inevitably, disillusionment was rapid and complete. Sadly, Coué returned to France, while Couéism became a subject for jokes: "My husband thought he was sicker and sicker until he saw Coué. Now he thinks he's deader and deader." However, Coué in his failure had served at least to demonstrate the enormity of the number of people who wish help. Could so many persons be considered psychiatric problems? Were so many Americans badly conditioned?

If the "cure" of about fifty percent of patients was enough to satisfy some people, it was not enough for Healy and Bronner. They had studied 675 delinquent boys and girls in Chicago and Boston and had found that 55 percent of them had committed crimes after supposedly having been reformed. It seemed clear to them that the methods for treating delinquents were inefficient and ineffective when only 45 percent were helped. They urged judges, lawyers, and public officials everywhere to give scientists the opportunity to employ their therapeutic techniques to help delinquents become healthy, useful members of society.

The therapeutic techniques that Healy and Bronner probably had foremost in mind for meeting the problem of delinquency were psychoanalytic. Although there had been some attempts at innovation, these techniques remained essentially unchanged during the twenties. Shortly after the War there had been some interest in integrating psychoanalysis and hypnosis into what was called "hypnoanalysis." The procedure of hypnoanalysis went somewhat as follows: The patient, under hypnosis, would recall a traumatic incident. The hypnotist would supply interpretations of it which the patient would evaluate until he seemed to find one acceptable to him. Then the hypnotist would give positive, forceful suggestions that all that they had discussed would be recalled when the patient awoke. Finally, in the waking state, the patient and hypnotist would go over the story, its interpretations, and its significance in past behavior and for future conduct.

But what general interest there was in hypnoanalysis soon diminished.

Not so the interest in psychoanalysis. Around 1924, William Alanson White, president of the American Psychiatric Association, recommended that psychiatrists shake up their concepts and take a fresh look at mental illness, with the formulations of psychoanalytic theory in mind to help them gain new insights. And by 1929 some schizophrenic and depressed patients in mental hospitals were being seen in psychoanalysis by analytically trained psychiatrists.

Most hospitalized patients, though, still received only custodial care. For a brief interval, many of them had found themselves subjected to teeth extractions and tonsillectomies. The rationale for these procedures came from Henry A. Cotton, a psychiatrist who believed that focal infections were responsible for mental illness and delinquency. Cotton claimed he had produced cures by removing the infected part of the body. Few people accepted his theory, but out of discouragement and in the remote hope that he might be right, they decided to give his procedures a trial. They felt rather wistfully that there was really little to lose and perhaps much to gain.

Then, in 1922, a study was reported by Kopeloff and Cheney. One group of fifty-eight mental patients had tonsils and teeth extracted, while sixty-two other mental patients constituted the control group of the experiment and were allowed to remain intact. No difference in improvement between the two groups was discernible. Apparently, there was nothing to support Cotton's theory. Another blind alley had been entered, but at least need no longer be explored.

In 1928, L. von Meduna, a Hungarian psychiatrist, speculated that an antagonism exists between epilepsy and schizophrenia. Out of six thousand schizophrenic patients studied by Meduna, only eight seemed to have epilepsy. He also observed that schizophrenics with convulsions have a tendency to recover. It therefore seemed logical to him to conclude that if he were to induce convulsions in schizophrenics, biochemical changes in their brains leading to their improvement might be produced. To induce seizures, Meduna began experimenting with intramuscular injections of camphor in oil. The results were promising but there were difficulties connected with the use of camphor. It brought about convulsions too slowly, thus causing the patients much distress, and also the onset and intensity of the seizure were decidedly unpredictable. We leave Meduna at the point where he began his search for a better convulsive agent than camphor.

It would appear that relatively little in the way of new developments in treatment occurred in the twenties. More people were becoming familiar with psychoanalysis and other personality and therapeutic orientations. More people were using these orientations with a greater variety of disturbances. The period seemed to be one of consolidation and dissemination rather than innovation.

PROFESSIONAL DEVELOPMENT

Tests were becoming big business, and psychologists were pleasantly torn between delight over their success and objecting to the extent of their commercialization. Tests were almost everywhere in use. Few children in schools could escape them. According to Goddard: "It is in the scientific classification of pupils that the most noteworthy results, for education, of the applications of differential and clinical psychology are found."

The task of the school psychologist was to detect and remedy what were thought to be "temporary" incapacities in learning. Through the use of his diagnostic techniques, he tried to differentiate between those who cannot and those who will not learn. At first this differentiation seemed easy because any child with an IQ below average "cannot" and all other children "will not." Unfortunately, this task became more and more difficult as the variables that affect intellectual functioning and IQ scores were recognized. Nevertheless, despite the mounting complexities in the decisions the school psychologist had to make, many schools continued to rely heavily upon him and his instruments to provide the information that would reduce the demands upon the teachers to exercise such responsibility and judgment.

A "new" application of testing developed in the field of vocational and industrial guidance. In 1920, Morris S. Viteles (b. 1898) set up a clinic for just that purpose at the University of Pennsylvania. The aim of vocational guidance, according to Viteles, was to supply scientific direction in the choice of occupations by children of working age, at that time fourteen to sixteen years. To achieve this aim required both an analysis of the demands of the job upon the individual and also an analysis of the individual's interests, competence, temperament, health, education, physical appearance, socioeconomic condition, and experience. Obviously, testing has an important role to play in this analysis of the individual.

James McKeen Cattell, formerly of Columbia University, took the lead in founding the Psychological Corporation in 1921. He was joined in this enterprise by a group of psychologists, some two hundred in number, who purchased shares of stock in the corporation. They were encouraged by reports from the British Institute of Psychology which indicated that psychological principles could be applied to increase industrial production and individual satisfaction. Far from being antithetical, production and employee satisfaction could go along very well together. The Psychological Corporation was to derive most of its income from the sale of tests, from consultations, and from the conduct of special studies and surveys for client firms. Its profits were intended for the promotion of psychological research. After a touch-and-go beginning, the Corporation eventually proved successful and became a giant supplier of tests as well as a moderating influence on extravagant and overly enthusiastic claims for diagnostic techniques.

The scope of the mental hygiene movement was also enlarged. Originally intended to promote the improvement of care for hospitalized mental patients, its aims now encompassed the prevention of mental illness and assistance of all those who suffered from any form of psychological malfunctioning. Beginning in 1919, and in keeping with its broadened range of operations, the National Committee for Mental Hygiene (NCMH) received $10,000 annually from the Commonwealth Fund. The purpose of this grant was to investigate the incidence, causes, treatment, and prevention of juvenile delinquency. This led, in 1921, to the establishment of the Division on the Prevention of Delinquency within the NCMH and also a Bureau of Children's Guidance at the New York School of Social Work.

From 1922 through 1926, the NCMH was engaged in conducting surveys of delinquency in New Jersey, South Carolina, Ohio, and Kentucky. During this period, demonstration child guidance clinics were arranged for communities which gave evidence of being willing to continue such psychiatric services on a permanent basis by providing the necessary funds. The first demonstration clinic was set up in St. Louis and was affiliated with the juvenile court. Its staff consisted of Thomas Heldt, psychiatrist; E. K. Wickman, clinical psychologist; and Mildred Scoville, Hester Crutcher, and Dorothy Wallace, psychiatric social workers. It was not considered successful because it failed to obtain adequate financial support from the community, although it did manage to struggle on for a number of years. Equally disappointing monetary fates awaited the demonstration child guidance clinics established in Norfolk and Dallas and a traveling clinic based at the University of Minnesota.

Despite these isolated instances, the trend was toward growth in the number of facilities offering psychological services. More fiscally fortunate were clinics in Minneapolis and St. Paul, both of which were outgrowths of the demonstration clinic at the University of Minnesota, Los Angeles, Cleveland, and Philadelphia. By legislative act in 1921, the Psychological and Psychopathic Clinic was established at the University of Hawaii, in 1925, James Drever organized the Psychological Clinic for Children and Juveniles at the University of Edinburgh, and in 1927, Cyril Burt helped form the Child Guidance Council in London.

Along the way a change in the functioning of child guidance clinics began to take place. Their attention was shifting from studies of delinquents and retardates to an examination of parent-child relationships. A similar enlargement of perspective can easily be traced in the development of the American Orthopsychiatric Association.

In December of 1923, Karl Menninger sent a letter inviting twenty-six fellow psychiatrists who seemed interested in "medical criminology, or disciplinary psychiatry, or orthopsychics" to meet with him in Chicago. This meeting was held the following month at the Institute for Juvenile Research, formerly called the Juvenile Psychopathic Institute. The Institute's change of name serves as another illustration of the broadened horizons in the field.

Among those present were Herman Adler, David Levy, V. V. Anderson, Lawson G. Lowrey, and George Stevenson. Together they made plans for the formation of "The Association of American Orthopsychiatrists." It should be noted that the term "orthopsychiatry" was substituted for Menninger's suggested term "orthopsychics." This was done in order to suggest subtly the medical nature of the group and so make it more inviting and acceptable to the medical profession. Evidently, psychologists were not the only ones concerned with status and recognition.

The first convention of the American Orthopsychiatric Association was held later that year, in June 1924, at the Institute for Juvenile Research. William Healy was selected as its first president.

Within six months the objectives of the association were sweepingly enlarged from medical criminology to "the study and treatment of problems of human behavior." Members of any interested profession were invited to participate in the organization. However, in the fear that prestige would be lost if members of the medical profession were not in control, active membership (eligibility to hold office) was restricted to psychiatrists. Quite sensibly though, and no doubt in order to promote the growth of the group, just two years later active membership was made available to psychologists, social workers, and other professional persons involved in the diagnosis and treatment of behavior disorders.

The membership of the American Orthopsychiatric Association increased from twenty-three in 1924 to eighty-three by 1929. Within its roster of early members these familiar names may be found: Augusta Bronner; Edgar Doll, who had taken over from Porteus as director of research at Vineland in 1925; Shepherd Franz; Henry Goddard; Adolf Meyer; and Lightner Witmer.

Another instance of widening scope occurred in 1921 when the *Journal of Abnormal Psychology* became the *Journal of Abnormal and Social Psychology*. Although practical considerations having to do with publishing costs may have entered into the reasons for this change of title, the reason given to the public was that social psychology, perhaps more than any other branch of the science, is interested in the forces underlying human behavior and is enriched by the findings of psychopathology.

A final example of how things were developing took place at Harvard in 1926, when Morton Prince appeared with a check for $75,000 from an anonymous donor. It was proposed that this gift be used to establish a "department of abnormal psychology" within the University as a means of bringing normal and abnormal psychology into a closer relationship. At Boring's suggestion, it was decided to protect the University in the event that abnormal psychology should cease to exist as a separate field by stating in the deed of gift that the new Harvard Psychological Clinic was to give instruction and conduct research in abnormal *and dynamic* psychology. In 1927, the Harvard Psychological Clinic was founded by Morton Prince.

The APA was not insensitive to these signs of change but vacillated in coming to decisions about them. At issue was the concern of many members that in enlarging the scope of the Association, its recently acquired, and still fragile, identity as a science might be threatened. To appreciate the fact that this concern was legitimate, we may note some of its grounds.

One of these was the embarrassing truth that mediums and spooks still tended to be associated with psychology in the minds of the general public. In a curious and almost desperate effort to dissociate psychology from what were claimed to be supernatural phenomena, the *Journal of Abnormal and Social Psychology,* in 1925, made a public offer of $5,000 to anyone who could produce supernatural events under rigid laboratory and scientific conditions. Forty-four persons responded to this offer in the hope of picking up some easy money. According to the opinion of the panel of psychologists acting as judges in this matter, only three of the respondents were genuinely interested, the remainder being cranks and phonies. Moreover, no one made further inquiry when informed of the conditions under which they would have to make contact with the nether or upper world. Somewhat hastily and presumptuously the offer was withdrawn, leaving many mediums, no doubt, grumbling to their ethereal associates about the unfairness of earthly psychologists.

A second consideration was that opposition from psychiatrists to the diagnostic function of clinical psychologists continued. Particular irritation centered around the diagnosis of mental retardation, which the medical profession contended was solely a medical responsibility.

Once again Shepherd Franz attempted to win peace with honor. He tried to achieve this desideratum by making a distinction between the abnormal and the pathological. For example, an IQ of 180 was abnormal but not pathological. He suggested that clinical psychologists were concerned only with deviations from the norm, the abnormal, and were content to leave to the medical profession the determination of whether pathology should be ascribed to these deviations. Franz also expressed the hope that interdisciplinary ill feelings were due only to semantic misunderstandings and that there would be harmony between the two professions once each understood the language of the other. He recommended that "psychological psychiatrists" and "psychiatric psychologists" play the role of mediators and translators between the disciplines. Unfortunately, the conflict went deeper than difficulties in communication.

For psychiatrists opposed psychologists engaging in treatment as well as diagnosis. In 1925, A. A. Brill published an article in a New York newspaper against the practice of psychoanalysis by anyone who was not a physician. About a year later, in 1926 in Vienna, one of Theodor Reik's patients sued him on the grounds of harmful treatment, also accusing him of quackery. Reik, who had his Ph.D. from the University of Vienna, was acquitted, but Freud, troubled by rumblings within the analytic ranks, published *The Problem of Lay Analysis* in an effort to settle this issue. That same year the New York Legislature passed a bill declaring lay analysis illegal, and the American Medical Association warned its members against any cooperation with lay analysts.

Freud's position was emphatically taken. Not only did he favor lay analysis but he strongly urged the separation of psychoanalysis from medicine: "psychoanalysis is not a particular branch of medicine. I do not see how anyone can refuse to recognize this. Psychoanalysis is a part of psychology."

Nevertheless, analysts within the United States took a position almost equally emphatic and in opposition to the stand taken by Freud. They insisted that the professional identity of analysts had to be attained and maintained within the medical profession. One compromise was proposed based upon the supposition that the analyses of children were easier and less professionally demanding than analyses of adults. Reluctantly, the New York Psychoanalytic Society, in 1929, temporarily acquiesced in the pleas of its brother organizations and agreed to permit lay analyses of children only.

The position of the APA may be described as springing from a desire to preserve its inoffensive, respectable appearance while decorously squelching and placating rising demands that it become involved in the professional problems of some of its members.

In 1921, the APA reaffirmed its objective as being the advancement of psychology as a science. Scrupulously avoided were any overt signs of enthusiasm for psychology as a profession. In keeping with its single-minded objective, the requirements for member status in the Association became a Ph.D. in psychology and published postdoctoral research of an acceptable nature. At the same time an APA committee recommended the formation of a Section of Consulting Psychology, the initiation of a program for the certification of consulting psychologists, and the elimination of the Section of Clinical Psychology. A group of dissatisfied clinicians banded together and formed the New York State Association for Consulting Psychology.

Events at the Carnegie Institute of Technology were probably not completely unrelated to the scientific spirit that pervaded the upper echelons of psychology. In 1924, the Division of Applied Psychology was discontinued by the Institute and its staff scattered. According to Bingham, first and only chairman of the Division, this was done to avoid competing with psychology in the graduate school of the University of Pittsburgh. Whatever the reason, Bingham packed his bags for New York City and the private practice of industrial psychology.

Meanwhile the certification program was not very successful . . . during its first two years only twenty-four psychologists applied for certificates . . . nor was the membership of the APA increasing so rapidly that it caused any alarm about overcrowding. Some psychologists, Wells for one, felt the standards for certification and membership were too high. They further believed the Association should assume the responsibility for setting ethical and professional standards for applied psychologists. The APA, however, by inaction made known that it felt things were going along just fine.

In 1924, the Clinical Section of the APA, which apparently had survived despite the earlier poor prognosis made for it, attempted to set standards. It recommended that a clinical psychologist should have a Ph.D. from an approved graduate school and four years of professional training, with at least one year of supervised experience in practical psychological diagnosis. These were high standards, everyone agreed, but it was felt that high standards were necessary. Furthermore, clinicians believed that some action had to be taken to prevent unqualified persons from engaging in testing, and there was incessant pleading with the APA to set up standards for the training programs that were needed. The pleas of L. Crane will serve as an example.

Crane argued that if psychologists were to receive the status and financial rewards they desired, a legal definition of their profession was necessary and a specific program of education in clinical psychology had to be inaugurated. He advocated a minimum of three undergraduate years followed by a four-year graduate course. The first two years of graduate training would stress courses in medicine; the next two years would stress testing, psychoanalysis, and topics of lasting interest, whatever they happened to be at the time. Upon successful completion of the program, the student would be awarded a Ps.D., doctor of psychology, with all rights and privileges attached thereto. The response to Crane's plea was not perceptible.

The Section of Consulting Psychology was changed to a Division in 1924, and in 1925 the APA became a corporation and purchased the journals of the Psychological Review Company. The purpose of incorporation was to relieve individual members of financial responsibility for the journals and to have that responsibility vested in a corporate body. It was also recommended that another class of membership, called Associate, be established in the Association. Requirements for Associate status were a Ph.D. in psychology and full time work in the field or sufficient distinction to be recommended for the associateship by the Council.

In 1926, Associate membership began in the APA; Alfred Adler was a visiting professor at Columbia; and Morton Prince generously gave the *Journal of Abnormal and Social Psychology* to the Association. The dues, which had been two dollars a year in 1919, were raised to ten dollars for members and six dollars for associates, with a subscription to *Psychological Abstracts* included. The following year the APA certification program was abandoned on the grounds of pervading disinterest. Besides, or so went the APA argument, the standards for certification were so high that those who could meet the qualifications did not need certification to attest to their competence.

Some psychologists were feeling uneasy about the effect the requirement of published research for election to member status was having on the composition of the Association. In 1928, sixteen members and 206 associates were elected; in 1929, six members and 222 associates were elected. Within three years the APA had more associates than members and the imbalance was growing. Obviously psychologists felt that it was desirable to belong to the APA, but perhaps not at the price of doing postdoctoral research.

Fernberger's analysis of the composition of the APA in 1928 showed that 616 members had Ph.D. degrees. Of that number, 324, or 53 percent, had received their doctorates from a total of just four universities: Columbia (135 Ph.D.'s), Chicago (80), Harvard (56), and Clark (50). Nineteen members were practicing industrial psychology and 104 were engaged in clinical work. Moreover, although approximately 77 percent of the membership of the APA held academic positions, 48 percent of the membership indicated research interests in some area of applied psychology.

What we see then, by the close of the twenties, is a shifting balance of forces within the American Psychological Association. A steadily increasing minority of clinicians was attempting to gain recognition within the organization and striving to shake it from a policy of complacent inaction in the face of increasingly urgent professional problems. There were disagreements among psychologists about their science and what direction they wished it to follow. Simultaneously the field was expanding and external pressures upon it were mounting. Society was demanding that psychologists apply their knowledge, skills, and techniques through many forms of service. Yet these demands also brought psychology into conflict with other professions in areas where the status and value of psychology had still to be demonstrated.

This was a far different psychology from that of twenty years before. As Dunlap wistfully put it: "The questions concerning introspection as present observation or memory; interaction *vs.* parallelism; two-level or multi-level attention; bidimensional or polydimensional feeling; and a host of other 'problems': who is willing to discuss these now?"

Joseph Jastrow could survey the field and say without fear of too much contradiction, "Psychology as we know it, along with many another discipline, is a twentieth-century achievement." Perhaps Jastrow stirred up more controversy with his opinion: "Yet of all the applications, that of clinical psychology appears to me the most momentous."

To a large extent, the changes within psychology had been and were effects directly, or more often indirectly, brought about by psychoanalysis. Thurstone, Leuba, Lashley, and Jastrow regarded the following contributions of Freudianism as having been most influential: its study of the basic and permanent tendencies in human nature; its emphasis on the demands of the organism and the behaviors by which these demands were satisfied; its determinism, focused particularly on the significance of childhood experiences as these affect adult behavior. G. Stanley Hall phrased his evaluation more personally: "I have the deepest appreciation of the service Freud has rendered our specialty by doing more to popularize and give zest to it among all sorts of intellectuals than any other man in the history of science."

Then there were the schools of psychology, some growing and some dying: behaviorism, gestalt, self psychology, structuralism, hormic psychology, associationism, functionalism. A representative of the expiring structuralist school, Madison Bentley, reflecting upon his feelings of isolation within his science voiced a moving plea for tolerance: "Our underlying notions are then useful . . . but we must remember that they represent less an ultimate truth than our own individual preferences. More is to be gained than men commonly acknowledge by a sympathetic insight into alien points of view and into the possible utility of concepts which one has not learned how to use. The history of the sciences is eloquent upon the enormous wastefulness of prejudice."

Mary Calkins held fast to her beliefs: "For with each year I live, with each book I read, with each observation I initiate or confirm, I am more deeply convinced that psychology should be conceived as the science of the self, or person, as related to its environment, physical and social." Yet here too the emphasis had changed—from a "self" that was introspective to a "person" in interaction with his world.

However, McDougall could not hide his disappointments under the strength of his convictions. Looking back on a career, which to most would appear outstanding in its accomplishments, he felt a keen sense of failure. From a detached, intellectual point of view, he claimed psychology was "the most difficult of the sciences, and the most unsatisfying of all fields of research." And all about him he observed the ironical fact that psychologists, seemingly unable to agree on an answer to any major question, were surrounded by an admiring public, eagerly seeking only immediate and dogmatic solutions to their problems. But these remarks were mere embellishments for what seemed to trouble him most . . . his corrosive belief that it was only his inability to contain his arrogance that had alienated people from him and produced little enthusiasm for his views. For reasons that he could never fathom, unlike his model William James, he had not been able to win the friendship of his readers. Somehow, he was convinced, he had failed to convey his humility and warmth, and so he was forced to remain in the awkward position of a leader virtually and pathetically devoid of followers.

To many psychologists, Bentley, Calkins, and McDougall were voices from a far distant past. Dominating psychology were behaviorism and psychoanalysis, with gestalt formulations challenging them both. Spokesmen for each school seldom neglected an opportunity to criticize their rivals. Yet Boring thought that probably every school has its serious errors: "the more you fight for the truth the less you see it."

Although Boring conceded that the leaders of the opposing factions were brilliant men, he felt the distinction of being right belonged to men who were less dazzling and extreme. The eclectics, the middle-of-the-roaders, really the majority of psychologists whose major interest, Boring felt, was in what was both meaningful and useful, would gather the most worthwhile fruits of these controversies between schools. There is a paradox in all this, that those who argue most vigorously for what they believe to be true are driven to some extent from the truth by the need to emphasize their position, but Boring concluded: "Psychology needs both judiciousness and effective prejudices, and I cannot resist the impression that we shall do well to cultivate and welcome both."

Disagreements, unsolved problems, and dissatisfactions were certainly to be found in abundance. But we must remember that these were only by-products, as a whole profession continued to make its almost revolutionary advance. In 1929, James McKeen Cattell was elected president of the Ninth International Congress of Psychology. His remarks, although a trifle chauvinistic, may serve to throw a positive light on the situation and help to explain the vitality of psychology within the United States: "Our people had curiosity, acquisitiveness, and energy with ever-increasing wealth. We were able to take over what we wanted from abroad; we were not bound by procedure and tradition. The psychologist has some reason to thank God when he is born a happy and irresponsible American child."

References

Adler, A. Individual psychology. *J. abnorm. soc. Psychol.,* 1927–28, 22, 116–122.

Adler, A. The cause and prevention of neuroses. *J. abnorm. soc. Psychol.,* 1928–29, 23, 4–11.

Allport, F. H. & Allport, G. W. Personality traits: their classification and measurement. *J. abnorm. soc. Psychol.,* 1921–22, 16, 6–40.

Allport, G. W. Personality and character. *Psychol. Bull.,* 1921, 18, 441–455.

Allport, G. W. The study of the undivided personality. *J. abnorm. soc. Psychol.,* 1924–25, 19, 132–141.

Allport, G. W. A test for ascendence-submission. *J. abnorm. soc. Psychol.,* 1928– 29, 23, 118–136.

Allport, G. W. The study of personality by the intuitive method: an experiment in teaching from *The Locomotive God. J. abnorm. soc. Psychol.,* 1929–30, 24, 14–27.

Ansbacher, H. L. & Ansbacher, Rowena R. *The individual psychology of Alfred Adler.* New York: Basic Books, 1956.

Beck, S. J. Rorschach's test in this anniversary year. In L. G. Lowrey & Victoria Sloane (Eds.) *Orthopsychiatry 1923–1948: retrospect and prospect.* New York: Amer. Orthopsychiat. Assoc., 1948.

Bentley, M. The major categories of psychology. *Psychol. Rev.,* 1926, 33, 71–105.

Berman, L. *The glands regulating the personality.* New York: Macmillan, 1921.

Bingham, W. V. D. Autobiography. In E. G. Boring, *et. al.* (Eds.) *A history of psychology in autobiography.* Vol. IV. Worcester, Mass.: Clark U. Press, 1952.

Boring, E. G. The psychology of controversy. *Psychol. Rev.,* 1929, 36, 97–121.

Brigham, C. C. *A study of American intelligence.* Princeton: Princeton U. Press, 1923.

Brigham, C. C. Intelligence tests of immigrant groups. *Psychol. Rev.,* 1930, 37, 158–165.

Brown, J. F. The methods of Kurt Lewin in the psychology of action and af-fection. *Psychol. Rev.,* 1929, 36, 200–221.

Burt, C. *The young delinquent.* New York: Appleton, 1925.

Burt, C. Autobiography. In E. G. Boring, *et. al.* (Eds.) *A history of psychology in autobiography.* Vol. IV. Worcester, Mass.: Clark U. Press, 1952.

Calkins, Mary W. Autobiography. In C. Murchison (Ed.) *A history of psychology in autobiography.* Vol. I. Worcester, Mass.: Clark U. Press, 1930.

Calkins, Mary W. & Gamble, Eleanor A. McC. The self-psychology of the psychoanalysts. *Psychol. Rev.,* 1930, 37, 277–304.

Cannon, W. B. *Bodily changes in pain, hunger, fear, and rage.* New York: Appleton, 1929.

Carmichael, L. A further study of the development of behavior in vertebrates experimentally removed from the influence of external stimulation. *Psychol. Rev.,* 1927, 34, 34–47.

Cotton, H. A. *The defective delinquent and insane.* Princeton: Princeton U. Press, 1921.

Cotton, H. A. The etiology and treatment of the so-called functional psychoses. *Amer. j. Psychiat.,* 1922, 2, 157–210.

Crane, L. A plea for the training of psychologists. *J. abnorm. soc. Psychol.,* 1925–26, 20, 228–233.

Davies, A. E. An interpretation of mental symptoms of dementia praecox. *J. abnorm. soc. Psychol.,* 1926–27, 21, 284–295.

Dodd, S. C. The theory of factors. *Psychol. Rev.,* 1928, 35, 211–234; 261–279.

Drever, J. Autobiography. In C. Murchison (Ed.) *A history of psychology in autobiography.* Vol. II. Worcester, Mass.: Clark U. Press, 1932.

Dunlap, K. The foundations of social psychology. *Psychol. Rev.,* 1923, 30, 81–102.

Dunlap, K. Autobiography. In C. Murchison (Ed.) *A history of psychology in autobiography.* Vol. II. Worcester, Mass.: Clark U. Press, 1932.

Durca, M. A. The province and scope of mental hygiene. *J. abnorm. soc. Psychol.,* 1927–28, 22, 182–193.

Edwards, A. S. Intelligence as the capacity for variability and versatility of response. *Psychol. Rev.,* 1928, 35, 198–210.

Eggen, J. B. Is instinct an entity? *J. abnorm. soc. Psychol.,* 1926–27, 21, 38–51.

Ellenberger, H. The life and work of Hermann Rorschach (1884–1922). *Bull. Menninger Clinic,* 1954, 18, 173–209.

Fernald, G. G. Character *vs.* intelligence in personality studies. *J. abnorm. Psychol.,* 1920–21, 15, 1–10.

Fernberger, S. W. Statistical analyses of the members and associates of the American Psychological Association, Inc. in 1928. *Psychol. Rev.,* 1928, 35, 447–465.

Franz, S. I. Cerebral-mental relations. *Psychol. Rev.,* 1921, 28, 81–95.

Franz, S. I. *Nervous and mental re-education.* New York: Macmillan, 1923.

Franz, S. I. Psychology and psychiatry. *Psychol. Rev.,* 1922, 29, 241–249.

Freeman, F. S. *Theory and practice of psychological testing.* New York: Holt, 1950.

Freud, S. *Beyond the pleasure principle.* London: Hogarth, 1942 (First German edition, 1920).

Freud, S. *Inhibitions, symptoms, and anxiety.* London: Hogarth, 1936. (First German edition, 1926.)

Freud, S. *The ego and the id.* London: Hogarth, 1927.

Freud, S. *The problem of lay analysis.* New York: Brentano's, 1927.

Freyd, M. Introverts and extroverts. *Psychol. Rev.,* 1924, 31, 74–87.

Garth, T. R. A review of racial psychology. *Psychol. Bull.,* 1925, 22, 343–368.

Garth, T. R. A review of race psychology. *Psychol. Bull.,* 1930, 27, 329–356.

Gesell, A. *The mental growth of the preschool child.* New York: Macmillan, 1925.

Gesell, A. *Infancy and human growth.* New York: Macmillan, 1929.

Gesell, A. Autobiography. In E. G. Boring, *et. al.* (Eds.) *A history of psychology in autobiography.* Vol. IV. Worcester, Mass.: Clark U. Press, 1952.

Goddard, H. H. *School training of gifted children.* Yonkers, N.Y.: World, 1928.

Goodenough, Florence L. *Measurement of intelligence by drawings*. Yonkers, N.Y.: World, 1926.

Guthrie, E. R. Measuring introversion and extroversion. *J. abnorm. soc. Psychol.*, 1927, 22, 82–88.

Hall, G. S. *Life and confessions of a psychologist*. New York: Appleton, 1923.

Hallowell, Dorothy K. Mental tests for pre-school children. *Psychol. Clinic*, 1927, 16, 235–276.

Harthshorne, H. & May, M. A. *Studies in deceit*. New York: Macmillan, 1928.

Healy, W. & Bronner, Augusta F. *Delinquents and criminals, their making and unmaking: studies in two American cities*. New York: Macmillan, 1926.

Heidbreder, E. F. The normal inferiority complex. *J. abnorm. soc. Psychol.*, 1927–28, 22, 243–258.

Hollingsworth, Leta S. *Gifted children: their nature and nurture*. New York: Macmillan, 1926.

Horton, L. H. Old and new in mental tests. *J. abnorm. Psychol.*, 1920–21, 15, 57–64.

Hull, C. L. *Aptitude testing*. Yonkers, N.Y.: World, 1928.

Hull, C. L. Quantitative methods in investigating waking suggestion. *J. abnorm. soc. Psychol.*, 1929–30, 24, 153–169.

Hull, C. L. Autobiography. In E. G. Boring, *et. al.* (Eds.) *A history of psychology in autobiography*. Vol. IV. Worcester, Mass.: Clark U. Press, 1952.

Hutt, R. B. W. The school psychologist. *Psychol. Clinic*, 1923, 15, 48–51.

Jastrow, J. Autobiography. In C. Murchison (Ed.) *A history of psychology in autobiography*. Vol. I. Worcester, Mass.: Clark U. Press, 1930.

Jones, E. The development of the concept of the super-ego. *J. abnorm. soc. Psychol.*, 1928–29, 23, 276–285.

Jones, E. *The life and work of Sigmund Freud*. Vol. III. New York, Basic Books, 1957.

Jones, Mary C. A laboratory study of fear: the case of Peter. *Ped. Sem.*, 1924, 31, 308–315.

Jung, C. G. *Psychological types or the psychology of individuation*. New York: Harcourt, Brace, 1925.

Kelley, T. L. *Interpretation of educational measurement*. Yonkers, N.Y.: World, 1923.

Kopeloff, N. & Cheney, C. O. Studies in focal infection: its presence and elimination in the functional psychoses. *Amer. j. Psychiat.*, 1922, 2, 139–156.

Kretschmer, E. *Physique and character*. New York: Harcourt, Brace, 1925.

Landis, C. Psychology and the psychogalvanic reflex. *Psychol. Rev.*, 1930, 37, 381–398.

Lehman, H. C. & Witty, P. A. Playing school: a compensatory mechanism. *Psychol. Rev.*, 1926, 33, 480–485.

Lowrey, L. G. The birth of orthopsychiatry. In L. G. Lowrey & Victoria Sloane (Eds.) *Orthopsychiatry 1923–1948: retrospect and prospect.* New York: Amer. Orthopsychiat. Assoc., 1948.

McDougall, W. The use and abuse of instinct in social psychology. *J. abnorm. soc. Psychol.,* 1921–22, 16, 285–333.

McDougall, W. A great advance of the Freudian psychology. *J. abnorm. soc. Psychol.,* 1925–26, 30, 43–47.

McDougall, W. Men or robots? In C. Murchison (Ed.) *Psychologies of 1925.* Worcester, Mass.: Clark U. Press, 1928.

McDougall, W. Autobiography. In C. Murchison (Ed.) *A history of psychology in autobiography.* Vol. I. Worcester, Mass.: Clark U. Press, 1930.

Merrill, Maud A. Oscillation of progress in clinical psychology. *J. consult. Psychol.,* 1951, 15, 281–289.

Mitchell, D. Private practice. In R. A. Brotemarkle (Ed.) *Clinical psychology: studies in honor of Lightner Witmer.* Philadelphia: U. of Pennsylvania Press, 1931.

Naccarati, S. & Garrett, H. E. The relation of morphology to temperament. *J. abnorm. soc. Psychol.,* 1924, 19, 254–263.

Oberndorf, C. P. (Ed. & Translator) Autobiography of Josef Breuer (1842–1925). *Int. J. Psychoanal.,* 1953, 34, 64–67.

Otis, A. S. *Otis Classification Test.* Yonkers, N.Y.: World, 1923.

Parsons, C. J. Children's interpretation of ink-blots. A study of some characteristics of children's imagination. *Brit. J. Psychol.,* 1917, 9, 74–92.

Piaget, J. *The language and thought of the child.* New York: Humanities Press, 1926.

Piaget, J. Autobiography. In E. G. Boring, *et. al.* (Eds.) *A history of psychology in autobiography.* Vol. IV. Worcester, Mass.: Clark U. Press, 1952.

Piaget, Jean. In Marjorie D. Candee (Ed.) *Current biography yearbook 1958.* New York: H. W. Wilson, 1958.

Pressey, S. L. A group scale for investigating the emotions. *J. abnorm. soc. Psychol.,* 1921, 16, 55–64.

Prince, M. The problem of personality: how many selves have we? In C. Murchison (Ed.) *Psychologies of 1925.* Worcester, Mass.: Clark U. Press, 1928.

Rich, G. J. A biochemical approach to the study of personality. *J. abnorm. soc. Psychol.,* 1928–29, 23, 158–175.

Riggs, A. F. *Intelligent living.* New York: Doubleday, 1929.

Rivers, W. H. R. *Conflict and dreams.* New York: Harcourt, Brace, 1923.

Rorschach, H. *Psychodiagnostik.* Bern: Huber, 1921.

Rorschach, H. & Oberholzer, E. The application of the interpretation of form to psychoanalysis. *J. nerv. ment. Dis.,* 1924, 60, 225–248; 359–379.

Rosanoff, A. J. A theory of personality based mainly on psychiatric experience. *Psychol. Bull.,* 1920, 17, 281–299.

Saudek, R. *Experiments with handwriting*. New York: Morrow, 1929.

Seashore, C. Autobiography. In C. Murchison (Ed.) *A history of psychology in autobiography*. Vol. I. Worcester, Mass.: Clark U. Press, 1930.

Spaulding, Edith R. The role of personality development in the reconstruction of the delinquent. *J. abnorm. soc. Psychol.*, 1921–22, 16, 97–114.

Spearman, C. General intelligence objectively determined and measured. *Amer. J. Psychol.*, 1904, 15, 201–292.

Spearman, C. A friendly challenge to Professor Thorndike. *Psychol. Rev.*, 1922, 29, 406–407.

Spearman, C. *The abilities of men*. New York: Macmillan, 1927.

Spearman, C. Autobiography. In C. Murchison (Ed.) *A history of psychology in autobiography*. Vol. I. Worcester, Mass.: Clark U. Press, 1930.

Spranger, E. *Types of men*. Halle (Saale): Niemeyer, 1928.

Stern, W. The theory of the constancy of intelligence. *Psychol. Clinic*, 1925, 16, 110–118.

Stevenson, G. S. Child guidance and the National Committee for Mental Hygiene. In L. G. Lowrey & Victoria Sloane (Eds.) *Orthopsychiatry 1923–1948: retrospect and prospect*. New York: Amer. Orthopsychiat. Assoc., 1948.

Symonds, P. M. *Diagnosing personality and conduct*. New York: Century, 1931.

Taft, Jessie, *Otto Rank*. New York: Julian Press, 1958.

Taylor, W. S. A hypnoanalytic study in two cases of war neuroses. *J. abnorm. soc. Psychol.*, 1921–22, 16, 344–355.

Terman, L. M. Symposium: intelligence and its measurement. *J. educ. Psychol.*, 1921, 12, 123–147; 195–216.

Terman, L. M. A new approach to the study of genius. *Psychol. Rev.*, 1922, 29, 310–318.

Terman, L. M. The mental test as a psychological method. *Psychol. Rev.*, 1924, 31, 93–117.

Terman, L. M. *et. al. Genetic studies of genius. Vol. I. Mental and physical traits of a thousand gifted children*. Stanford: Stanford U. Press, 1925.

Thorndike, E. L. A constant error in psychological rating. *J. applied Psychol.*, 1920, 4, 25–29.

Thorndike, E. L. Intelligence and its uses. *Harper's Magazine*, 1920, 140, 227–235.

Thorndike, E. L. On the organization of intellect. *Psychol. Rev.*, 1921, 28, 141–151.

Thorndike, E. L. *et. al. The measurement of intelligence*. New York: Columbia U. Press, 1929.

Thurstone, L. L. The mental age concept. *Psychol. Rev.*, 1926, 33, 268–271.

Thurstone, L. L. The absolute zero in intelligence measurement. *Psychol. Rev.*, 1928, 35, 175–197.

Thurstone, L. L. Autobiography. In E. G. Boring *et. al.* (Eds.) *A history of psychology in autobiography*. Vol. IV. Worcester, Mass.: Clark U. Press, 1952.

Thurstone, L. L., Leuba, J. H., Lashley, K. S., & Jastrow, J. Contributions of Freudianism to psychology. *Psychol. Rev.*, 1924, 31, 175–218.

Thurstone, L. L. & Thurstone, T. G. A neurotic inventory. *J. soc. Psychol.*, 1930, 1, 3–30.

Tolman, E. C. Can instincts be given up in psychology? *J. abnorm. soc. Psychol.*, 1922–23, 17, 139–152.

Twitmyer, E. B. The correction of speech defects. In R. A. Brotemarkle (Ed.) *Clinical psychology: studies in honor of Lightner Witmer.* Philadelphia: U. of Pennsylvania Press, 1931.

Vaughan, W. F. The psychology of compensation. *Psychol. Rev.*, 1926, 33, 467–479.

Vaughan, W. F. The psychology of Alfred Adler. *J. abnorm. soc. Psychol.*, 1926–27, 21, 358.

Viteles, M. S. Vocational guidance and job analysis. *Psychol. Clinic*, 1924, 15, 157–182.

Voelker, P. F. Function of ideals in social education. *Teach. Coll. Contr. Educ.*, 1921, No. 112.

Wallin, J. E. W. The nature of G, as seen by the clinical psychologist. *Psychol. Clinic*, 1929, 18, 196–198.

Watson, J. B. *Behaviorism.* New York: People's Institute, 1924.

Watson, J. B. What the nursery has to say about instincts. Experimental studies on the growth of the emotions. Recent experiments on how we lose and change our emotional equipment. In C. Murchison (Ed.) *Psychologies of 1925.* Worcester, Mass.: Clark U. Press, 1928.

Watson, J. B. Autobiography. In C. Murchison (Ed.) *A history of psychology in autobiography.* Vol. III. Worcester, Mass.: Clark U. Press, 1936.

Watson, J. B. & Raynor, Rosalie. Conditioned emotional reactions. *J. exp. Psychol.*, 1920, 3, 1–14.

Webb, E. Character and intelligence. *Brit. J. Psychol. Monogr. Suppl.*, 1915, III.

Wells, F. L. Attesting psychologists for public service. *Psychol. Rev.*, 1924, 31, 328–335.

Wells, F. L. *Mental tests in clinical practice.* Yonkers, N.Y.: World, 1927.

Wentworth, Mary M. Two hundred cases of dementia praecox tested by the Stanford Revision. *J. abnorm. soc. Psychol.*, 1923–24, 13, 378–384.

Winkler, J. K. & Bromberg, W. *Mind explorers.* New York: Reynal & Hitchcock, 1939.

Witmer, L. Intelligence—a definition. *Psychol. Clinic*, 1922, 14, 65–67.

Witmer, L. Psychological diagnosis and the psychonomic orientation of analytic science. *Psychol. Clinic*, 1925, 16, 1–18.

Witty, P. A. & Lehman, H. C. Drive: a neglected trait in the study of the gifted. *Psychol. Rev.*, 1927, 34, 364–376.

Woodworth, R. S. Dynamic psychology. In C. Murchison (Ed.) *Psychologies of 1925*. Worcester, Mass.: Clark U. Press, 1928.

Wyatt, H. G. Intelligence in man and ape. *Psychol. Rev.,* 1926, 33, 375–384.

Wyatt, H. G. The recent anti-instinctive attitude in social psychology. *Psychol. Rev.,* 1927, 34, 126–132.

Young, P. C. Hypnotism. *Psychol. Bull.,* 1926, 23, 504–523.

Young, P. C. The nature of hypnosis: as indicated by the presence or absence of post-hypnotic amnesia and rapport. *J. abnorm. soc. Psychol.,* 1927–28, 22, 372–382.

Zilboorg, G. & Henry, G. W. *A history of medical psychology*. New York: Norton, 1941.

6

Shared Values

1930-1939

THROUGHOUT THE WORLD during the thirties there was ample reason for feelings of bewilderment and despair. Within the United States millions of people were unemployed or attempting to adjust themselves to greatly reduced incomes, while the prospects for their conditions to be improved by their country's recovery from the Great Depression were bleak indeed. The financial situation elsewhere was little or no better. Under such dire circumstances economic competitions and antagonisms between nations were intensified, and governments felt it necessary to exercise more than ordinary initiative in efforts to surmount their internal problems.

The United States set about righting its domestic affairs in a peaceful manner through such steps as the ending of Prohibition, commencing a system of social security, adopting minimum-wage and maximum-hours laws, and spending unprecedented sums for the construction of public works. However, other countries sought to stimulate their economies and rouse the spirits of their people through appeals to a fierce nationalistic pride, by stepping up the production of armaments, and by military conquests. Starting in 1931, when Japan invaded Manchuria, the decade was marked by wars and a succession of triumphs for dictatorial forms of government: Adolf Hitler became Chancellor of Germany in 1933; Spain's civil war began in 1936 and ended with the consolidation of Franco's power; Japan invaded China in 1937; and in 1939 Germany annexed Austria, Italy invaded Ethiopia, Germany seized Czechoslovakia, Russia attacked Finland, Germany attacked Poland, and Great Britain and France declared war on Germany.

In particular the Hitler regime, with a cold disregard of human life and a ruthlessness unmatched in history, had repercussions upon eugenics and psychology. Shortly after assuming power Hitler ennacted sterilization laws covering mental deficiency, epilepsy, schizophrenia, manic depressive psychoses, Huntington's chorea, severe alcoholism, and hereditary blindness, deafness, and deformity. Some idea of the zeal with which these laws were enforced can be gained by noting that in a period spanning close to thirty years and involving some thirty states in the United States, approximately 20,000 sterilizations had been performed, while in a period of about four years, approximately 225,000 sterilizations were performed in Germany, in many instances in utter violation of the rights of the individual and the intent of the laws. Accordingly, in much of the Western world outside Germany, even reasonable and humane eugenic measures lost the esteem of persons whose overriding concern was now the welfare of the individual rather than the common welfare, though in this instance there is no real incompatibility between the interests of the individual and those of society.

Even more directly related to psychology were the effects produced by Hitler's policies of anti-Semitism and his intolerance of any opposition, which resulted in closing most of the centers for psychological research in Germany and Austria. Many psychologists suffered greatly in the upheaval, though fortunately a sizeable number managed to emigrate to the United States, where assisted by their American colleagues, they secured positions in their profession and unquestionably contributed to the preeminence which psychology in the United States now enjoys.

Among the sciences it was physics, however, that achieved the greatest prestige and which had findings of the most ominous significance when, in 1939, man succeeded in splitting atoms of uranium, thus releasing gigantic quantities of energy. Compared with what was happening outside the laboratories, this momentous event attracted little public notice. For the attention of the world was on the progress of a war unlike any other in mechanization and destructiveness. After a mere twenty years men were once again killing each other and sacrificing themselves in a struggle where human dignity was at stake. During such a time there seems little point in questioning the meaning of life, for it appears all too short and precious, and instead the more prevalent form of this persistent question becomes one of giving significance to death.

NORMAL PERSONALITY FUNCTIONING

The deaths of a number of prominent psychologists—Freud, Adler, Rank, McDougall, and Stern—contributed to the atmosphere of general gloom of this decade. Yet of more enduring importance were the many exciting innovations and the auspicious intermarriages between various points of view within psychology, as well as between psychology and other sciences.

In 1930, Freud's mother died, and the following year his friendly relationship with Ferenczi became impaired. Ferenczi felt that in the conduct of therapy he should be playing a less passive and a more affectionate or maternal role, to the extent of sometimes kissing his patients in a motherly fashion. Freud disapproved of this behavior, and their friendship, which had existed for over thirty years, was officially acknowledged by both parties to be strained. Two years later Ferenczi died.

In that same year, 1933, the German Society for Psychotherapy was taken over by the Nazis. Kretschmer resigned his presidency of the Society, but Jung accepted the position. Jung's chief function became that of discriminating between Aryan and Jewish psychology and emphasizing the superior value of the former. Although he resigned in 1940, Jung had held the position long enough to inspire a great deal of justifiable resentment. Just seriously considering acceptance of a position of this kind would have been sufficient to create such an effect.

Germany "abolished" psychoanalysis in 1934, and Eitingon managed to escape and settle in Palestine. It was a time of much physical suffering and many bitter disappointments for Freud. However, he undoubtedly derived some comfort from seeing his daughter, Anna, attain a position of eminence in psychoanalytic circles.

In 1937, Anna Freud published *The Ego and the Mechanisms of Defense*. Her book focused on the use of defenses in normal growth and as a means of dealing with external, as well as internal, threats to the organism. Among the defenses noted were: fantasy in thought and action, e.g., daydreaming and playing; identification with the aggressor, e.g., a boy displaying the mannerisms and personality characteristics of his father as a device for seeming to be less afraid of him; and asceticism, a defense prominent during puberty and adolescence when a person seeks to control his impulses by repudiating them and avoiding situations which might arouse them, such as staying away from dances, movies, or dates.

When Austria joined with Germany in 1938, the lives of Freud and all other Jews in the country were in danger. Yet circumstances were still such that the Nazis were at times willing to appear to be reasonable men of good will. Therefore, after Mussolini and President Roosevelt made requests for the safe treatment of Freud, the Nazis consented to allow him and his family to leave Vienna. First, however, Freud had to undergo the formality of intimidation and the confiscation of his property. Further, as a final galling indignity it was demanded that he sign a document stating he had been treated with fairness and courtesy. Being a realist, Freud did not hesitate to put his signature to the release but added, as a way of gilding the lily of his endorsement, "I can heartily recommend the Gestapo to anyone."

Accompanied by Ernest Jones, Freud left for England, where he died the following year, 1939. A study by Park in 1931 had attempted to assess the influence of Freud on psychology. Park reported that of fifty popular texts in general psychology published between 1910 and 1930, only four failed to mention Freud; no text after 1917, with the exception of Dunlap's, ignored psychoanalysis. She concluded, "Thus the status of Freudianism in academic psychology seems to be rather firmly established."

Within psychoanalysis the ideas of Melanie Klein, although given little serious notice in the United States, were attracting favorable attention in England. Melanie Klein (1882–1960) was the youngest child in a Viennese family. Her father was a dental surgeon, so it is not too surprising that she hoped to pursue a career in medicine. But this plan was abandoned when she became successively engaged at seventeen, married at twenty-one, and then the mother of three children. She attended the University of Vienna and went into analysis with Ferenczi and then Karl Abraham. Her marriage was unhappy, her older son died in early manhood, and she became estranged from her daughter. Around 1921, she began formulating her own ideas about analysis. She went to England in 1926, and her first book, *The Psycho-analysis of Children,* was published in 1932.

Melanie Klein believed that children exhibit details of their unconscious fantasy life when engaged in free, undirected play. Therefore, she thought, since play may be considered equivalent to the verbal free associations produced by adults, children as young as two or three can be analyzed and their unconscious conflicts interpreted to them.

From her psychoanalyses of children, Melanie Klein began to evolve theoretical formulations of her own. It seemed to her that the child in early infancy feels that he is in serious danger. He experiences this fear as a persecutory anxiety. Later in his development, between four to nine months, this fear changes from an anxiety about being harmed to an apprehension that he may harm loved ones by swallowing or incorporating them. This fear is experienced as a depressive anxiety. Actually, according to Klein, the persecutory anxiety is produced by a projection of the infant's own intense aggression and sadism, and the depressive anxiety is a form of guilt brought about by his recognition of his hostile feelings. Some analysts, when they contemplated the innocent faces of babies sleeping in their cribs, found it difficult to agree with Melanie Klein, but then one never knew. They did find it much easier to accept her suggestion of the possibility of psychoanalyzing youngsters through play, and they recognized this as a definite contribution to the study and treatment of children.

Meanwhile, Alfred Adler was still busy broadening his theory and casting it in a more positive mold. The concept of the striving for superiority was now thought of as a longing for perfection and fulfillment which is evidenced in all behavior, a desire through which the personality expresses itself throughout all its psychological functioning. As can be seen, Adler's views mellowed with the years. He had moved from basing his theoretical position upon the presence of an actual organ inferiority underlying behavior to one in which the emphasis was placed almost entirely upon the person's perceptions of himself and his external environment.

More specifically, Adler now believed that early in life the child sets a goal for himself which imposes a unity upon his actions. This setting of a goal is universal, each person is compelled to do this by his innate striving for perfection. But the particular goal selected by each person is unique and determined uniquely by the individual's inherited equipment and his perceptions and interpretations of himself and his world. By the age of five the child has developed his *style of life,* which has been considerably influenced by his appraisals and conceptions of his bodily functioning, strength, and vitality. This style of life is the pattern—the means or method—through which the individual seeks to achieve perfection or superiority. It supplies consistency and stability to the person's behavior; these characteristics, we might add, are to be regarded, in part, as advantageous since they contribute to the person's sense of identity. However, the maintenance of this stability and consistency may be purchased at the cost of excluding or distorting whatever threatens to be incompatible or challenging to the style of life, or in other words, at the cost of resistance to personal change and distorted perceptions of reality. (The Spanish philosopher Miguel de Unamuno [1864–1936] beautifully phrased ideas very similar to Adler's: "To propose to a man that he should be someone else, . . . is to propose to him that he should cease to be himself. . . . A man can change greatly, almost completely even, but the change must take place within his continuity.")

Further, Adler thought the unique goal of the individual could be either normal or pathological. A normal goal is one dominated by social feeling, a goal based on interest in reality, interest in others, and cooperative actions. In contrast, the pathological goal is private and self-centered, with the individual preoccupied, not with benefiting others, but with obtaining something from them. Of course, it is through a normal goal that the person best serves his own interests as well as those of his society. Finally, toward the close of his life Adler came to regard feelings of inferiority, not as abnormal in and of themselves, but instead as an inescapable condition of being human which provides the impetus for much that is desirable, as well as undesirable, in mankind.

In 1935, Alfred Adler and his family moved to the United States. His children Kurt and Alexandra became, like their father, psychiatrists. While on a lecture tour in Scotland in 1937 Adler died suddenly from a heart attack.

At the same time that Adler was modifying his formulations, Otto Rank was placing a similar emphasis on the more constructive aspects of human functioning. He was now discussing and making central to his theory his concept of *will:* "a positive guiding organization and integration of a self which utilizes creatively as well as inhibits and controls the instinctual drives . . . (something) that acts not merely reacts." In the light shed by this concept, resistance in analysis, as well as a child's refusal to obey his parents, though often frustrating to those who encounter or provoke the opposition, may be viewed positively as a conflict between wills, in which the patient or child attempts to assert his own individuality in the face of what he perceives as demands for his submission.

Conversely, Rank saw both positive and negative aspects in acquiescence. Through submission to the ideas of another, the person gains a measure of safety and security because he does not alienate that individual, but in so doing he sacrifices some of his uniqueness. Unlike Adler, who focused on the benefits of cooperation, Rank stressed the need for self-assertion and made the striving to assert one's will basic. From birth on throughout life, the individual struggles to separate himself from others and to express his own feelings and ideas. This growth in autonomy is far from easy. Each advance away from the influence of others eventuates in feelings of guilt for having estranged them, feelings of loss, and perhaps a fear of being totally abandoned; yet each act of compliance results in a sense of guilt and self-reproach for having betrayed or compromised one's self, while often eliciting a fear of losing one's own individuality.

Admittedly a difficult process and yet, Rank insisted, within each person, regardless of his normality or abnormality, this conflict and the striving for independence are to be found. Its ideal resolution, he conceived as an artistic, creative integration in which the person accepts his own will as right without feeling guilt for self-expression, and still maintains relationships with others in which their wills are accepted, when it is reasonable to do so, without feeling a loss of self.

Coincident with the development of his theory, a resolution seemed to be occurring in Rank's personal life. Although he continued to experience periods of depression and still found it necessary to undertake frequent transoceanic voyages between Paris and New York, in 1934 he decided to "settle" in New York City. He taught at the Graduate School for Jewish Social Work and lectured at the New York School of Social Work, Stanford, Philadelphia, Cleveland, Rochester, and Buffalo. Unfortunately, his marriage had not been happy, and with the arrival of his wife in the United States he appeared to suffer more intensely from feelings of depression. Three years later, in 1939, there was a divorce, Rank remarried, seemed briefly happy, and that same year died.

Among the other psychologists who made their way to the United States was Kurt Lewin. His description of personality functioning aroused much excitement and interest. Lewin, who was successively at Stanford, Cornell, and the University of Iowa during this period, saw each individual existing in a world of his present perception which he called the life space. A person's life space is everything that exists for him and that has some bearing on his current behavior. It includes needs, persons, objects, memories of the past, and thoughts of the future as they are perceived in the present. Lewin believed that as the person develops, his life space tends to become differentiated into various regions of phenomena or facts which are more or less connected or kept firmly apart.

Heightening the fascination of psychologists with Lewin's ideas were his ingenious diagrams for representing the life space, which tended to be elliptically shaped and which contain the person (P), arrows ("vectors" that represent forces in a given direction), plus and minus signs ("valences" that indicate whether the object is attractive or repulsive), and lines (boundaries) demarcating certain areas (regions and barriers within the life space). Human functioning was understood in terms of needs arising from within the person that arouse tensions which confer positive valences on those regions perceived to be instrumental in satisfying the needs, and negative valences on regions perceived as threatening to increase tensions. Movement or locomotion is supposed to be toward positive and away from negative valences. Lewin pointed out that his diagrams represent a topological space, i.e., representations of magnitudes are completely arbitrary and only ordinal relations are fixed. Therefore his "vectors" are not the same as the mathematician's vectors and can not be used in any quantitative way.

McDougall, who in 1927 had gone to chair the Psychology Department at Duke, could not understand why so many psychologists were excited about Lewin's work. He himself was not impressed and saw only one merit in the theory: its recognition of the existence within the person of "springs" of motivating energy. The theory as a whole he regarded as "hopelessly inadequate." "All the multitude of personal pecularities . . . Lewin's theory requires us to interpret in terms of his basket of potatoes, one differing from another merely in respect of size, position in the group, and thickness of its skin." All in all, McDougall failed to appreciate the significance of Lewin's work as a stimulus to the growth of an experimental social psychology, and it appears that he was still finding it difficult to effect the creative integration that Rank cherished.

For his own theory of hormic psychology, McDougall had words of praise and hope for success. It seemed to him that almost everyone now agreed behavior was purposive, and so he saw a possibility for the eventual acceptance of many of the other ideas he had championed. Although he now minimized instincts, they were still present in his theory to explain the energy source or motivating impulse for behavior. His concept of behavior, though, was quite different from what was commonly understood by the term. "Hormic activity is essentially mental activity, involving always cognition or awareness, striving initiated and governed by such cognition, and accruing satisfaction or dissatisfaction."

Essentially, hormic psychology saw behavior as occurring in the following sequence. An impulse or energy manifestation or instinct within the organism is channeled into approaches toward a goal, a striving, which is guided by a cognitive activity or awareness of the present situation. Once this activity begins, it tends to persist until the goal is reached or attained. Progress towards the goal and its attainment are experienced as pleasurable; frustrations and failures are experienced as disagreeable or painful. Activity terminates when the goal is reached and remains terminated until some new impulse arises, and the organism once again strives to obtain satisfaction.

The terms "horme" and "hormic" had been introduced by P. T. Nunn in 1920 to refer to both conscious and unconscious drives in animals, including man. By adopting the term McDougall acknowledged that hormic processes could be unconscious; but even then they involved, no matter how dimly, some foresight or knowledge of the goal by the person. All man's activities, McDougall insisted, are in pursuit of some goal which is foreseen and which man, instinctively or by his nature, desires to achieve. McDougall recognized that his emphasis on instincts, rather than on external stimuli, as the source for the arousal of behavior antagonized his colleagues and made it more difficult to predict what behavior would occur. However, when they questioned him as to why he allowed this room for uncertainty to exist, he justified his point of view by citing the principle of indeterminacy in physics as evidence that even in the most esteemed of sciences exact predictability was being abandoned as an attainable goal.

Until his death, McDougall continued to espouse unpopular views, often simply because they were unpopular and he felt they deserved an opportunity to be heard: he began experimentation on Lamarckian evolution to see if learning could be passed from one generation of rats to those following; he welcomed J. B. Rhine to Duke for research on clair-voyance and mental telepathy; and he provided a faculty position for William Stern at a time when Stern was no longer in favor in psychology.

Stern had fallen from grace because of his attacks on the Rorschach and because he represented armchair philosophy and was proud of it. He was still talking about the person: "an individual, unique whole whose activity is goal directed, who is related to the self, is open to the world, and who lives and experiences." Stern agreed with other psychologists that the person has certain potentialities, such as character and intelli-gence, which to become actualized require appropriate interactions with the outer world. But since Stern held firmly to his opinion that psychol-ogy is the science of the experiencing person, and so does not in itself include the environment, he insisted that psychology is only a *partial* science of the person—a conviction that was not likely to win him many followers among psychologists.

During this period there was much talk in psychology about traits of character, and Stern maintained that they could be described in-trinsically (a person's attitude toward something), comparatively (how one person's attitude compared with the way others held that attitude), and personally (how the attitude related to the individual's total char-acter). Stern defined character as the person's disposition to act or to will changes and exert influences in the world, a definition that coincides with popular usage but which makes the term virtually a synonym for personality.

For Gordon Allport (b. 1897), of Harvard University, character is a quite different concept and is defined as the evaluation of personality in ethical terms; and personality is "the dynamic organization within the individual of those psychophysical systems that determine his unique ad-justments to his environment." According to Allport, personality is a definite something of the nature of a psychophysical system. His concep-tion contrasts markedly with a behavioristic and social formulation of personality, which had been advanced by Vernon, among others. They asserted that personality is simply behavior that is socially evaluated, and therefore it ceases to exist when there is no one available to judge a per-son's actions; all that we then have is a person exhibiting behavior. (However, it is reasonable to argue that the person himself can evaluate his own behavior according to standards he has adopted from others.)

In Allport's schema the concept which is introduced to provide for the consistency and uniqueness which he stressed is to be found in every personality is the trait: "a generalized and focalized neuropsychic system (peculiar to the individual)" that initiates and guides adaptive and ex-pressive behavior. What gives maturity to the personality is, for Allport, the operation of the principle of functional autonomy.

By functional autonomy, Allport means that an individual may be motivated to continue engaging in an activity for entirely different reasons or purposes than those which originally cause his involvement. In other words, behavior may no longer be motivated by the gratification of instincts or early needs or tensions, and becomes largely independent of them. An activity is now pursued because it has become interesting, rewarding, and stimulating in its own right. What makes it so is the continuous challenge it presents to the individual to perfect his performance while engaging in it. This is, of course, very similar to Woodworth's idea that mechanisms may become drives.

Woodworth, by the way, was still trying to promote a reconciling and unifying definition of psychology. It troubled him to see belligerent schools of thought since he felt strongly that all psychologists are sincere in their beliefs, are competent investigators, and are searching as best they can for the truth. He suggested that psychology be defined as the study of the individual organism's activities, especially in relation to the environment. Woodworth hoped psychologists would rally round his definition, but many insisted on taking more specialized positions. Yet, at least in terms of general principles, some unification was being achieved.

Many personality theorists could agree that what is most important to know is not the objective situation in which a person finds himself but the person's perceptions of that situation. This phenomenological approach in understanding human behavior was becoming more and more popular. For example, around 1934, a psychiatrist Paul Schilder (1886–1940) developed the concept of the body image, the individual's conceptualization of his body and its boundaries. Schilder conceived of the body image as an evolving, changing picture affected by emotional disturbances and everyday events; in turn, the individual's body image strongly affects his experiencing of himself and his environment. To illustrate these interactions, Schilder urged his audience to imagine an injured person. For such a person, he predicted, everything is perceived as closer to his body and as about to touch his wound. Among others with phenomenological leanings that we have met are Stern, Rank, Lewin, Adler, McDougall. They constituted a large and growing group.

Of more significance, it was possible for two major unifying developments to begin because of the very fact that somewhat definite and "opposing" schools in psychology had become established and had gained recognition. Let us first examine the early steps in the direction of integrating and making more compatible the two major systems, psychoanalysis and behaviorism, and then view an interest of psychologists to reach out to embrace formulations from other disciplines, particularly cultural anthropolgy.

It had been argued by some behaviorists that the concept of emotion should be eliminated from psychology as superfluous. After all, their argument went, emotions are only behavior; *ergo* when behavior is understood, emotions will be understood without having to bother about them specifically. Buttressing their contention were the disappointments experienced in evolving a satisfactory theory of emotions. Cannon's theory, Lashley pointed out, had run into some difficulties. To be sure, experimentation had demonstrated the localization of motor centers for emotional expression in the hypothalamus, but no evidence had been found to indicate the existence of special centers for "feeling tone." Nor, for that matter, were there any other areas of the brain where existence of a neurological basis for affect could be demonstrated.

But unfortunately for those who contended for parsimony, it no longer seemed feasible to throw out emotions when they seemed more important than ever in understanding behavior. The results of at least nine studies agreed that recall of the pleasant occurred more frequently than recall of the unpleasant, regardless of whether the items were school grades, nonsense syllables paired with odors, or previous experiences. Of more significance, even the behaviorists were starting to become involved with the investigation of feelings.

Clark Hull had not been frustrated for long by the ban on the continuation of his hypnosis research at Yale. After publishing *Hypnosis and Suggestibility* (1933), he turned his full attention to "pure" research and learning theory. Around the same year, 1933, the Institute of Human Relations was established at Yale to bring together ideas from psychology, anthropology, psychiatry, and sociology. The learning theory being developed by Hull provided a framework for integrating the formulations and concepts of the various disciplines at the Institute.

Among Hull's colleagues at the Institute were: Neal Miller (b. 1909), who had a Ph.D. from Yale and a training analysis at the Vienna Institute of Psychoanalysis in 1935–1936; O. H. Mowrer (b. 1907), who received his doctorate from Johns Hopkins in 1932 and arrived at Yale as a Sterling fellow in 1934; Robert Sears (b. 1908), who had spent the interval between earning his Ph.D. from Yale in 1932 and his return there in 1936 as an instructor at the University of Illinois; and John Dollard (b. 1900), who obtained his doctorate in sociology from the University of Chicago in 1931. Together these men tried to interrelate Hullian learning principles and psychoanalysis.

One of Hull's major principles is that the tendency for a reaction to occur is strengthened whenever the response is closely associated with the reduction of a need, i.e., whenever the response is reinforced. The concept of anxiety, of great importance in psychoanalysis, can be considered a learned response whose reduction is reinforcing the organism. Mowrer thought that since anxiety generally occurs in advance of an actual danger, it can be viewed as an anticipatory reaction which motivates the organism to cope with a potential threat and thereby diminishes the likelihood of any harm. According to his formulation, those actions which reduce anxiety are reinforced or tend to be learned.

The crowning achievement of this Yale group during the thirties was the publication of *Frustration and Aggression* in 1939. L. W. Doob (b. 1909), who had obtained his Ph.D. from Harvard in 1934, joined with the others in writing this work. Its major hypothesis is that aggression is always a consequence of frustration.

Very briefly, their ideas run somewhat as follows: If we assume that an individual is being frustrated, his tendency to make aggressive responses varies directly with the amount of frustration. However, even with much frustration, there may be no display of aggression in overt behavior. It has then been inhibited, and the likelihood of this inhibition taking place depends upon the amount of punishment the person expects to receive if he expresses his hostility openly. These inhibited aggressive responses tend to be displaced, or expressed in some modified form. But no matter how the person expresses his aggression, whether displaced or directed at the frustrating object, any expression will lessen the probability of other aggressive responses being aroused. By these few principles, these psychologists attempted to explain a variety of behaviors, such as delinquency and adolescent turmoil, in terms of differing manifestations of aggression in response to some frustration.

Frustration itself was analyzed in an article by Saul Rosenzweig, Mowrer, *et. al.* (Incidentally, Rosenzweig [b. 1907] was not a member of the Yale group but obtained his Ph.D. from Harvard and was employed as a research psychologist at Worcester State Hospital.) They regarded the frustrating situation as being brought about by external and internal deprivations, privations, and other conflicts. In this context, people are seen as differing in two respects: one, they differ in their capacities to tolerate frustration; and two, they differ in their reactions to frustration. Now it is also possible to evaluate such a reaction along four dimensions: (1) its adequacy or inadequacy in coping with the situation; (2) its specificity or nonspecificity (a nonspecific reaction to frustration would be feeling tired or falling asleep); (3) its directness or indirectness in relation to the frustrating object; and (4) its perseverativeness or defensiveness. The defensive reaction can be further broken down into aggression directed at some external object (extrapunitive reaction), aggression directed at the person himself in the form of self-condemnation or guilt (intrapunitive reaction), and situations in which the aggression might be repressed or the frustration denied (impunitive reaction). With the help of this analysis a way now seemed open for launching an experimental attack on the problem.

A very different analysis of frustration was being made at Harvard by Henry A. Murray. Murray (b. 1893) received an A.B. in History from Harvard in 1915, an M.D. from Columbia in 1919, an M.A. in Biology from Columbia in 1920, a Ph.D. in Biochemistry from Cambridge in 1927, and finally training in psychoanalysis. He became director of the Harvard Psychological Clinic in 1928.

Murray's two basic concepts were those of need and press. A need was defined by him as a construct, or hypothetical concept, representing a force in the brain region which organizes perception and action so as to modify an unsatisfactory situation. Needs may be aroused by internal processes, but generally they tend to be elicited by circumstances in the environment, or press, that affect in some way, favorably or unfavorably, the well-being of the person. Murray tentatively listed twenty needs, including achievement, affiliation, aggression, autonomy, deference; he took note of some sixteen forms of press, among them danger, loss, family insupport, sex, inferiority. When the individual perceives a press, a need is aroused which eventuates in some pattern of behavior for reducing the tension (need) thus generated; this interactive process between needs and press is called a *thema*. We can see that, in contrast to the hypothesis of the Yale group, Murray saw aggression as only one of the possible needs which might be aroused by a frustrating press (though, of course, it can be argued that the other needs which appear in response to some frustration, such as abasement, are varients of, or defenses against, aggression). In any case the important point is that psychoanalytic concepts were being assimilated into the mainstream of psychology. Let us now consider the press exerted upon psychologists by the work of the cultural anthropologists.

During the early thirties, Edward Sapir (1884–1939) seemed to express the self-confidence of most cultural anthropologists when he claimed their discipline is of great value in specifying which forms of behavior might be universal and which forms seem to be inherited and which acquired. On the basis of anthropological investigations already completed Sapir described a different way of looking at personality: "A personality is carved out by the subtle interaction of those systems of ideas which are characteristic of the culture as a whole, as well as of those systems of ideas which get established for the individual through more special types of participation, with the physical and psychological needs of the individual organism, which cannot take over any of the cultural material that is offered in its original form but works it over more or less completely so that it integrates with those needs."

By "culture" Sapir meant what Ralph Linton (1893–1953), a fellow anthropologist, defined as the "sum total of the behavior patterns, attitudes, and values shared by members of a given society." Linton pointed out that no individual can be fully aware of all his culture or participate in all its ramifications. Nevertheless, the members of a culture are differentiated into families and age and sex categories, and demands are imposed upon those in each category for performing certain tasks according to certain procedures. Therefore, Linton claimed that with knowledge of the culture and the categories to which an individual belonged, a foundation would be provided for predicting the behavior of the person in a given situation.

The idea that a culture requires its members to act in certain prescribed ways was carried a step further by Ruth Benedict (1887–1948), who stressed that a specific culture tolerates the expression of only certain personality characteristics and behaviors while the appearance of deviations from these are considered abnormalities. Therefore, what is normal or abnormal may be viewed as relative to the particular cultural setting. In the same vein, Abram Kardiner (b. 1891) offered the concept of a basic personality type. Supposedly, the primary institutions (the prescribed patterns for obtaining food, dealing with aggression, forming families) result in a modal kind of personality structure for that culture. This basic personality, Kardiner suggested, attains uniqueness by the individual's idiosyncratic ways of coping with the primary institutions in order to ameliorate their tyranny.

However, not everyone thought that culture is only tyrannical. Some felt it is not actually such a bad chap and cited instances where a culture might even allow its members an approved opportunity or two for expressing in one medium what it prohibits in another. Drawing upon Adler, Beaglehole thought that when a culture represses a segment of behavior, it is forced to offer a socially approved compensation for what is repressed through media such as the dance, art, and religious ceremony.

The studies of cultures were also clarifying the extent to which human behavior is learned. Among others, Margaret Mead (b. 1901) reported how sex behaviors, which many had considered to be innate patterns of response, appear to be products of social learning. On the island of New Guinea, Mead studied three cultures. She noted that both males and females among the Arapesh were gentle and cooperative, among the Mundugumor both sexes were violent and aggressive, and among the Tchambuli there seemed to be a reversal of the behaviors found in Western cultures since the males were artists and dancers while the females provided the food and dominated the household (Some psychologists are uncertain that this really differs from a pattern observed in the United States!). Evidence such as Mead's is most compelling. It was generally agreed that the anthropologists had established the point that behaviors which some had thought to be instinctive or inherited are actually capable of modification by the culture and that they might be completely a product of learning.

Anthropologists also vigorously criticized those psychologists who had postulated qualitative differences between the mentalities of primitive and civilized men. They argued that what distinguishes primitive societies from those called civilized is the lack of a written tradition, which thus makes cultural transmission dependent upon the memories of some members of the group. But they did not consider this illiteracy sufficient cause to justify hypothesizing a dichotomy in intellectual functioning between these peoples and "modern" mankind. For one thing, it is obvious that the various primitive cultures differ considerably from each other. Furthermore, in some respects, e.g., the kinship system among the Australian aborigines, their customs and practices are more complex than those found in Western societies. Accordingly, it would no longer do, anthropologists warned, to make a distinction between cultures on the basis of primitiveness. Nor would it be possible to claim knowledge of a culture by superficial observations of the living habits of its people and the mechanical conveniences they enjoyed. Just as psychologists had discovered in the case of individuals responding to stimuli, anthropologists had discovered with cultures that they have to be studied as wholes, against their ecological backgrounds, and with knowledge of their training methods, norms, and deviations.

Most psychologists responded to admonitions from anthropologists with good grace, feeling, no doubt, that the criticisms were surely directed at members of the profession other than themselves. There is, after all, ample room in the environment for the concept of a culture, and it fitted nicely into justifications for the significance of acquired, as against innate, behaviors. Perhaps as a humorous paradox, T. L. Kelley suggested that cultural changes passed on from one generation to the next could be viewed profoundly as an instance of the inheritance of acquired characteristics. Unfortunately, heredity and Lamarckian evolution were serious matters among psychologists in the thirties, so it is unlikely that many relaxed sufficiently to laugh at Kelley's little joke.

Clearly, the contributions of cultural anthropology created much excitement in the social sciences and psychiatry, and we shall consider them further in the sections and chapters that follow. A related development was experimentation concerning the effects of social variables on psychological processes, such as remembering and perception. In 1932, Bartlett illustrated that a person's recollection of the events of an incident is distorted in the direction of agreement with his cultural values and expectations, and in 1935, Sherif published one of the first studies of a type which aimed to show the influence of a group in shaping an individual's perception.

Sherif hypothesized that perceptual patterns are molded in different ways in different cultures. Therefore what a person perceives individually might be altered when he engages in the "same" act of perceiving within a group. Sherif tried to demonstrate this by an experiment involving autokinetic movement (This refers to the phenomenon that a person observing a stationary pinpoint of light in a totally darkened room will report, after a few moments, that the light appears to be moving.). Sherif obtained estimates of autokinetic movement when a person sits in a darkened room alone and also when groups of people participate in making estimates aloud. Within the group setting the estimates tended to converge toward a common standard, i.e., a social norm of the extent of movement seemed to become established. Whether this represents an alteration in perception or a change in reported judgments is not clear. But nevertheless, Sherif was successful in demonstrating experimentally the effects of social variables on psychological processes. The hope for a simple stimulus-response formulation of behavior, which had seemed so feasible only twenty years before, had now, under the impact of various psychoanalytic and interpersonal considerations, become virtually untenable.

DIAGNOSTIC TECHNIQUES

During the thirties a deluge of tests rained down upon psychologists and the public. Much of this inventiveness centered in the United States. On the European continent what conduciveness there had been for the growth of psychological testing was fast being dissipated by the repressive measures of dictatorial regimes.

For example, in 1936 the Central Committee of the Communist Party of the Union of Soviet Socialist Republics formally abolished the construction and use of psychological tests. The Committee based its proclamation on the work in genetics done by I. V. Mitchurin and T. D. Lysenko, who believed inheritable characteristics could be induced by the individual's experiences or environmental manipulations. This meant that Mitchurin and Lysenko supported Lamarck's rather disreputable doctrine that acquired changes could be passed on to succeeding generations. It therefore seemed fruitless to study or test for innate abilities among the Bolsheviks since by placing an individual in a suitable environment it would be possible to change him to such an extent that he could perform any human practicable task. And their theory predicted a considerable dividend because after one person had learned a task his descendents could learn it even more easily.

Within a democracy, despite one's faith in the potency of the environment, there are limits to how free one can be in manipulating fellow citizens. Since environments cannot be strictly controlled and people cannot simply be moved hither and thither, it still makes sense to do testing whether one believes in partly inherited or wholly acquired intellectual functioning. During 1936, the most frequently used tests in the United States were the Stanford-Binet, Porteus Mazes, Arthur Performance Scale, Healy Picture Completion, Pintner-Paterson, Stanford Achievement, Merrill-Palmer, Gesell Developmental Schedules, and Kuhlmann-Anderson. Up through 1936, the six tests that had the largest numbers of studies published about them were the following: the Stanford-Binet, with about 141 studies, ranked first; the Rorschach, with 68 studies, had come up rapidly to capture second place; the Bernreuter Personality Inventory; Seashore Measures of Musical Talent; Strong Vocational Interest Blank; and American Council on Education Psychological Examination for College Freshmen. Other tests were emerging in profusion so let us note the essentials of what was happening.

Most psychologists engaged in the field of test construction considered themselves, and were considered by others, to be psychometricians. Their efforts were directed at devising techniques which would arrange or order persons along a continuum from little (least) to more (most) of the trait, ability, or attribute that they hoped to measure. In the general classification of intellectual functioning their testing methods seemed to be working satisfactorily. But in the evaluation of most other characteristics of the person, psychometricians were encountering difficulties. Simultaneously, clinical psychologists, frequently referred to as psychometrists and not too happy about their identity, were impatiently casting about for techniques that would assess "latent" personality functioning. Troubled by what they felt was a lack of professional status, the clinicians hoped that through the use of more global and less statistical personality measures they would earn the understanding and respect of their psychiatric colleagues.

Within psychology as a whole, the atomistic, molecular approach to behavior was fading into disrepute, and a molar, dynamic approach emphasizing interactions and interrelations between variables was in the ascendant. To meet the need for global measures and as an expression of this changing orientation, relatively unstructured tests emerged which imposed, in the main, far greater demands than heretofore upon the interpretative skills and judgment of the persons administering them. Now, let us examine this picture more closely.

Two well-received performance scales appeared early in the decade. In 1930, Grace Arthur (b. 1883) published the Arthur Point Scale of Performance Tests. Intended primarily for use with children between the ages of six to sixteen years, Form I of the Scale was composed of eight restandardized tests from the Pintner-Paterson, plus the Kohs Block Designs, plus the Porteus Mazes. Arthur planned her Scale to correlate highly with the Stanford-Binet, and it seemed to do so satisfactorily with children up to twelve years of age. In 1934, the Cornell-Coxe Performance Ability Scale was published. It covered the same age range as the Arthur and was composed of seven restandardized tests from various sources. Ethel Cornell (b. 1892) and W. W. Coxe (b. 1886) constructed their Scale so that it would have little correlation with the Stanford-Binet, and in this they seemed to be successful. The two scales were thus designed to serve different purposes: the first to be a nonverbal substitute for Binet revisions; the second to supplement them.

The most popular Binet revision, the Stanford-Binet, was published in revised form in 1937. Tests were provided at age levels from two years to a Superior Adult III category, including items for those levels which had been absent from the 1916 revision, eleven and thirteen years. There were two equivalent forms of the scale, L and M, the letters presumably referring to the first initials of its authors Lewis Terman and Maud Merrill (b. 1888). The revision was standardized on a sample of about three thousand American-born white children ranging in age from one and a half to eighteen years, with efforts to control the influence of geographic location and socioeconomic status.

Criticisms of the 1937 Revision were similar to those made for the 1916 Scale. There were too many verbal items. The test was of questionable value with adults. The use of "mental ages" at the upper end of the Scale was misleading. The test items were a hodgepodge.

Nevertheless, it was agreed that the 1937 Revision was a marked improvement over its predecessor, and the Scale was widely and quickly accepted by clinical psychologists. Early studies encouragingly reported "constancy" with children of school age, i.e., ordinarily IQs did not vary more than 5.5 points from one administration to the next.

Efforts to evaluate the significance of scatter on the Stanford-Binet continued to prove fruitless. There was no consensus with regard to any quantitative measure of scatter, nor had any numerical computation of spread of scores revealed any significant differences between groups of children thought to be normal, feebleminded, delinquent, or neurotic. It had been found, however, that scores on the vocabulary subtest seemed less impaired by mental illness than scores on the other items. Harriet Babcock (1877–1952) thought it might be advantageous to make use of this finding as a means for determining the extent of intellectual deterioration in psychiatric disturbances.

In the early thirties, Babcock's Deterioration Test attracted the attention of psychologists working in state hospitals. The test involved administering the vocabulary items of the Stanford-Binet to obtain an estimate of the patient's pre-illness level of overall intellectual ability, and then administering twenty-four tests sampling speed of response and capacity for learning to obtain a measure of current mental functioning. The discrepancy between the two estimates was supposed to indicate the extent, if any, of mental deterioration.

J. McV. Hunt warned of two difficulties in evaluating test results and experimental findings when the test was used with psychiatric patients: one, there was an alarming tendency for psychologists to naively accept psychiatric diagnoses and nosology as factual when, in reality, both the classification scheme and the diagnosis were relative to the predilections, training, skills, and biases of a particular psychiatrist; and two, most psychologists were ignoring the problem of the patient's motivation. Therefore, samples of the same diagnostic grouping might not be comparable, and the nomenclature might be, to a great extent, unreliable and invalid. Further, in most studies it was virtually impossible to determine whether the patient could not or would not perform the task in question or was simply not interested in what was being asked of him. The relevance of Hunt's remarks for tests such as the Babcock was obvious.

Mental deterioration was given some consideration by Wechsler when he published his intelligence scale, the Wechsler-Bellevue, in 1939. Deterioration was evaluated by comparing the scores on subtests which supposedly did not decrease with increasing age against the scores on those subtests which did decrease with the passage of time. But this diagnostic feature was tentative and just so much frosting on the cake. For Wechsler had presented psychologists with an instrument designed to measure effectively the intellectual functioning of adults.

David Wechsler (b. 1896) had received his Ph.D. from Columbia in 1925. At first his published interests centered in evaluating the significance of the psychogalvanic reflex, but later he turned to the problems of measuring intelligence. In 1932, Wechsler accepted the position of Chief Psychologist at Bellevue Psychiatric Hospital in New York and while there developed his test. It was composed of a Verbal and a Performance Scale with five subtests in each, respectively: information, comprehension, arithmetic similarities, and memory span for digits; object assembly, picture arrangement, block design, digit symbol, and picture completion; plus a vocabulary test as an alternate.

The Wechsler-Bellevue was standardized in 670 white children from seven to sixteen years and 1,081 white adults aged from seventeen to seventy years, all of whom resided in New York City and surrounding areas. Efforts were made to control for education and occupation, and the scale was intended for use with persons from ten to sixty years of age.

Wechsler defined intelligence as an *"aggregate or global capacity of the individual to act purposefully, to think rationally and to deal effectively with his environment,"* a definition that indicated his support of Spearman's two-factor theory. He rejected the mental age concept in favor of point scales: an IQ value of 100 was assigned to the mean score of an age group; an IQ value of 90 was assigned to a score that is minus one probable error from the mean; this done, it became possible to calculate IQ tables for conversion of scores for a particular age group on the Verbal, Performance, and Full Scale into IQ estimates. Therefore, in the case of adults the score obtained by an individual is compared with the scores of others of approximately the same age; in contrast, on the Stanford-Binet the adult's score is evaluated only in relation to the successes obtained by children and adolescents.

By virtue of the way the IQ tables were constructed, the classification of intelligence on the Wechsler-Bellevue is symmetrical. Approximately 2 percent of the population—the group considered "defective"—are assigned IQs of 65 and below. Approximately 2 percent of the population—the group considered "very superior"—obtain IQs of 128 and above.

In his development of the scale Wechsler found that scores on the subtests, depending upon which specific subtest is involved, begin to decrease gradually between the ages of fifteen and twenty-two years, and fall more rapidly after age thirty-five. Wechsler's findings indicated to some psychologists that intellectual abilities continue to grow until early adulthood and then decline. But to other psychologists Wechsler's results only illustrate again that intellectual growth varies with the specific ability and the means by which it is assessed.

Kuhlmann introduced another revision of the Binet in 1939 but it was far overshadowed in popularity by the Stanford Revision and the Wechsler-Bellevue. The California Tests of Mental Maturity, group scales of intelligence, were introduced around 1937. They reflected the view of Thorndike and Thurstone that intelligence is composed of independent abilities or factors. Intended primarily for school children, the California Tests sample factors of visual acuity, motor coordination, auditory acuity, memory, spatial relationships, reasoning, and vocabulary.

Around 1938, Thurstone came out with his Primary Mental Abilities Test. Based on the results of his factor analytic research, his group scale was supposed to measure reasoning, word fluency, verbal comprehension, number facility, spatial perception, and rote memory.

Also in 1938, Gesell and Helen Thompson provided developmental schedules for the evaluation of infants between four and fifty-six weeks of age. Meanwhile research studies were indicating that it was not possible to predict later intelligence scores accurately from scores made on tests administered in infancy.

Around 1936, Edgar Doll introduced a novel developmental schedule, the Vineland Social Maturity Scale, intended to measure social competence. Designed for use with persons from infancy to thirty years of age, the Vineland is unique in that its scoring is based on an interview with someone well acquainted with the person rather than the person himself. There are 117 items, grouped in age levels, ranging from "balances head" to "directs or manages work of others." The scores on the scale are expressed in terms of Social Age, which, when divided by the chronological age, produce a Social Quotient (SQ). Doll's rationale for this new use for division is that some individuals, such as delinquents, may be high in intellectual level but low in social maturity, and vice versa. However, with preschool children the items are so similar to those found on the Gesell that the Vineland provides a means for estimating their developmental levels when it is not possible actually to test them.

The Strong Vocational Interest Blank made its appearance in 1938. Earlier in the decade, in 1931, a somewhat similar test, the Allport-Vernon Study of Values, was first published. The Allport-Vernon is based on Spranger's typology and is therefore a device that attempts to discover the value systems of an individual, i.e., his preference for aesthetic, theoretical, economic, social, political, and religious values.

Among the many personality inventories introduced in this period were the following: Thurstone Personality Schedule; Bernreuter Personality Inventory; Bell Adjustment Inventory; Rogers Adjustment Inventory; Humm-Wadsworth Temperament Scale; The California Test of Personality; Aspects of Personality; Maller Personality Sketches; and the Guilford Inventory of Factors STDCR (social introversion, thinking introversion, depression, cycloid tendency, and rhathmyia, i.e., carefree disposition). In most of the inventories the person is confronted with straightforward questions, such as "Are you troubled with shyness?" His task is simply to answer each item as truthfully as possible by checking Yes, No, or ?

One of the difficulties with some of the inventories is that they seem to be measuring more than they are supposed to measure. A "simple" test of extraversion-introversion was found by the Guilfords to contain a minimum of eighteen group factors, such as impulsiveness, and interest in self. Another difficulty with the inventories is that they do not seem to be measuring the same thing, even when it is reasonable to expect that they would do so, and it then becomes a problem to know what it is they are measuring. Moore and Steele reported a study in which they used the Thurstone Personality Schedule, Allport's Ascendence-Submission Test, Laird's Personality Inventory, Neymann-Kohlstedt Submission Test, June Downey Test, and the Pressy X-O Test; they found little correlation between the results on any two tests.

A third difficulty with the inventories is that the scores can easily be faked. Kelly, Miles, and Terman, using the Stanford Test of Masculinity-Feminity, observed that their subjects, both male and female, would obligingly shift their scores considerably in either direction when asked to respond to the items as they thought a member of the other sex would. The transparency, or obviousness, of the inventories is an issue which troubled many clinicians greatly, not only because the person may choose to misrepresent himself, but also because certain items may be alarming to someone who is oversensitive to his being asked questions which have to do with abnormal behavior.

Rosenzweig suggested that an experimental rather than a statistical attitude in test construction would greatly improve matters. Instead of asking people Yes-No questions that it is hoped will prove related to personality, he urged the development of techniques based on well-defined hypotheses which yield performances or actual behaviors that can be evaluated. If, however, his test-constructing colleagues should persevere in asking questions, he strongly recommended that they at least regard the responses as raw data in need of interpretation, and not as necessarily valid answers.

Yet even if success in measuring traits had been more demonstrably achieved, a number of psychologists would still have regarded the psychometric approach to personality as in fact bankrupt. "Too atomistic," would have been the contention of some. There is a need for qualitative as well as quantitative knowledge would have been the argument of others. The demand was fast growing for global, qualitative test procedures which were both simple and disarming in the behavioral tasks they impose upon those taking them.

Graphology certainly provided a sample of behavior for interpretation, and Robert Saudek, a leading graphologist, enjoyed considerable favor among psychologists. Saudek had founded the journal *Character and Personality*, which was later called the *Journal of Personality*. One of his interesting studies showed that identical handwriting could be produced by different persons. Such an occurrence is rare—Saudek guessed that the chances of it happening were one in ten thousand—but happen it did in some cases of identical twins and even between people not related or known to one another.

Saudek's death in 1935 was undoubtedly a setback to graphology and probably made it more difficult for the field to gain acceptance in the United States. However it is doubtful that Saudek's efforts could have altered the outcome much. Graphology's easy corruptability and consequent notoriety dampened what little appeal it might have had as a diagnostic technique.

A few psychiatrists were suggesting diagnostic procedures. In 1930, Appel thought it would be a good idea to ask children to draw a house, or persons, or members of their family and then obtain their comments about their drawings. He found this procedure helped him to understand the child's unconscious problems. The same was true when he had children make ink blots and noted their comments about them. In 1932, Schwartz reported on his use of pictures that illustrated children in different kinds of social situations. He would ask the youngsters to describe the pictures and answer questions about them. Along the same lines, David Levy claimed he found it profitable to present children with dolls representing the members of the family and then observe how they played with them. Not only was this technique diagnostic, but Levy thought some of the children derived therapeutic benefits from just expressing their feelings in play. Although Levy seemed to have shifted his interests from the Rorschach, his former student Samuel J. Beck was enthusiastically following up this work.

Samuel Beck (b. 1896) had concentrated upon the classics during his first three undergraduate years at Harvard. He was prevented from entering his fourth year by a lack of money and so took a job as a newspaper reporter in Cleveland. That job lasted ten years, of which the last three were spent by Beck in covering the criminal and juvenile courts. His career in journalism is regarded by Beck as a profitable interlude in which his skills in analyzing information objectively and precisely were sharpened. He returned to Harvard in 1926 and obtained his B.A. His M.A. and Ph.D. were received from Columbia in 1927 and 1932. During his graduate school days he spent a year as a Commonwealth Fund Fellow at the Institute for Child Guidance in New York, where he met Levy and became acquainted with the Rorschach; there followed a year as psychologist at the Jewish Board of Guardians in New York; and three years as senior resident psychologist at Boston Psychopathic Hospital. In 1933, Beck became a research associate at Harvard Medical School, and the following year was awarded a fellowship which enabled him to study the Rorschach with Oberholzer in Zurich. Beginning in 1936, Beck headed the clinical psychology laboratory at Michael Reese Hospital in Chicago.

In 1930, a study conducted by Beck, one involving diagnosis of the feebleminded using Rorschach's ink blots, was the first published research about the Rorschach in the United States. Other studies with the instrument quickly followed, and Beck's research efforts were soon joined by those of Marguerite Hertz (b. 1899) and Bruno Klopfer. The initial problems in developing the test, as Beck saw them, were: one, obtaining statistical norms so that good form responses could be specified and "rare" detail areas of the blot delineated; and, two, testing patients representing a variety of diagnostic categories so that their differential personality patterns could be ascertained.

By 1935, there was still no standardized way to administer the test or score its responses, and the studies reporting positive findings about its reliability and validity were few. Yet Hertz concluded her survey of the Rorschach literature with the prediction that the test would grow in popularity because: "(it) is another form of the free association technique which has been found useful for describing personality in the past." Appropriately enough, though perhaps inevitably, the "useful" in the last statement was not quantified.

It seemed reasonable to expect little encouragement from studies or experimentation with the Rorschach until some agreement could be reached on how to administer, score, and interpret the test. Tending to make such an agreement more and more difficult to achieve was the fact that as familiarity with the technique increased so did the complexities of scoring and interpreting it.

Some psychologists remembered that Rorschach had made distinctions within the categories introversion and extraversion. He distinguished an active or voluntary introversion from a passive or pathologic introversion. The former is exemplified by a poet and the latter by a catatonic patient. Similarly, the active extravert, e.g., the socialite, is to be distinguished from the passive extravert, e.g., the manic individual. Implicit in Rorschach's distinction is the issue of how much control the person is able to exert over his behavior. Perhaps, it was thought by some of Rorschach's followers, this control could be evaluated by the appropriateness of form in color and movement responses.

On a somewhat broader scale, Beck took note of some general principles. All Rorschach determinants (color, form, movement) are dependent upon the person's ability to organize stimuli into a meaningful relationship. Moreover, all responses having the same determinant involve the same psychological process. However the same determinant does not always have the same interpretative significance and can represent behaviors of differing social value. For example, movement always indicates the "inner ability to create fantasy" but might be overtly expressed in artistic productions, daydreams, or delusions. The psychologist skilled in the use of the Rorschach, Beck concluded, is supposed to be able to make these meaningful differentiations.

In 1937, Beck published a manual for the Rorschach and introduced several innovations: an organization score (Z); the substitution of the term "Experience Balance" for *Erlebnistypus;* a classification scheme for content categories; and some normative tables for determining good form responses and rare details. That same year also saw Klopfer and Kelley provide instructions for administering the Rorschach.

During the early thirties shading determinants had not been formally recognized by American psychologists. Back in Switzerland, though, H. Binder had been stressing their significance and by 1937 they could no longer be ignored. Binder believed an emphasis on the dark shadings indicated a dysphoric mood, while a touch of euphoria is evidenced by percepts determined by light shadings. On the other hand, Klopfer thought shading responses indicated sensitivity or a cautious desire for contact with the environment. Whatever their meaning, all Rorschach experts agreed they now had to be scored.

Meanwhile the Rorschach was encountering criticism from psychologists on three counts. It was too subjective in administration, scoring, and interpretation. It was of questionable reliability. It was of dubious validity.

Yet much to the consternation of its critics, the test grew in popularity. There simply was no other technique which allowed clinicians to make statements about global personality functioning; in time it was hoped that the legitimate objections to its use would be proven groundless. Encouraging its users were occasional positive reports, such as the one by Hertz and Rubenstein. They reported a Rorschach record had been presented to three experts, Hertz, Beck, and Klopfer, who made their interpretations "blind," i.e., they had seen neither the patient nor his case history. Happily, their interpretations were very much in agreement and were substantiated by the case history material. It surely seemed that with increasing experience, equal successes could be had by all serious students of the Rorschach.

So enthusiastic had been the response of clinicians to the Rorschach that one of its early and most severe critics made an ambivalent attempt to "jump on the bandwagon." If psychologists wanted ambiguous stimuli, well then William Stern was willing to supply them and go those ink blots one better. Stern asked his colleague Karl Struve to make three pictures of clouds of unsurpassable nebulosity. These cloud pictures had neither symmetry, nor contours, nor backgrounds. They were just broad expanses with internal variations in shading. Probably Stern intended his cloud pictures to be a bitter joke. If so, he was successful, for few clinicians took his test seriously.

In 1935, Christiana D. Morgan and Henry Murray presented the Thematic Apperception Test. The TAT consists of thirty pictures, mostly of people in a variety of situations, and a blank card. The person is supposed to make up a story about each picture which describes what has happened, what is happening, what will happen, and what are the feelings of the characters. Only twenty cards are to be administered to any one person, ten at a sitting, with the selection of cards determined by the individual's sex and age. Each story is recorded verbatim and analyzed for its thema, i.e., the interaction of needs, press, and outcome. Obviously, the TAT is a time-consuming procedure and has the additional disadvantage of taxing the clinician's stenographic powers to the limit. Nevertheless, it was received with enthusiasm when its cards became available in 1936 as a promising technique for determining the individual's conflicts and attitudes.

Some interest was evidenced in two techniques offered by Margaret Lowenfeld. Her Mosaic Test (1931) requires the person to make a design from tiles of differing geometric shapes and colors. She hoped the designs produced by the individual would yield information about his personality functioning and aid in establishing a psychiatric diagnosis. At the time, however, she regarded the test as still being in an early stage of development and therefore best restricted to experimental uses and continued investigation. Her other procedure was the World Test (1939). This test asks the person to construct an environment using settings and models of people, animals, houses, and other *objets d'art*. Naturally, once the scene is made a story can be elicited about it. Like the Mosaic Test, the World Test was in need of considerable study in order to ascertain its usefulness.

Another device that had possibilities as a diagnostic technique, in particular as an instrument to evaluate the blind, was the tautophone, described in 1939 by Shakow and Rosenzweig. The tautophone is based on Skinner's verbal summator, which had been used to study latent speech. An individual hears a voice speaking conversationally but unintelligibly and has to guess what he thinks the voice is saying. It was hoped that his guesses would reveal something about the way he functioned as a person.

The Bender-Gestalt Test made its appearance in 1938. Lauretta Bender (b. 1897), a psychiatrist who received her M.D. in 1926 from the State University of Iowa, became a member of the faculty at New York University in 1930, and in 1936 married Paul Schilder. Her test is composed of nine geometric designs based on figures devised by the Gestalt psychologist Max Wertheimer in his work on perception. The person is told simply to copy them to the best of his ability. It was thought that disturbances in the process of perception and reproduction would indicate pathology, and more specifically organic brain disease and schizophrenia. Furthermore, in using her test with children, Bender found a chronological progression in the accuracy with which the figures could be reproduced. The test therefore had potential value in assessing the level of maturation of visual motor coordination, in addition to its possibilities for helping in psychiatric diagnosis, and was quickly accepted for use.

In 1939 L. K. Frank (b. 1890) proposed the term "projective methods" for those techniques, such as the Rorschach, the TAT, and the tautophone, where the meaning of the material is not determined by the tester but by "the personality who gives it, or imposes upon it, his private idiosyncratic meaning and organization." Therefore, according to Frank, what made a test projective was not the test itself but the method by which its results were evaluated. Any test can be considered projective if the individual's performance is analyzed and interpreted in terms of its processes and configurations; the *projective method* can be applied to behavior elicited by any scale and by any situation.

The tests thus far presented, while impressive, were not the only methods put forth during the thirties for diagnosing human behavior. Some advocated the evaluation of personality by an investigation of the functioning of the endocrine glands. Charles Dickens was one of many notables treated to a postmortem glandular analysis: insufficient parathyroids, an overstrained thyroid, overtaxed adrenals, and an excess pituitary. Few psychologists were receptive to this approach.

Research papers of more lasting interest to clinicians were those about individual differences in electroencephalographs (EEG). Hans Berger, a German neuropsychiatrist, after fifteen years of trying, was the first to be successful in recording electrical activity from the intact human head. This event took place in 1929. In 1934, at Harvard Medical School the first record of human brain waves in the United States on an ink writer came from the cortex of the physician Hallowell Davis.

A large number of EEG studies followed, so that by 1939 certain findings about the technique were generally accepted. Among them were the following: Whether or not the person is psychotic, an unstable EEG pattern indicates emotional instability; conversely, a stable pattern indicates emotional stability. Predominantly alpha type patterns are associated with passive dependent persons; nonalpha type patterns are associated with active, driving individuals. A feebleminded person without brain damage can have a normal EEG. Epileptics tend to have abnormal EEGs. Patients treated at a psychoanalytic institute have the same EEGs during and after their analyses that they had before their treatment began. It is not possible to separate a normal from an abnormal EEG solely on the basis of specific factors—the pattern of the record as a whole has to be evaluated.

Thus from the perspective of the various procedures discussed in this section, it appears that while the thirties may have been a time of desperation in the world at large, never before had clinical psychology experienced so productive a period in the development of diagnostic techniques. From the seeds of ideas, satisfactions, dissatisfactions, and needs sown in previous decades a rich crop of new instruments had grown. The immediate task was to harvest, process, and digest them.

DIAGNOSTIC FORMULATIONS

The flaming controversy about the structure of intelligence had dwindled to a flicker, and most psychologists were content to sit back and let it burn itself out. Thorndike had never been a willing combatant and had sufficient integrity to follow his own advice that "the time spent in replying to an attack could better be employed in doing a relevant experiment." Spearman and Thurstone, however, carried on gamely.

On the sidelines it was advocated by some psychologists that the concept of intelligence be eliminated from psychology. They noted matter-of-factly that the IQ could be viewed as merely an index of certain types of adaptation, whenever definite relationships between IQ and those adaptations could be demonstrated. Since intelligence scales sample heavily what the person has learned, they can be regarded as a form of achievement test. Therefore, it was concluded, the concept of intelligence should be abandoned because all that was being done in testing intelligence was simply sampling what the person had achieved as a basis for predicting what he would achieve.

Most psychologists were willing to part with their instincts, but were not so eager to lose their intelligence. Thurstone had devised a new statistical technique, multiple-factor analysis, which he believed was a scientific method capable of resolving the issue of the structure of intelligence, among other problems.

According to Thurstone, Spearman's two-factor methods of factor analysis encounter difficulties in dealing with group factors (factors common to some, but not all the variables) and more than one general factor. In contrast, he claimed multiple-factor analysis asks how many factors have to be postulated to account for the experimentally given table of correlations and imposes no restrictions on the number of group and general factors.

In his APA presidential address in 1933, Thurstone discussed some of the early results of using his multiple-factor analytic method. He had analyzed sixty adjective traits and had found five factors. Perhaps, he suggested, this meant that it is possible to describe and study the complexity and variety of man along only five dimensions. Similarly, he had factor-analyzed psychotic symptoms and found five clusterings, which he named catatonic, manic, depressive, cognitive, and hallucinatory. Perhaps, he thought, this meant that psychiatric disturbances could be reduced to five syndromes. But more work would be needed before definite statements could be made, and the important point in Thurstone's opinion was that these results gave merely an inkling of the contributions which might be expected through use of the method of multiple factor analysis.

The following year, Thurstone launched another experimental attack on the structure of intelligence. Fifty-seven tests sampling intellectual functioning were administered to 240 students in eighth grade, high school, and college. During factor analysis of the results, a correlation of less than .40 was used as a critical value to eliminate a test from participation in a factor.

Six "primary" factors or mental abilities emerged from the data: (1) number, or ability to perform numerical calculations; (2) verbal comprehension; (3) space, or the ability to manipulate an object about in space by using one's imagination; (4) word fluency, or the ability to think of isolated words rapidly; (5) reasoning; and (6) rote memory. There were also possibly two other factors but they were "not yet sufficiently clear," a perceptual factor and a deductive factor. In addition, Thurstone discovered that the tests were intercorrelated, and concluded there was a general factor but only of a "second-order."

Spearman insisted that the "second-order" general factor found by Thurstone was not "second-order" at all but was really the primary general factor he had been talking about over the many years. It was becoming increasingly evident to all concerned and especially to the bystanders that factor analysis is an arbitrary method.

Thomson, an internationally recognized expert on factor analysis, publicly expressed his doubts that the procedure was worth much. Stephenson suggested that instead of factor-analyzing tests, psychologists should factor analyze people by giving a large number of tests to a small number of persons and then obtain the factor saturations for the individuals; it might be that this method would help uncover personality types.

Thurstone acknowledged that there is no single unique result from a factor-analytic study and attempted to evaluate three criteria which had been proposed for deciding whether the results of one's analysis are valid.

The first criterion is the invariance of results, or the claim that the factorial structure has to remain constant under differing methods of factor analysis. Thurstone felt this criterion did not work out too well because the factor loadings change with the additions and removals of tests supposedly measuring the same thing. Also the correlations seem to fluctuate depending upon the particular sample of subjects.

The second criterion is the psychological meaningfulness of the results. In practice this meant that it should be possible to discern some common factor among those correlated items which clustered on tests. This seems to place a large burden on the ability of the experimenter to perceive similarities among diversities, and also appears to be a fairly arbitrary procedure in its own right.

The third criterion is the practical value of the results, the usefulness of a factor in describing an individual and its superior meaningfulness in comparison with the unanalyzed test score. This should be sufficient to repay the efforts made to obtain it. To put it differently, do the results of a factor analysis have any application or make any real difference to anyone? In the final analysis this is what seems to count most.

Other things being equal, most clinicians seemed to value a scale which yielded a profile of mental abilities over one which furnished a single estimate of intelligence. It would have been of significance to them if one theory of the structure of intelligence produced a scale which differed in structure from another. Yet not too surprisingly, one scale based on Spearman's theory, the Wechsler-Bellevue, was just as capable of yielding a profile as Thurstone's Primary Mental Abilities Tests. Therefore, it did not seem to make much difference in the appearance of scales whether one subscribed to Spearman's or Thurstone's theory of intelligence. When the smoke of battle cleared, the fine distinction between a general factor and specific factors *versus* specific factors and a second-order general factor had an evanescent subtlety which was unimpressive to those not personally involved in the dispute.

A similar truce, born of futility, seemed to have been reached in another quarter of psychology. Pacific overtures were drifting across the no man's land separating the camp of the nature-heredity-organicists from that of the nurture-stressing environmentalists. The environmentalists had entered the thirties coming on strong. But just when nature seemed to be on the run and very little appeared to be inherited any more, a sensible reconciliation was effected. Let us see what happened.

The nurture position with respect to intelligence had appeared to many to gain irresistible strength after Beth L. Wellman (1895–1952) reported that children of average intelligence and above who attended nursery school had a mean increase of about 5 IQ points over those who did not attend a preschool. Other studies indicated that feebleminded mothers could have children of normal intelligence, retarded children who were properly trained could become socially useful adults, and children who at one time seemed of average ability could later score in the feebleminded range if reared in a depriving environment. Far from being "constant," IQs could vary 5 to 20 points and more. Wellman reported the case of a child who at three years earned an IQ of 89, at ten years scored 149, and at thirteen years was estimated to have an IQ of 132. It seemed clear to Wellman, as well as to other psychologists, that IQs should be dated; that the particular tests by which they were obtained should be noted; and that marked losses in IQ could come from deprived environments, while IQ gains could come from enriched environments.

In further support of the nurture position, it had been found that Negroes living in the North scored higher on intelligence tests than those remaining in the South. However, the nature camp attempted to vitiate this finding by the hypothesis of selective migration, i.e., those Negroes who left the South tended to be more intelligent than those who remained. In 1935, Otto Klineberg evaluated the evidence for selective migration and found it lacking. It appeared that Negroes who came North were not on the average superior to those in the South but instead obtained higher scores after living in the more favorable Northern environment.

At first each bit of evidence in support of environmental effects on intellectual functioning was marshalled in favor of the "alternative" that intelligence was acquired, and not innate. The nature camp was on the defensive, but it counterattacked at every opportunity. Terman expressed his conviction: "That the major differences between children of high and low IQ, and the major differences in the intelligence test scores of certain races, as Negroes and whites, will never be fully accounted for on the environmental hypothesis."

Even in the case of mongolism, which generally was believed to be genetically determined, advocates of nurture argued that the disorder might be produced by some environmental deficiency *in utero*. Then in 1935, the British psychiatrist Lionel Penrose reported two cases of mental retardation produced by a genetically determined deficiency of phenylalanine hydroxylase. This deficiency resulted in an incomplete oxidation of the amino acid phenylalanine which could be detected by the presence of phenylpyruvic acid in the urine. If the disorder were detected shortly after birth, preventive measures could be taken to avoid irreparable intellectual damage.

Thus toward the close of the thirties victories could be claimed by both sides of the nature-nurture controversy. The studies on deprived and enriched environments had cast serious doubt on the validity of the

1930 White House Conference committee's definition of feebleminded-ness: social incompetence due to arrested mental development from organic causes. Still it was clear, if for no other reason than the small percentage of retardates accounted for by phenylpyruvic oligophrenia, that the environmental position was not able to explain all cases of mental subnormality. A synthesis between the nature-nurture positions was in order.

Steps in effecting such a synthesis had been taken throughout the decade. Witty and Lehman, in 1933, had tried persuasion to bring the two groups together. They noted that although most psychologists had rejected the term "instincts," the term "maturation," as applied to the development of behavior due to normal processes of growth entirely uninfluenced by learning, was being given a definition which sounded definitely familiar. Few studies could be found, they pointed out, in unequivocal support of the nature position. Even the fact that IQ scores of near relatives are more highly correlated than those of distant relatives might be explained on the basis of more similar environments with more close consanguinity. They concluded that it is futile to attempt to dichotomize behavior into learned or innate categories. Most behaviors are due to interactions between heredity and environment, and both are essential to a full understanding of growth.

The integration of nature-nurture positions was exemplified by an American Orthopsychiatric Association meeting on aging held in 1939. George Lawson, a member of a panel which discussed this topic, em-phasized that senescence has a double aspect. Biologically, there are declines in the functioning and performance of some abilities, but usually not in all of them; nor are abilities impaired at the same rate. Psycho-logically, there is a transition from autonomy and self-sufficiency to in-creasing dependence upon others; but this is often determined by enforced retirements from occupations as well as by impaired functioning. It thus appears that chronological age, in and of itself, has little predictive value for assessing the ability of the person to perform a useful function in society, and that senility is the product of an interaction between bio-logical and environmental effects. Therefore, the helplessness, the despair, and the worthlessness so frequently experienced by the aged, and which usually were considered their unavoidable lot, might well be prevented. Such dreadful and unnecessary psychological consequences of aging would probably not take place if the elderly were assisted to find some task in keeping with their abilities and if employers were flexible about retire-ment ages.

A similar integrative process was at work in areas of personality func-tioning other than the intellectual. Many of these areas had been domi-nated, by default, by psychiatry, and so were weighted in favor of organic, hereditary explanations. A strong reaction against this traditional position was displayed during the thirties in contemporaneous theoretical formulations.

Adler's revised personality theory buttressed and fitted into the modern functional architecture. He had traveled some distance from the notion that neurosis is caused by the inferiority of some organ. Now he saw the neurotic as a person lacking in social interest, as someone whose symptoms are unconsciously motivated artful creations intended to protect his self-esteem. Through his use of safeguarding mechanisms, the neurotic strives to avoid coming to grips with the problems of life and confronting his basic feelings of worthlessness. Yet to the trained observer, Adler for one, the patient constantly reveals his feelings and his means of dealing with them. His attitudes and mechanisms are apparent in his verbalizations, his expressions, his mannerisms, his movements, his posturings. When such a person is being seen in therapy, his task must be to correct his methods of distorting his world and to grow to accept a mature view of it. For only by doing this is he then able to derive a feeling of true worth through benefiting his fellow man. But Adler was not the only psychiatrist who stressed the significance of the social environment in the genesis of neurosis.

Expressive in its very title of the emphasis of the thirties upon culture was Karen Horney's popular book *The Neurotic Personality of Our Time* (1937). Horney (1885–1952) had received her M.D. from the University of Berlin in 1911 and began her psychoanalytic training in 1914. This included a personal analysis with Karl Abraham and Hanns Sachs. In 1920, she became an instructor at the Psycho-Analytic Institute in Berlin. Coming to the United States in 1932 she assumed the position of associate director of the Chicago Psychoanalytic Institute. However she became increasingly dissatisfied with the insistence in psychoanalysis that psychosexual development was genetically determined and universal in nature, and broke with the Chicago group. From 1934, she practiced privately in New York and taught at the New School for Social Research and the New York Psychoanalytic Institute.

Horney held that "neuroses are generated by disturbances in the interhuman relationships." She insisted that many of Freud's theoretical formulations were "culture-bound," true only with reference to his particular time and place of practice. Not only might much of his theory be invalid in the United States of the thirties, but what modern psychiatrists would consider a neurotic is probably quite different from what would have been considered a neurotic in Freud's day and age. Thus Horney accepted the contention of cultural anthropologists that what determines whether a behavior is neurotic depends upon the standards and values of the culture in which it occurs.

The culture of the United States, she asserted, was based on individual competition, which caused people to feel isolated and hostile. What made adjusting to this culture more difficult even than its competitiveness were its many inconsistencies. On the one hand people were urged to achieve and get ahead; on the other hand their ethics held up meekness, humility, and brotherly love as virtues. On the one hand advertising, movies, books, and magazines stimulated sexual and material needs; on the other hand the country's economy and its moral and legal codes frustrated these needs and restricted their expression. On the one hand there was supposed to be freedom of the individual; on the other hand there were endless streams of written and unwritten social prohibitions. It was Horney's opinion that within this uniquely confusing culture a new sort of neurotic had emerged.

Horney took pains to make it clear that her discussion did not relate to all kinds of neurosis. She excluded hysteria, obsessions, and compulsions, and even further she differentiated between situational and character neuroses; the former occurring in relatively intact personalities as a reaction to some conflict or stress in reality; the latter, character neuroses (which had already been discussed to some extent by Franz Alexander, Wilhelm Reich, and Erich Fromm, among others) are attributable, in Horney's phrase, to an "insidious chronic process" of personality deformations. Her theory was directed to explaining these character neuroses, which, she thought, were especially prevalent in the United States at the time.

Beginning at the beginning, Horney noted that a child is at first helpless and utterly dependent upon his parents. If their love for him is not genuine, the child senses this and reacts to his rejection and to the demands of his parents with feelings of basic hostility. This hostility is repressed for a variety of reasons: in order to maintain parental protection; to minimize fears of punishment, abandonment, and complete loss of love; and to avoid feelings of guilt. However, if the child continues to experience a lack of affection from those persons with whom he comes in contact, or if the rejection by his parents is severe, a feeling of being isolated develops and his hostility is projected onto the world about him. Horney calls this feeling of being alone in a hostile, frightening, dangerous environment "basic anxiety."

Once the child acquires this feeling of basic anxiety he begins a process of adopting defenses or maneuvers to alleviate it. He may withdraw from people, become submissive, strive to gain affection, or attempt to gain power and prestige. Usually two or more of these forms of incompatible striving are adopted by the neurotic in his now chronic efforts to gain reassurance. Therefore no matter how successfully he has fulfilled the dictates of one striving, he will have betrayed the dictates of at least one other and so feels constantly conflicted and torn. Moreover, his strivings, in and of themselves, by their persistence and intensity actually serve to alienate people. The rejections that ensue only make matters worse for the neurotic. Being highly sensitive to any rebuff and perceiving the requests of others as demands, and these demands and those of the culture as burdensome impositions, his feelings of basic anxiety are intensified, which in turn produces an intensification of his neurotic patterns of behavior, causing more people to become alienated from him, and so on, and so on. This entire process is thus a vicious circle in which the individual's very struggles to achieve his ends frustrate him and in consequence only cause him to struggle harder.

In Horney's formulation symptoms no longer define a neurotic disorder. Instead she saw certain forms of repetitive and inept behavior that are perceived by the individual, for better or worse, as part of himself. What seems to make a person neurotic is his belief, or the belief of responsible people, that his behavior is unsatisfying, distressing, inefficient, and/or maladaptive. According to Horney, "the absence or presence of symptoms is often irrelevant for the nature of a neurosis." This broadening of the concept of neurosis makes virtually everyone suspect of being a neurotic. In fact, it was claimed that all Americans are probably neurotic, and that they suffer from this disorder because of the neurotic culture in which they live. It is at this point that from the rear a pot shot was fired by the nature camp; of course, said this proponent of heredity banging away at the bird of culture on the wing, all human beings are neurotic since, "it's just the way our phylum is."

The concept of cultural relativism was applied not only with reference to the forms of behavior that constitute neurosis. What constitutes schizophrenia, for example, may also be viewed as relative to a particular culture. According to Devereux, it is not true, as was formerly maintained, that the schizophrenic has reverted to a primitive or immature level of thinking. Instead it appears to be the case that he is unable or refuses to think in the manner or patterns demanded by his society. He is aware of his environment, not withdrawn from it, but rather than using the values and purposes shared by the members of his culture to make sense of his world, he interprets events according to his own private, limited, and idiosyncratic code. Therefore what might be considered schizophrenic behavior in one community may not be considered unusual or abnormal in another, and, conversely, the normal behavior of one culture may be the psychotic behavior of another. Inevitably, cultural relativism led to the seriocomic proposal that a country might well benefit its schizophrenic population by distributing them around among those peoples of the earth who find their behavior perfectly acceptable.

During the thirties, emotional disturbances thus seemed to be everywhere and nowhere, depending upon the cultural frame of reference of the moment. Even speech and reading disorders, if one believed what the experts were now saying, were no longer caused by physical defects, unfavorable attitudes toward learning, and inappropriate habits. Instead they were thought to be produced by unconscious conflicts, and when these conflicts were resolved by psychotherapy, these children were supposed to be able to learn to read and to speak correctly without the need for special tutoring. Thus clinicians, who had been laboring in the hard field of remedial teaching, found the value of their work questioned and themselves facing what amounted to a Hobson's choice: either they would have to begin abandoning their efforts in this area or they could give up their role as tutors and assume the responsibilities of functioning as psychotherapists.

As would be expected, the concept of psychosomatic illness was one which was attracting considerable attention. Ulcers, asthma, skin rashes, etc., which formerly had been classified as physical ailments, were now thought to be partially determined and exacerbated by tensions and unconscious conflicts and desires. Murray reported that the following unconscious wishes were especially important in the etiology of psychogenic or psychosomatic disorders: (1) to avoid something, (2) to atone for something, (3) to injure someone, (4) to elicit sympathy or support, (5) to die, and (6) to gratify one's sexual desires. Although many people understood psychosomatic disturbances to mean that psychological problems could produce certain physical illnesses, the major significance of the concept was to emphasize that all disturbances are psychosomatic, that any sickness or injury or trauma has psychological consequences which have an important bearing upon the course of treatment. This way of looking at afflicted persons is well expressed in Goldstein's statement: "The aphasic is not a man with altered speech but an altered man."

Kurt Goldstein (1878–1965), whose theoretical position came to be called holistic and organismic, obtained his M.D. from the University of Breslau in 1903. During the First World War, while serving as director of the Military Hospital for Brain-Injured Soldiers, he observed that the behavior of the brain damaged is more concrete than normal; these soldiers seemed bound more tightly to the immediate stimulus situation and found it more difficult to consider future possibilities or to see relationships between different stimuli. Goldstein used observations such as these to help in the formulation of his general theory. In 1930, he accepted the position of professor of neurology and psychiatry at the University of Berlin, but with the rise of Nazism, left Germany in 1933 and went to Amsterdam. While there Goldstein wrote *The Organism*, which appeared in an English translation in 1939. He arrived in the United States in 1935 and became clinical professor of neurology at Columbia University.

For Goldstein the only motive of the organism is the inborn, somewhat abstract, striving for self-actualization, or in other words the individual's strivings to realize his potentialities and to express himself. All other motives such as thirst, hunger, sex, and affiliation are simply ramifications of this one basic master motive. Put simply, Goldstein saw the person born into his world with certain innate potentialities. These potentialities are sometimes frustrated and sometimes promoted by his environment. If the organism (person) is to get anywhere, he has to come to terms with his environment and achieve some sort of stability and balance. But this coming to terms is a continuing process both because the organism's striving for self-actualization persists and because the stimulation from the world is always changing.

For the most part Goldstein saw self-actualization as essentially good and the environment in which man functioned as limiting and frustrating. Thus, like Rousseau, Goldstein looked at man and discerned his basic, worthwhile potentialities distorted and thwarted by a world that is, for the most part, oppressive.

The emphasis upon nurture in the etiology of the neuroses received additional support from experimental studies within psychology. Working with animals, some psychologists had been able to produce neurotic-like behavior by frustrating their charges or forcing them to attempt to make impossible discriminations. Rats could be made to exhibit such "learned disorganized behavior" when the experimenter blocked the paths they had taken to get to food. They could be "cured," or made to attempt once again to traverse these paths, by increasing the strength of their drive or by periods of food deprivation. Although these findings were not crucial, the deliberate creation of disturbed behavior in cats, rats, dogs, sheep, and other domestic animals was certainly very interesting, and they demonstrated that neuroses might indeed be brought about by situations in which the person could do no right.

A prime target of both those who argued for the tremendous formative significance of the culture and those who contended that neuroses are learned was Freud. He was criticized by the first group for his neglect of interpersonal variables, by the second group for his emphasis on unconscious functioning, and by both groups for the tenacity with which he and his followers held to a view of a naturally evolving progression in psychosexual development. Yet Freud's influence was established and pervasive.

Early in the decade Freud's predilection for affixing proper names borrowed from mythology to complexes led to what soon assumed the proportions of a fad. In addition to the Oedipus complex and the Electra complex, there were proposals to inaugurate Medea, Clytemnestra, Jehovah, Belshazzar, and Manfred complexes, and Fritz Witels suggested Phaedra, Heracles, and Amphitryon. In line with the *Zeitgeist* Henry Starr offered a Prometheus complex for an urging in the direction of an ideal too far above the level of the individual's social group, an urge which therefore has to be repressed because of cultural taboos. Such supplements to the contemporary nomenclature were fashionable and entertaining for a few years, but were not too lasting and did seem needlessly confusing.

In the meantime, Freud, despite advanced age and poor health, had been far from idle, unproductive, and subdued. Though he still paid homage to constitutional predispositions to certain kinds of personality functioning, his attention continued to be directed to their psychological characteristics, as was illustrated in 1931 in his discussion of three libidinal types whose physical bases went unmentioned. Persons of the erotic type are mainly interested in being loved. The narcissistic type is preoccupied with self-preservation and self-assertion, and tends to be confident and aggressive. Those of the obsessional type are dominated by their superegos and fears of not being loved. Freud recognized, however, that only rarely would it be possible to find a person who embodied the characteristics of only one type, and that usually a person would evidence two or all three dispositions with, perhaps, the features of one more prominent than any other.

Though Freud's typology aroused interest within psychoanalytic circles, the *Zeitgeist* was not propitious for its more wide-spread acceptance. The trend was to attack or belittle suggestions of inborn differences and to concentrate upon observable, measurable behavior. Thus although Jung's introversion-extraversion dichotomy was popularly accepted as descriptive of important individual differences, the supposed constitutional foundation for these traits was minimized or rejected outright.

Even less interest was displayed in other typologies which made their appearance during this period. Among them were Jaensch's integrated and disintegrated perceptual types, Kroh's extensive and intensive attentional types, and Kretschmer's cycloids and schizoids. Each of these typologies has differentiations similar in essence to those of Jung's introversion-extraversion. Kretschmer's typology, since it is related to physique, is the most easily tested. Katherine Campbell reported that height and weight curves for populations of patients suffering from dementia praecox and manic depressive psychosis are highly similar. Her study was one of several that failed to support Kretschmer's observations.

In fact so adverse was the reaction to any organic etiology for "functional" disturbances that some research by Kallmann in support of a genetic determination of schizophrenia was criticized for the "Teutonic thoroughness" with which its author had conducted his study. Franz Kallmann (b. 1897), the recipient of that irrelevant reproach, was a German psychiatrist, who in 1936 accepted a position at the New York Psychiatric Institute. His work, published in 1938, carefully noted the occurrence of schizophrenia among near and distant relatives of a sample of 1,087 schizophrenic patients, and concluded that the psychosis is in part conditioned by general tissue defects having germ-plasm determiners. In other words, schizophrenia is to some extent genetically determined.

Kallmann's conclusion was disputed on the familiar grounds that people who are closely related have similar environments, an argument of some merit. Unfortunately, in attempting to vitiate organic explanations the implication was fostered that parents were to be held solely accountable for the psychological disturbances of their offspring. This "accusation" was becoming more grave as more severe disorders were thought likely to occur in childhood. In regard to this we should note that although psychoses in children had been recorded in the nineteenth century, it was not until the late twenties and early thirties of the twentieth century that psychiatrists considered certain patterns of symptoms to be indicative of schizophrenia as modified by childhood. Therefore, while the presence of schizophrenia among the very young is capable of being interpreted by a hypothesis of organic defect as well as one of nurture, the tendency at the time of which we are writing was to attend more closely to whatever evidence supported an environmental explanation, particularly evidence having to do with pathological interpersonal relationships within the family.

While the symptoms of schizophrenia in childhood generally appear to be fewer and more simple than those manifested by adults afflicted with this psychosis, they are fully as dramatic and heart-rending. In making such a diagnosis, psychiatrists agree that no single symptom is definitive and the total behavioral picture of the child has to be considered. The forms of behavior indicative of this most severe disorder are seclusiveness, bizarre speech, anomalies of thinking, greatly reduced interest in the environment, regressive activities, and disturbances in the expression of emotions. By the end of the thirties, and even earlier as we shall soon see, it was widely believed that the most helpful course to adopt in treating childhood schizophrenia is to remove the child from the disturbed environment of the family and to place him in a setting that would be therapeutic.

As the decade came to a close there existed a considerable consensus supporting the position that heredity, with few exceptions, should not be considered a sole causative factor of mental abnormalities. The most reasonable view seemed to be that the individual's genetic endowment provides certain potentialities or capacities whose realization or fulfillment are dependent upon his environmental experiences. It was generally agreed that the individual is best understood as a unitary functioning organism. Accordingly, emotional stresses and strains could have a damaging effect upon bodily functioning, and physical ailments and disabilities could have a damaging effect upon the person's view of himself and his psychological functioning. It appeared that in any disorder, the person's symptoms are most enlighteningly understood in relation to the cultural setting and their effects upon and meanings to a striving, adjusting individual.

TREATMENT FORMULATIONS

It is ironic that while the nurture position was in ascendance a minor revolution in the psychiatric treatment of hospitalized mental patients was taking place. Within the span of a few years vigorous and bold techniques were inaugurated to benefit psychotics. Although the effectiveness of the assault might be debatable, its sincerity and good intentions are unquestioned. And, at the very least, sustained efforts were being made on the behalf of patients who might otherwise have simply languished.

In 1934, L. von Meduna found in metrazol the convulsive agent he had been seeking for the alleviation of schizophrenia. It produced seizures rapidly, though unfortunately there was a fifteen-second delay from the injection of the solution and the appearance of the convulsion. Despite this disadvantage, the administration of metrazol or convulsive-irritative therapy with schizophrenic, and shortly thereafter, melancholic, and manic-depressive patients became a widespread practice.

Metrazol therapy was soon to be supplanted by electro-shock therapy. Two Italian psychiatrists V. Cerletti and L. Bini found, in 1937, that they could induce convulsions by passing a current through the temporal regions of the patient's head. Loss of consciousness was immediate, the seizure was usually not very severe, and ordinarily the cost of the treatment was low. In 1939, Lothar Kalinowski and Renato Almansi introduced the method to the United States.

Another form of shock treatment was discovered by the Viennese psychiatrist Manfred Sakel. Sakel had been treating the withdrawal symptoms of morphine addiction by injecting doses of insulin sufficient to produce coma, or hypoglycemic shock. Pleased with his success in making the withdrawal more bearable, he thought it might also be helpful to give hypoglycemic shocks to schizophrenics. He began his work with psychotic patients in 1933, and in 1938 demonstrated his insulin shock method in the United States. The therapy did seem to be effective in certain cases.

Generally, either insulin or metrazol shock was used in the treatment of psychoses. But sometimes, and especially with patients who were particularly disturbed or unresponsive to one or the other, the two types of shock treatment were combined, the metrazol following the insulin.

Narcosis therapy was used with agitated or excited patients as a means of inducing prolonged sleep and making them more accessible to what was said to them by members of the staff. The principal drug for this purpose was sodium amytal. In some cases the conflicts of the patients could be discussed with them during the period of awakening, a time when they seemed most amenable to suggestion.

The most drastic of these new procedures, psychosurgery, was first performed by the Portuguese neurologist Egaz Moniz. Originally, Moniz had hoped to abolish chronic delusions by injecting alcohol into the prefrontal lobes, the area of the brain which was thought to be the locus of intellectual activity. But his technique underwent an evolution and by 1936 it consisted of severing the fiber tracts connecting the prefrontal lobes with the thalamus. Refinements and variations on this basic strategy soon followed. The outcome of Moniz's early operations demonstrated that while the content of delusions might be little changed, the patient's feelings about his delusions, along with his feelings about almost everything else, had become bland and apathetic. Psychosurgery was introduced to the United States in 1937 by W. Freeman and J. W. Watts.

All these shock and surgical methods shared at first in lacking a demonstrable rationale, but, nevertheless, apparently possessing an ability to effect improvements in some psychotic patients. The formulations which originally led to their development were quickly found to be groundless. There was little support for Meduna's hypothesis that epilepsy and schizophrenia are antagonistic, and Moniz's early work soon demonstrated that the prefrontal lobes are not *the* locus of cognition. In order to provide some basis for their continued use, aside from the simple fact that they were of some help, a variety of psychological explanations were offered—the shock treatments punish the patient and relieve him by subjecting him to the experiences of his own death and rebirth, or perhaps the superego functions are located in the prefrontal lobes and are surgically isolated or removed—which by their very abundance and equal plausibility pointed to the absence of any definitive explanation.

More importantly, the results of studies evaluating the therapeutic outcomes when these techniques were employed were equivocal. Yet, for two major reasons, their use continued and expanded: one, there was little else to choose from in treating psychotics; and two, the introduction of the techniques had raised morale among the staffs of mental hospitals, generating a feeling that something positive was being done by them in behalf of their patients. This was a benefit not to be lightly dismissed.

Despite the fact that psychoanalysts were attempting to adapt their method to the treatment of psychotics, Freud believed such efforts were doomed to failure. He contended that these patients did not have enough remnants of a normal ego intact to be able to cooperate in the manner needed for an effective psychoanalysis. His point of view about the futility of these efforts was shared by Paul Schilder but for a different reason. Schilder believed that since schizophrenia was an organic illness, no form of psychotherapy would be of much value in ameliorating the condition. Freud's and Schilder's pessimism was not shared by many workers in the field. On the contrary, the growingly popular attitude was that psychotherapy could be quite helpful if it were only made available.

This widespread belief in the beneficial effects to be derived from psychotherapy should be seen in the light of other prevailing conditions, such as the appreciation of the importance of social variables and the enthusiasm for psychological etiologies in general. Taken together they constituted a situation which was highly receptive to the development of psychotherapeutic approaches and produced a generation of clinicians who were most attentive to the latest thinking of the leaders in this area: Freud, Jung, Adler, and Rank.

Drawing on his vast experience as an analyst, Freud expressed his opinions on a variety of issues. He felt that the neuroses, since they did not involve a repudiation of reality as severe as that found in the psychoses, were most amenable to psychoanalysis, especially in those cases where their onset seemed to be brought about by some recent trauma. He acknowledged the possibility that the constitutional strength of an instinct might be of less significance than its strength at a given moment, i.e., the present might be of more significance in a given case than the past. He conceded that the fixing of a termination date for an analysis could be effective if it were employed at just the proper time. His feelings about this practice, however, were essentially negative and he referred to it as a "blackmailing device."

Freud thought the question as to when an analysis could be considered completed had to be tempered by practical considerations. The analysis should not be pursued until the patient is a psychologically perfect human being. That would be expecting too much. A more reasonable standard for termination is that the patient's condition is improved, even though there may still be a chance for the recurrence of symptoms. However, speaking ideally, possibly when the basic theme that is unconscious is brought into awareness and fully explored, the wish for a penis in the case of women and the struggle against passivity or the fear of castration in the case of men, possibly then the analysis could be judged to be truly ended. Yet in another vein Freud seemed to feel that no analysis ever really comes to an end. Once begun, analysis is an interminable task in which both patient and analyst continue throughout life to examine their own feelings, conflicts, and problems.

Such concepts as ego functioning, defense mechanisms, and resistances, including the fear of recovery itself, appeared to be assuming an ever larger place in Freud's thinking: "Our therapeutic work swings to and fro during the treatment like a pendulum analyzing now a fragment of the id and now a fragment of the ego. . . . Our object will be not . . . to demand that the person who has been 'thoroughly analyzed' shall never again feel the stirrings of passions in himself or become involved in any internal conflict. The business of analysis is to secure the best possible psychological conditions for the functioning of the ego; when this has been done, analysis has accomplished its task."

In the meantime Freud's former colleague Jung had been concentrating much of his therapeutic work on patients who were middle-aged. Many of these cases complained chiefly that they felt their lives were empty and meaningless. It seemed clear to Jung that this neurosis, like all others, is an attempt to compensate for, and draw attention to, neglected or repressed aspects of the personality. Perhaps, he thought, in the second half of life sexuality and self-assertion are of less importance than earlier and are not as significant as is a drive to express a spiritual or "natural religious function." What the middle-aged have repressed that is now causing them so much anguish, assuming their development has proceeded satisfactorily up to this time, are their spiritual yearnings and their need to relate to a being superior to man. As these needs and wishes obtrude into consciousness, they are regarded as bad and the patient feels guilty and worthless because he experiences them. But fortunately relief can be obtained and this conflict can be resolved if the person confesses or acknowledges his repressed yearnings and frankly discusses them with the honest, warm human being who is typified by his Jungian analyst.

As Jung saw it, the early stage of this type of analysis would deal with the contents of the personal unconscious, examining those problems and conflicts which are specific to this individual. As the analysis progressed, and especially in its later stages, the collective unconscious material would come into prominence and be discussed, an examination of those problems and conflicts shared by all mankind. Working together, patient and analyst form a relationship in which both might become changed as they consider the spiritual problems of man or search for new meanings to give to the patient's life: "Psychotherapy then becomes freed from its clinical origins and ceases to be a mere method for treating the sick. It is now of service to the healthy as well, or at least to those who have a right to psychic health and whose illness is at most the suffering that tortures us all."

In contrast, Adler's concept of therapy seemed to reach its end about where Jung regarded his as just beginning: "Individual psychology considers the essence of therapy to lie in making the patient aware of his lack of cooperative power, and to convince him of the origin of this lack in early childhood maladjustments." According to Adler, the prime task of the therapist is to enlist the patient's cooperation in the psychotherapeutic process, to provide the experience of contact with an understanding and accepting fellow human being, and to help the patient transfer the favorable attitudes of the therapeutic relationship to his dealings with other persons.

Not cooperation, but self-expression is what came first with Rank. The individual taking joy in the expression of his own views and yet, so at ease with himself and certain of his identity, that he can attend to and accept the will of another without self-reproach. Rank did not claim that as a therapist he could "make" the patient aware of his problems, principally because he did not believe that the therapist is the best judge as to what those problems are. "Psychology does not deal with facts as science does," he said, "but deals only with the individual's attitude toward facts." Therefore, Rank asserted that in therapy the person is not so much taught or convinced, but only is helped to experience his own understanding and knowledge of himself. Since Rank saw the individual as striving to assert his own thoughts and feelings, his resistance in analysis is not regarded as something to be broken by the therapist, but as a positive force which can be turned into a beneficial agent in self-development. The task of the therapist is to provide a relationship in which the patient can learn to use that force constructively and assert his will without feeling excessively guilty or fearful about it.

Freud, Jung, Adler, and Rank all shared a belief in the far-reaching importance of the relationship that develops between the therapist and his patient. Although differing in the details of what they considered is the ideal form of this alliance, all agreed that it is a vehicle by which the goals of an analysis are reached and that at least a minimum of co-operation must exist if the person is to be helped. But such an awareness was not confined to these leaders. Talk of "the relationship" blossomed in profusion everywhere in the literature of this period.

For many, such as the psychiatrist John Levy (1897–1938), the relationship was of importance mainly because it can be assumed that the patient will use the same tactics and defenses he usually employs with others in relating to the therapist. However, there is a big difference in the reaction he will obtain. The therapist will not respond in the same way as other people have done to these maneuvers. Rather than becoming emotionally upset or involved, the therapist will only understand, clarify, and interpret the person's feelings and needs, which produces a different kind of relationship from any the person has ever experienced. Then, gradually, and in some manner not quite clear, the patient's maladaptive attitudes will "drop off" and in their place effective functioning will be restored. Levy called this approach "relationship therapy," but we should note that by this term he meant that it is essentially the relationship that is treated. A quite different stance was taken by others who saw the treatment relationship as so significant and meaningful that they regarded it as a therapy in and of itself.

This was a position taken, to some extent out of necessity, in the social work profession, where depth analysis was thought to be seldom feasible or desirable. Although this ruled out explorations of unconscious motivation and conflict, it still allowed the effective attachments of the client to the case worker to be employed in what was called "supportive therapy": a conscious attempt to alleviate the patient's hunger for protection, help, and solicitude. The social worker attempted to achieve this objective through an expression of interest and a deliberate giving of advice, encouragement, and affection, all of which was predicated on the assumption that the client would be able to move from the close, dependent attachment that was to be engendered and on toward greater self-reliance and personal freedom.

While this conceptualization appealed to many members of the mental health professions, some psychologists, psychiatrists, and social workers expressed doubt that supportive therapy was the right or even a satisfactory way to go about helping people. They were convinced that they saw in this approach a view of the person as weak, dependent, and infantile in his needs. In contrast, the beliefs of Rank, for one, depicted the individual as striving for independence and needing to assert himself. It was Rank's view that struck Frederick Allen as more meaningful and which dictated his interpretation of what constituted the most favorable therapeutic relationship.

Frederick Allen (1890–1964) had earned his A.B. and Master's degrees in psychology from the University of California. For about three years he worked as a school psychologist and then entered Johns Hopkins to study medicine. He received his M.D. in 1921, became a psychiatrist, and in 1925 assumed the position of director of the Philadelphia Child Guidance Clinic.

Allen felt that as a therapist his task was above all to accept and respect the person as he is at the moment, without feeling any need to change him or assume the responsibility for directing his decisions. He did not see himself, nor did he wish others to see him, as omnipotent. Allen's cardinal assumption, emphasized again and again, is that respect for the individual as he exists, respect for his ability to help himself and to take responsibility for his own life, would be of most benefit to the person and enables him to carry over the healthier modes of self-expression brought about through the therapeutic relationship into interactions with others.

The relationship between the therapist and the patient is valuable, in Allen's opinion, not because it is a re-experiencing of past events, but because it is a meaningful reality satisfying in the present. Since within this relationship, Allen, in line with his assumptions, minimized the giving of interpretations and advice and stressed the activity of the patient and the receptivity of the therapist, his colleagues called his approach "passive therapy." However Allen disliked this term and felt that it embodied a misunderstanding of his concept of the therapist's proper role. In 1933, he attempted to clarify his position by writing: "I am interested in creating a natural relation in which the patient can acquire a more adequate acceptance of himself, a clearer conception of what he can do and feel in relation to the world in which he continues to live. . . . I am not afraid to let the patient feel that I am interested in him as a person."

Though Allen's work was mostly with children, he felt there was nothing to prevent his formulations from applying equally to adults. His ideas had some effect, and the psychologist Carl Rogers, whom we shall encounter later, was one of those favorably impressed, but on the whole we can say that Allen's concepts, deceptively simple in appearance, could not compare with Freud's in popularity or in the following and enthusiasm they generated.

Throughout the thirties there was considerable development in those psychotherapeutic techniques and methods which reflected the significance attached to interpersonal variables. The growing importance of the therapeutic relationship is but one manifestation of this point. There are two others: (1) increasing interest in the treatment of children and (2) in the use of group therapy. (At the same time what interest there had been in hypnosis as an aid to treatment declined. Some experimentation did continue . . . for example, Friedlander and Sarbin suggested a standard method for trance induction and a scale for measuring depth of hypnosis in order to allow comparison between the results of different studies in this area . . . but little attention was given to the therapeutic uses of hypnosis. Possibly this occurred because, except in wartime, there is less concern about the rapid alleviation of symptoms and more concern about effecting changes in basic personality functioning, the latter presumably requiring a long and deliberate involvement by the patient.)

In 1931, the first residential treatment center for children in the United States, the Emma Pendleton Bradley Home, was established. It was designed to serve severely emotionally disturbed and psychotic children ranging from five to twelve years of age. What made the Bradley Home unique were its attempts to make an entire environment therapeutic, not only by judicious selection and indoctrination of all its personnel, but also by having rules, procedures, furnishings, and rooms constructed to meet the needs of the children, rather than of the institution.

By and large, play therapy was the form of treatment children received when they were seen individually. Its usefulness had been amply demonstrated by the pioneering efforts of Anna Freud and Melanie Klein. In their formulations play served two major functions. It is an appropriate or natural medium by which the child can express his unconscious fantasies and conflicts. Moreover, the therapist, by virtue of his superior skills, can use play as a means of favorably impressing the child and winning his confidence and admiration. The first function is, of course, by far the more important of the two. It is through a relatively free and expressive form of play that the child seems to communicate with his therapist.

David Levy offered some additional observations and comments of interest about play therapy. He saw no reason why play could not be deliberately made to serve as a diagnostic technique. The therapist could choose toys and materials that would be likely to draw the child out or be pertinent to his case; employ them in creating and describing a situation, usually interpersonal; and then encourage the child to react to it. Further, Levy was convinced that play alone could provide the child with therapeutic benefits, simply because it allowed the expression of feelings and impulses. He called this "release therapy."

Another important addition during the thirties to the repertory of psychotherapeutic methods was group therapy. We may recall some of the group approaches of the early 1900's, such as the Emmanuel Movement, which were tentative forerunners of this "new" kind of treatment. One of the pioneers of that period, Joseph Pratt, was still active in the field though in a somewhat different way. In 1930, he established a clinic at the Boston Dispensary using his class method to help, not tubercular patients this time, but persons who complained of physical ills when nothing organically wrong could be detected. While Pratt seems to have become more psychiatrically oriented over the years, his influence on work with groups was not extensive and was confined to only a very few colleagues.

In 1931, L. C. Marsh, a psychiatrist, began to publish accounts about the use of group treatment with schizophrenics. Marsh had the idea of establishing a therapeutic community and relied heavily in his treatment upon generating a healthy enthusiasm among the members of his groups, something we might perhaps surmise from his credo: "By the group have they been broken; by the crowd shall they be healed." He claimed that he had been involved in working with groups since 1900, and that another psychiatrist by the name of E. W. Lazell antedated him. But it cannot be said that either of these men had much effect on the field.

Someone who did have a very significant effect was Jacob Levy Moreno. It is he who introduced the term "group therapy" in 1932. Moreno was born in 1892 in Roumania. During his childhood he had a love for the theater and he would act out elaborate, improvised dramas. He received his M.D. from the University of Vienna in 1917, and while there acquired a distaste for psychoanalysis. At the beginning of his career, Moreno used group discussions in an attempt to rehabilitate prostitutes. Later, in 1922, he founded a spontaneity theater in Vienna in which individuals were encouraged to throw themselves freely into specified roles in a given situation and to improvise both their lines and their actions as they went along. Subsequently this method, called "psychodrama," was developed as an approach to the diagnosis and treatment of psychological problems.

Moreno left Austria for the United States during the late twenties and began practicing psychiatry in New York. He defined group therapy as follows: "a method of psychotherapy which combines the technique of assignments with the technique of spontaneous treatments." This somewhat unusual definition originated in Moreno's attempt to work out a therapeutic approach to the classification or grouping of criminals in prison. His idea was to evaluate prisoners individually and then to group them so that social and personal ameliorations would be produced by the interactions of appropriately arranged personalities. To implement his interests Moreno developed sociometric techniques. A sociometric technique attempts to measure preferences of the members of a group for one another, usually by asking each member to name those in the group with whom he would like, or not like, to be involved under a specified set of circumstances. It was this work which led Moreno, in 1937, to establish the journal *Sociometry*.

In 1934, the psychiatrist S. R. Slavson began what he called "activity group therapy," a form of treatment intended specifically for use with emotionally disturbed children. His idea was to help youngsters about eight to eleven years old by placing them in a group and allowing them to freely engage in constructive, destructive, and other expressive activities, all with a highly permissive therapist in attendance. The atmosphere of the activity group is that of a "social club," refreshments are served, and outings may be held. However, Slavson believed that the group functions as a secondary family and that the therapist comes to be seen as a substitute parent. The group members become increasingly important to each other, and insight is gained, not by interpretations from the therapist, but mainly through the reactions of the children to the behavior that takes place in the group.

Paul Schilder was also very enthusiastic about group therapy and his enthusiasm seemed to infect others. By the end of the thirties, almost everyone in the mental health field had heard of the method and quite a few had tried their hands at it. As generally understood, group therapy involved seeing in a group a small number of persons with problems who were encouraged to express their feelings to each other and to the therapist present. The therapist undertook to clarify the expressions and interactions of the members, including, of course, any comments or actions that related to himself.

Few clinical psychologists spoke out on the subject of therapy during this period but those that did seem to have been swimming against the mainstream of interest and experimentation in interpersonal and group psychotherapy. Their approaches to treatment were still geared to their conviction that they were dealing with problems in learning, and thus they emphasized the value of making use of principles of conditioning. Tendler, for example, urged his fellow clinicians to pursue work in psychotherapy and offered his method of treatment by "detensors." The clinician was to reduce his patient's tensions by presenting him with relaxing ideas (reassurances, comforting explanations), by advocating new and delightful situations (e.g., telling people to go on vacations or trips), and by helping him to avail himself of persons who might be of assistance (e.g., advising that they confide in their friends, with members of the clergy, or with the clinical psychologist). Knight Dunlap recommended the breaking of habits such as stuttering, thumb-sucking, and masturbation by "negative practice." This procedure required the person deliberately to repeat the habit so that it eventually could be brought under conscious control and thus be eliminated. Mowrer advised a form of apparatus for treating eneuretics similar to one devised by the German pediatrician M. Pfaundler in 1904. Whenever the child urinates in bed, the urine serves to complete an electrical circuit which rings a bell that awakens him. According to Mowrer's information, thirty eneuretic children had been treated by the bell-ringing technique and all abandoned the habit without substituting any other that was maladaptive.

These conditioning approaches made no great appeal to American psychiatrists and social workers. Nor were they especially inspired by the offer of psychologists to subject psychotherapy to scientific investigation. These proposed contributions from psychology were interesting, to be sure, but they implied, as Carl Rogers pointed out, a belief that psychotherapy is a process which can be examined and refined by scientific methods. Yet at that time probably a majority of those who worked in the area of psychotherapy felt strongly that treatment is largely an art, that it loses an essential something in the very process of being experimentally dissected and studied. They believed deeply in the worth of what they were doing, were personally convinced of its value, and on occasion even argued that such deep conviction is necessary for psychotherapy to be most effective. Far from a questioning of the effectiveness of psychotherapy, the major concern of this period appeared to be to see this form of treatment extended to the mentally retarded, the psychotic, to anyone who might be benefited or feel benefited by its use.

Despite such enthusiasm, there were few who claimed that psychotherapy was always successful. Healy, who had been among those who led in advocating therapy for juvenile delinquents, was also among those who led in reporting that outcomes had been most discouraging. However, he held the disorder and not the treatment responsible for these disappointing results, and he concluded that the prognosis for children with "abnormal personalities" was in general not good. Healy and Franz Alexander had conducted another investigation. Although their research had to be curtailed during the Depression due to a lack of funds, they had been able to devote about nine months to psychoanalyses of five criminals. The results of their study in Healy's estimation were: "The material obtained bearing upon unconscious motivation is extremely illuminating; the curative results in the face of long-standing internal conditionings and external vicissitudes were meagre."

A verdict such as Healy's was sobering to many members of the mental health professions, but elicited from others contentions that the treatments described in these studies had not been long enough or else were not of the proper kind to produce the desired changes. In fact, the variety of different therapeutic methods and techniques, the growing emphasis upon the significance of the personality and the experience of the therapist in the course and outcome of treatment, and the complexities arising from subtle variables in this relationship enabled anyone who believed strongly in a particular form of therapy to explain, quite sensibly, instances of failure as attributable to some fault in the large constellation of method and other interacting variables. Often enthusiasts conveyed the impression that some measure of success could be obtained with any patient, regardless of his condition, if he were matched with the appropriate practitioner and seen for a sufficient length of time. They held to this belief with such tenacity and seemed so impervious to contradictory evidence that some members of the mental health professions began to wonder if this were not an indication of an absolute and unshakable resistance to the idea that psychotherapy might sometimes be ineffective. Gregory Zilboorg was one who gave some thought to this intraprofessional matter.

Zilboorg (1890–1959) was a psychoanalyst who obtained his M.D. from Columbia in 1926. By 1938, he could safely proclaim, "Ours is an age of psychology," and yet at the same time entertain some misgivings about this attainment. His apprehension was based on his concern as to why psychology had become so popular, and why so many people had attached so high a value to psychoanalysis and psychotherapy. His answer was not a very flattering one. Zilboorg believed that a large number of persons, including members of the mental health professions, had a repressed demand for individual perfection. By virtue of their own narcissism they felt they could attain excellence or help others to change for the better simply by the use of words. These words were, perhaps not too unconsciously, endowed with magical properties and powers (a belief, which we may recall, Freud referred to as the "omnipotence of words"). Therefore, Zilboorg argued, in order to satisfy their own emotional needs they had made psychotherapy into a form of dogmatism, maintained by rationalizations and intellectual insights and dedicated to the perpetuation of the delusion that its practitioners are capable of improving anyone.

Accordingly, Zilboorg urged his colleagues to evaluate themselves unsparingly and to recognize and accept their limitations. In particular, he advocated caution and restraint in acquainting the public with what they had to offer. It is all too easy, he noted, to oversell psychology, not only to people in general, but to those who seek to apply it professionally as well.

Thus we see by the close of this decade that some serious doubts were being considered about the desirability of the supposed triumph of psychotherapeutic approaches. These reservations appeared to be dismissed rather quickly, however, in the excitement and challenge of innovations and the ever-increasing variety of groups to whom, it was claimed, these techniques could profitably be applied. The modern conception of mental illness encompassed any degree of maladjustment from childhood through old age. While there was some question about the universality of these disorders, there was a general feeling of confidence that they could be treated satisfactorily by some form of psychotherapy. What, then, could the disturbed person expect in the way of professional assistance? If a child, he might engage in play, either individually or in a group; he might practice habits negatively or be conditioned; and certainly he would encounter practitioners, perhaps of widely differing therapeutic orientations, but virtually all of whom would treat him with respect, acceptance, and, to the best of their professional knowledge and skill, with understanding. If an adult, there would, of course, be no play therapy in our sense of the term, but an impressive number of psychotherapies would, nevertheless, be available to him. The adult, hospitalized psychotic would be more likely to encounter treatment with insulin and electroshock therapies than an understanding relationship alone. But even with these patients there was a growing conviction as to the intrinsic effectiveness of psychotherapy and its superiority to other forms of treatment whenever it could possibly be utilized.

PROFESSIONAL DEVELOPMENT

Hunter, in his presidential address before the APA in 1931, expressed a view shared by most of his colleagues: "Psychology seeks to describe and explain, to predict and control, the extrinsic behavior of the organism to an external environment which is predominantly social." The disputes between various schools of psychology no longer seemed to arouse the emotion or even the interest that they had done only a few years before. It was as though most psychologists had tacitly reached an agreement that speculations and polemics are not the means by which their profession can be advanced, and so had decided to unite in developing experimental methods and the objective study of human behavior. Guthrie had observed that: "The extent to which psychologists are divided into schools measures the extent to which psychology is not a science, but a field for speculation." So it seemed reasonable to hold that investigation should take precedence over argumentation, since when facts and natural laws are established they will be binding on all psychologists and all schools of thought.

Of course this agreement about certain principles did not mean that by the end of the thirties the schools and all controversies had vanished from psychology. Obviously they did not, and even in the midst of this relative accord Yerkes, for example, claimed that psychology should be restricted to the systematic study of the self and its relations to other selves, while the study of various organisms should be a different discipline called psychobiology. However it did mean that psychologists agreed they shared in pursuing the goal of attempting to understand human behavior through means as objective ("reproducible") as possible. Therefore they turned from arguing about what they should or should not study and began to seek to establish certain basic rules by which all scientific investigations and theoretical constructions, regardless of particular opinions and persuasions, could be conducted.

Naturally there were misgivings and recognized limitations. Skraggs noted that the more specific and manipulable problems became, the more they became simplified and restricted in scope. Conversely, the more problems were treated globally, the more difficult it became to appraise and delineate their variables objectively. Nor was this awareness of probably unavoidable restrictions on the acquisition of so-called truth confined to psychology. Within the physical sciences similar trends were dramatically apparent. Beliefs were changing from determinism to indeterminism; from certainty to probability; from an insistence on a rigorous and pure objectivity to a skeptical recognition of possibly ubiquitous subjectivity; from absolute to relative statements; from axioms to productive hypotheses as the most worthwhile fruit of science.

So psychologists began turning once again to philosophy, but this time to the philosophy of science, for help in erecting firm methodological foundations for their discipline.

An essential need, it was agreed, was for clear definitions of terms. Bridgman and Stevens suggested that terms and constructs should be defined operationally, i.e., according to specifiable, "public," and repeatable operations. "To experience," Stevens asserted, can be operationally defined as "to react discriminatively." Since these operations are always changing, all concepts require constant and continuing definition, and any term not capable of being specified by shared and repeated observations would, in Steven's opinion, best be ejected from the body of science.

Hull, in his APA presidential address of 1936, described what most psychologists could subscribe to as an ideal model for building theories: a set of explicit postulates with operationally defined terms and a deduced series of interlocking theorems. If the statements or hypotheses derived from the theorems failed to be supported by facts, the theoretical system was to that extent false and in need of revision or abandonment. If it is not possible to derive testable hypotheses from a theory or to relate observations to it, such a theoretical system, according to Hull, is scientifically meaningless.

Although no theory in psychology at that time satisfied the rigorous standards advocated by Hull, the majority of those in his audience concurred that his criteria were worthy objectives and that whenever possible they would strive to implement them. There was thus a ground swell of harmony within psychology and, as we know, attempts to integrate the findings of this science with those of related disciplines. Psychologists, as they looked about themselves and examined the development of their profession, had ample cause for satisfaction.

The science of psychology had continued to grow and the United States had become its leader in sheer volume of research and in professional expansion. During the forty years between 1894 to 1933, there had been 138,820 titles of studies listed in the *Psychological Index;* of these 41 percent were in English, 29 percent were in German, 13 percent were in French, with the remainder distributed among several other languages. If numbers of publications and increase in the number of members of the American Psychological Association are any criteria of professional vitality, the facts are striking: in 1894, 1,312 papers were published while in 1933 there were 6,286; in 1930, there were approximately 1100 and in 1939, approximately 2200 members of the APA.

Nevertheless, Fernberger's conclusions about the APA in 1931 applied just as forcefully to the organization in 1939. He felt the Association had succeeded very well in giving psychologists a group consciousness, an identity, and prestige in the academic world. Due to its high standards for membership, it had made APA affiliation both an honor and an economic necessity, since employers favored applicants who had this distinction. Further, the Association performed an important scientific service through its ownership and publication of a balanced group of journals. Certainly here are reasons enough for self-congratulation, though Fernberger did see a persistently vexing debit side: "the Association has completely and signally failed at every direct attempt to control psychology or psychologists, whether . . . in matters of terminology, technique, or personnel." These were urgent matters, and equally as pressing, in Fernberger's opinion, was the need for the APA to assume the responsibility to formulate some sort of legal definition of psychologists.

Other psychologists, particularly clinicians, were even more strongly dissatisfied with this situation. It is somewhat of a paradox that this distress was especially acute among clinical psychologists at a time when their self-confidence and success were higher than ever. Although the role of the clinical psychologist as a constructor, administrator, and interpreter of tests was increasingly accepted and respected by other professions (In 1931, Augusta Bronner and in 1936, Edgar Doll were elected to the presidency of the American Orthopsychiatric Association.), many clinicians felt this function was restrictive and even distasteful. Tulchin declared in 1930: "The clinical psychologist is just beginning to get recognition and help in his attempt to emerge from the IQ-indicator stage and to develop a technique in treatment of behavior and personality problems. . . . The psychologist is no longer satisfied with the mere giving of tests."

Tulchin gave the following reasons for the clinician's discontent: (1) a wish to break free of the rigid adherence to standardized testing procedure, which apparently was invoked to set limits on what seemed the pursuit of the major objective, that of understanding a person; (2) a recognition, and evidently the lack of it by others, that the individual patient cannot be expected to confine the expression of his emotional reactions to his meetings with a psychiatrist, and therefore the psychologist also should have the right to deal with these reactions when they are expressed in his office; (3) the belief of clinicians that they should be involved in the actual conduct of treatment since they were already participating in the planning of treatment for specific patients and were doing research on psychotherapy; (4) due to the fact that clinicians were engaged in remedial teaching, they were in a strategic position to deal with school maladjustments "while ostensibly tutoring" (That Tulchin should feel it necessary to point out a subterfuge which would enable the clinician to broaden his role without attracting undue attention indicates the likelihood of considerable resistance to such a change, probably stemming from the medical profession.); and finally (5) the unhappiness of clinicians over the growing demands made upon them to undertake vocational counseling as well as testing, demands that they did not feel they could satisfy because "The sooner we recognize the fact that there are few vocational tests of real worth the better."

Wallin offered some additional reasons. He noted with justifiable concern that there was a growing tendency for psychologists to be relegated to "second-string" jobs, while physicians took over the positions of heads of clinics and bureaus. As one might expect, along with inferior positions of responsibility went lower salaries, running perhaps from $1200 to $3000 a year. Yet there was nothing diabolical in all this. At the heart of the problem Wallin saw an absence of standards, regulations, and a prescribed program of training for clinical psychologists. Phony psychologists were able to advertise their services in the daily press so that, as far as the public was concerned, being called a psychologist was not always a guarantee of competence. Moreover, those who presumed to function as "mental-testers" were often persons of relatively limited ability who had received very little, if any, training. Under these deplorable circumstances students were better advised to get out of clinical programs than to pursue a career in this profession. But Wallin saw a much more sensible and desirable alternative than that. He urged psychologists to meet their responsibilities in this area promptly. Satisfactory training standards would have to be set up and enforced, and better jobs would have to be created by arousing the public to the pressing need for them and through favorable state legislation. Wallin preferred that the universities should assume these responsibilities but other clinicians felt they should be assumed by the American Psychological Association.

The APA still wavered, seemingly ambivalent about venturing into non-academic professional problems, and in consequence, in 1930, the Association of Consulting Psychologists was formed. This organization was in effect an extension and expansion of the New York State Association of Consulting Psychology, which had been in existence since 1921. The new name indicated its intention to reach out for membership beyond the boundaries of the state of New York.

In 1931, the Clinical Section of the APA made an effort to establish a prescribed training program in clinical psychology that, it was hoped, would be accepted by the universities. A special Committee on Standards of Training for Clinical Psychologists was appointed.

At that time there were approximately eight hundred psychologists in the United States engaged in clinical work. The need for them to offer their professional services in the area of treatment was formally recognized the following year, 1932, when the Executive Committee of the Association of Consulting Psychologists established a subcommittee on psychotherapy.

The APA Committee on Standards of Training published its report in 1935. It defined clinical psychology as "that art and technology which deals with the adjustment problems of human beings." The Committee recommended that before a person could be called a clinical psychologist he must have a Ph.D. degree and a year of supervised experience (fifteen hours of clinical work a week for forty weeks). An M.A. degree and a year's experience would entitle the person to be called an assistant psychologist. Following publication of the report, the Committee, considering its task finished, disbanded.

In the same year Poffenberger, president of the APA, exhorted the Association to accept the responsibility of setting up a "hallmark" for the qualified psychologist and establish conditions or standards for defining his competence. Poffenberger pointed out that the composition of the Association was changing; 530 members of the APA had jobs with no academic affiliation, and too many were unemployed and finding it difficult to obtain positions, particularly in a university setting. Therefore, if psychologists were going to get work during the economic depression, an even larger number would have to consider expanding their services to include applications of their science and they would have to look for such employment in clinics, schools, courts, and mental hospitals. Psychology, he claimed, was compelled to revise its image and become an applied as well as a pure science. At the same time, psychologists had to insure that both the public and their own reputations were protected from damage by incompetents.

Poffenberger's concern about unemployment and the Depression should not obscure the fact that despite the prevalent economic adversity the number of clinics and clinical positions was increasing. In 1930, there were about 500 clinics in the United States offering psychiatric services, of which about 125 were child guidance centers staffed by psychiatrists, psychologists, and social workers. By 1936, there were approximately 676 psychiatric clinics, and, in addition, about 87 psychoeducational clinics (compared with 20 in 1914) affiliated mostly with universities and colleges and directed by psychologists.

Within psychiatric clinics the major activities of the clinical psychologists were diagnostic testing and interviewing. Nevertheless, a sizable percentage, approximately 44 percent of clinicians, were engaged in remedial teaching and about 35 percent reported that they conducted therapeutic interviews with persons suffering from mild personality disorders. Within the psychoeducational clinics and state hospitals there was a similar distribution. Obviously, the majority of clinical psychologists were not active in psychotherapy, and some, contented that this was so, even felt the name of their profession should be changed to Consulting Psychology to avoid any implication that they were involved in treatment.

In 1936, the Department of Psychology at Columbia University established a tentative curriculum for clinical psychologists which consisted of two years of graduate work and one year of internship. Just such a three years training program was endorsed as a satisfactory model by the Boston Society of Clinical Psychologists in 1937.

Also in 1937 Witmer retired from the University of Pennsylvania. Earlier in the decade he had proposed another goal for the field he had named and helped create: "psychonomic personeering . . . clinical psychology oriented toward the creation of a personal character of surpassing superiority." This objective, like many proposed by Witmer, had merit but seemed inopportune and attracted little interest.

Out of a sense of futility the Clinical Section of the APA disbanded in 1937 and the American Association of Applied Psychology was formed. The new AAAP swallowed up the Association of Consulting Psychology and organized itself with four sections or divisions: consulting psychology, clinical psychology, educational psychology, and business and industrial psychology. The Association also began publishing a journal, the *Journal of Consulting Psychology*.

Toward the close of the decade the situation in clinical psychology as a profession had reached the following state of affairs. Some clinical psychologists still made up a small but distinct minority group within the APA. Some 888 members and associates of the APA, or approximately 40 percent of the Association, did not hold academic positions, and of this number about 270 were clinical psychologists. The trend was that an increasing number of psychologists were going into the clinical field and that an increasing number of clinical positions were available to them. This was especially true in the United States and proportionately not less so in England, where the number of child guidance clinics has increased from four in 1929 to twenty by 1939.

Nevertheless, more psychologists were looking for jobs than there were positions to be filled. The situation was particularly acute in universities and in large metropolitan areas, especially New York City. Although some skeptics suggested the problem was confined to the more desirable positions in the more desirable locations, the matter seemed one of genuine concern to those out of work, and several factors could be adduced to explain why unemployment existed. To some extent the Depression had probably slowed expansion in psychiatric and psychological facilities and academic positions. Moreover, the influx of psychologists from Europe undoubtedly pre-empted some jobs that might otherwise have been held by Americans. But what was most distressing was that some employers reported that they were unable to offer a position to someone who claimed to be a clinical psychologist because he was poorly trained and had little to contribute professionally.

The clinical psychologist was still thought of primarily as a diagnostician or mental-tester, but there was much talk about having him engage in psychotherapy. Any such proposal encountered major opposition from psychiatrists and the medical profession in general. There was also considerable discussion about getting state legislatures to ennact certification laws for psychologists and this also aroused strong antagonism from physicians. Little could be accomplished in either of these directions until clinicians defined their role to their own satisfaction, saw high standards of training adopted by their profession, and gave evidence of their professional maturity by formulating and following an explicit code of ethics.

Once again the APA took the lead by setting up a Committee on Scientific and Professional Ethics in 1938. However, the APA still seemed unwilling to come to grips with the issue and took a compromising stance. The Committee reported, in 1940, that it would be premature to devise a code of ethics, yet it recommended that a standing committee be formed to handle ethical infractions.

Still, clinicians were undeterred in their determined and concerted efforts to include psychotherapy within their role definition. This was certain to introduce a number of serious problems. Measures were called for to meet the all-too predictable opposition from the medical profession. Criteria for the selection of clinical psychology trainees would have to be set. Graduate students were going to have to be more carefully screened by the universities in order to filter out those who seemed unsuited to function as psychotherapists. The universities would have to establish graduate-level courses in methods of treatment.

Referring to the selection of trainees, Carl Rogers recommended that students in clinical psychology must have the ability to enter into warm human relationships, give evidence of an interest in people as individuals, and have a sincere desire to be of help to others. Further, their training should assist them to gain insight into their own motives and needs, while developing their integrity and maturity. Rogers' recommendations were eminently desirable, and all psychologists could agree that everything should be done to see that they were put into practice.

The war in Europe had thrust the responsibility for the scientific progress of psychology upon the United States. Mixed with the pride of American leadership went the sobering recognition of an obligation to the science, not to particular points of view. Gordon Allport, in addressing the APA as its president in 1939, advised his colleagues to be tolerant of their differences and to avoid authoritarian attitudes. The test of a particular point of view, he observed, rested not on discourse and the most forceful argumentation in its behalf but on its success in predicting, understanding, and guiding human action.

In the world at the end of the thirties when so many men had taken up arms to settle their grievances, psychologists did well to remind themselves that they belonged to an international fraternity and shared in a scientific discipline with its purposes and values.

References

Adams, D. K. William McDougall. *Psychol. Rev.*, 1939, 46, 1–8.

Adler, A. Individual psychology. In C. Murchison (Ed.) *Psychologies of 1930.* Worcester, Mass.: Clark U. Press, 1930.

Allen, F. H. Therapeutic work with children. *Amer. j. Orthopsychiat.*, 1934, 4, 193–202.

Allen, F. H. Otto Rank. *Amer. j. Orthopsychiat.*, 1940, 10, 186–187.

Allport, G. W. *Personality: a psychological interpretation.* New York: Holt, 1937.

Allport, G. W. The psychologist's frame of reference. *Psychol. Bull.*, 1940, 37, 1–28.

Allport, G. W. & Vernon, P. E. A study of values. Boston: Houghton Mifflin, 1931.

Anderson, J. E. The limitations of infant and preschool tests in the measurement of intelligence. *J. Psychol.*, 1939, 8, 351–379.

Ansbacher, H. L. & Ansbacher, Rowena R. *The individual psychology of Alfred Adler.* New York: Basic Books, 1956.

APA Clinical Section. Guide to psychological clinics in the United States. *Psychol. Clinic*, 1935, 23, 9–140.

Appel, K. E. Drawings of children as aids to personality studies. *Amer. j. Orthopsychiat.*, 1930–31, 1, 129–144.

August, H. E. Newer attitudes toward mental subnormalities. *Amer. j. Orthopsychiat.*, 1935, 5, 49–56.

Axelrode, Jeanette. Some indications for supportive therapy. *Amer. j. Orthopsychiat.*, 1940, 10, 264–271.

Bartlett, F. C. *Remembering: a study in experimental and social psychology.* Cambridge U. Press, 1932.

Beaglehole, E. A note on cultural compensation. *J. abnorm. soc. Psychol.*, 1938, 33, 121–123.

Beck, S. J. The Rorschach Test and personality diagnosis. I. The feebleminded. *Amer. j. Psychiat.*, 1930, 10, 19–52.

Beck, S. J. The Rorschach method and the organization of personality. *Amer. j. Orthopsychiat.*, 1933, 3, 361–375.

Beck, S. J. Problems of further research in the Rorschach Test. *Amer. j. Orthopsychiat.*, 1935, 5, 100–115.

Beck, S. J. Psychological processes in Rorschach findings. *J. abnorm. soc. Psychol.*, 1936–37, 31, 482–488.

Beck, S. J. *Introduction to the Rorschach method.* Monograph No. 1. Amer. Orthopsychiat. Assoc., 1937.

Beck, S. J. Personal communication. 1963.

Bender, Lauretta. *A visual motor gestalt test and its clinical use.* New York: Amer. Orthopsychiat. Assoc., 1938.

Benedict, Ruth. *Patterns of culture.* Boston: Houghton Mifflin, 1934.

Bernreuter, R. G. The measurement of self-sufficiency. *J. abnorm. soc. Psychol.*, 1933–34, 28, 291–300.

Binder, H. The "light-dark" interpretations in Rorschach's experiment. *Ror. res. Exch.*, 1937, 2, 37–42.

Blanchard, Phyllis. Psychogenic factors in some cases of reading disability. *Amer. j. Orthopsychiat.*, 1935, 5, 361–374.

Bradley, C. *Schizophrenia in childhood.* New York: Macmillan, 1941.

Bryngelson, B. A method of stuttering. *J. abnorm. soc. Psychol.*, 1935–36, 30, 194–198.

Burrow, T. The economic factor in disorders of behavior. *Amer. j. Orthopsychiat.*, 1939, 9, 102–108.

Byrn, D. The problem of human types: comments and experiment. *Char. Personal.*, 1936–37, 5, 48–60.

Campbell, Katherine J. The relation of the types of physique to the types of mental diseases. *J. abnorm. soc. Psychol.*, 1932–33, 27, 147–151.

Cattell, R. B. The status of applied psychology in England. *J. consult. Psychol.*, 1939, 3, 76–79.

Chidester, Leona. Therapeutic results with mentally retarded children. *Amer. j. Orthopsychiat.*, 1934, 4, 464–472.

Corsini, R. J. *Methods of group psychotherapy*. New York: McGraw-Hill, 1957.

Crane, H. The limitations of psychometrics in clinical practice. *J. abnorm. soc. Psychol.*, 1931–32, 26, 199–202.

Dashiell, J. F. Some rapprochements in contemporary psychology. *Psychol. Bull.*, 1939, 36, 1–24.

Davis, P. A. Development of electroencephalography: retrospect and outlook. *Amer. j. Orthopsychiat.*, 1940, 10, 710–718.

Devereux, G. A sociological theory of schizophrenia. *Psychoanal. Rev.*, 1939, 26, 315–342.

Doll, E. A. A genetic scale of social maturity. *Amer. j. Orthopsychiat.*, 1935, 5, 180–190.

Dollard, J., Doob, L. W., Miller, N. E., Mowrer, O. H., & Sears, R. R. *Frustration and aggression*. New Haven: Yale U. Press, 1939.

Dunbar, H. Flanders. *Emotions and bodily changes*. New York: Columbia U. Press, 1938.

Dunlap, K. *Habits: their making and unmaking*. New York: Liveright, 1932.

English, H. B. & Killian, C. D. The constancy of the IQ at different age levels. *J. consult. Psychol.*, 1939, 3, 30–32.

Fantham, H. B. Charles Dickens: a biological study of his personality. *Char. Personal.*, 1933–34, 2, 222–230.

Farber, M. L. A critique and an investigation of Kretschmer's theory. *J. abnorm. soc. Psychol.*, 1938, 33, 398–404.

Finch, F. H. & Odoroff, M. E. Employment trends in applied psychology. *J. consult. Psychol.*, 1941, 5, 275–278.

Frank, L. K. Projective methods for the study of personality. *J. Psychol.*, 1939, 8, 389–413.

Freeman, F. S. *Theory and practice of psychological testing*. New York: Holt, 1950.

Freeman, W. & Watts, J. W. *Psychosurgery*. Springfield, Ill.: Charles C Thomas, 1942.

Freud, Anna *Technic of child analysis*. New York: Nerv. & Mental Disease Publishing Co., 1928.

Freud, Anna *The ego and the mechanisms of defence*. London: Hogarth, 1937.

Freud, S. Analysis terminable and interminable. *In Collected papers*. Vol. 5. New York: Basic Books, 1959.

Friedlander, I. W. & Sarbin, T. R. The depth of hypnosis. *J. abnorm. soc. Psychol.*, 1938, 33, 453–475.

Gesell, A. & Thompson, Helen *The psychology of early growth*. New York: Macmillan, 1938.

Gitelson, M. Section on "play therapy." 1938. *Amer. j. Orthopsychiat.*, 1938, 8, 499–524.

Goldstein, K. *The organism*. New York: American Book Co., 1939.

Gray, J. S. An objective theory of emotion. *Psychol. Rev.,* 1935, 42, 108–116.

Guilford, J. P. Introversion-extroversion. *Psychol. Bull.,* 1934, 31, 331–354.

Guilford, J. P. & Guilford, Ruth B. An analysis of the factors in a typical test of introversion-extroversion. *J. abnorm. soc. Psychol.,* 1933–34, 28, 377–399.

Guthrie, E. R. On the nature of psychological explanations. *Psychol. Rev.,* 1933, 40, 124–137.

Hall, C. A comparative psychologist's approach to problems in abnormal psychology. *J. abnorm. soc. Psychol.,* 1933–34, 28, 1–5.

Harris, A. J. & Shakow, D. The clinical significance of numerical measures of scatter on the Stanford-Binet. *Psychol. Bull.,* 1937, 34, 134–150.

Healy, W. & Bronner, Augusta F. The child guidance clinic: birth and growth of an idea. In L. G. Lowrey & Victoria Sloane (Eds.) *Orthopsychiatry 1923–1948: retrospect and prospect.* New York: Amer. Orthopsychiat. Assoc., 1948.

Hertz, Marguerite R. The Rorschach Ink-Blot Test: historical summary. *Psychol. Bull.,* 1935, 32, 33–66.

Hertz, Marguerite R. & Rubenstein, B. B. A comparison of three "blind" Rorschach analyses. *Amer. j. Orthopsychiat.,* 1939, 9, 295–314.

Horney, Karen *The neurotic personality of our time.* New York: Norton, 1937.

Hull, C. L. Mind, mechanism, and adaptive behavior. *Psychol. Rev.,* 1937, 49, 1–32.

Hunt, J. McV. Psychological experiments with disordered persons. *Psychol. Bull.,* 1936, 33, 1–58.

Hunter, W. S. The psychological study of behavior. *Psychol. Rev.,* 1932, 39, 1–24.

Isaacs, Susanna. Obituary: Melanie Klein 1882–1960. *J. child Psychol. Psychiat.,* 1961, 2, 1–4.

Jung, C. G. *Modern man in search of a soul.* New York: Harcourt, Brace, 1933.

Kallmann, F. J. *The genetics of schizophrenia: a study of heredity and reproduction in the families of 1,087 schizophrenic families.* New York: Augustin, 1938.

Kardiner, A. *The individual and his society.* New York: Columbia U. Press, 1939.

Kelley, T. L. The inheritance of mental traits. In C. Murchison (Ed.) *Psychologies of 1930.* Worcester, Mass.: Clark U. Press, 1930.

Kelly, E. L., Miles, Catherine C., & Terman, L. M. Ability to influence one's score on a typical pencil-and-paper test of personality. *Char. Personal.,* 1935–36, 4, 206–215.

Klein, Melanie. *The psycho-analysis of children.* New York: Norton, 1932.

Klineberg, O. *Negro intelligence and selective migration.* New York: Columbia U. Press, 1935.

Klopfer, B. The shading responses. *Ror. res. Exch.,* 1938, 2, 76–79.

Klopfer, B. & Kelley, D. M. The technique of the Rorschach performance. *Ror. res. Exch.,* 1937, 2, 1–14.

Kunkel, F. Sex and society. *J. abnorm. soc. Psychol.*, 1932–33, 27, 1–28.

Lashley, K. S. The thalamus and emotion. *Psychol. Rev.*, 1938, 45, 42–61.

Lawson, G., *et al.* Section meeting, 1939. Old age and aging. *Amer. j. Orthopsychiat.*, 1940, 10, 27–87.

Lazell, E. W. The group treatment of dementia praecox. *Psychoanal. Rev.*, 1921, 8, 168–179.

Levy, D. M. Release therapy. *Amer. j. Orthopsychiat.*, 1939, 9, 713–736.

Levy, J. Relationship therapy. *Amer. j. Orthopsychiat.*, 1938, 8, 64–69.

Lewin, K. *A dynamic theory of personality.* New York: McGraw-Hill, 1935.

Linton, R. Culture, society, and the individual. *J. abnorm. soc. Psychol.*, 1938, 33, 425–436.

Louttit, C. M. The nature of clinical psychology. *Psychol. Bull.*, 1939, 36, 361–389.

Lurie, L. A., Schlan, Leah, & Freiberg, Margaret. A critical analysis of the progress of fifty-five feeble-minded children over a period of eight years. *Amer. j. Orthopsychiat.*, 1932, 2, 58–69.

Lutz, J. Über die Schizophrenie im Kindesalter. *Schwiez. Arch. Neurol. Psychiat.*, 1937, 39, 335–372; 1937, 40, 141–163.

MacLeod, R. B. William Stern (1871–1938). *Psychol. Rev.*, 1938, 45, 347–353.

Maller, J. B. Forty years of psychology. *Psychol. Bull.*, 1934, 31, 533–559.

McDougall, W. The hormic psychology. In C. Murchison (Ed.) *Psychologies of 1930.* Worcester, Mass.: Clark U. Press, 1930.

McDougall, W. Dynamics of the gestalt psychology. Part III. *Char. Personal.*, 1936–37, 5, 61–82.

McFadden, J. H. The will-o'-the-wisp "intelligence." *Psychol. Rev.*, 1932, 39, 225–234.

Mead, Margaret. The use of primitive material in the study of personality. *Char. Personal.*, 1934–35, 3, 3–16.

Mead, Margaret. *Sex and temperament.* New York: Morrow, 1935.

Meyer, M. That whale among the fishes: the theory of emotions. *Psychol., Rev.*, 1933, 40, 292–300.

Moreno, J. L. Application of the group method to classification. New York: National Committee on Prisons and Prison Labor, 1932.

Morgan, Christiana D. & Murray, H. A. A method for investigating fantasies: the Thematic Apperception Test. *Arch. Neurol. Psychiat.*, 1935, 34, 289–306.

Moore, Elan H. A note on the recall of the pleasant *vs.* the unpleasant. *Psychol. Rev.*, 1935, 42, 214–215.

Moore, H. & Steele, Isabel Personality tests. *J. abnorm. soc. Psychol.*, 1934–35, 29, 45–52.

Mowrer, O. H. A stimulus-response analysis of anxiety and its role as a reinforcing agent. *Psychol. Rev.*, 1939, 46, 553–565.

Mowrer, O. H. & Mowrer, Willie Mae Eneuresis: a method for its study and treatment. *Amer. j. Orthopsychiat.,* 1938, 8, 436–459.

Murray, H. A. Visceral manifestations of personality. *J. abnorm. soc. Psychol.,* 1937, 32, 161–184.

Murray, H. A., et. al. *Explorations in personality.* New York: Oxford, 1938.

Newell, H. W. Play therapy in child psychiatry. *Amer. j. Orthopsychiat.,* 1941, 11, 245–251.

Nunn, P. T. *Education; its data and first principles.* London: Arnold, 1920.

Oberndorf, C. P. Dr. Karen Horney, *Int. j. Psychoanal.,* 1953, 34, 154–155.

Park, Dorothy G. Freudian influence on academic psychology. *Psychol. Rev.,* 1931, 38, 73–85.

Penrose, L. S. Two cases of phenylpyruvic amentia. *Lancet,* 1935, 228, 23–24.

Poffenberger, A. Psychology and life. *Psychol. Rev.,* 1936, 48, 9–31.

Poffenberger, A. T. Specific psychological therapies. *Amer. j. Orthopsychiat.,* 1939, 9, 755–760.

Potter, H. W. Schizophrenia in children. *Amer. j. Psychiat.,* 1933, 12, 1253–1270.

Purdy, D. M. The biological psychology of Kurt Goldstein. *Char. Personal.,* 1936–37, 5, 321–330.

Rank, O. *Will therapy* and *Truth and reality.* New York: Knopf, 1950.

Report of Committee of Clinical Section of American Psychological Association. *Psychol. Clinic,* 1935, 23, 1–140.

Report of Committee on Clinical Training of Psychologists. *Amer. j. Orthopsychiat.,* 1940, 10, 166–171.

Rhine, J. B. Some selected experiments in extra-sensory perception. *J. abnorm. soc. Psychol.,* 1936–37, 31, 216–228.

Rogers, C. R. Three surveys of treatment measures used with children. *Amer. j. Orthopsychiat.,* 1937, 7, 48–57.

Rogers, C. R. Needed emphases in the training of clinical psychologists. *J. consult. Psychol.,* 1939, 3, 141–143.

Rosenzweig, S. A basis for the improvement of personality tests with special reference to the M-F battery. *J. abnorm. soc. Psychol.,* 1938, 33, 476–488.

Rosenzweig, S., et. al. Frustration as an experimental problem. *Char. Personal.,* 1938–39, 7, 126–160.

Sapir, E. Cultural anthropology and psychiatry. *J. abnorm. soc. Psychol.,* 1932–33, 27, 229.

Saudek, R. Can different writers produce identical handwritings? *Char. Personal.,* 1933–34, 2, 231–245.

Schilder, P. The somato-psyche in psychiatry and social psychology. *J. abnorm. soc. Psychol.,* 1934–35, 29, 314–327.

Schilder, P. *Psychotherapy.* New York: Norton, 1938.

Schwartz, L. A. Social-situation pictures in the psychiatric interview. *Amer. j. Orthopsychiat.*, 1932, 2, 124–133.

Shakow, D. The functions of the psychologist in the state hospital. *J. consult. Psychol.*, 1939, 3, 20–23.

Shakow, D. Clinical psychology: an evaluation. In L. G. Lowrey & Victoria Sloane (Eds.) *Orthopsychiatry 1923–1948: retrospect and prospect.* New York: Amer. Orthopsychiat. Assoc., 1948.

Shakow, D. & Rosenzweig, S. The use of the tautaphone ("verbal summator") as an auditory apperceptive test for the study of personality. *Char. Personal.*, 1939–40, 8, 216–226.

Sherif, M. A study in some social factors in perception. *Arch. Psychol.*, 1935, No. 187.

Shuey, H. A new interpretation of the Rorschach Test. *Psychol. Rev.*, 1933, 40, 213–215.

Skinner, B. F. The verbal summator and a method for the study of latent speech. *J. Psychol.*, 1936, 2, 71–107.

Skodak, Marie Children in foster homes: a study of mental development. *Univ. Iowa Stud. Child Welf.*, 1936, 16, No. 1.

Skraggs, E. B. The limitations of scientific psychology as an applied or practical science. *Psychol. Rev.*, 1934, 41, 572–576.

Spearman, C. Thurstone's work re-worked. *J. educ. Psychol.*, 1939, 30, 1–16.

Starr, H. E. Promethian constellations. *Psychol. Clinic,* 1933, 22, 1–20.

Stephenson, W. Correlating persons instead of tests. *Char. Personal.*, 1935–36, 4, 17–24.

Stern, W. On the nature and structure of character. *Char. Personal.*, 1935–36, 4, 270–289.

Stern, W. Cloud pictures: a new method for testing imagination. *Char. Personal.*, 1937–38, 6, 132–146.

Stevens, S. S. The operational definition of psychological concepts. *Psychol. Rev.*, 1935, 42, 517–527.

Stogdill, R. M. Neurosis as learned behavior. *Psychol. Rev.*, 1934, 41, 497–507.

Sundberg, N. D. A note concerning the history of testing. *Amer. Psychol.*, 1954, 9, 150–151.

Taft, Jessie. *Otto Rank.* New York: Julian, 1958.

Tendler, A. D. A reorientation in psychotherapy. *Psychol. Clinic,* 1933, 21, 253–259.

Terman, L. M. Autobiography. In C. Murchison (Ed.) *A history of psychology in autobiography.* Vol. II. Worcester, Mass.: Clark U. Press, 1932.

Terman, L. M. & Merrill, Maud A. *Measuring intelligence.* Boston: Houghton Mifflin, 1937.

Thurstone, L. L. Multiple factor analysis. *Psychol. Rev.*, 1931, 38, 406–427.

Thurstone, L. L. The vectors of mind. *Psychol. Rev.,* 1934, 41, 1–32.

Thurstone, L. L. *Primary mental abilities.* Chicago: U. Chicago Press, 1938.

Town, Clara H., *et. al.* Report on the survey of training and duties of clinical psychologists. *Psychol. Exch.,* 1933, 2, 109–114.

Tryon, R. C. Multiple factors *vs.* two factors as determiners of ability. So-called group factors as determiners of abilities. *Psychol. Rev.,* 1932, 39, 324–351, 403–439.

Tulchin, S. H. The psychologist. *Amer. j. Orthopsychiat.,* 1930, 1, 39–47.

Unamuno, M. de *The tragic sense of life.* New York: Dover, 1954.

Vernon, P. E. The biosocial nature of the personality trait. *Psychol. Rev.,* 1933, 40, 533–548.

Vernon, P. E. & Allport, G. W. A test for personal values. *J. abnorm. soc. Psychol.,* 1931–32, 26, 231–248.

Wallin, J. E. W. Shall we continue to train clinical psychologists for second string jobs. *Psychol. Clinic,* 1929–30, 18, 242–245.

Wechsler, D. *The measurement of adult intelligence.* Baltimore: Williams & Wilkins, 1939.

Wellman, Beth L. The effect of preschool attendance upon the IQ. *J. exper. Educ.,* 1932–33, 1, 48–69.

Wellman, Beth L. Our changing concept of intelligence. *J. consult. Psychol.,* 1938, 2, 97–107.

West, R. Is stuttering abnormal? *J. abnorm. soc. Psychol.,* 1936–37, 31, 76–86.

Winter, J. E. The postulates of psychology. *Psychol. Rev.,* 1936, 48, 130–148.

Witmer, L. Psychonomic personeering. *Psychol. Clinic,* 1930, 19, 73.

Wittman, Phyllis. The Babcock deterioration test in state hospital practice. *J. abnorm. soc. Psychol.,* 1933–34, 28, 70–83.

Witty, P. A. & Lehman, H. C. The instinct hypothesis *vs.* the maturation hypothesis. *Psychol. Rev.,* 1933, 40, 33–59.

Witty, P. S. & Theman, Viola. The psychoeducational clinic. *J. appl. Psychol.,* 1934, 18, 369–392.

Woodworth, R. S. Dynamic psychology. In C. Murchison (Ed.) *Psychologies of 1930.* Worcester, Mass.: Clark U. Press, 1930.

Woodworth, R. S. The future of clinical psychology. *J. consult Psychol.,* 1937, 1, 4–5.

Yerkes, R. M. Concerning the anthropocentrism of psychology. *Psychol. Rev.,* 1933, 40, 209–212.

Zilboorg, G. Overestimation of psychopathology. *Amer. j. Orthopsychiat.,* 1939, 9, 86–94.

7

To The Victors

1940-1949

THE WAR IN EUROPE had taken a dramatic turn of events, becoming markedly different from the trench warfare that had been anticipated. By 1940, the British army had been driven from the Continent, and Germany had conquered Denmark, Norway, the Netherlands, Belgium, and France; meanwhile her ally Italy had launched an invasion of Greece. Within the next year Germany conquered Bulgaria, Yugoslavia, and Greece. The German army invaded Russia and in North Africa pressed its advance toward the Suez Canal. The German Air Force continued its bombing of Great Britain, and the lurking hulls of German submarines filled the waters of the Atlantic. Then, in December of 1941 Japan attacked the United States, and what had been a European war became World War II.

After a series of further victories the tide soon turned against Germany, Italy, and Japan, and in 1945 they surrendered unconditionally (Italy had surrendered earlier, in 1943.). The war had been an extremely savage and costly one. Approximately sixteen million men in the armed forces had been killed and many more millions wounded. Uncounted millions of civilians, including women and children, had died in bombings and the vicious persecutions conducted by the Nazis.

The United States emerged from the war the most wealthy and power-ful nation on earth and deeply resolved not to repeat its mistakes of the post-World-War-I period. Accordingly, it eagerly joined and hopefully supported the United Nations, an organization dedicated to seeking ra-tional, peaceful solutions to world problems. For a moment, but only for a moment, there seemed to be peace.

This illusion was quickly dispelled when civil war was renewed in China, and the U.S.S.R. made clear its intention to promote communism whenever possible—a policy which the United States found it necessary to oppose with growing determination. All too swiftly it appeared that one enemy had been replaced by another. By 1949, two great coalitions of nations confronted each other: the nations of the West led by the United States and including Great Britain and France *versus* the nations of the East led by the Union of Soviet Socialist Republics and including the recently established Communist regime in China. Each of the leaders of these blocs possessed atomic weapons and thus the capacity to ex-terminate each other, and, it was widely feared, everyone else besides.

Yet World War II and its aftermath were not without some positive results. They had had an enormous vitalizing effect on the American economy. Billions of dollars in aid were extended by the United States to countries all over the world and vast sums were spent in rejuvenating the nation. One highly desirable consequence was the G.I. Bill, which pro-vided veterans with an opportunity to acquire a college education with-out cost. Not too surprisingly, enrollments in schools of higher learning for the academic year 1949, which numbered 2,659,021, were nearly double what they had been ten years before. Many of these students chose to specialize in psychology, perhaps encouraged to do so by the favorable publicity which psychology earned through its contributions to the mili-tary effort and its applications in other fields, notably mental health.

Moreover, the fruits of the research stimulated by the war were many and diverse: electronic devices of all sorts, jet aircraft, miracle drugs, antibiotics, insecticides, rockets, detergents, and atomic energy. Taken all in all there had been ten years of rapid change—for individuals, for na-tions, and for the profession of clinical psychology.

NORMAL PERSONALITY FUNCTIONING

The field of investigation which Freud found when he began his epoch-making discoveries bore little resemblance to the one which he left. Within the framework of the relative sophistication of his followers and their formidable obligation to digest his wisdom and knowledge, few could expect to attain his stature. Yet reactions to his contributions, including sharp dissent, continued, and even among those who considered themselves Freudian in orientation there were shifts in emphasis and movement into areas which were thought to have previously been neglected.

Many psychoanalysts focused upon the functioning of the ego. In so doing they were drawn into the task of integrating their findings with those of psychology as a whole. They were supported by Anna Freud's observations that these ego processes defend against external as well as internal stimuli, and by the formulations of Hartmann, Kris, and Loewenstein concerning the autonomy of ego functions. These ideas were leading to a different psychoanalytic conception of human development in which instinctual forces were held to be less powerful and considerably less dominant than had been thought.

The organism was now conceived of as having been endowed from birth both with instinctual impulses (id) and "apparatuses" or structures for motility, perception, and memory (ego). Even without conflict or a need to control these impulses the ego processes function to adapt the individual to his environment, which includes interpersonal relationships. The autonomy of the ego was proclaimed in theory by departing from the previous belief that it derived its energy gradually from the id. Instead, both ego and id were thought to be differentiated from a common matrix, and the processes of each have their own supplies of energy. Furthermore, in these analytic circles a concept was developed similar to functional autonomy but called "neutralization of drives."

Neutralization of drive energy refers to a progressive process whereby energy associated with instinctual gratification becomes divorced from this aim and serves the function of environmental adaptation. For example, though painting might have originally provided pleasurable gratification through giving expression to smearing impulses, it could later come to serve as a vehicle for the communication of feelings and a source of livelihood. Through neutralization, energy associated with functioning of the id would become associated with ego functioning.

The concept of neutralization served to bring the present more sharply into focus and to stress its importance in understanding the individual . . . although the past was still emphasized and it was still agreed that the essential structure of personality is formed by the time a child is five or six years old. Another idea which sharpened the significance of the present was the suggestion that a stimulus of little relevance in one stage of development might become decisive at a later stage. For example, a child might see a nude woman early in his life when this would have little meaning for him, but later this memory might be reactivated and contribute to the development of fear of castration.

A similar swing corrective of a previously held extreme position became evident in relation to the importance attached to the gratification of drives. Not only instinctual gratifications but also their frustrations, as well as the maturation of perceptual equipment, were now seen as necessary for psychological growth and the development of interpersonal relationships. An optimal balance between satisfactions and deprivations is needed if the child is to become mature in all respects.

Despite these modifications, psychoanalytic theory was encountering much criticism from cultural anthropologists. By means of cross-cultural studies it had been found that infants can be subjected to widely varying child-rearing practices and still seem to develop into "normal" adults. Two major conclusions emerged: one, though the child's early experiences might predispose him to acquire certain personality characteristics, his later experiences could actualize, modify, or nullify them; and two, overt practices of child-rearing are of much less significance for personality development than the attitudes, feelings, and motives communicated to the child by the parental figures in the course of their caring for him. Both these empirically supported conclusions were swiftly recognized and incorporated into psychoanalytic teaching.

"There is no psychology of man in a vacuum . . . only a psychology of man in a certain concrete society and in a certain social setting within this concrete society." These are the words of Otto Fenichel (1897–1946) in his book *The Psychoanalytic Theory of Neurosis* (1945). Fenichel felt a great love for psychoanalytic theory and a great fear that in trying to meet the enormous demand for therapeutic services psychoanalysis would be modified and compromised until its uniqueness as a form of treatment was lost. He had taught at the Berlin Psycho-Analytic Institute before leaving Germany in 1933. After teaching analysis in Oslo and Prague, Fenichel arrived in the United States in 1938 and spent his few remaining years in California. Fenichel concluded from his studies that the Oedipus complex is not universal and inevitable but that it is a product of family structure and influences. Therefore he hypothesized that when the composition of the family departs from the Western model of a nuclear family structure with an authoritarian father and a passive mother, the pattern of the Oedipus complex changes . . . thus taking another step toward making psychoanalytic theory accessible to the findings from cultural anthropology by suggesting certain modifications of the theory to make it conform to findings already available.

Freud's death instinct, or instinct of aggression, was also revised to make it compatible with results of experiments and more current points of view. In 1942, Karl Menninger asserted that the aggression instinct is fostered and intensified by frustrations of the love instinct. Such frustrations are produced by parents who are unconsciously rejecting their children. A vicious circular process is set in motion that produces children who, when they grow up and become parents, in turn, unconsciously reject their children. If this vicious circle is to be broken, Menninger recommended that people should become aware of their aggressive impulses and cultivate their expressing their love. Karen Horney, it would seem, might easily have returned to the psychoanalytic fold. But of course she did not, and was joined by others, including Fromm and Sullivan, who shared with her the conviction that man's personality is largely a function of his culture.

Erich Fromm (b. 1900) grew up in Germany, received his Ph.D. from the University of Heidelberg in 1922, and trained as an analyst in Munich and at the Berlin Psychoanalytic Institute. In 1933, he came to the United States and lectured at the Chicago Psychoanalytic Institute before entering private practice in New York.

In 1941, Fromm saw man as, by his very nature, a being in need of experiencing a sense of belonging and relatedness. Yet with each gain in his growth as a unique person, with each step forward in his awareness of separation from his natural environment, he comes to feel more lonely, isolated, and uncertain of the desirability of his supposed progress. His life may easily come to seem empty and meaningless, and the temptation is to fill this void by conformity and submission to others. But at the same time he is reluctant to part with his individuality. A choice has to be made: "to unite himself with the world in the spontaniety of love and productive work or else to seek a kind of security by such ties with the world as destroy his freedom and the integrity of his individual self."

Naturally Fromm favored the selection of the alternative of personal growth and social usefulness. But coming from Germany, Fromm was acutely aware that a whole people seemed to have sacrificed their freedom in order to gain a feeling of security and a sense of identity through submission to a totalitarian regime. Obviously, the more healthy choice is not always made and with consequences that may be calamitous and catastrophic. Therefore, Fromm believed, in view of the dangers confronting democratic forms of government, an immediate need of men is to have "faith in life and in truth, and in freedom as the active and spontaneous realization of the individual self."

Although Harry Stack Sullivan shared Fromm's appreciation of the importance of interpersonal relations, his approach to the subject was from a different direction. Though it may be argued whether man inherently needs to relate to others, it cannot be disputed that from birth on he is involved in interpersonal situations. For Sullivan "the relatively enduring pattern of recurrent interpersonal situations which characterize a human life" is personality.

Sullivan (1892–1949) obtained his M.D. from the Chicago College of Medicine and Surgery in 1917. He studied under the psychiatrist William Alanson White, and from 1923 until 1930 was connected with the Medical

School of the University of Maryland. During that period Sullivan conducted studies of schizophrenia, pioneering in its psychotherapeutic treatment and interpreting its etiology primarily in terms of disturbed relationships in the patient's early childhood. In 1933, Sullivan became president of the William Alanson White Foundation, and in 1936 became director of the Washington School of Psychiatry. The journal *Psychiatry,* which began publication in 1938, served as the chief vehicle for the communication of his ideas.

Sullivan defined psychiatry as the study of interpersonal relations, "the study of processes that involve or go on between people." This rather ambitious and certainly overinclusive definition contains an implication which Sullivan recognized and explicitly discussed: the individuality of the person is not itself the object of scientific scrutiny. Instead, it is the interactions between the person and others, including those with the scientist or therapist, which are to be observed, studied, and interpreted. Thus what the person says or does has meaning only insofar as it is related to someone else. The therapist or scientist can no longer consider himself passive or neutral and let it go at that. He has to understand what effects he might have, including what effect his attempts to have no effect at all might have, within the field of the individual's personality.

From the very beginning, it was thought, interpersonal interactions are of paramount importance. According to Sullivan, the self-system, the sanctioned potentials which the person seeks to develop and integrate, originate in the infant's empathic sensing of the mothering one's feelings (For example, the infant is supposed to be able to sense his mother's feelings of anxiety or her affection for him. To a large extent, these feelings are thought to be communicated by the way in which the mother feeds, holds, in short, interacts with her child.). Further, the self-system is built up over the course of years from the child's appraisals of how significant people seem to regard him. When the organism experiences biological frustrations and insecurities, a tension or anxiety is felt. This anxiety sets up disruptions in the process of communication and disturbs integrative actions and growth. Ordinarily, efforts are made to alleviate tensions and anxiety through the satisfaction of needs and through regaining a feeling of security. But when these efforts fail, the individual tends to resort to feeling apathetic or sleepy. Thus indifference, drowsiness, selective inattention, withdrawal, and distortions of reality are seen more as means whereby the person prevents an overwhelming feeling of tension or anxiety from coming into his awareness and less as defenses against instinctual impulses.

The various stages of development described by Freud were perceived by Sullivan as representative of modes of interaction between the child and others. For example the anal stage centers around the activities of toilet-training in which the child's retention and elimination of feces can produce melodramatic interpersonal reactions, and is not simply a time when the anus serves as a zone of special sensitivity and gratification.

While the self-system has its foundation in infancy, it continues to grow in scope, complexity, and integration throughout childhood and adolescence. Sex roles, cultural values, and occupational goals are some of the conceptions that are supposed to accrue to it. Clearly, Sullivan regarded personality as capable of changes and modifications throughout the normal course of development, and during this growth it is interpersonal variables that are of major importance, particularly the relationships between mother and infant, parent and child, and between child and peers and authority figures.

Since the self-system functions to safeguard a feeling of security and to protect the person from feeling anxious, Sullivan claimed it tends to exclude information incongruous with its state of organization. A similar conceptualization was advanced by Prescott Leckey in his book, *Self-consistency* (1945). Leckey regarded personality as an organization of consistent values: consistent because the individual resists accepting information inconsistent with his values and assimilates experiences that correspond with his beliefs. In the same vein, Angyal conceived a symbolic self that tends to falsify and distort reality with the result that the person's behavior is often based upon or guided by unreliable and inappropriate information. In ways such as these the concept of the self was finding its way back into psychology.

Hilgard, in his presidential address before the APA in 1949, pointed out that feelings of guilt have to be understood in relation to a self-concept since guilt feelings indicate that the person conceives of himself as capable of either good or bad choices. The individual's defense mechanisms also imply a self-reference in the sense that they protect the person against a loss of self-esteem. Therefore Hilgard believed it is necessary to obtain a picture of the individual's self-concept, "his image of himself," in order to understand him fully.

But to ask the person simply what he thinks of himself does not constitute a satisfactory way of obtaining information about his self-concept. Even if the person wants to be honest and cooperative, unconscious factors will distort his reported self-concept because not all that he "thinks" about himself is in awareness. It seemed to Hilgard that the best way to avoid both conscious and unconscious bias is to infer the self-concept from observations of a person's behavior, whether by noting his performance in interviews or on projective techniques.

Many psychologists agreed with Hilgard that a self-concept is important, but disagreed with his contention that the self has to be inferred. It is a simple matter to avoid this difficulty, they claimed. All one has to do is restrict the self-concept to consciously held thoughts, feelings, and strivings which the person readily acknowledges as his own. Other psychologists felt that such a restricted concept of the self is not very sophisticated, but it became apparent that regardless of which self psychologists wanted to talk about, they at least were discussing once more a self. William James and Mary Calkins would have been pleased.

At least four factors contributed to this renewed interest in the self. Two of them we have already noted and discussed: the growing attention paid both to ego functioning and to interpersonal relationships. A third was the experimental demonstration of support for the hypothesis that man exists in a world of his own perceptions. A fourth was the increasingly popular belief in the dignity and uniqueness of the human being. Let us now briefly consider the last two factors.

Everyone agreed that perception is a function of maturation, and in 1940 Heinz Werner more specifically described what that might mean. In general, Werner saw mental development as progressing from products of perception and conceptualization that are diffuse, labile, and indefinite to those that are more differentiated, integrated, stable, and definite. To the child, objects have a personal meaning. They appear alive and expressive, and their fine details do not seem to be perceived. As the child grows, his perceptions become more discrete and less influenced by personal feelings and needs. However, these maturational changes seem to be more a matter of degree rather than being discriminable into two distinct types of perception, one occurring only in childhood, the other occurring only among adults. A number of studies which investigated the effects of needs and feelings upon perception supported the view that these effects are found normally in adulthood. We shall mention only two of them.

In 1943, Schafer and Murphy had subjects learn names for each of four outlined faces presented tachistoscopically. Whenever two of the faces were presented the subjects were regularly rewarded with money, while presentation of the other two was regularly accompanied by "punishment," taking money from the subjects. A rewarded and a punished face were then combined along their common profile into a single ambiguous figure. When these were presented, the subjects more frequently called out, "perceived," the name of the rewarded face than the name of the punished face.

In 1948, McClelland and Atkinson, after establishing a set by projecting faint pictures onto a screen, projected blanks and asked three groups of hungry naval trainees what they thought these "faint pictures" might be. The more hungry the naval trainee, the less he tended to see food but the more he tended to see objects related to food, e.g., plate, spoon, fork. This finding was interpreted as indicative of an inhibition against thinking about food itself when hungry.

Because of the insights gained from such experiments, psychologists began to talk enthusiastically about "a new look in perception," referring to the demonstrations of the influence of values and needs upon perceptual processes and hence the artificiality of demarcating content areas within psychology. As Bruner and Cecile Goodman put it in 1947: "For too long now, perception has been virtually the exclusive domain of the Experimental psychologist with a capital E." It seemed clear to them that a full understanding of perception would require the cooperative efforts of psychologists specializing in different fields of research.

A similar conclusion might have been reached in every area of psychology. There was no longer much question that the individual is an organism, an integrated whole, who cannot be broken up into separate functions or processes that are fully understood when in isolation from one another. The "new look in perception" had given support to the position of those psychologists who had argued for more emphasis upon the self. Some of these psychologists defined the self as a conceptual system describing the person organized from his perceptions of his environment, especially those related to his experiencing of the attitudes and feelings of others toward him, which in turn affect his subsequent perceptions. But regardless of the particular definition employed, their experimental findings were compelling most psychologists to entertain a much broader conception of the stimulus and response than before.

During the preceding forty years of psychology a picture of man had emerged as a higher form of animal (some psychologists would stop here) whose behavior is determined in large part by thoughts and feelings and impulses of which he is not aware, who unknowingly distorts his world on the basis of his needs and fears, and whose lifelong patterns of responding have been laid down during the first five years of his development as an individual. Now a reaction antithetical to this conception of man was mounting. Adding impetus to this reaction were the very real prospects for human annihilation made vivid by the recent spectacle of destruction in which millions of egos and selves perished. What was felt to be needed was that man should experience a sense of responsibility for his own actions, and then strive to live by an ethics based upon an appreciation of the worth of every human being. Perhaps at the crux of the matter is the need for each individual to refute the apparent meaninglessness and insignificance of his own life.

Man's significance, dignity, worth, and responsibility for his behavior had certainly always been emphasized by religion, but such ideas had seldom found a place within textbooks of psychology. The time seemed ripe for them to make an appearance and with force.

Sullivan pointed out that even the lowest level of human integration is far superior to the most highly developed organism that is not human. Man as a species is unique, and by virtue of his uniqueness is set apart from other organisms. Even the genius and the idiot, Sullivan asserted, are more similar to each other because of their shared humanness than either is to any nonhuman member of the animal kingdom.

Of course James, Freud, Adler, Jung, Rank, etc. had each in his own way discussed the uniqueness of man. But where before this uniqueness was taken mostly for granted and his continuity with other forms of animal life had to be made explicit and stressed, now the continuity of man with other forms of animal life had come to be taken for granted and a need was felt to make his uniqueness vivid and of great consequence. But of course while many psychologists experienced this need there were many others who did not.

According to some psychologists what makes man unique are his needs, especially the upper range of his needs, and his ability to deal creatively with his environment. Abraham Maslow (b. 1908) described the person as possessing a hierarchical structure of needs, which in ascending order are: physiological; safety; belongingness and love; esteem; and finally self-actualization, the same term, though in a more restricted sense, as that used by Goldstein to indicate a striving for completion and the fulfillment of potentialities. Physiological needs are basic, shared with other organisms, and demanding, if the individual is to survive, of relatively immediate gratification. But with their satisfaction, the next higher group of needs in the hierarchy emerge to dominate conscious functioning and to serve for a time as the immediate motivation of behavior; with its satisfaction the next higher need emerges, and so on. Therefore, as the lower needs are satisfied, the person becomes free to manifest the higher ones. Conversely, it must also be noted that when the lower needs remain chronically unsatisfied, the person may never have the opportunity to express those which are more altruistic, lofty, and human. In a land where people starve and fear for their lives the need for self-actualization may not be too apparent.

In 1948, John Anderson presented an overall picture of the nature of children which is shared by many of his colleagues in developmental psychology and which can also be taken in principle as descriptive of the nature of man. He depicted the child as an active energy system coping with and creating his world . . . not at all a passive organism victimized by stimuli from his environment. This child responds selectively, ignoring as well as attending to stimuli. His past is largely forgotten, and he lives in a present where he retains from his previous experiences those events which have been repeatedly encountered in the form of cultural values, persistent family attitudes and problems, and in general the more or less successful patterns of adjustment. The child as thus conceived evidences resiliency and a substantial capacity for tolerating and recovering from stresses and frustrations.

Anderson's description of the child may easily be substituted for one of the self. In it the pendulum of ideas is seen swinging back to a self theory, though one both less abstract and less extreme than that of the late nineteenth and early twentieth centuries. Psychoanalysis had discarded the rational adult self capable of free will. Behaviorism also represented a reaction against self psychology and against indulgence in the whole class of mentalistic concepts. But here was the self again—a less rational self than its predecessor, more aware of its environment, less capable of pulling itself up by its own bootstraps, and with a history of development. As such, it represented a formidable reaction against determinism by the unconscious as in psychoanalysis, and against the bundle of habits or empty organism as in behaviorism.

DIAGNOSTIC TECHNIQUES

While personality theories were proliferating and in some measure integrating, diagnostic techniques were also increasing in quantity, complexity, and comprehensiveness. Some idea of the number of psychological tests in use in 1940 was provided by Buros, who published appraising reviews of about 325 testing instruments and who listed approximately two hundred others. Only a small proportion of these techniques were employed to any great extent by clinicians. The remainder were either instruments devised for use in other areas of applied psychology or were tests that did not enjoy much popularity.

With war already raging in Europe and Asia, psychologists were once again called upon to develop group tests for the evaluation of military personnel. In 1940, a committee of psychologists consisting of Walter Bingham (chairman), C. C. Brigham, H. E. Garrett, L. J. O'Rourke, M. W. Richardson, C. L. Shartle, and L. I. Thurstone formed an advisory group to the Adjutant General. These psychologists assisted in the development of the Army General Classification Test, a group test administered to approximately ten million servicemen during the course of the war. A number of other tests were devised for use in the selection of naval officers, pilots, instructors, and candidates for assignment to training in particular skills.

To meet the special demands of wartime, a variety of screening devices and modifications of existing procedures were produced, among which were a Personal Inventory of 145 items for detecting psychiatric disturbances, the Kent EGY tests for a rapid evaluation of intelligence, a group administered Rorschach, and shorter forms of the TAT. At the other extreme were highly elaborate situational tests, which included lengthy stress interviews and subjecting men to diabolical frustrations. These were used to select from among candidates those best fitted for the dangerous, precarious, highly important work of the Office of Strategic Services.

Hardly a male adult of military potentiality within the United States escaped psychological testing. It was estimated that during 1944 sixty million standardized tests were administered to twenty million persons. Examining these figures more closely: the College Entrance Examination

Board and American Council on Education administered 26,781,759 tests
to 11,493,407 persons; the Adjutant General's Office gave 4,993,142 tests
to 2,302,919 persons; the Bureau of Naval Personnel 9,000,000 tests to
1,250,000 persons; the Army Air Force 10,000,000 tests to 400,000 persons;
the Civil Service Commission 1,800,000 tests to 1,120,000 persons; and
the Bureau of Medicine and Surgery 240,000 tests to 80,000 persons.

Within Great Britain the principal test for purposes of military classification was the Raven Progressive Matrices. This is a nonverbal test of
homogeneous items, in which the person is required to select the missing
section that will complete a sequence of designs. In each item there is
some logical principle of progression, and this principle becomes increasingly more difficult to detect. The test was devised by L. S. Penrose and
J. C. Raven, and was first published in 1938 as a technique for measuring
general intelligence that would minimize the effect of culture and education. Although based on Spearman's theory of intelligence and thus designed to measure *g* or the ability to perceive relationships, more specifically "insight through visual survey," the Progressive Matrices did not
prove too effective in predicting success in most training courses. However, it did seem quite useful as a predictor of performance in visual
signaling and the operation of radar sets.

Surprisingly, in view of official declarations against their use, diagnostic
techniques even managed to survive and find a place in Nazi Germany.
Ostensibly, testing had been abandoned in 1942, probably for two reasons: one, because, in essence, psychological testing is a democratic procedure since selection for positions is on the basis of an individual's
psychological functioning and skills rather than on his membership in a
favored political party or social group; and two, because there was a wish
to deny the presence of psychological problems within the German armed
forces. Nevertheless, somewhat clandestine psychological testing went on
within the German slave-labor program. Individual industrialists sanctioned testing as a method of placing laborers in proper jobs and insuring
worker satisfactions. Approximately 425,000 slave laborers were given
group placement tests patterned after those used in the American Army
in World War I. It is satisfying from a scientific point of view, but chill-
ing from another perspective, to note reports that the slave laborers who
had been assigned to their jobs on the basis of testing had a higher productivity than those slave laborers who were assigned arbitrarily.

Publication of the Wechsler-Bellevue was propitiously timed, since the
war created a great demand for the evaluation of adult intellectual functioning. It rapidly assumed the position of the leading individually
administered adult intelligence scale. Its appeal to clinicians was increased
in 1941 when Wechsler hypothesized that certain patterns of scatter among
subtest scores might be useful in the diagnosis of organic brain disease,
schizophrenia, mental deficiency, juvenile delinquency, and psychoneuro-

sis. Almost immediately a flurry of research was stimulated aimed at assessing the instrument's validity as a diagnostic tool in psychiatry. An early evaluation of these studies by Rabin in 1945 indicated that the various measurements of Wechsler-Bellevue scatter and patternings might differentiate between groups of individuals who manifested certain psychiatric disturbances but they were not sensitive enough to warrant a diagnosis in a specific case on their evidence alone.

Nevertheless the Wechsler-Bellevue fulfilled its major objective of providing a measure of adult intellectual functioning. In 1949, the similarly constructed Wechsler Intelligence Scale for Children (WISC) was published. The WISC had been standardized on 2200 children: 100 boys and 100 girls at each age level from five through fifteen years. This standardization sample consisted of white youngsters only and was controled so as to represent proportionately geographic areas in the United States, urban and rural populations, and occupational classification of the fathers. Clinicians liked its division into subtests and into Verbal and Performance Scales, and before long the WISC challenged the Stanford-Binet as the most popular individually administered intelligence scale for children, particularly in age ranges above eight years.

For use in testing infants, the developmental-intelligence scale constructed by Psyche Cattell (b. 1893), daughter of James McKeen Cattell, won a position of leadership. This scale included items at each age level from two through thirty months. It was designed to overlap with the Stanford-Binet so that testing could be extended upward and downward between the two instruments. Standardization was based on 1,346 examinations of 274 white children of North European stock living in the Boston area. Since Cattell's scale provided standardized administration and scoring procedures, it was a decided improvement over Gesell's Developmental Schedules, which lacked both. Yet even at the time of its introduction in 1940 Cattell acknowledged its dubious reliability and validity. Research seemed to make it clear that until children reach school age their IQ's as measured by tests are not very reliable or predictive of scores which they may obtain later.

There are three rather disparate occurrences which we shall take notice of before proceeding to a consideration of some techniques for determining personality in general. Among other devices introduced during this period for the evaluation of intellectual functioning were the group administered Stanford Achievement Tests (1940) and Forms R, S, and T of the Otis Classification Test (1941). The Kuder Preference Record appeared in 1942 and consisted of 168 items selected to provide a measure of the person's interest in nine areas: artistic, clerical, computational, literary, mechanical, musical, persuasive, scientific, and social service. In 1947, the Educational Testing Service was established at Princeton, New Jersey, merging and coordinating the functions formerly performed by the Graduate Record Office, the College Entrance Board, and the Cooperative Test Service.

The Minnesota Multiphasic Personality Inventory (MMPI), constructed by the psychologist Starke Hathaway and the psychiatrist J. C. McKinley, began to receive attention around 1940. It eventually consisted of 550 statements which a person taking the test has to categorize as *True, False,* or *Cannot Say,* e.g., "I very seldom have spells of the blues." The responses to such statements were initially standardized on 1500 normals, 220 psychopaths, and 50 hypochondriacs but were soon extended to sample nine diagnostic groupings: depression, hypochondriasis, hypomania, hysteria, masculinity-femininity, paranoia, psychasthenia, psychopathic personality, and schizophrenia. Although the MMPI was intended primarily to assist in differential psychiatric diagnoses, its 550 items and its scales, which could be regarded as descriptive of personality characteristics, provided a large field for exploration and tempted the ingenuity of clinicians to devise other uses for the Inventory.

A great deal of activity centered around projective techniques, particularly the Rorschach. From 1930 through 1938, approximately 142 articles had been published on clinical applications of the Rorschach; from 1939 through 1947 there were 436 publications on this one projective technique alone. A significant event in the development of this test occurred in 1942 when Klopfer and Kelley published their scoring system, which included a major innovation, the scoring of animal and inanimate movement responses.

Bruno Klopfer, born in Germany in 1900, the son of an authoritarian banker, has expressed the belief that his poor vision made it necessary for him to develop his abilities to concentrate on and think carefully about a problem. He received his Ph.D. from the University of Munich in 1922. Then for about a year Klopfer had an analysis with Jung, and while in Zurich spent his time profitably between analytic sessions by studying the Rorschach. When later asked how he could study and master so complex a test in so short a time, he replied, "Well you see, it wasn't so complex, till I made it complex."

Klopfer came to the United States in 1934 and worked with Franz Boas as a research associate in anthropology at Columbia University. He began teaching the Rorschach and two years later founded the Rorschach Institute and the *Rorschach Research Exchange,* a publication that changed its name in 1949 to the *Journal of Projective Techniques.* In 1946, he was appointed associate clinical professor at UCLA. The scoring system proposed by Klopfer and Kelley was widely adopted, rivaling that of Beck's in popularity. Beck described and explained his method of scoring in two volumes published in 1944 and 1945. The major difference between the two systems was that Beck scored only human movement responses. (Although not as commonly adopted as the two just mentioned, there were other scoring systems, notably those of Marguerite Hertz and Zygmunt Piotrowski.)

The Rorschach, consisting as it does of ambiguously structured ink blots, seemed at first to be an ideal culture free instrument, and as such suitable for evaluating the personality functioning of diverse peoples. However, it soon became clear that it is not as culture free as had been thought, and even if it had been, the psychologist who administers and interprets it is not. Although the anthropologist Jules Henry discussed the Rorschach with reference to its use in cross-cultural studies, his comments have the same relevance whether the subjects are natives of the United States or Pilaga Indians of Argentina.

Henry thought that with persons who are not test-wise a reason has to be given for their being tested, and it has to be one that does not clash with their particular culture. If the psychologist, through ignorance of a person's value system, unwittingly justifies the test administration for reasons that conflict with what the person feels is right, then the results, supposing that testing is still allowed to take place, will probably be invalid. Furthermore, to make meaningful interpretations, the psychologist has to have some frame of reference for evaluating responses in a particular culture, including knowledge of the language and its nuances, and of the emotions associated with a particular flora and fauna, e.g., among some inhabitants of the United States a donkey is a good omen and an elephant a bad one. Henry concluded that valid Rorschach interpretations can only be obtained after the psychologist has immersed himself in the culture in which he wants to do testing.

Following the war a number of projective techniques made their debut. There was still interest in graphology, though relatively little. Somewhat more attention was given for a time to Dollard and Mowrer's Discomfort-Relief Quotient. This was a method of measuring "tension" in a document by dividing the number of words it contained indicating Discomfort by the number of Discomfort plus Relief words. However, enthusiasm for this method was far less than for certain drawings and other projective devices that we shall mention.

The Rosenzweig Picture-Association Study for Assessing Reactions to Frustration consisted of twenty-four cartoons (This test is usually referred to as the Rosenzweig Picture-Frustration Study.). Each cartoon depicts two people in frustrating circumstances in which the character at the left verbalizes a statement that is frustrating in itself or helps describe the frustration. The person taking the test is asked to write in what he thinks the other character will say about the unhappy turn of events. His responses are thought to reveal something about his tolerance of frustration; the direction his aggression might take (toward the environment, against himself, or perhaps an attempt to appear nonchalant and avoid any expression of hostility); and also his reaction type (defensive, overwhelmed by frustration to the point of helplessness, or persisting in attempts to overcome the obstacle and achieve gratification of his need).

David Rapaport (1911–1960) brought the Szondi Test to the United States when he emigrated from Hungary but it did not attract much interest until after the war. Constructed by Lipot Szondi, a psychiatrist, the test is composed of forty-eight facial photographs of (European) psychiatric patients. There are six photos in each of eight psychiatric categories: passive male homosexuals, male sadistic murderers, hysterics, epileptics in the intraparoxysmal phase, catatonic schizophrenics, paranoid schizophrenics, manic-depressive depressed, and manic-depressive manic. A person taking the test is asked to pick the two photos he likes most and the two he dislikes most in each of six sets. It was supposed that his selections indicate the strength of his own latent tendencies to the pictured conditions. Those pictures he liked were believed to represent tendencies available for expression in overt behavior; those he disliked were thought to indicate characteristics that are repressed or sublimated; those he did not select were supposed to be tendencies that were already overt. Szondi's rationale was that the eight syndromes represent genetically determined basic drives and that the person responds to the photos according to the relationships between his own drives and those of the patients pictured. A *Szondi Newsletter,* established in 1949, made it possible for those interested in the test to communicate with one another.

E. S. Schneidman's Make-A-Picture-Story Test (MAPS) requires people to construct a picture and then tell a story about it. The sentence completion test provides the person with the stem of a sentence which he is asked to finish. Karen Machover's Draw A Person Test (DAP) requests that the individual draw a picture of a person and then one of a person of the other sex. These drawings are analyzed for evidence of anxiety about certain body parts, for suspiciousness, for inadequacy, for insecurity, etc. In J. N. Buck's House-Tree-Person Test (HTP) the person has to draw a house, a tree, and a person on a sheet of paper. G. S. Blum's Blacky Test asks the person to tell a story and answer questions about pictures of a cartooned dog family, each picture depicting one or more dogs in a situation related to, supposed to arouse the idea of, some aspect of personality functioning derived from psychoanalytic theory, e.g., the Oedipus complex, anal and oral impulses, etc.

Of inventiveness and activity, then, it can be seen there was plenty. But of validity, there was all too little evidence. Guilford, evaluating the role of psychology in aviation during the war, concluded that its major contributions had been rather undramatic. Psychologists did improve training procedures by suggesting techniques that made it possible for persons to get immediate knowledge of how well they were performing. But a variety of personality tests were found to have little value in predicting success in pilot training. Such objectively scored personality inventories as the Bernreuter, MMPI, and Guilford-Martin, had validity coefficients around .20. Projective techniques fared no better. Neither the Rorschach nor the TAT were of much use in making predictions about pilots. In fact, intuitive clinical judgments were found inferior in validity to objective scores. What did seem to be of some help in predicting who would make the better aviators was biographical information about them . . . not exactly clinically demanding data.

However, in rebutting the negative verdict of their critics, clinicians quite legitimately pointed out that they had been given no chance to go about their job properly. They had been expected to predict success in pilot training without first being given an opportunity to find out what are the personality characteristics of the successful military pilot. Under the unrelenting pressures of war there had not been the time to gain this knowledge.

That "new look" in perception was introducing other variables for the clinician to ponder upon while evaluating his test results. Some experiments indicated that transitory deprivations and frustrations could distort an individual's perceptions. For this reason it seemed important to know a person's experiences just prior to administering a projective test to him. Could it be that recently frustrated drives would turn up in his responses to projective techniques? Of course things would be much simpler if the tests proved insensitive to situational variables. Everyone hoped they were not. But, unfortunately, the evidence indicated that they were. For example, when the person had become angry with the Examiner or had recently seen nude photos, his responses to the Rorschach differed from what they were when he approached the test situation with more poise and less provocation. Accordingly, the individual's performance came to be seen as a function of both current and relatively enduring response patterns, and the task of the clinician was now to discover approximately how much weight should be given to each.

There was even some question as to whether the techniques actually furnished any unique information about the person. In the opinions of Rosenzweig and others they did not: "The view is indeed current that the projective techniques serve in large measure not to elicit new facts regarding the personality, but to underscore certain knowledge already available from history and interview and thus to indicate the degree and type of relevance these aspects may have in the patient's actual present approach to his environment."

"The literature abounds with signs proposed as indicators of this or that trend or characteristic," said H. F. Hunt after reviewing publications in psychodiagnostics. The Rorschach was the favored projective technique for evolving signs, such as the presence or absence of movement responses, or the number and type of color responses that would help in making differential diagnoses. There were signs for schizophrenia, signs for suicide, signs for homosexuality, signs for brain damage, signs for mental deficiency, signs for hysteria, signs for depression, signs for obsessions, signs for paranoia, but very few signs for normality. Moreover, irritation was growing over a swelling mass of studies of dubious value for making predictions.

Despite criticisms and discouraging reports, many clinical psychologists retained their enthusiasm for projective techniques and the method. There were, admittedly, some obvious asides asking whether the person or the clinician had been doing the projecting, but such sarcasms did not diminish the ardor of some clinicians for their ink blots, pictures, and drawings. It was generally felt by the group favoring these devices that the psychometric tradition had, to be sure, yielded standardized personality tests, but that these were capable only of telling the extent of an individual's deviation from a norm—rather dry stuff. In contrast, projective techniques were regarded as an avenue into the fascinating private world of the individual, where he was continuously engaged in creating, maintaining, and defending his perceptions and beliefs.

Thus to some psychologists it seemed that psychological testing had arrived at a time of full flowering. In their view the ultimate tests for the evaluation of personality had been developed, and while much remained to be done to understand them fully, these instruments were, so to speak, inviolable. Their conviction was not shared by many other psychologists, who, though they admired these creations, were still poking about seeking to discover if their plot of land were in need of weeding and the rotation of crops.

DIAGNOSTIC FORMULATIONS

Despite the growing number of disputed points, such as those concerning projective tests, some areas of general agreement were being established. The formerly heated nature-nurture controversy was one of these, with each side now recognizing some validity in the position of the other. Exaggerated claims that mentally deficient children can be brought up to an average level of intellectual functioning by being reared in suitable environments were generally discounted, as were adamant assertions that the IQ is a completely stable index of native ability. Some fifty studies agreed that attendance at nursery school could raise the mean IQ of children by about five or six points. Environmental effects, it was concluded, can mildly to markedly impair, and alternatively can to a similar degree improve, the level of intellectual functioning. Presumably, though, the functioning of the basic neurophysiological processes involved in intelligence cannot be radically improved by experiences later in life, e.g., as far as we know, even with the best that can be provided by the environment, a mongoloid child will remain intellectually subnormal.

Another controversy that had persisted over the years was also drawing to a close. In 1940, Cyril Burt demonstrated that the results of any one factor analysis can easily be transformed into the results of another. Hence the disagreement between Spearman and Thurstone about the structure of intelligence was shown to be largely a product of two different statistical methods, as well as the restricted range of scores in Thurstone's University of Chicago sample. At any rate, Spearman acknowledged the existence of certain group factors and Thurstone wound up with a general factor, though he considered it of a second order.

Nevertheless, the search for factors or abilities went on. Guilford found *g*, verbal, numerical, spatial, memory, speed of perception, fluency, and alertness factors in intelligence, and also uncovered some leads in the direction of others. Meanwhile Thurstone, after second thoughts about the matter, decided to eliminate the induction factor. He also had his doubts about the perceptual and deductive factors, but dealt with these less drastically.

In 1948, Thurstone explained that first order factors represent primary abilities, which function as media for the expression of intellect and are probably connected with separate organs of the body. The second order factors are supposed to be representative of more central and universal parameters influencing the activities of the primary factors. By this time Guilford had discovered twenty-seven factors in human abilities. Among them are space (awareness of spatial arrangement in which reference to the body is important), visual memory, rote-memory, reproductive-memory, and mechanical knowledge.

Oddly enough, Thurstone's earlier conclusions were used to justify a course of social action, not in the United States, but in Great Britain, Spearman's own country. Using, or perhaps it is more accurate to say "misusing," Thurstone's initial finding that there is no general ability factor, the British Education Act of 1944 set up a tripartite classification of secondary schools for three types of children: grammar schools for the literary or abstract type; technical schools for the technical or mechanical type; and "modern schools" for the practical or concrete type. Cyril Burt, in describing this system a few years later, reported that in his judgment it had not really worked well.

How to define intelligence was still a lively issue. Stoddard, in 1943, offered: "intelligence is the ability to undertake activities that are characterized by (1) difficulty, (2) complexity, (3) abstractness, (4) economy, (5) adaptiveness to a goal, (6) social value, (7) the emergence of originals, and to maintain such activities under conditions that demand a concentration of energy and a resistance to emotional forces."

Garrett disapproved of Stoddard's definition. He suggested that intelligence should be considered an attribute of behavior, not an ability; "an intelligent person does not possess 'intelligence' but rather exhibits the capacity to act intelligently (make a high score) when faced by tasks demanding the use of symbols (words, diagrams, numbers, mazes) in their solution."

In keeping with Werner's theory of perceptual development, Garrett hypothesized that as a person grows older, intelligent behavior gradually becomes differentiated and changes from being fairly unified and general into a loosely organized grouping of abilities or factors. Garrett's hypothesis is supported by evidence which indicates decreasing intercorrelations between various tests of ability as age increases. Probably the basis for this developmental trend, Garrett suggested, is to be found in the differential effects of maturation, in divurging interests, and in concentration on the cultivation of certain skills or talents to the neglect of others. From such a hypothesis it could be predicted that tests that yield a single score, such as the Stanford-Binet, are most useful with children, while tests providing part scores, such as the Wechsler-Bellevue, are most useful with adolescents and adults.

If intelligence is an attribute of behavior, it follows that what is intelligent depends upon the frame of reference of those who propose to evaluate the behavior. Some psychologists did not like a relativistic concept of intelligence, but there seemed to be no getting away from it. Doll, in his definition of mental deficiency, asserted that the primary criterion of mental subnormality is social inadequacy, which certainly would seem to vary depending upon the criteria of adequacy prevailing in a particular society. Incidentally, Doll's complete definition of mental deficiency runs as follows: a social incompetence due to mental subnormality of constitutional origin which is evidenced over the course of development and at maturity which is essentially incurable.

In the majority of mental defectives, a "constitutional origin" of their retardation has not been specifically identified and their subnormality is assumed to be genetically determined. They are called "garden variety" defectives or, according to Strauss and Lehtinen, "endogenous" defectives. However, Strauss and Lehtinen distinguished another group of mental defectives, the exogenous, which they thought is made up of those who are brain-injured and which might comprise from perhaps 15 to 20 percent of all retardates. When examined as children by neurologists, signs of their possessing defective neuromotor systems sometimes showed up. Generally, though, the neurological reports are negative, supposedly because the symptoms are relatively minor and subtle. Instead of being evident in pathological reflex functioning, these abnormalities are observed in the psychological examinations of perceptual processes, thinking, and other complex forms of behavior. Since the diagnosis of exogenous mental deficiency usually rests on evidence solely from psychological tests, the etiology of the syndrome seems wrapped in a process of circular inference and is of questionable validity, at least until some external criterion of brain-injury can be found to substantiate and rescue it. But this does not diminish the accomplishments of Strauss and Lehtinen in the identification of children with cognitive disturbances.

At the other extreme of the continuum of intellectual functioning Terman and Oden reported on the results of their follow-up of a group of gifted children. Most of these children retained their superior standing into adulthood, possessed better than average physiques and health records, and did well in college and in their chosen professions. Rates of divorce, sickness, and mental illness were about the same as in the general population.

On the basis of her study of approximately thirty children who earned IQ's of 180 and above on the Stanford-Binet, Leta Hollingworth (1886–1939) concluded that these children tend to feel, and actually are, isolated by their unusually high level of intellectual functioning. They are likely to be social misfits, in part because they do not appreciate fully their own superior abilities, and for this reason experience much unhappiness. Apparently, an extremely high IQ may be, in its own way, as much a social liability in the United States as one that is low. In any case, it appears that those children who have the best prospects for developing well-rounded personalities and achieving "good" adjustments in our society possess IQ's between 125 and 155. In intelligence, as well as in many other characteristics, it seems to be possible to have too much of a good thing.

Turning from the subject of intelligence, we may note that the issue of whether personality is constitutionally determined was being examined with new vigor. A fresh empirical attack upon these variables was inaugurated by William Sheldon, even though typologies based on relationships between physical characteristics and personality were no longer fashionable. Sheldon (b. 1899) was raised in Rhode Island on a farm owned by his father, a naturalist and breeder of animals. He received his Ph.D. in psychology from the University of Chicago in 1926 and his M.D. in 1933. For about two years he studied psychiatry abroad, mostly with Carl Jung. In 1938, he went to Harvard, and, after a period of service in the Army during the war, in 1947 accepted the position of Director of the Constitution Laboratory, College of Physicians and Surgeons, at Columbia University.

During the early stages of Sheldon's research project he sought to determine the principal variables that account for variation in physique using the nude photographs of four thousand male college students and the considered opinions of several judges. The task of the judges was to detect primary components of physique, i.e., characteristics which could be used to rank each and every subject, that are reliable, and that could not be accounted for by combining two or more other variables. Three major components were found to satisfy these criteria: ectomorphy, which refers to a thin, lightly muscled body with a flat chest, fragile appearance, and a large central nervous system in proportion to size; mesomorphy, which is seen in a muscular physique with well-developed bones; and endomorphy, which is characterized by softness, relatively large body cavities containing the viscera, and underdeveloped bones and muscles. Generally, Sheldon noted, an individual exhibits all three of the components to some degree and so it is possible to classify him by rating him on a seven-point scale with respect to each of them. Thus there are theoretically 343 patterns of physique, or somatotypes, and in his early studies Sheldon identified 76 of these.

In another phase of his research Sheldon attempted to isolate the major components of temperament. After concluding that fifty personality traits seemed to adequately describe an individual, an intensive study of thirty-three young men was conducted, during which each subject was rated on each trait. These rating scores were intercorrelated and three primary clusterings of personality traits emerged: cerebrotonia, a term which describes the inhibited, introverted, controlled, secretive, self-conscious, and perhaps thoughtful person; somatotonia, which describes one who is energetic, extraverted, aggressive, inclined to be noisy, and brave; and viscerotonia, which describes an individual who is sociable, relaxed, and preoccupied with seeking companionship, comfort, and food.

A study of two hundred male college students, which took about five years, sought to discover what relationships could be found between physique and temperament. Sheldon claimed that his results indicated high correlations between ectomorphy and cerebrotonia, mesomorphy and somatotonia, and endomorphy and viscerotonia. These findings are similar to those reported by Kretschmer during the twenties, and, just as Kretschmer had done, Sheldon investigated the relationship between physique and psychiatric disturbances and also found significant positive correlations . . . between endomorphy and affective psychiatric disturbances, e.g., manic-depressive psychosis, and between ectomorphy and heboid disorders, as, for example, schizophrenic reaction, hebephrenic type.

However, unlike Kretschmer, Sheldon offered explanations for his correlations that recognized the importance of environmental interactions and mediators, as well as constitutional predispositions. Thus he thought it likely that cultural stereotypes about the personality characteristics of people with certain physiques might play some part in shaping the behavior of the individual to fit the stereotype (the "tall, silent type"); or it could be that certain body builds might restrict the person to certain patterns of action, as in the case of the frail individual who would not be encouraged to participate in sports and so might turn to a compensatory interest in books and ideas.

Sheldon's reasonable explanations made his work more acceptable than it might have been had he insisted on genetic determiners alone for physique and personality characteristics. Although few psychologists were convinced that the correlations between the variables are as large as he claimed, they appreciated the worth of his classification of physiques as a research tool, and admitted that, at the very least, Sheldon's studies served as a reminder that the bodies of people might have some bearing on how they function as personalities.

Of course organic disorders are often cogent illustrations that physical changes have dramatic consequences for behavior. One of the significant findings of this decade was the discovery, around 1940, that alcoholic psychoses are by no means due wholly to the direct effects produced by the consumption of alcohol but are largely traceable to vitamin B deficiencies. Jolliffe described four possible factors in evaluating the indirect effects of alcoholic intake on nutrition: (1) the irritating action of alcohol on the gastric mucosae; (2) its interference with the absorption and utilization of vitamins; (3) the substitution of vitamin-free alcohol for vitamin-containing food; and (4) an increased requirement for vitamins because of the large number of calories provided by alcohol. This advance in understanding the etiology of alcoholic psychoses made high vitamin diets and adequate nutrition essential in the treatment program of these disorders.

On the other hand, support, if support were needed, for emphasis upon the significance of interpersonal relationships came from two unexpected sources. A number of studies agreed that relatively few neuroses were induced among children or adults who had been subjected to frequent bombings. It was thought that their experiences had been made less traumatic by the fact that they had been shared with others and also by the mutual support and encouragement which they both received and gave. Here were persons able to endure considerable stress when given the company of their fellow human beings. Moreover, several studies of institutionalized children substantiated the clinical impression that mothering is essential for satisfactory personality development. Particularly in the case of infants, deprivations of warm, human contacts seemed to have damaging effects on their physical growth. While the experimental procedures in some of these studies left something in the way of rigor to be desired, it was generally conceded, even by the most severe critics, that mothering, if not mothers, is very important.

The importance of parent-child relationships was also emphasized by findings in studies of prejudice. Much of this research was spurred by the war's demand for a unified America, and one of its noteworthy products was an impressive amount of information on the nature of the authoritarian personality. An authoritarian person, it was shown, while submitting to those in positions of power and glorifying the values and virtues of his particular in-group, depreciates and even vilifies the characteristics and beliefs of members of out-groups; perceives the world as dangerous and unpredictable; and finds it difficult to tolerate ambiguous situations. Unconsciously, such persons appear to have hated their parents and felt worthless, though they vehemently deny these feelings and at the same time displace their hostility toward people belonging to minority groups. Complicating their problems even further is their need to justify their attitudes and actions within a culture that values democratic ideals. Often their justifications rest upon rationalizations and projections of their own conflicts, which make their aggressive attacks seem strikingly unrealistic and irrational.

Although the plight of an authoritarian personality is deplorable, the sympathies of most social scientists lean toward the defense of the persecuted minorities, who suffer not only obvious abuses and assaults but who also, it was thought, may fall prey to psychosomatic diseases induced by the tensions engendered by their being discriminated against. Yet, it is also true, as Bruno Bettelheim observed, that the victims of bigotry likewise deal in stereotypes. Addressing himself specifically to antisemitism, Bettelheim noted that frequently Jews caricatured the people who persecuted them in pictures indicative of distortions of their own inner conflicts. Moreover, while no one could deny the sufferings of the Jews or the tragic death that befell such vast numbers of them during the war, Bettelheim suggested that despite these tortures and humiliations, they derived some narcissistic gratification from being persecuted. After all, the Jewish victims might "reason," they must be of some importance and potential power to be dealt with so brutally by those in authority.

Let us now briefly examine a severe disorder in which the parents of the patients seemed to be, almost without exception, persons of high intelligence and possessed of an objectivity bordering on coldness. In 1943, the psychiatrist Leo Kanner described the syndrome of early infantile autism, a psychotic disturbance of childhood characterized by virtually no relationships with people and a fascinated preoccupation with inanimate objects. The primary criteria for the diagnosis of this condition are "from the start an extreme autistic aloneness," failure to use language for communication, and an obsessive insistence on sameness. Secondary criteria are onset of these symptoms before three years of age and evidence of average, or better, intellectual functioning in certain areas. After Kanner's delineation of the syndrome, other psychiatrists began reporting the diagnosis of early infantile autism among children they had observed, but some wondered if this disorder was a form of schizophrenia rather than a specific illness.

Meanwhile, there was still considerable controversy about the etiology and the nature of schizophrenia. One question had to do with the fact that usually whenever a group of schizophrenics is compared with a group of normals on the performance of a task, they do less well.

Does this mean that this psychosis necessarily eventuates in a deterioration of the abilities under study? If so, schizophrenia could be viewed as a disease affecting the functions of the cortex. This appeared to be the conclusion of Lauretta Bender, who, impressed by the impaired functioning of schizophrenic children, suggested that the disturbance might consist of a "developmental lag of the *biological processes* from which subsequent behavior evolves by maturation at an embryological level." However, J. McV. Hunt and Cofer questioned whether there are actual impairments in the abilities of schizophrenics, and suggested the hypothesis that the deficits in performance are more probably attributable to impaired motivation.

Sullivan proposed that the term schizophrenia should be reserved as a label for those psychotic disorders of living which have an acute, traumatic onset, while the term dementia praecox could be retained to refer to an organic, degenerative psychosis which has an insidious onset and poor prognosis. Similarly, Darrah believed that dementia praecox implies a schizoid prepsychotic personality which progresses toward deterioration, while schizophrenia is the correct diagnosis when the prepsychotic personality seems to have been adequate and there has been an abrupt onset followed by a milder, nondeteriorating course.

Bellak thought one could detect a continuum of etiological factors in cases of schizophrenia ranging from the completely organic to the completely psychogenic. Duval and Hoffman noted that soldiers evidencing symptoms of dementia praecox had, typically, an abrupt onset, a stormy course, and a better prognosis than patients who manifest the illness in civilian life; they suggested that the best diagnosis for the military disorder might be somewhere between hysteria and acute schizophrenia.

At any rate a new distinction was being drawn between types of schizophrenic patients. On the one hand are those who evidence a long history of poor psychological adjustment which eventually culminates in hospitalization; in the etiology of such cases organic factors are thought to predominate and the prognosis is poor. On the other hand are those who seemed to make an overtly satisfactory psychological adjustment prior to hospitalization and in whom the psychotic onset is sudden and usually contemporaneous with some trauma. Psychogenic factors are thought to predominate in the etiology of this form and the prognosis is good.

It was hoped that clarifications of these subtypes of schizophrenia would help explain and prevent conflicting experimental results as well as being of assistance in the evaluation of the validity of psychological tests. Of course the fact that practically every large medical teaching center had its own unique nomenclature did make for some additional difficulties in appraising research results and in obtaining consistent information about diagnostic techniques used with psychiatric patients. The American Psychiatric Association had attempted to remedy this problem in 1933 by publishing the *Standard Classified Nomenclature of Disease*. Unfortunately, that manual was intended to meet the needs of mental hospitals which treated civilian patients so that when World War II broke out only about 10 percent of the military psychiatric cases could be satisfactorily diagnosed. The *Nomenclature* had no category for combat neuroses, and relatively minor personality disorders had to be classified either as psychopathic personalities or as psychoneurotics because there were no appropriate labels for them and they had to be called something from the manual.

An Army revision of the *Nomenclature* was adopted in 1945 by all branches of the armed forces and, in 1946, by the Veterans Administration. In 1948, a revised *International Statistical Classification* was adopted. Thus during the forties at least three major nomenclatures enjoyed some degree of popularity. In addition, almost all the psychiatric teaching centers had their own varying emphases and diagnostic groupings. Some order had to be brought into this chaos, and as the decade drew to a close a committee established by the American Psychiatric Association was hard at work on this problem.

It was against this background that clinical psychologists attempted to validate their instruments, assess the functioning of patients manifesting various psychiatrically diagnosed disturbances, and evaluate the effects of different treatment procedures.

TREATMENT FORMULATIONS

Insulin and electroshock, both singly and in combination, continued to be used in the treatment of schizophrenia, manic-depressive psychoses, and melancholia. For chronic psychoses, psychosurgery was becoming popular and enthusiastic accounts of it were not uncommon in the daily press and in magazines.

It appeared that the prefrontal lobes are involved in planning, persisting at a task, thinking about the future, and functions related to conscience. What contributed to this impression was the fact that patients who have lobotomies are less inhibited, find it difficult to contemplate prospective courses of action, and are less able to sustain attention for any considerable period of time. There was some question whether such impairments in the patient's functioning outweighed the improvements in behavior produced by the surgery. Even more serious was the question as to whether really any benefits at all are derived from the operation or whether whatever favorable changes might be observed were traceable to the good effects of the care the patient received before and after his lobotomy.

Toward the end of the forties a study was conducted by the staff at Greystone State Hospital in New Jersey with the collaboration of a research team from Columbia University. A group of chronic schizophrenic patients had topectomies performed. (A topectomy is a refinement of lobotomy in which only a few selected areas of the prefrontal lobes are severed.) A control group of similar chronic schizophrenic patients was prepared for surgery, wheeled into the operating room, did not have topectomies, but did have their heads bandaged, and received postoperative surgical care. Neither the patients nor those ministering to them knew which persons had had the operation and which were controls. It was found that favorable changes occurred just as frequently among the nonoperated controls as among the schizophrenic patients who had received topectomies. Therefore, the study concluded, there is no justification for the use of topectomies in the treatment of schizophrenia.

Although the decade was closing on a disappointing note as far as psychosurgery was concerned, psychotherapy was benignly thought of by almost everyone. Clinical psychologists, social workers, teachers, clergymen, and other professionals were being attracted to this area in ever greater numbers. Kraskin, an optometrist, recommended that his colleagues engage in the practice of psychotherapy since ocular problems are exacerbated by emotional problems and sometimes even engendered by them; "There is more in this than meets the eye," one might say. Schwing, a nurse and lay analyst, urged members of the nursing profession to treat psychotic patients. Her own work was primarily with schizophrenic women with whom she aimed to function as a giving mother-substitute.

Psychiatrists were far from delighted by this trend toward psychotherapeutic intervention by nonmedical persons. Some were sufficiently alarmed to instigate an attempt to induce general practitioners into accepting the role of psychotherapists. Their hope seemed to be that by enlisting the help of the kindly family doctor proprietary rights to psychotherapy could be fixed exclusively within the province of medicine. However this was not easy to accomplish, if for no other reason than because psychotherapy had little appeal to physicians who were already burdened by the pressures of their ordinary practice.

Yet the demands for psychotherapy were unmindful of distinctions between professions, and the public was concerned only that the need for this service was becoming ever greater, while relatively few persons were available to supply it. Karen Horney suggested that in certain cases the individual might be able to analyze himself. After all, self-analysis was good enough for Sigmund Freud, William James, Alfred Adler, and John B. Watson, among countless others. Through a planned system of self-treatment involving introspection, meditation, reading, prayer, work, etc., Horney believed that the person might be able to gain greater self-understanding, improve his social adjustments, and in general become more relaxed and satisfied. She called this consciously directed self-analysis "autonomous therapy."

Group therapy was a method particularly suited to meet the need for more psychotherapy caused, in part, by the war and its aftermath. In consequence this approach experienced an acceleration in growth.

In 1942, Moreno established a Psychodramatic Institute in New York, and Slavson helped found the American Group Psychotherapy Association. Like everything else, group therapy became more complex and differentiated. Slavson described four types: play or release group therapy; activity group therapy; interpretive group therapy, in which the personality functioning of the individual members of the group is discussed; and group work, in which, Slavson thought, there may not be too much "therapy" but which helps the person socially and educationally. In 1947, Moreno founded the journal *Sociatry,* later named *Group Psychotherapy.* He was notable as a vigorous and untiring proponent and proselytizer for this form of treatment.

As group therapy became more widely used, its unique advantages and disadvantages became more clear. Among the advantages claimed for the method are the following: it is of help to resistant or reserved patients who might find it difficult to participate in, and obtain benefit from, individual sessions; it quickly helps persons who may take comfort from their discovery in the group that they are not alone in their unhappiness and their struggle toward self-improvement. The group also provides opportunities for its members to reassure and support one another, and to offer to each alternative solutions to their problems; moreover, it allows the leader of the group to observe and explore the interactions of his patients.

Among the disadvantages reported in connection with the use of group therapy are the following: the therapist cannot devote as much time as he might like to a particular patient; the therapeutic experience is less intense and more superficial than in individual therapy; hostility tends to be acted out in the group and may be injurious to some members; a resistant member may interfere with the efforts of others to gain self-understanding, as well as thwarting his own treatment; and one member may copy the symptoms of another. Despite such disadvantages, its economy and specific values made group therapy the treatment of choice under many circumstances, especially in institutional settings.

Another line of attack for meeting the demand for services was the development of methods for abbreviating the duration of individual psychotherapy. In 1941, Berliner discussed the possibilities of brief psychoanalysis. The psychoanalyst, instead of dealing extensively with repressed content or id material, might deliberately choose to focus on the ego and those aspects of superego functioning readily accessible to awareness. By this means the analyst could hope to shorten the course of treatment and so become able to serve more patients than he could otherwise.

A method of treatment called semantic therapy, which is a special branch of general semantics (This has to do with the study of human responses to signs [anything that is perceived to have significance] and symbols [anything that is *intended* to communicate significance]), began to receive some attention from psychologists around 1940. One of its exponents and a leading popularizer of the subject, Alfred Korzybski (1880–1950), claimed that maladjustments are often the result of emotionally charged, inaccurate interpretations of experiences. The person thus uses symbols irrationally, and has to be helped to evaluate them intelligently and precisely. Korzybski mentioned four general rules which, if acquired by the person, would help him to examine his behavior correctly. They are as follows.

(1) The symbol has to be dated, i.e., an event or the action of a person has to be specified in time. For example, a father is not always cruel; the patient has to note those times and circumstances when his father did treat him harshly, and by this means may be led to see his own responsibility for the punishments he received and become aware, perhaps, that his father possessed more positive characteristics and positive feelings toward him. In short, an equation such as Father=cruelty has to be recognized as false; the correct equation is Father=cruelty when. . . .

(2) The symbol is not all-inclusive, i.e., a partial resemblance to an object does not necessarily signify that object, and the patient has to make this differentiation. This rule has relevance to the concept of transference. The person has to discriminate and realize when his reactions to an individual are being determined by some aspect of the individual or their relationship which elicited an emotional response based on feelings toward someone else.

(3) The symbol has to be indexed, i.e., an individual has to be specified and distinguished from other members of his group. This rule bears on the subjects of prejudice and stereotypic thinking. The patient has to recognize that simply because he has had unpleasant experiences with, let us say, his mother, he is not justified in feeling an antipathy toward all women.

(4) The symbol is not the object and therefore should not of itself elicit an emotional response. This means that the person should learn to control his feelings when reacting to words, pictures, and thoughts. Excessive affective reaction is not only inappropriate but may do great harm to onself.

Korzybski believed that by a thoroughly rational evaluation of symbols, the person would be helped to face his problems objectively, clearly, expeditiously, and successfully.

As would be expected, there was at this time an awakened interest in narcoanalysis and hypnosis. Narcoanalysis or narcosynthesis seemed to be particularly useful in treating combat or traumatic neuroses. Sodium amytal or pentothal sodium was administered to produce a light narcosis, during which the patient re-enacted the occasion of his trauma. This was followed by interviews which aimed at synthesizing the material in awareness. The method was particularly effective in alleviating feelings of guilt and in consequence soldiers could often be returned to their duties in a relatively short time.

By the early part of the decade, some agreement had been reached about the nature of hypnosis. A number of experts in this field felt that hypnotic behavior should be regarded as a form of meaningful, goal-directed striving, in which the general goal is to behave like a hypnotized person as this role is continuously defined by the hypnotist (through his suggestions and commands) and understood by the subject.

Hypnosis as a form of treatment, or hypnotherapy, seemed to have six major uses: (1) to allow relaxation and rest by employing prolonged hypnosis; (2) to remove symptoms by direct suggestions that they disappear; (3) to bring about by direct suggestions the disappearance of the attitudes underlying the symptoms; (4) the abreaction of traumatic experience, or a reduction of emotional tension by recalling the incident; (5) specialized techniques, e.g., anesthesia during what would otherwise be the extremely painful exercise of muscles to prevent their atrophy while bedridden; and (6) hypnoanalysis.

Two of the better-known proponents of hypnoanalysis were the psychiatrist Lewis Wolberg and the clinical psychologist Robert Lindner (1914–1956). As expounded by them hypnoanalysis is a method integrating hypnosis within a psychoanalytic approach. First, the patient is taught how to be hypnotized and to experience a deep trance state. Free associations in the "normal" state are then elicited, and whenever resistances are encountered, hypnosis is resorted to in order to clarify or circumvent them. With the patient once again in the "normal" state there are syntheses of material and attempts to reeducate him, that are then reinforced by posthypnotic suggestions. The goals of this treatment are the same as those generally attributed to psychoanalysis: to uncover the unconscious motives for behavior, to enable the patient to experience an abreaction, and to strengthen the healthy aspects of ego functioning. Lindner believed that hypnoanalysis is most successful with cases of alcoholism, anxiety neurosis, homosexuality, and somnambulism, but is contra-indicated for psychoses.

As the forties came to a close, there occurred a perceptible waning in enthusiasm for the use of both hypnosis and procedures involving drugs. The feeling was that these were largely techniques adopted as expedients during wartime and best confined to the battlefield and its victims. Few civilian patients seemed to give evidence of the same dramatic improvement that had been shown by soldiers, and in peacetime there is less urgency and more concern for thoroughness and lasting effects, desiderata presumably related directly to the length of treatment.

Here, too, exceptions could be found. Some analysts contended the treatment could be shortened and still be effective. Franz Alexander and Thomas French advocated variations in psychoanalytic technique to abbreviate the therapy and reported pleasant results when this is done. They recommended enlisting the cooperation of those persons in a strategic position to ameliorate environmental pressures on the patient, setting a time limit for the end of analysis, manipulating the frequency of analytic sessions, and accepting the validity of the apparent improvements produced after even one meeting.

Within this context we may note two forces at work: (1) the greater weight given to expediency as sufficient reason for demanding a briefer form of therapy in view of the large number of cases in need of this service in comparison with the small number of available therapists; (2) a growing conviction that persons might be changed through corrective emotional experiences within a short time, which implied a belief in the resiliency of human beings. These forces and the need of many clinicians for a form of psychotherapy closely identified with, and offered under the aegis of, their own profession provided a fertile set of circumstances which combined to predispose many of them to accept the eloquently expressed and thoughtfully developed ideas of Carl Rogers.

In 1940, Carl Rogers described the process of psychotherapy in terms that included the following: establishment of rapport; the client freely expresses his feelings; the client experiences a recognition and acceptance of his spontaneous self; the client, aided by the support of the therapist, makes responsible choices, gains insight through assimilated interpretations, and grows into independence. In 1942, Rogers stated: "Effective counseling consists of a definitely structured, permissive relationship which allows the client to gain an understanding of himself to a degree which enables him to take positive steps in the light of his new orientation."

Roger's approach, called "nondirective therapy" due to its prohibitions of counselor interpretations, probing, and giving of advice, emphasized the significance of the therapeutic relationship as in itself a growth experience. Its stress upon the importance of feelings over intellectual insights, upon the present rather than the past, and upon the role of the counselor in assisting the client to grow in individual expression and independence gave notice of its indebtedness to the formulations of Otto Rank and Frederick Allen.

The originator of nondirective therapy, Carl Rogers (b. 1902), was a middle child in a large, close-knit, conservative family. His parents prohibited dancing, cards, sodas, movies, and all other frivolous, enticing activities: "So I was a pretty solitary boy, who read incessantly, and went all through high school with only two dates."

Rogers entered the University of Wisconsin majoring in agriculture. During his junior year he went to China for six months to attend an international World Student Christian Federation Conference. On this trip he began to admit to himself more frankly his doubts about organized religion and about his dependence upon his parents. Following his graduation from Wisconsin, he married and entered Union Theological Seminary. After two years he left Union for Teacher's College at Columbia and the field of clinical psychology.

At Columbia, Rogers was influenced by the ideas of John Dewey, enjoyed the atmosphere of free thought, interned at the Institute for Child Guidance, and learned to work with children under Leta Hollingworth. He accepted a position as psychologist at the Society for the Prevention of Cruelty to Children in Rochester, New York, in 1928, became director of the Society in 1930, and received his Ph.D. in 1931. That year a test developed by him, *A Test of Personality Adjustment,* was published. It is a paper and pencil test which samples a child's wishes, aspirations, affection for members of his family, and the areas in which he feels a discrepancy between what he is and what he would like to be. In 1939, Rogers helped establish and served as director of the Rochester Child Guidance Center. His book, *The Clinical Treatment of the Problem Child,* was published and received favorable reviews. A major theme of this book, that treatment may become a science if we are willing to subject it to careful examination, is recurrent throughout his work. From 1940 to 1945, he was professor of psychology at Ohio State University, and in 1945, he accepted the positions of professor and executive secretary of the Counseling Center at the University of Chicago.

Rogers pointed to four major principles which his many years of clinical experience had taught him: one is that authorities are not always right; a second is that coercion in therapy or counseling is never more than superficially effective; a third is that the client, not the therapist, is most aware of direction of movement in psychotherapy; and a fourth is that there is a discoverable orderliness in the process of counseling and therapy.

At first Rogers believed that the nondirective approach was appropriate for only a select group of clients. The person has to be under some degree of tension and must want to be helped. He has to have some capacity to cope with life and to express his feelings. He must be of at least dull normal intelligence, be between ten to sixty years of age, be free of excessive instability or severe organic impairment, and be reasonably independent of close family control. He also has to be able to plan his contacts with his counselor and keep them as scheduled.

By 1946, Rogers was speaking of his approach as "client-centered therapy," an unfortunately rather presumptuous term since all psychotherapists feel that they place the well-being of their clients at the center of their efforts. The cardinal assumption of Rogerian therapy, which is perhaps a more felicitous label of his approach, is the existence within the individual of forces that potentially make for his growth. These forces are supposed to be spontaneous in their working and in their capacity to integrate and creatively reorient the organism, the person. Thus, an individual's behavior is determined not only by the influences to which he has been previously exposed but also by his current integrative and creative insights. The role of the therapist is to provide a setting in which these constructive forces can operate, to create a relationship in which the client feels understood and free to understand and alter himself. In keeping with this new assumption, or hypothesis, all admonitions as to the suitability of particular kinds of clients for nondirective therapy were here abandoned in favor of trying this new method with anyone and everyone rather than presume it is not applicable.

In his presidential address before the APA in 1947, Rogers emphasized the importance of perceptions in the behavior of the person. Like Lewin, he argued that behavior is not immediately determined by organic or environmental factors as such but rather by the individual's perceptions of these. He contended that when changes occur in the individual's perceptions of himself and the world about him, there will be related changes in his feelings and his manner of interacting with others.

From Roger's point of view, psychological maladjustment represents a more and more extensive denial to awareness of significant experiences so that these denied percepts cannot be integrated into the structure of the self. Failure to integrate what should have been integrated produces a state of psychological tension. When the person is able to integrate all his self-perceptions into a conscious concept of self, Rogers believed there will result a feeling of comfort which may be thought of as psychological adjustment. Rogerian therapy, he proposed, is one means—for him the best one—by which this comfort or adjustment can be attained.

Major criticisms leveled at the Rogerian approach are that it seems superficial and places inordinate demands upon the client to assume responsibility for himself. Frederick Thorne contended that some patients are better served by directive techniques, and that the therapist has a responsibility to evaluate continuously how much potential the person has for effective self-regulation. It seemed to Thorne that the crucial factor in therapy is not the method adopted but the skill with which a particular method is used. Directive and nondirective approaches both have a place, depending upon the needs of the person at the time. Accordingly, Thorne advocated an eclectic method of psychotherapy which has as its goal the replacement of emotional-compulsive behavior by rational-adaptive action. Emotional reactions are handled in the initial phases of therapy and later the patient is to be in certain respects reeducated or trained. Throughout the course of treatment, any available technique or method may be used if and when it is appropriate.

A similar viewpoint as to how the therapist can best meet his responsibilities is expressed in the following statement: "From beginning to end, to the best of his ability, the psychiatrist tries to avoid being involved as a person—even as a dear and wonderful person—and keeps to the business of being an *expert*." That is Sullivan's description of the role of the therapist. Sullivan regarded the therapist as a participant observer, an expert in the field of interpersonal relationships whose tasks are to respect his patient and to demonstrate his expertness by his understanding in the interview. This interview is serious business. There is to be no joking or fooling around, and if the patient digresses from his task, he is to be brought back to it. Through listening and skillfully asking questions, the therapist gains an understanding of the patient and of the nature of the interaction that is going on between the two of them. Sullivan de-emphasized free associations, except when they might prove useful in overcoming silences or resistances. However, when an interview seems to lag, Sullivan did urge the therapist to ask himself in what way he has caused the patient to experience anxiety as a result of which he finds it difficult to continue the discussion. At the conclusion of his evaluative or therapeutic interviews, the therapist tells his patient what he has learned, prescribes a course of action, and later assesses the possible effects of his plan on the patient's life.

From experiences gained in his work with schizophrenics, Sullivan advocated a therapeutic relationship grounded on mutual respect, and urged the therapist to refrain from arousing the patient's anxiety by making "deep" interpretations.

From experiences gained in his work with schizophrenics, the psychiatrist John Rosen advocated a therapeutic relationship grounded on an active, nurturant, maternal role for the therapist, a role which requires him to offer "deep," direct interpretations of the patient's behavior.

Despite these islands of dissent, there were pacific atolls of psychotherapeutic agreement. Almost everyone concurred that the environment is important and so there was general rejoicing for the term "milieu therapy," popularized around 1947 by Bruno Bettelheim and Emmy Sylvester, both at the Sonia Shankman Orthogenic School of the University of Chicago. Milieu therapy referred to a thoughtful creation, selection, and arrangement of physical surroundings, personnel, and general procedures so that virtually everything around the patient would make a positive contribution to his mental health. Within an institutional setting, this called for as pleasant and optimally stimulating a physical plant as possible, friendly interpersonal relationships, flexibility in schedules and routines, and opportunities such that each patient could experience a meaningful involvement with at least one member of the staff. Although milieu therapy made its first headway in residential treatment centers for children, it was speedily adopted as the treatment of choice in mental hospitals where it could often be said to be provided without any noticeable disruption of previous routines.

Estes observed: "There now appears to be almost complete agreement among therapists of all schools that the social relationship between therapist and client is critical with respect to whether there will occur the thinking and doing on the part of the client which are essential for his improvement." It remained true, however, that the significance attributed to the relationship varied from one approach to another.

According to Estes, transference phenomena resulted from a fusion of four variables: the repetition compulsion (In general, this refers to a need to repeat a behavior pattern or to think about an incident again and again in order to allay anxiety. With specific reference to transference, it points to a need to perceive and to relate to people in the present as one has perceived and related to them in the past.); the infantile neurosis (the unresolved conflicts of childhood, particularly those related to one's parents); early experiences with significant persons which have an influence upon later reactions to others; and current social relationships that affect what and how rapidly the person learns. It seemed to Estes that Rogers, Alexander, French, and a number of other therapists were stressing the last variable and neglecting all the rest. But, he conceded, it was still a matter for conjecture whether dealing with the other three variables was really essential in order that the person should be helped.

Among clinical psychologists there was general agreement that psychotherapy should be recognized a proper function of their profession and that it should be offered to all who might benefit from it regardless of socioeconomic status, race, religion, creed, level of intelligence, and severity of disturbance. Not all psychologists were enthusiastic about this program. Brotemarkle noted drily that clinical psychology had originated in a case of bad spells and was now encountering a spell of bad cases. Hathaway questioned the effectiveness of psychotherapy and wondered how often improvement is a matter of a "hello-goodby" social situation in operation; "hello" referring to the client's need to begin by giving his reasons for seeking help, and "goodby" referring to his need to tell his counselor at the end of their meetings that he has been helped. Walter Bingham, rather than favoring that psychology become embroiled with psychiatry about the right of clinicians to practice psychotherapy, declared: "We should thank them (the psychiatrists and social workers) for their willingness to relieve us of all responsibility for therapy, thereby freeing the psychological profession for the more congenial and, I sincerely believe, more socially useful task of augmenting the productivity and the happiness of the mentally well."

But these were voices trying to stay an onrushing tide. Far from heeding those who advocated the erection of a stout wall between counseling and psychotherapy, the majority were engrossed in seeking to remove any obstacle that would bar the psychologist from attempting to help an individual deal with any psychological problem. There was some merit to their argument.

To those who accept the basic principle of integration and appreciate the implications of an organismic philosophy, the separation of a person into problem areas seems artificial and arbitrary. A woman who faces a vocational problem, *ipso facto,* has a personal problem. A child who is doing poorly in school has, if nothing else, an emotional response to his educational difficulties. A man with a broken leg has feelings about his injury and the effects it may have upon his ambitions.

Furthermore, it did not seem possible any longer to conceive of psychotherapeutic influences magically confined within the four walls of the therapist's office. They were seen to be everywhere—in diagnostic evaluations, in talking with friends and enemies, in eating and drinking, in dancing, in sports, in arts and crafts, in listening to music, in scrubbing floors, in any activity that may be pleasurable or by any stretch of the imagination instuctive. As the implications of such a point of view became accepted, the number and complexity of the variables which have to be considered in helping the person and in evaluating the effectiveness of psychotherapy swells to the point of encompassing every facet of his life, and restrictions as to who may do therapy seem almost impossible to impose.

The professional literature burgeoned with case histories, descriptions of new therapeutic approaches and techniques, and research that tested the concepts of therapy, both old and new. Between January 1948 and August 1949, there were over four hundred publications on psychotherapy. Too much of this research ended where it should have begun. All too frequently it took the form of a therapist announcing that he was doing something and then demonstrating that he did it, but failing to show whether or not the technique he employed was related to variables outside of therapy or whether it had any usefulness. But still the volume of research and publication mounted. More and more links were forged between the therapeutic process on the one hand and learning theory, perception, and social interactions on the other. Psychology was aggressively extending itself into psychiatry, while psychiatry was hardly less aggressively extending itself into psychology.

PROFESSIONAL DEVELOPMENT

This robust growth is aptly illustrated by the changes in the profession during this decade. To begin with, the situation in the APA in 1939 was critical. There were 618 members and 1909 associates. Everyone knew what the roadblock to status as a member was—the requirement of postdoctoral research, published and of an acceptable quality. If this requirement had been eliminated, there would have been 1759 members and 768 associates. In 1940, a committee was appointed to review this matter.

In 1941, the AAAP had 615 members. Despite an occasional stone thrown at the APA, these members were looking to that organization for leadership and support in dealing with professional problems. Their expectations were soon to be fulfilled. That very year William Malamud and Walter S. Hunter, who had been working as members of the Committee on Problems of Neurotic Behavior under the National Research Council, issued a report urging cooperation between psychiatrists and psychologists in the interests of national defense. Their report was sent to the Surgeon General and it probably helped pave the way for the recognition of military clinical psychology.

In 1942, following spade-work by a subcommittee of the National Research Council on Survey and Planning in Psychology with Robert M. Yerkes as chairman, the APA and the AAAP began to make plans for a constitution that would be acceptable to both groups and which would lead to the incorporation of the latter within the former. The following year a joint convention was held and an APA-AAAP constitution committee was appointed. Under the leadership of Yerkes a new constitution was drafted.

The new association was to be "federal." Eighteen divisions of the new APA were to be established, each representing a special-interest group, and provision was made for the addition and dissolution of divisions as needs changed and developed.

Henceforth, the objectives of the APA were to be "to advance psychology as a science and as a means of promoting human welfare." It was intended, therefore, that it should devote more attention to the professional problems of its members. As a tangible expression of its professional interest, the APA was to publish a new journal, *American Psychologist,* devoted largely to that area.

The new constitution established two classes of membership in the APA: fellow, which required the Ph.D. plus acceptable research or professional experience in psychology; associate, which required either two years of graduate work in psychology or a year of graduate work and a year of professional experience. Both fellows and associates could vote in the organization and hold office, but associates were restricted to holding relatively minor positions. Provisions were also made for student and division affiliates, who would not be eligible to vote or hold office and would not be considered members of APA. The APA governing body was to be the Council of Representatives, with a Board of Directors as its administrative agent. The Board consisted of six members of the Council plus the elected executive officers of the APA.

In 1944, the APA voted to accept the constitution. At the same time the AAAP voted to go out of existence and to transfer its membership to the APA. Dues were raised from $10 to $15 for fellows, and from $8 to $10 for associates. The *American Psychologist* began publication in 1946, and in 1948 the dues were raised to $17.50 for fellows and $12.50 for associates.

Approximately 1710 psychologists had served in the armed forces of the United States during World War II, their average age being about thirty-two. Many of them had been involved in devising methods for the selection and training of personnel. Others worked in the designing of extremely complicated instrument panels which needed to be adapted as closely as possible to human sensory capacities and limitations so that they could be most effectively read and operated. Clinical psychologists had not only to make diagnoses as to the fitness of men or their suitability for particular assignments, but over half of them also engaged to some extent in counseling and psychotherapy. The contributions made by psychologists obviously cover a broad range. We shall point at random to just two of them. The adjustment of a recruit was likely to be facilitated by the book *Psychology for the Fighting Man,* by Boring and others, and upon his leaving the service he could find help in making the transition to civilian life in the companion book *Psychology for the Returning Serviceman,* also by Boring and his associates. An outstanding contribution by a psychologist to the war effort was the suggestion by Walter Miles that men could secure and maintain adaptation of their vision to darkness by wearing red goggles. It would be difficult to overestimate the significance of Miles' simple prescription for men who had to be able to perform their duties under ordinary illumination and then emerge abruptly ready to function efficiently at night.

As we have already seen, even before the conclusion of the war in 1945 psychologists were making ready to deal with their postwar problems with brisk competence. The keynote was sounded in Gardner Murphy's presidential address before the APA in 1944, in which he declared that psychology was on the threshold of becoming an integrated, dynamic science. This was a time, he suggested, not only for integrating the various areas of psychology, but also for exercising the freedom to become immersed and involved in all its ramifications, and to apply the findings of psychology to the great problems which confront nations. If we look for a moment beyond the obvious content of Murphy's speech, we can appreciate better its significance as an indication of the confidence that psychologists now had in their science.

In the period after the war Murphy devoted much of his energy to the Society for the Psychological Study of Social Issues, which was founded in 1936 and of which he was president in 1937–38, and to UNESCO. Many of his colleagues shared a similar concern about meeting their responsibility as psychologists to assist in the alleviation of international tensions and the preservation of peace. Essentially, they worked to create an atmosphere in which men would be willing to strive toward a goal of maximum social justice. Therefore they emphasized that aggression cannot be dismissed as an unfortunate consequence of human nature, and so the irritants which provoke it must be faced. (It is of interest to note that William James in 1904 identified himself as a philosopher to his audience, and then proceeded from a premise that there is a "rooted bellicosity" in man to argue that the hope for a lasting peace rests in directing this militancy into a warfare against injustice and nature.)

As one might expect, public interest in psychology and clinical psychology had never been higher. A constantly increasing number of college students majoring in psychology attested to that interest and to the growing prestige of the profession. Approximately 53 percent of those affiliated with the APA in 1945 expressed an interest in the clinical field, thus proving the vision of Cattell, who predicted years earlier that there would come a day when the majority of APA members were engaged in nonacademic work. Yet, as we pointed out earlier, there were not enough clinical psychologists to meet the demand.

A few facts will show the extent of the problem which confronted psychology at that time. There were sixteen million veterans of World War II and four million veterans from previous wars. Forty-four thousand neuropsychiatric patients were in the hospitals of the Veterans Administration. The VA claimed that it alone needed 4,700 clinical psychologists and vocational counselors. The states asserted that they required 2,100 vocational advisers. At the moment there were 1,500 positions in vocational guidance waiting to be filled while there were only 1,000 vocational counselors in the entire United States. It was clear that something had to be done and done quickly to train clinical psychologists and counselors, set up acceptable professional standards, and accomplish this without resorting to shortcuts that might do injury to the public or the hard-won reputation of psychology.

A joint APA and AAAP committee, with David Shakow serving as its chairman, had foreseen the emergency and decided in 1944 that rather than attempt to develop new schools or departments, the training of clinicians should be entrusted to the existing graduate programs in psychology. Through the cooperation of the VA and the U.S. Public Health Service, funds became available to assist in clinical training. A four-year graduate program was proposed: the first year or so would be needed to provide the student with a foundation in the science, research methodology, and theory; in the second or third year practicums and internship training would be introduced; and the fourth year would include completion of the doctoral dissertation.

In its essentials, that was the graduate program endorsed by the APA for clinical psychologists. Standards were set for graduate departments, and the APA assumed responsibility for evaluating training facilities and informing the VA and the USPHS which universities and other schools were meeting its criteria. In 1946, the National Institute of Mental Health began its program of training grants. During 1948, the NIMH awarded $212,000 for graduate training in clinical psychology.

By requiring the doctorate for clinicians seeking employment in its installations the VA was helping to raise professional standards in clinical psychology. Moreover, by providing training facilities, personnel to assist in the training, financial support for trainees, and job opportunities for graduates of clinical programs, it was fostering the development of graduate programs and exerting a strong influence upon the type of clinician produced: one experienced in working with hospitalized male adults, but usually with little experience in working with outpatients and especially with women and children.

The APA Committee on Training in Clinical Psychology reported in 1947 that a graduate program for clinicians should include general psychology, statistics, psychotherapy, psychodynamics, diagnostic methods; an internship or externship, and training in research methods; as well as courses in related disciplines, e.g., anthropology, clinical medicine, physiology, and sociology.

This emphasis on a well-rounded background in psychology, coupled with a decision not to add to the length of graduate education, ensured that the student would gain his knowledge of psychological principles at the cost of some proficiency in clinical techniques . . . an outcome not altogether pleasing to everyone. A conference sponsored by the APA was held at Boulder, Colorado, in 1949 to consider training policies. Although the conferees recommended continuing the solid grounding in principles and techniques, they urged graduate schools to experiment in their training approaches with different kinds of departures from the core of an approved curriculum.

The upshot of all this activity and interest was that within an incredibly brief period of time there was a great increase in graduate education in clinical psychology. During 1947, twenty-two universities had a total of 210 trainees in the VA training program for clinical psychologists. By 1949, there were forty-two schools in the United States offering the doctorate in clinical psychology, and each of them had far more applicants than it could accommodate. Thus psychologists were faced with the difficult, though really not too unpleasant, task of selecting students with outstanding intellectual abilities and personalities fitted to clinical work. No one questioned any longer the drawing power of psychology, and of clinical psychology in particular.

The prospects for clinical psychology were brightened further by developments in the attempt to obtain legal recognition for psychologists. Legislation was being sought to enact two types of law: licensing and certification. A licensing law restricts the performance of certain functions or practices to members of a specified profession. A certification law restricts the use of a title, e.g., "psychologist," to persons who meet certain standards specified by statute and whose qualifications in these respects satisfy an official board of examiners. Since psychologists would engage in activities that are also performed by members of equally qualified and reputable professions, licensing laws did not seem feasible, nor on the whole did they seem advisable in view of possible complications arising from a premature defining of the psychologist's role.

The first general certification law for psychologists was enacted by the state of Connecticut in 1945; it required possession of a Ph.D. degree and one year of professional experience. Certification for clinical psychologists went into effect in Virginia in 1946, and required the Ph.D. and five years of professional experience.

By 1949, *school* psychologists were certified in eleven states: Arizona, California, Connecticut, Delaware, Florida, New Jersey, New York, Ohio, Pennsylvania, Wisconsin, and Wyoming. Registries for school psychologists were maintained by seven other states: Illinois, Indiana, Maryland, Minnesota, North Dakota, Oregon, and Utah.

The APA favored certification over licensing, but the bills for both forms of legislation ran into stiff opposition from the medical profession. William Menninger expressed the position of many of his fellow psychiatrists when he spoke on behalf of taking a conciliatory attitude in both psychiatry and psychology. He stated his belief that "clinical psychology is essential to the best practice of psychiatry." However, he added that he felt the major contributions of clinical psychologists would be made in the areas of diagnostic testing and research. Although most psychiatrists could accept the idea of psychologists performing psychotherapy in medical settings, they tended to agree that psychologists should be barred from engaging in independent private practice. Menninger concurred with this point of view and justified his position by saying that physicians are trained to feel what may be called a life-and-death responsibility for their patients, and he doubted that psychologists shared an equally deep and genuine concern in this matter.

Since certification of psychologists in each and every state was not likely to become readily available, it was decided in 1946 to establish certification within the profession by setting up as a certifying authority the American Board of Examiners in Professional Psychology (ABEPP). This Board was to consist of nine fellows of the APA, who would serve three-year terms and administer the standards decided upon for professional competence. In order to protect the APA from possible damage suits arising from allegedly improper actions by a certifying body, the ABEPP was organized as a separate corporation in 1947.

The requirements for an ABEPP diploma or certificate in clinical, counseling, or industrial psychology were: satisfactory professional, moral, and ethical standing; membership in APA; a doctorate in psychology; five years of professional experience; and the passing of written and oral examinations (A "grandfather" clause, which expired at the end of 1949, waived examinations for those of sufficient experience who also were able to satisfy other requirements.). In 1949, the first ABEPP written examinations were held.

Thus toward the close of the forties there could be no doubting that the United States held the position of professional leadership. Among other countries of the world there was comparatively little professional activity, and what little there was centered on teaching, research, and diagnostic testing.

Psychologists were regrouping and attempting to reestablish their field in Germany and Scandinavia. In Zurich, Switzerland, the C. G. Jung Institute was founded in 1948. In England, clinical psychology was moving forward with research and experimentation related to chemotherapy, nutrition, and personality characteristics, but the position was still maintained that psychotherapy is alien to the role of the clinician. Hans Eysenck, one of England's leading clinical psychologists, gave his American colleagues the following reasons for viewing psychotherapy as inappropriate for their profession: (1) treatment is a medical problem; (2) therapy dilutes the clinician's specialization of function, which is diagnosis and research; and (3) psychotherapy spoils objectivity and forces the psychologist involved in its practice to become biased in its favor.

For the most part, then, the enthusiasm among clinical psychologists in the United States for psychotherapy was of relatively recent origin and was not necessarily shared by clinicians elsewhere. But, of course, psychology in the United States had become to a large extent an applied field and so was quite different from what it was in other countries. Some 54 percent of the positions open to psychologists in the United States were now nonacademic. Clinical psychology and counseling alone accounted for 43 percent of all psychological positions, both filled and available. Salaries for a psychologist with a Ph.D. had risen from approximately $3400 in 1940 to $6400 in 1949, and in that year 250 Ph.D. and 1350 M.A. degrees in psychology were awarded. There were now approximately 149 graduate departments that offered clinical training with a total registration of approximately 5600 students, half of whom were majoring in clinical psychology. Practically all these budding clinicians had been attracted to the field by the prospects of doing psychotherapy. The membership of the APA had increased from 4500 members in 1946 to 6735 at the close of the decade, and there were 1047 members in the Clinical Division alone.

The APA by adopting the position that psychotherapy is an integral function of the clinical psychologist showed that it recognized the possibility of and was prepared for whatever interprofessional conflict might prove necessary in defense of this stand. The Association did this from a feeling of respect for the integrity and quality of its membership, and with confidence in the ability and competence of psychologists to meet fully their obligations and responsibilities.

References

Adorno, T. W., *et. al. The authoritarian personality*. New York: Harper, 1950.

Alexander, F. & French, T. M., *et. al. Psychoanalytic therapy*. New York: Ronald, 1946.

Anderson, J. E. Personality organization in children. *Amer. Psychol.*, 1948, 3, 409–416.

Angyal, A. *Foundations for a science of personality*. New York: Commonwealth Fund, 1941.

Ansbacher, H. L. Testing, management, and reactions of foreign workers in Germany during World War II. *Amer. Psychol.*, 1950, 5, 38–49.

APA & AAAP Committees on Graduate and Professional Training. Subcommittee report on graduate training in clinical psychology. *J. consult. Psychol.*, 1945, 9, 243–266.

APA Committee on Training in Clinical Psychology. Recommended graduate training program in clinical psychology. *Amer. Psychol.*, 1947, 2, 539–558.

Bartlett, F. C. Visitor to America. *Amer. Psychol.*, 1947, 2, 372–374.

Beck, S. J. *Rorschach's test: Vol. I. Basic processes; Vol. II. A variety of personality pictures*. New York: Grune & Stratton, 1944, 1945.

Bellak, L. *Dementia praecox*. New York: Grune & Stratton, 1948.

Bender, Lauretta. Childhood schizophrenia: a clinical study of one hundred schizophrenic children. *Amer. j. Orthopsychiat.*, 1947, 17, 40–56.

Benton, A. L. The experimental validation of the Rorschach test. *Brit. j. med. Psychol.*, 1950, 23, 45–58.

Berliner, B. Short psychoanalytic therapy: its possibilities and limitations. *Bull. Menninger Clin.*, 1941, 5, 204–213.

Bettelheim, B. The dynamism of anti-semitism in gentile and Jew. *J. abnorm. soc. Psychol.*, 1947, 42, 153–168.

Bettelheim, B. & Sylvester, Emmy. A therapeutic milieu. *Amer. j. Orthopsychiat.*, 1948, 18, 191–206.

Bingham, W. V. D. Autobiography. In E. G. Boring, *et. al.* (Eds.) *A history of psychology in autobiography*. Vol. IV. Worcester, Mass.: Clark U. Press, 1952.

Black, J. D. A survey of employment in psychology and the place of personnel without the Ph.D. *Amer. Psychol.*, 1949, 4, 38–42.

Blum, G. S. A study of the psychoanalytic theory of psychosexual development. *Genet. Psychol. Monogr.*, 1949, 39, 3–99.

Bordin, E. S. Counseling methods: therapy. *Ann. rev. Psychol.*, 1950, 1, 267–276.

Brennan, M. & Gill, M. M. *Hypnotherapy.* New York: Josiah Macy, Jr., Foundation, 1944.

Britt, S. H. & Morgan, Jane D. Military psychologists in World War II. *Amer. Psychol.,* 1946, 1, 423–437.

Bruner, J. S. & Goodman, Cecile C. Value and need as organizing factors in perception. *J. abnorm. soc. Psychol.,* 1947, 42, 33–44.

Buck, J. N. The H-T-P technique: a qualitative and quantitative scoring manual. *J. clin. Psychol.,* 1948, Monogr. Suppl. No. 5.

Buros, O. K. (Ed.) *The 1940 mental measurements yearbook.* Highland Park, N.J.: Mental Measurements Yearbook, 1941.

Burt, C. *The factors of the mind.* London: U. London Press, 1940.

Burt, C. The inheritance of mental ability. *Amer. Psychol.,* 1958, 13, 1–15.

Cantril, H. Psychologists working for peace. *Amer. Psychol.,* 1949, 4, 69–73.

Cattell, Psyche. *The measurement of intelligence of infants and young children.* New York: Psych. Corp., 1940.

Columbia-Greystone Associates. *Selective partial ablation of the frontal cortex.* New York: Hoeber, 1949.

Committee of National Research Council. *Psychology for the returning serviceman.* New York: Infantry Journal. Penguin Books, 1945.

Committee on Nomenclature and Statistics of the American Psychiatric Association. *Diagnostic and statistical manual mental disorders.* Washington: Amer. Psychiat. Assoc., 1952.

Darrah, L. Should we differentiate between schizophrenia and dementia praecox? *J. nerv. ment. Dis.,* 1940, 91, 323–328.

Deri, Susan. *Introduction to the Szondi Test: theory and practice.* New York: Grune & Stratton, 1949.

Doll, E. A. The nature of mental deficiency. *Psychol. Rev.,* 1940, 47, 395–415.

Doll, E. A. The essentials of an inclusive concept of mental deficiency. *Amer. j. men. Def.,* 1941, 46, 214–219.

Dollard, J. & Mowrer, O. H. A method of measuring tension in written documents. *J. abnorm. soc. Psychol.,* 1947, 42, 3–32

Duval, A. M. & Hoffman, J. L. Dementia praecox in military life as compared with dementia praecox in civil life. *War Med., Chicago,* 1941, 1, 854–862.

Ellis, A. The validity of personality questionnaires. *Psychol. Bull.,* 1946, 43, 385–440.

Estes, S. G. Book review: *Psychoanalytic therapy. J. abnorm. soc. Psychol.,* 1947, 42, 137–142.

Eysenck, H. J. Training in clinical psychology: an English point of view. *Amer. Psychol.,* 1949, 4, 173–176.

Fenichel, O. *The psychoanalytic theory of neurosis.* New York: Norton, 1945.

Fernberger, S. W. On election to membership in the APA. *Psychol. Bull.,* 1940, 37, 312–318.

Fischer, R. P. & Hinshaw, R. P. The growth of student interest in psychology. *Amer. Psychol.,* 1946, 1, 116–118.

Fitts, P. M. German applied psychology during World War II. *Amer. Psychol.,* 1946, 1, 151–161.

Frank, L. K. *Projective methods.* Springfield, Ill.: Charles C Thomas, 1948.

Freeman, F. S. *Theory and practice of psychological testing.* New York: Holt, 1950.

Freeman, W. & Watts, J. W. The frontal lobes in their relationship to the ego and the future. *N. C. med. J.,* 1941, 2, 288–290.

Freeman, W. & Watts, J. W. *Psychosurgery.* Springfield, Ill.: Charles C Thomas, 1942.

Frenkel-Brunswik, Else & Sanford, R. N. Some personality correlates of anti-semitism. *J. Psychol.,* 1945, 20, 271–291.

Fromm, E. *Escape from freedom.* New York: Rinehart, 1950.

Garrett, H. E. A developmental theory of intelligence. *Amer. Psychol.,* 1947, 2, 372–374.

Grinker, R. R. & Spiegel, J. P. *Men under stress.* Philadelphia: Blakiston, 1945.

Guilford, J. P. Human abilities. *Psychol. Rev.,* 1940, 47, 367–393.

Guilford, J. P. Some lessons from aviation psychology. *Amer. Psychol.,* 1948, 3, 3–11.

Hall, C. S. & Lindzey, G. *Theories of personality.* New York: Wiley, 1957.

Hall, Margaret E. Current employment requirements for school psychologists. *Amer. Psychol.,* 1949, 4, 519.

Harrower-Erickson, Molly R. & Steiner, M. E. Modifications of the Rorschach method for use as a group test. *J. genet. Psychol.,* 1943, 62, 119–133.

Hartmann, H., Kris, E. & Loewenstein, R. M. Comments on the formation of psychic structure. *Psychoanalytic study of the child,* 1946, 2, 11–38.

Hathaway, S. R. & McKinley, J. C. A multiphasic personality schedule (Minnesota): I Construction of the schedule; II A differential study of hypochondriasis. *J. Psychol.,* 1940, 10, 249–254; 255–268.

Hathaway, S. R. & McKinley, J. C. *The Minnesota Multiphasic Personality Inventory.* New York: Psych. Corp., 1943.

Hathaway, S. R. Clinical methods: psychotherapy. *Ann. rev. Psychol.,* 1951, 2, 259–280.

Heiser, K. F. Survey of departments giving instruction in clinical psychology. *Amer. Psychol.,* 1950, 5, 610–619.

Henry, J. Rorschach technique in primitive cultures. *Amer. j. Orthopsychiat.,* 1941, 11, 230–234.

Hertz, Marguerite R. Modification of the Rorschach Ink Blot Test for large scale application. *Amer. j. Orthopsychiat.,* 1943, 13, 191–211.

Hilgard, E. R. Psychologic preferences for divisions under the proposed APA by-laws. *Psychol. Bull.,* 1945, 42, 20–26.

Hilgard, E. R. Human motives and the concept of self. *Amer. Psychol.,* 1949, 4, 374–384.

Hollingworth, Leta S. *Children above 180 IQ.* Yonkers, N.Y.: World, 1942.

Horney, Karen. *Self analysis.* New York: Norton, 1942.

Hunt, H. F. Clinical methods: psychodiagnostics. *Ann. rev. Psychol.,* 1950, 1, 207–220.

Hunt, J. McV. & Cofer, C. N. Psychological deficit. In J. McV. Hunt (Ed.) *Personality and the behavior disorders.* New York: Ronald, 1944.

Hunter, W. S. Psychology in the war. *Amer. Psychol.,* 1946, 1, 479–492.

Hutt, M. L. & Milton, E. O. An analysis of duties performed by clinical psychologists in the Army. *Amer. Psychol.,* 1947, 2, 52–56.

Jolliffe, N. The influence of alcohol on the adequacy of the B vitamins in the American diet. *Quart. j. Alcohol,* 1940, 1, 83.

Kanner, L. Autistic disturbances of affective contact. *Nerv. Child,* 1943, 2, 217–250.

Katz, E. The constancy of the Stanford-Binet IQ from three to five years. *J. Psychol.,* 1941, 12, 159–181.

Kent, Grace H. Emergency battery of one minute tests. *J. Psychol.,* 1942, 13, 141–164.

Klopfer, B. & Kelley, D. M. *The Rorschach technique.* Yonkers, N.Y.: World, 1942.

Korzybski, A. H. *Science and sanity.* Lancaster, Pa.: Science Press, 1941.

Kraskin, L. H. Psychotherapy for optometrists. *Amer. j. Optom.,* 1940, 17, 402–413.

Krugman, M. Recent developments in clinical psychology. *J. consult. Psychol.,* 1945, 9, 342–353.

Lecky, P. *Self consistency.* New York: Island Press, 1945.

Lindner, R. M. Hypnoanalysis. In P. L. Harriman (Ed.) *Encyclopedia of psychology.* New York: Citadel Press, 1946.

Machover, Karen. *Personality projections in the drawing of the human figure.* Springfield, Ill.: Charles C Thomas, 1948.

Maslow, A. H. A theory of human motivation. *Psychol. Rev.,* 1943, 50, 370–396.

Maslow, A. H. Some theoretical consequences of basic need-gratification. *J. Personal.,* 1948, 16, 402–416.

McClelland, D. C. & Atkinson, J. W. The projective expression of needs: I. The effect of different intensities of the hunger drive on perception. *J. Psychol.,* 1948, 25, 205–222.

McLean, H. V. Psychodynamic factors in social relations. *Ann. Amer. Acad. polit. Sci.,* 1946, 244, 159–166.

McNemar, Q. A critical evaluation of the University of Iowa studies of environmental influences upon the IQ. *Psychol. Bull.,* 1940, 37, 63–92.

Menninger, K. *Love against hate.* New York: Harcourt, Brace, 1942.

Menninger, W. C. The relationship of clinical psychology and psychiatry. *Amer. Psychol.,* 1950, 5, 3–15.

Miles, W. R. Red goggles for producing dark adaptation. *Federation Proc.,* 1943, 2, 109–115.

Miller, J. G. Clinical psychology in the Veterans Administration. *Amer. Psychol.,* 1946, 1, 181–189.

Monroe, Ruth. Inspection technique: a modification of the Rorschach method of personality diagnosis for large scale application. *Ror. res. Exch.,* 1941, 5, 166–190.

Moreno, J. L. *Who shall survive?* New York: Beacon House, 1952.

Murphy, G. The freeing of intelligence. *Psychol. Bull.,* 1945, 42, 1–19.

Myrdal, G. *et. al. An American dilemma.* New York: Harper, 1944.

Orlansky, H. Infant care and personality. *Psychol. Bull.,* 1949, 46, 1–48.

O. S. S. Staff Assessment of men. New York: Rinehart, 1948.

Otis, A. S. *Otis classification test: revised Forms R, S, T.* Yonkers, N.Y.: World Book, 1941.

Pratt, J. H. The group method in the treatment of psychosomatic disorders. *Sociometry,* 1945, 8, 323–331.

Rabin, A. I. The use of the Wechsler-Bellevue scale with normal and abnormal persons. *Psychol. Bull.,* 1945, 42, 410–422.

Raimy, V. C. Self-reference in counseling interviews. *J. consult. Psychol.,* 1948, 12, 153–163.

Ribble, Margaret A. Disorganizing factors of infant personality. *Amer. j. Psychiat.,* 1941, 98, 459–463.

Robinson, Mary F. What price lobotomy? *J. abnorm. soc. Psychol.,* 1946, 41, 421–436.

Rogers, C. R. *Measuring personality adjustment in children nine to thirteen years of age.* New York: Teachers College, Columbia U., 1931.

Rogers, C. R. *The clinical treatment of the problem child.* New York: Houghton Mifflin, 1939.

Rogers, C. R. The process of therapy. *J. consult. Psychol.,* 1940, 4, 161–164.

Rogers, C. R. *Counseling and psychotherapy.* New York: Houghton Mifflin, 1942.

Rogers, C. R. Significant aspects of client-centered therapy. *Amer. Psychol.,* 1946, 1, 415–422.

Rogers, C. R. Some observations on the organization of personality. *Amer. Psychol.,* 1947, 2, 358–368.

Rogers, C. R. A theory of therapy, personality, and interpersonal relationships, as developed in the client-centered framework. In S. Koch (Ed.) *Psychology: a study of a science.* Vol. 3. New York: McGraw Hill, 1959.

Rogers, C. R. *On becoming a person.* Boston: Houghton Mifflin, 1961.

Rosen, J. N. The treatment of schizophrenic psychoses by direct analytic therapy. *Psychiat. Quart.,* 1947, 21, 3–38.

Rosenzweig, S. Projective techniques: their progress in the application of psychodynamics. In L. G. Lowrey & Victoria Sloane (Eds.) *Orthopsychiatry 1923–1948: retrospect and prospect.* New York: Amer. Orthopsychiat. Assoc., 1948.

Safir, M. A. Certification versus licensing legislation. *Amer. Psychol.,* 1950, 5, 105–106.

Salter, A. *Conditioned reflex therapy.* New York: Creative Age, 1949.

Sarason, S. B. *Psychological problems in mental deficiency.* New York: Harper, 1949.

Schafer, R. & Murphy, G. The role of autism in a visual figure-ground relationship. *J. exp. Psychol.,* 1943, 32, 335–343.

Schneidman, E. S. The Make-A-Picture-Story (MAPS) projective personality test: a preliminary report. *J. consult. Psychol.,* 1947, 11, 315–325.

Schwing, G. *Ein Weg zur Seele des Geisteskranken.* Zurich: Rascher, 1940.

Sheldon, W. H. *The varieties of human physique: an introduction to constitutional psychology.* New York: Harper, 1940.

Sheldon, W. H. *The varieties of temperament: a psychology of constitutional differences.* New York: Harper, 1942.

Sheldon, W. H. Constitutional factors in personality. In J. McV. Hunt (Ed.) *Personality and the behavior disorders.* New York: Ronald, 1944.

Sheldon, W. H. *Varieties of delinquent youth: an introduction to constitutional psychiatry.* New York: Harper, 1949.

Shipley, W. & Kent, F. The insulin-shock and metrazol treatments of schizophrenia with emphasis on psychological aspects. *Psychol. Bull.,* 1940, 37, 259–284.

Simmel, E. Otto Fenichel. *Inter. j. Psychoanal.,* 1946, 27, 67–71.

Snyder, W. V. The present status of psychotherapeutic counseling. *Psychol. Bull.,* 1947, 44, 297–386.

Spitz, R. A. Hospitalism: a follow-up report: *Psychoanalytic Study of the Child,* 1946, 2, 113–117.

Staff, Psychological Research Project (Pilot) Psychological research on pilot training in the AAF. *Amer. Psychol.,* 1946, 1, 7–16.

Stoddard, D. G. *The meaning of intelligence.* New York: Macmillan, 1943.

Strauss, A. A. & Lehtinen, L. E. *Psychopathology and education of the brain-injured child.* New York: Grune & Stratton, 1947.

Sullivan, H. S. *Conceptions of modern psychiatry.* Washington: William Alanson White Psychiatric Foundation, 1947.

Sullivan, H. S. *The interpersonal theory of psychiatry.* New York: Norton, 1953.

Sullivan, H. S. *The psychiatric interview.* New York: Norton, 1954.

Symonds, P. M. The sentence completion test as a projective technique. *J. abnorm. soc. Psychol.,* 1947, 42, 320–329.

Szondi, L. *Szondi Test: experimentelle Triebdiagnostik.* Bern: Hans Huber, 1947.

Terman, L. M. & Oden, M. H. *The gifted child grows up: twenty-five years' follow-up of a superior group.* Stanford: Stanford U. Press, 1947.

Thorndike, R. I. "Constancy" of the IQ. *Psychol. Bull.,* 1940, 37, 167–186.

Thorne, F. C. A critique of nondirective methods of psychotherapy. *J. abnorm. soc. Psychol.,* 1944, 39, 459–470.

Thorne, F. C. Principles of directive counseling and psychotherapy. *Amer. Psychol.,* 1948, 3, 160–165.

Thurstone, L. L. Psychological implications of factor analysis. *Amer. Psychol.,* 1948, 3, 402–408.

Vernon, P. E. Psychological effects of air-raids. *J. abnorm. soc. Psychol.,* 1941, 36, 457–476.

Vorhaus, Pauline G. Bruno Klopfer: a biographical sketch. *J. proj. Tech.,* 1960, 24, 232–237.

Wechsler, D. *WISC Manual.* New York: Psych. Corp., 1949.

Wellman, Beth L. IQ changes of preschool and nonpreschool groups during the preschool years: a summary of the literature. *J. Psychol.,* 1954, 20, 347–368.

Werner, H. *Comparative psychology of mental development.* New York: Harper, 1940.

White, R. W. A preface to the theory of hypnotism. *J. abnorm. soc. Psychol.,* 1941, 36, 476–505.

Wolberg, L. R. *Hypnoanalysis.* New York: Grune & Stratton, 1945.

Wolff, W. *Diagrams of the unconscious.* New York: Grune & Stratton, 1948.

Wolfle, D. The reorganized American Psychological Association. *Amer. Psychol.,* 1946, 1, 3–6.

Wolfle, D. Testing is big business. *Amer. Psychol.,* 1947, 2, 26.

8

Questions, Doubts, and Responsibility

1950-1959

THIS WAS A PERPLEXING DECADE, distinguished by both prosperity and recession, by duplicity and a sinister form of patriotism, and by a great deal of general bewilderment. Consider what occurred in 1950 when the army of North Korea invaded South Korea and the United Nations intervened with force to halt the aggression. Technically, the Korean War was not a war—for want of a better term President Truman referred to it as a "police action." Yet in this police action the United States alone incurred 157,530 casualties, of which 54,246 were deaths. A convoluted use of language was a prominent feature of the fifties.

Another of the less commendable distinguishing properties of the decade was anti-intellectualism. Distrust of persons who were learnèd as well as moderate and conscientous was fanned by the position adopted by many intellectuals that the manufacture and testing of atomic weapons ought to be stopped, a point of view that struck some Americans as distinctly subversive of the best interests of the United States. A few instances of treason by educated individuals contributed to a hysterical feeling that the nation had been betrayed by its liberals and that Communists had infiltrated the government. In some places oaths of loyalty to the United States were required, and it could happen that a mere insinuation of socialistic leanings was sufficient to wreck a career.

Naturally, psychologists were troubled when suspiciousness became so prevalent, and especially when at some universities the signing of a loyalty oath was required of faculty members. Aside from objecting to the futility of expecting Communist agents to reveal themselves by refusing to sign such an oath, there was resentment at the imputation cast upon their patriotism and at what was perceived as a threat to academic freedom. The furor was greatest at the University of California, with Edward Tolman as the leading and most eminent dissenter.

During this time psychologists were also becoming more actively involved as shapers of social legislation and legal briefs. Their counsel was being sought to assist the judiciary in the consideration of the social consequences of a law, a matter which, as the noted jurist Louis Brandeis emphasized, is of great importance. The results of a psychological investigation could thus become of far-reaching significance in evaluating the effects of laws and their implications upon people.

For example, in 1943 Hawaii passed a statute prohibiting the teaching of languages other than English below the age of ten years in public schools. This law was based on the alleged fact that bilingualism in children could produce academic retardation and emotional disturbances. In a brief which successfully contested the law, psychological findings were introduced to show that bilingualism, in and of itself, did not result either in emotional disturbances or in intellectual retardation, and that while some retardation in academic achievement might be attributed to bilingualism, these effects could be circumvented by improved and already available methods of teaching.

Now the Supreme Court at one time had ruled that racially separated but equal public school facilities were constitutional. In legal briefs contesting the constitutionality of separate but equal facilities, psychological studies were used to point out that separate, even if equal, facilities were discriminatory and eventuated in undesirable social and psychological consequences. Further, when a poll of 849 anthropologists, sociologists, and psychologists was taken, of the 517 social scientists who responded, 90 percent claimed that in their (expert) opinion enforced segregation would have detrimental effects even if equal facilities were provided. These results and others like them led the Supreme Court, in 1954, to reverse its earlier ruling and to decide that the doctrine of separate but equal facilities was unconstitutional, that the public school system within the United States should be racially integrated. It would be difficult to illustrate a more significant case at law in which psychologists participated. However, as might have been expected, this did not increase the esteem with which psychologists were regarded in certain quarters.

Fortunately, this wave of anti-intellectualism was not long-lasting. It suffered a marked reverse when Russia placed a satellite in orbit around the earth in the autumn of 1957. Intellectuals suddenly became important and could bask in being regarded as a valuable national asset. Talk turned to how programs might be instituted to utilize the gifted effectively, to the need for concentrating extra effort and funds in promotion of the sciences, to missile lags, to the restoration of American prestige in the eyes of the world, and to the care which had to be taken to create and to preserve a favorable image. Newspapers and magazines frequently referred to this period as an age of anxiety, and they published cartoons depicting the analyst's couch and vending machines dispensing tranquilizers. There is little doubt that this was a time of fear and what were, in part, reactions to it—the "beat" generation, the popularity of adult westerns, and rock-and-roll music—as well as being a time of accelerated advances in science and technology—the Salk and Sabine antipolio vaccines, electronic computers, automated machinery, transistors, and new profundities in the theory of relativity.

Within psychology the integrating and synthesizing tendencies of the previous years continued. A method-oriented formulation of what constituted a science had to a large extent replaced the content-oriented conception. Although a few psychologists were still uneasy about the study of, for example, extrasensory perception, there was general agreement that what defines a science is not the subject being investigated but the method by which those working in an area obtain and order their data. Any topic may become part of science if the "scientific method" is used in its exploration.

The "modern" views on matters with special relevance to clinical psychology were the following: both heredity and environment are essential, interactive, and ubiquitous, and the question is not which is more important than the other but to determine how these variables affect human behavior and growth; frustrations and gratifications are each necessary to some degree for optimum psychological development; mental health does not imply freedom from worry and anxiety but an ability to tolerate and deal effectively with one's problems and fears; and the results of any psychological evaluation represent only a sample of the individual's functioning obtained on a given test at a given time under certain circumstances.

Of course there were still different emphases and points of view. Probably there will always be a place in psychology for the kind of "tough-minded" experimental emphasis so highly esteemed in the natural sciences. Just, in the same way, as there will always be a place for the "tender-minded" humanistic emphasis so evident in the arts. But particularly in this decade, when so many Americans seemed tormented with problems of conformity, identity, self-expression, and despair, there was a heightened interest in those who stressed that man is a being unique in nature and focused upon the scientific study of his distinctive needs, feelings, beliefs, and potentialities.

As an aside, we might remark that perhaps psychoanalysis occupied a middle-ground position of a tough-minded humanism.

NORMAL PERSONALITY FUNCTIONING

As psychoanalysts directed more of their attention to ego processes, some of the results and conclusions of experimental psychology were woven into the fabric of the theory. The writings of many psychoanalysts during this period were, to a large extent, either embroideries or restatements of both empirical findings and behavioristic theories that related to the child's early development. Perhaps the most widely discussed analytic author of this period was Erik H. Erikson (b. 1902), who had graduated from the Vienna Psychoanalytic Institute in 1933 before settling in the United States.

In essence, Erikson integrated and extended a psychosocial theory of development with Freud's psychosexual theory. In this amalgamation each psychosexual stage is supposed to confront the individual with social demands or tasks, which are considered universal—for example, the acquisition of a relative sense of trust in one's world, in the functioning of one's own body, and in others. However, the form of the typical solutions for each interpersonal conflict varies from one culture to another. Furthermore, although the traditional psychoanalytic model ends with the attainment of genital sexuality, Erikson went further to postulate later crises of adjustment extending into old age. The successful resolution of one developmental crisis or problems increases the likelihood, but does not guarantee, a successful resolution of the next, while an unsuccessful resolution appreciably reduces an individual's chances of dealing appropriately with subsequent stages of development.

Erikson characterized each phase of the life cycle as a more or less successful attempt to deal with a specific central conflict that had now become prominent. He believed, however, that the resolution of the conflict is not an either-or matter, though it is in healthy growth weighted toward the positive or desirable alternative. Since this general perspective is extended through adulthood, it is assumed that the normal developmental crises of parents will interact with the normal developmental crises of their children.

The specific alternative outcomes at each stage in growth are identified as follows: in the oral-sensory stage, a basic sense of trust *vs.* mistrust; in the muscular-anal stage, a sense of autonomy or independence *vs.* shame and doubt; in the locomotor-genital stage, a sense of initiative *vs.* guilt; in latency, a sense of industry or accomplishment *vs.* inferiority; in puberty and adolescence, a sense of identity *vs.* role or identity diffusion; in young adulthood, a sense of intimacy or friendship and love *vs.* isolation; in adulthood, a sense of generativity or productivity *vs.* stagnation; in old age, a sense of integrity *vs.* despair and disgust. Of particular interest, and requiring special mention, is Erikson's concept of identity.

When he speaks of identity, Erikson refers to the awareness of continuity in one's development, self-knowledge, and a sense of consistency between what one has been and what one wishes to become. This concept seemed especially meaningful to many persons of middle and higher social status in the United States where discontinuity appeared rife. Breaks in the life cycle and with one's past were evident in such diverse forms as mobility, the nuclear family structure, unconscious motivation, modern art and architecture, divorce, and concern about the preservation of one's individuality. The intellectuals, the college-educated were troubled about conformity and how a person can maintain his uniqueness in spite of the pressures toward conforming, and about the meaning of life and how one is to carry on even when life seemed to have no meaning. The old answers were no longer satisfactory. Here were new answers— some, perhaps, not so much new as newly discovered and bandied about in popular discourse and publications. Thinking to obtain them, many persons were turning to psychoanalysis, psychotherapy, Zen Buddhism, and existentialism.

Existentialism emerged from the latter half of the nineteenth century or rather was rediscovered in the writings of the Danish philosopher and theologian Soren Aabye Kierkegaard (1813–1855). Kierkegaard's theme, and that of other existentialists, is how an individual is to understand his situation in the world. Although existentialists do not tend to see man's situation as an easy or enviable one since he is alienated from nature and aware of his limited existence, they strongly emphasize the worth and significance of each person as a unique and irreplaceable being. The major, if not the only, problem facing each person is to exist as an individual, to be oneself, to fulfill one's potentialities. Unlike other organisms, man is regarded as free to determine his actions, to become aware of himself as a-part from other beings, to be reflective, to question his own behavior, and to ponder the reason for his existence. This very freedom places upon a person responsibility for *becoming,* for his own genuineness or authenticity. To refuse this freedom, to attempt to escape this responsibility, produces, perhaps, temporary relief but will eventuate in a state of boredom mingled with dread and despair. To accept this freedom and responsibility and genuinely to strive to bring one's potentials to fruition is the only means by which a person may provide his life with meaning.

Existential thought appears in the writings of psychologists such as

Erich Fromm, Gordon Allport, Rollo May, and Carl Rogers. Very much as Goldstein had stated earlier, Rogers declared: "The organism has one basic tendency and striving—to actualize, maintain, and enhance the experiencing organism." This striving is in the direction of increasing differentiation and integration, self-government, autonomy, and, in a broad sense, socialization, and away from control by external forces. For Rogers, as for Lewin, "Behavior is basically the goal-directed attempt of the organism to satisfy its needs as experienced, in the field as perceived."

Karen Horney also saw the individual as striving for growth and self-realization, and, in a sense, so did Erich Fromm. To fully understand man, Fromm contended, it is necessary to understand the needs that arise from the conditions of his existence. These needs are for relatedness or productive love; transcendence or creativeness; security or rootedness; identity; and a stable frame of reference or a consistent perception of the world. These are human needs, not found in other organisms, and the forms in which they are expressed are determined by the mores of the social order in which a person lives. Fromm believed that all known societies have failed in some degree to meet the basic needs of man's existence, and he sketched as his ideal a psychologically perfect society, Humanistic Communitarian Socialism. In such a Utopia every person would have an equal opportunity to become fully human, everyone could gain "a sense of self by experiencing himself as the subject of his powers rather than by conformity."

Gordon Allport introduced the term proprium, "the regions of our life that we regard as peculiarly ours . . . and which make for inward unity." Once the individual's basic needs are satisfied, he is free to grow, to become. Therefore, Allport pointed out, people strive not only to reduce their tensions but to maintain some kinds of them. This maintenance of tensions falls within the province of propriate strivings and includes endeavors to attain one's goals, realize one's values, perfect one's behavior, and pursue one's interests.

Thus existentialism as a development within psychology emphasized the responsibilities of the individual to himself, rather than his responsibilities to his fellow man. Obviously, when there was so much concern about conformity, such a point of view was of consequence to a sizable portion of the public. But just as psychoanalysis was unfortunately distorted by some persons into a rationalization for sexual license, so existentialism was often distorted into a rationalization for a perverse negativism and a groping for egocentric experiences. All too frequently overlooked was what existential writers demonstrated by the simple fact of their writings, and that is that self-actualization takes place within a social context. So it would seem that one valuable way to provide meaning for one's own life is to be of help in providing meaning to the lives of others.

Closely allied with existentialism is a view of man as actively dealing with his environment and capable of initiating constructive changes in his functioning. However, some psychologists expressed this view who are not ordinarily associated with existentialism. George Kelly (b. 1905) asserted that the ordinary man performs in much the same way as does the scientist, in the sense that both have theories and personal constructs, both test hypotheses, and both weigh whatever evidence they perceive for the purpose of predicting and controlling their world. Kelly envisioned the growth of a person as the development of a unique system of constructs, capable of change and of varying degrees of integratedness, fragmentation, or incompatibility. To understand a person, one has to understand his constructs, and to understand a construct, one has to understand the two construct poles that form it. For example, a person may believe that women are gentle and males are not; thus he has certain expectations about the ways individuals of each sex should behave when an act to which he would apply the construct "gentleness" is involved. Moreover, a person not only makes predictions, but directs his own behavior so that it will be appropriate to the events which he anticipates.

Under nonthreatening, experimental conditions in which the person has an opportunity to validate his constructs, they may undergo modifications. Kelly believed that man has the conceptual freedom to alter his construct system and realize his personal resources, that man can invent and make his own ideas. Unlike some psychologists who saw man dismayed by his finite existence or striving to filfull himself within his environment, Kelly focused upon man attempting to deal with his environment actively and creatively by making representations of it through which he comes to understand it better. His model of man is very similar to an ideal held up by some of the philosophers of old as the best means to a good and happy life: man as the curious seeker of knowledge, truth, and understanding.

Another Kelly, Everett Lowell Kelly, reported that after years of research on the consistency of adult personality he had been most impressed by its flexibility. While values and vocational interests professed by adults seem relatively stable, self-ratings and certain attitudes are less so. Further, when the results are seen in broader perspective, there is evidence of much change in all measured variables. Kelly concluded: "Our findings indicate that significant changes in the human personality may continue to occur during the years of adulthood. Such changes, while neither so large nor sudden as to threaten the continuity of the self-percept or impair one's day-to-day interpersonal relations are potentially of sufficient magnitude to offer a basis of fact for those who dare to hope for continued psychological growth during the adult years."

As we can see, man was coming to be regarded by some psychologists and psychoanalysts as less driven and irrational in his behavior and as more capable of reason, modification, and the exercise of responsibility.

Before we go on to consider the views of man that were emerging from "tough-minded" experimental studies, it is of interest to note that both modern existentialism and science do not attribute any purpose to the universe, although, of course, they differ considerably in their attitude about this. Nevertheless, many persons, influenced by science and existentialism, felt their religious beliefs shaken (though it is difficult to determine whether the influence came before the feeling). So widespread was this skepticism that even members of the clergy questioned the existence of God in public. One of the few psychiatrists who spoke out strongly for religion as essential to the well-being of man was Carl Jung.

It seemed to Jung that man and psychology were neglecting a "natural religious function" that exists within the collective unconscious of each of us, ignoring at their peril a powerful need to relate one's inner being to one's conscious world. Through religion, man is provided with the means to give expression to his inherited and unconscious experiences, his archetypes: the God-image or archetype of the self, the archetype of the great mother, the archetype of the old wise man. Each person, Jung believed, needs to experience these archetypes within himself and to feel their correspondence with the particular forms his own religious upbringing gave to them: "Too few people have experienced the divine image as the innermost possession of their own souls. Christ only meets them from without, never within the soul; that is why dark paganism still reigns there." In order to express the strength of his conviction that a deep belief in a Supreme Being satisfies an unconscious need of man, above the entrance to his house Jung had these words carved: "Called or not called, God is present."

Let us now consider some of the studies of this decade that are relevant to the issue as to what is the nature of man. The physiologist Hans Selye of the University of Montreal concluded that the living organism, including man, adjusts to stresses of all kinds by a general adaptation syndrome. Any stress, whether due to infection, extremes of temperature, injury, fatigue, or psychological conflict, produces physiological changes which elicit a definite reaction pattern. The goal of this reaction is to restore inner equilibrium. It is composed of a general response, common to all forms of stress, and a specific response peculiar to the particular form of stress afflicting the organism at any one time. There are three stages in this reaction.

Selye called the relatively brief first stage "the alarm reaction." The organism reacts to the stress with increased activity of the autonomic nervous mechanisms and an outpouring of glandular secretions. If the organism successfully maintains the production of these secretions and still survives, the next stage, that of adaptation occurs. In adaptation a homeostatic balance to the stress is sustained, and the organism is relatively insensitive to further stresses of the same kind. But this represents a successful adjustment to what is still an abnormal situation. If the stress persists, the organism becomes less able to tolerate other stresses and enters the third and final stage, physiological exhaustion. In this terminal stage homeostatic mechanisms no longer function effectively and symptoms of illness appear.

One test of Selye's theory consisted in housing rats in refrigerators. At first there was a short period of disruption which showed in disturbed mating and feeding habits. But the rats survived in their ice box and thereafter appeared to carry on "normally." Finally, as they were forced to maintain their adjustment to their polar environment, the rats suffered physiological exhaustion, became ill, and died. This study is a clear demonstration of the general adaptation syndrome.

Selye's work has a number of implications, of which we shall mention but two. The first is that the organism may be better able to tolerate a continued stress if supplied with substances that compensate for the physiological strain that it endures. There has been some support for this deduction in that the use of glandular extracts in the treatment of human rheumatoid arthritis and other complaints has been found helpful. The second implication is that man's appearance of health and vitality in a stressful environment may be deceptive, that an apparently successful adjustment to psychological pressures may mask progressive physiological debilitation that culminates in illness and premature death.

While Selye was reminding psychologists of the frailty, as well as the sturdiness, of human beings, another way of looking at man was gaining in popularity. This was to depict him as a glorified electronic computer, a system into which information is fed through statements. In order to understand man, one has to understand the information that is being introduced and to analyze how much it reduces the number of alternatives that confront him. At times the statements may be meaningless or equivocal. Specifically, Bateson, *et. al.* spoke of double-bind communication, a statement which places a person in a situation where no matter what he does he cannot feel satisfied, such as "I don't want you to feel that I'm forcing you to do this." Such messages may foul the system. At any rate, man can be seen as an exceedingly complex, elegant mechanism who has his inputs, outputs, communication channels, programmings, servomechanisms, and feedbacks, and who sometimes gets his wires crossed.

A huge number of empirical studies supporting, challenging, and extending these and other theories were being published. There were, for examples chosen almost at random, studies of empathy, rigidity, perceptual defense, creativity, and subliminal stimulation. The last of these, subliminal stimulation, is, as we shall soon make clear, particularly pertinent to our discussion.

Subliminal stimulation refers to experiments in which ideas or commands, e.g., EAT POPCORN, were flashed at speeds so fast that the person claimed to be unaware of their meanings, yet gave evidence of having believed them or acted in some way to carry them out. These findings, if confirmed, would have implications for advertising and other forms of persuasion. Yet it is obvious that they might also lead to serious abuses, and that in any case their use raises ethical issues. It can be contended that ordinarily a person recognizes an idea or suggestion as coming from an external source and is free to evaluate it critically. But supposedly in subliminal stimulation (if this does really occur) the person is not cognizant of the external source, and the idea is accepted by him as his own. Thus by influencing him without his knowledge, his right to evaluate information is violated. This was a particularly sensitive matter at that time, not only because of the dangers posed to civil liberties in the United States which were the product of extreme reactions to the threat of Communist infiltration, but also because so much was heard about "brain-washing" during and especially after the Korean War.

A small, but damaging percentage of United States soldiers taken prisoner in Korea were known to have cooperated with the enemy. This was disheartening news to the American public and a strong demand for an explanation was voiced. Inquiries into the experiences of the men after they had been captured disclosed a certain similarity in the way some soldiers had been handled. They had not been beaten or tortured physically but had been placed in isolation with little to see or hear or do. Shortly after their solitary confinement began, they started to experience hallucinations, difficulties in thinking and concentration, and a feeling of helplessness, futility, and abandonment. This was followed by a childlike dependence upon the generosity and sympathy of their captors and by a receptivity to thoughts and suggestions given to them.

Before the Korean War brain-washing had been inferred when political prisoners in various Communist nations abjectly confessed to the crimes with which they were charged. So complete were these confessions that it was thought the prisoners had been drugged or that their "minds had been broken" by compelling them to examine their darkest fears. To help evaluate the veracity of the more recent reports from Korea, controlled laboratory investigations into the effects of sensory deprivation were carefully planned. Beginning around 1952, dogs were reared in isolation, college student volunteers were bundled and bandaged on couches in soundproof rooms, and some subjects were suspended in tanks of water kept at body temperature. On the basis of the results from the research conducted with dogs, Hebb concluded: ". . . the normal development of behavior depends on a normal perceptual environment. The animal, reared in isolation is a permanent screwball at maturity: motivationally, socially, intellectually abnormal."

The studies of human beings cut off from virtually any external stimulation confirmed the fact that within a short period a person becomes highly suggestible and experiences hallucinations, and delusions. Moreover, after his removal from the experience of being deprived, suggestions and propaganda were far more lasting in their effects than were any of the other changes that had been produced. In other words, although the subjects were no longer in isolation and although they did not seem to be abnormal in their behavior, they continued to profess beliefs that had been suggested to them. It seemed clear that the organism requires a certain amount of stimulation from his environment in order to function normally, realistically, and critically.

From a different line of research came additional demonstrations of the significance of central stimulation in motivating the organism and further intimations that man might one day be controlled with relative ease and economy. Around 1954, W. R. Hess succeeded in permanently implanting electrodes in the brains of living cats. This made it possible to stimulate the brain electrically while the organism is in a "normal" unanesthetized state. Evidence soon accumulated from studies with rats and cats about the effects of such stimulation. It appeared that the electrical stimulation of certain areas of the brain that induce eating responses could also motivate the organism to perform learned instrumental acts which had been reinforced by food. According to the findings of James Olds, rats would learn to press a bar and would continue to do so with electrical stimulation of portions of their brains serving as a powerful reward and, apparently, their only one. Neal Miller reported the discovery of other areas where stimulation served as punishment. At the very least, such findings demonstrated that the organism could be motivated by direct central stimulation, as well as by drive or tension reduction.

The response of the press to photographs of rats performing tasks while wearing implanted electrodes was to envision a day when men would labor for electrical stimulation rather than money. This dream or nightmare of the control or dehumanization of man was reinforced by the successes of Skinner and his followers in shaping behavior.

B. F. Skinner had abundantly demonstrated that a response pattern can be "shaped" or built up by quickly reinforcing any initial crude approximation of the final behavior desired, and by following this up with a careful scheduling of reinforcements of each closer and closer approximation to the particular response wanted. In this way animals could learn to perform acts not at all normally characteristic of their species. Chickens could play a minor league variety of baseball. Pigeons could play a game of ping-pong before climbing into the cockpit of a missile to give their all for psychology and country. Children sitting in front of teaching machines that almost immediately informed them of the correctness of each of their responses to questions seemed to learn certain academic subjects with an efficiency ordinarily considered beyond their reach. Human behavior, Skinner asserted, could be analyzed in terms of its schedules of reinforcement and many activities could be modified and manipulated by altering these schedules.

Experiments on verbal conditioning supported Skinner's contentions. A casual "mmm-hmmm" or "good" uttered by the psychologist as the person speaks serves to increase the frequency of any verbal response temporally associated with it. Hostile verbalizations, references to the past, the use of plural pronouns can all be reinforced and increased in frequency during the span of a single interview with the person reporting no awareness of what has been taking place and the reinforcement usually consisting simply of "mmm-hmmm" or "yes" or "good."

It might be remarked, somewhat facetiously, that while these experiments implied that man was less free, or human, than had been supposed, other studies implied that monkeys, at the very least, were more human than had been thought. Many psychologists have believed a child's love for his mother is a learned or secondary drive acquired by associating the mothering figure to the drive reductions produced by feeding. Fromm, however, as spokesman for a dissident group, argued that among the unique needs of man are productive love or relatedness and rootedness or security. Both of these views are challenged by Harry Harlow's experiments with macaque monkeys.

Groups of infant monkeys had been nursed on man-made, inclined models of monkey "mothers." Some of these "surrogate mothers" were constructed of bare wire. Others were covered with foam rubber and terry cloth. Regardless of whether or not the infant monkey had been nursed on the wire "mother," he preferred to spend much of his time clutching to and resting on a terry cloth "mother." When strange and presumably frightening objects were introduced into the room, the infant monkey would run to the model and press himself against the foam rubber. Only after a time would he begin to explore the situation, and always the "mother" remained the base to which he retreated or returned whenever he appeared disturbed.

Harlow believed that his experiments supported Watson's suggestion that love is an innate emotion elicited by cutaneous stimulation of the erogenous zones of the skin. He also thought that his work made it clear that love is not unique to man and also that this emotion is more dependent on tactile than on oral stimulation.

As the decade closed the crush of research caused one reviewer to cry out, "Gad, what a mess!" Many of the studies contradicted each other or were fragmentary. So much was coming out so rapidly that the content of one experiment or theory was hardly assimilated before another experiment or theory appeared to refute or extend it. Relatively new statistical techniques, such as nonparametric methods, were often un-

familiar and evoked skepticism when their use led to statistically significant results. There were theories in abundance, journals in profusion,
and like an awesome iceberg the published research represented but a
small fraction of all the investigations conducted.

Some terms had become so popular that they had lost their distinctive
meaning. For example, most psychologists in using the term "dynamic
psychology" wished to imply that they were speaking of the causes of
behavior, especially motivation. But as English and English pointed out,
" 'dynamic' is often a mere cliché to imply that something is happening of
which the speaker approves." Other long-honored concepts seemed to
have become so refined, so exclusively specified in terms of their operations, and so intertwined that they were threatened with extinction. Cofer
concluded his review of the literature on motivation with the statement:
"motivation, as a distinctive concept, coordinate to other psychological
concepts, may well disappear." Blake and Mouton decided from their
survey that, "As an independent, isolated compartment, personality is
on its way to oblivion."

Nevertheless, there were terms that served as rallying cries for many
psychologists. "The organism! The self! Psychodynamics! Identity! Interpersonal relations! Reinforcements! Feedbacks!" To list but a few. However, this should not obscure the fact that the majority of psychologists,
regardless of their particular area of interest, continued to value precision
in measurements, in formulations, and in technology as the best means
for understanding man. A minority disagreed, often eloquently arguing
that the essence of what they were seeking to study and understand in
man became lost in the very act of scientific scrutiny. Perhaps unwisely,
this disagreement was sometimes phrased in the form of an alternative,
exhorting psychologists to choose one position or the other. William
McDougall had succinctly asked it this way: "Men or robots?"

Obviously this issue—whether an essential dignity of man becomes lost
in the process of reducing his behavior to relatively small units—has
troubled some psychologists for many years, even before the fifties. William
James, as we know, grappled with this problem, and it may be that he
had it in mind when he offered this apologia for all the questions that
after a lifetime of inquiry still remained unanswered: "What has concluded that we might conclude in regard to it?" Yet it is clear that at
least one conclusion can be offered. We are certain that it is possible to
put together a portrait of man from the results of the various approaches
that have been taken to study him that is more complete and accurate
than any that can be assembled from the findings of one method alone.
Accordingly we can say, as do most psychologists, that there is no question
of choosing between alternatives. But rather it is a question of whether
we ourselves are free to welcome all knowledge that advances our understanding of human behavior.

DIAGNOSTIC TECHNIQUES

Although the number of available tests increased markedly during the fifties, the clinical psychologist remained loyal to those techniques and their modifications which had been developed during the thirties and forties. Buros in 1953 listed 793 mental tests, an increase of approximately 250 instruments in a span of about ten years. With so many tests appearing so rapidly, it was small wonder that the clinician preferred to rely upon those that, if not altogether tried and true, at least were familiar and of some demonstrated value.

And these tests certainly seemed to have been tested, if number of publications is any criterion. Through 1951, there had been 1219 publications dealing with the Rorschach, 493 with the Stanford-Binet, 371 with the Wechsler-Bellevue, and a respectable demonstration of interest in the TAT and MMPI. Amid all this research, interest in some tests seemed to die, e.g., the Szondi, in the light of generally negative evaluations, while interest in others held up stubbornly despite the many criticisms heaped upon them.

Speaking relatively, the intelligence scales were a solid rock for the clinician, a place of refuge and security in an otherwise ambiguous world of perception. Only one individually administered scale in this field made its debut in the fifties and attained wide popularity. In 1955, the Wechsler Adult Intelligence Scale (WAIS) was published.

The WAIS had the same structure as its forebear the Wechsler-Bellevue. It was standardized on a population of 1700 persons of both sexes ranging in age from sixteen to sixty-four years, with an additional 475 persons sixty or more years old. This sample was stratified, with a proportionate selection of cases representing different occupational groups, levels of education, geographic locations, and urban *vs.* rural populations within the United States. A noteworthy feature of the standardization sample was that 10 percent of it was nonwhite.

Wechsler did not alter his definition of intelligence and remained firm in his adherence to Spearman's theory of its structure. The Wechsler-Bellevue and the WAIS seemed to resemble each other factorially, with g, verbal comprehension, performance organization, and memory. However, the age range of persons who made the highest score on the WAIS was 25–29, while on the Wechsler-Bellevue it had been 20–25. What does this mean? Well, it does not mean that people are still getting smarter at a later age than formerly, and in order to understand what Wechsler thought it may mean, we have to consider two of his concepts.

The concept of ability, according to Wechsler, refers to the nature and manner in which certain mental operations are performed; intelligence refers to the relevance and relation of those operations to certain goals and ends. It would seem to follow from this distinction that, for example, a person may have great ability in performing arithmetical computations but if nothing of any value is gained from his additions and subtractions, his dedication of long hours to this work would not be considered very intelligent. Since Wechsler believed that intellectual ability does not increase beyond the age of fifteen or sixteen years, he attributed the gains in scores on his tests found after those ages to increased familiarity with the culture and a rise in educational level, both of which contribute to make a person's behavior more intelligent. Presumably, the population used in the standardization of the WAIS is more attuned to the culture and better educated than the population used in the standardization of the Wechsler-Bellevue.

Despite discouraging reports concerning the validity of patterns of scatter when the Wechsler-Bellevue was used to make psychiatric diagnoses, Wechsler in his new test still offered patterns of subtest scores for differentiating anxiety states, organic brain disease, delinquency, schizophrenia, and mental deficiency. He suggested that a difference of fifteen IQ points between the Verbal and Performance Scales was probably significant clinically, and advised his colleagues to take two or more scaled score units from the mean as a measure of scatter. Furthermore, he recommended that the clinician employ the method of successive sieves in arriving at a diagnosis: one test pattern would be used to identify a percentage of a diagnostic group, then another test pattern would be employed to filter out a percentage from the previous percentage, then another, and another. For example, the first sieve might be finding a difference of twenty or more IQ points between Verbal and Performance Scale scores; the second sieve might be scores in Picture Completion and Object Assembly lower than scores in Picture Arrangement and Digit Symbol; the third sieve could be doing better on Vocabulary and Comprehension than on Similarities and Digit Symbol. The hope was that after such a series of siftings the clinical psychologist would be able with high likelihood to bake a diagnostic cake composed of clearly identified ingredients.

The following techniques which received a great deal of attention during the fifties will serve to demonstrate the diversity of the clinical area of those years and the tenacity of old truths, even though for a time they may have been ignored.

Price and Deabler reported in 1955 that the perception of a visual aftereffect is useful in discriminating between those who have suffered brain damage and those who have not. This test requires the individual to stare at a spinning Archimedes spiral. When the spinning is stopped, the "normal" person "sees" the spiral expanding or contracting, but the person with central nervous system pathology does not seem to experience this aftereffect. A later study claimed that children perform in the same manner as those who are brain-damaged. Subsequent research, however, challenged these findings and led psychologists to question the validity of earlier reports. A reason for this skepticism was that a study was done in which children were presented with balloons with Archimedes spirals painted on them. They were asked to describe what seemed to happen to the spirals when the balloons were inflated and deflated. Once a child's way of describing what he saw was ascertained, he was tested for the aftereffect and he seemed to be able to see it, although he put his report in his own words. It was thought probable that the children in the earlier study had also perceived the aftereffect but had not been able to communicate what their experience had been in a way which the psychologist had understood owing to their idiosyncrasies of expression.

Q-sorts enjoyed some popularity, particularly as a research technique for Rogers and his followers. The Q-sort consists of a number of descriptive statements, usually having to do with feelings and personal beliefs, which the person has to arrange along a continuum from those which are most to those which are least appropriate as applied to himself. The person is usually asked to sort these statements at least twice, first according to their relevance to the kind of person he thinks he is (Self-concept sort), and second according to their relevance to the kind of person he would like to be (Ideal Self sort). The extent of the discrepancy between the "Self" and "Ideal" sorts serves as a measure of the person's self-satisfaction. The closer the correspondence between the two sorts, the greater, supposedly, is the individual's self-satisfaction and the better is his psychological adjustment. Unfortunately, it was soon found that psychotics and others who are obviously maladjusted often have high correlations between their two sorts. This prompted the ready explanation that these individuals are very defensive, but, of course, this also raised the question of how one is to know when the person has been honest and when he has been defensive.

An attempt had been made to solve this problem in the case of the MMPI by having items that have been designed to detect on the one hand either carelessness or poor comprehension and on the other hand intentional falsification of responses. As mentioned earlier, the amount and quality of the research on this instrument are impressive and high hopes were held for it as an objective means for making a psychiatric diagnosis. This goal was, for the most part, abandoned during the fifties, and the scales were regarded as descriptive of personality patterns rather than immediately diagnostic of the specific disorders for which they were named. Therefore, like practically everything else, the interpretation of the MMPI had become more complex while at the same time more uses were proposed for it than those for which it had originally been intended. Hathaway and Meehl published an *Atlas* for help in its interpretation. This consisted of a collection of 968 short case histories with one or more associated MMPI profiles for each. Items from the Inventory were used by Janet Taylor to construct a scale of manifest anxiety, which was employed in a number of studies to identify groups of individuals supposedly differing in drive level as a means of testing Hullian learning theory. Barron took 69 items from the MMPI and made an ego-strength scale that appeared to differentiate between groups of patients who would or would not benefit from psychotherapy. And by 1959, there were almost two hundred different scoring keys for the MMPI attempting to assess characteristics ranging from dependency to baseball talent.

Despite these indications of acceptance, the MMPI, of course, was not without its critics. A major criticism, directed not only at this technique but also at others of its kind, was offered by Edwards, who pointed out that people frequently respond to questionnaires so as to appear in a socially favorable light.

Edwards noted quite sensibly that some of the items on personality inventories require an individual to admit to or deny characteristics or forms of behavior that differ greatly from what is culturally approved. Thus Edwards thought it probable that many individuals yield to the tendency to select the alternative which is more desirable as descriptive of themselves. As one way of dealing with this problem, which he hoped would prove successful, Edwards designed the Edwards Personal Preference Schedule. The Schedule is intended to measure fifteen of a person's needs on the basis of his choices between 225 paired comparison statements. Each pair of alternatives had been matched so that they were approximately equal in social desirability, and Edwards recommended to his fellow psychologists that in the future they consider this variable in constructing tests.

In 1957, Dement and Kleitman described an ingenious and objective method to determine when the person is dreaming. While the individual is in a light sleep, as defined by EEG criteria, the usual slow drift of the eyes is sometimes replaced by rapid conjugate eye movements, as measured by electro-oculograms. This rapid conjugate eye movement is apparently a valid indication that dreaming is taking place. Findings from this research indicated that dreams last from three to fifty minutes (much longer than had been thought) and occur at intervals of 70–104 minutes throughout the night (more frequently than had been believed). The technique thus proved to be a valuable tool in investigations of dream activity and of dreamers.

As we have seen, questions about the validity of diagnostic instruments were a prominent issue during this decade. In specific terms, Margaret Lowenfeld, even after her test had been in use for twenty-five years, still regarded it as being in its beginning stages of development. Studies of the test in the United States indicated that cultural factors probably would have to be considered in interpreting the designs constructed by the persons who take it. The intervening years of research, instead of simplifying matters, had only added more variables that have to be taken into account in the complex task of interpretation, and Lowenfeld could no longer keep from doubting that her hope that hers would prove a reasonably simple and useful technique for the evaluation of personality would be fulfilled. Somewhat more encouraging were the results from investigations of the Bender-Gestalt. They indicated that reasonably valid Mental Ages from five to ten years could be estimated from the drawings of the designs. Below the Mental Age of five, the drawings were too crude to allow discriminations; above the Mental Age of ten, the task was not difficult enough to be discriminating. Moreover, the test appeared to have some value in distinguishing between psychotic and nonpsychotic adults, and supplies clues for the detection of central nervous system pathology when used in a battery of tests.

Examining the subject of validity more generally, the concept itself was being analyzed and its ramifications more fully appreciated. In 1952, the APA Committee on Test Standards attempted to clarify some of the problems involved in validating diagnostic techniques. They distinguished between four kinds of validity. *Criterion* or *predictive validity* refers to the correlation between test results and some subsequently obtained criterion measures, such as success in training or therapy or school. *Concurrent* or *status validity* refers to the correlation between test scores and some external criterion available at about the time the test is taken, such as a psychiatric diagnosis, or ratings by teachers or therapists. Content validity refers to the extent to which test items sample the universe of content specified by the instrument's purpose, as an intelligence scale samples intellectual behavior but not feelings about oneself or other persons. *Congruent* or *construct validity* refers to the degree to which the test measures the psychological variable it is supposed to measure, as when there is a demonstrated correlation of the test with other tests of accepted validity, or when scores on the test correctly predict differences in behavior deducible from the same theory that led to the test's construction.

As an illustration of construct validity, the following example may be cited: in theory, people who are authoritarian are supposed to be rigid in their psychological functioning. Therefore, those who score high on a test of authoritarianism should be more rigid in their behavior than those who score low. If an experiment is conducted which substantiates that prediction, its results would illustrate construct validity of the test, as well as the validity of the theory itself. However, failure to support the prediction would indicate the test or theory or both lack validity.

Further, it should be noted that the congruent or construct validity of a test is no guarantee that it also has predictive validity. A test may measure a certain characteristic very well, but that characteristic may have no demonstrable relationship to something else in which we are interested. Thus knowledge of scores on our test of authoritarianism may not help us to predict grades in school or success in a course of training because whether the person is authoritarian or not may not be related to his academic or vocational accomplishments.

The distinction between predictive and construct validities is pertinent to one's judgment of the Rorschach, which had been severely censured for the failure of its scores to relate to certain predictive criteria, such as improvement in psychotherapy and successful performance as an airplane pilot. Yet some clinicians, in spite of these statistical failures, felt the Rorschach was a valuable instrument and of great help to them in their work. Far from being persuaded to abandon the test, clinical psychologists in greater numbers than ever became convinced that their interpretation of the Rorschach must depend less on the significance of specific test scores than on their acumen, sensitivity, and understanding of subtle aspects of the entire testing situation.

This shift, moving the emphasis from scores to an emphasis on the total set of circumstances in evaluating the Rorschach, is exemplified in Schafer's *Psychoanalytic Interpretation in Rorschach Testing* (1954). Schafer argued that content, test scores, expressive movements, the person's verbal comments or asides, the qualitative aspects of his verbalizations, the relationships between one response and another are all to be analyzed and integrated in an attempt to comprehend the individual's defenses, conflicts, and interpersonal reactions. In general, he viewed the situation in which the taker of the Rorschach finds himself as a challenge to the individual's ability to relax his defenses, to "regress in the service of the ego" and meet the demands imposed upon him for imaginative productions.

The number and complexity of variables that had to be taken into account increased not only in the interpretation of tests, but in their construction as well. When selecting a standardization sample the psychologist had to consider the relevance of his population's age, sex, geographic distribution, educational level, personality characteristics, socioeconomic status, racial and ethnic composition, mental health, and quite possibly other variables in addition to these. Items on tests had to compensate for response biases, i.e., the general tendency of people to agree with statements, especially with clichés; to mark extreme positions on degree-of-agreement scales; to describe themselves in socially desirable terms; to deny symptoms; and to develop sets so that their responses are determined more by the kind of answers they have previously given than by the immediate question. Furthermore, the hypothesis of "levels" suggests that the ambiguity or definiteness of a test might be related to the extent to which unconscious processes would normally be expected to affect responses to its items. This means that the less ambiguous psychological tests, such as intelligence tests, would be expected to tap higher levels of conscious functioning than the more ambiguous projective techniques.

By the close of the fifties, clinical psychologists as a group seemed to be trying to catch their breath while attempting to assimilate the vast amount of new information that had been accumulating. Being an extremely self-critical group, they berated their research. "One cannot read in detail the contemporary literature in diagnostics without being overwhelmed by the tremendous expenditure of time, money, and labor involved in bringing forth inconclusive or trivial results," said Ann Magaret. "A large number of publications mostly making little or no contribution to theory or practice," was the judgment of E. L. Kelly. Yet much had been learned.

The consensus about factor analysis echoed Hebb's remarks: "Factor analysis remains a powerful tool for simplifying correlational data, but it now seems clearly not to be a means of discovery, and it is not reasonable to expect that it can transcend the limitations of the original test data or be a substitute for new experimental analyses."

Attempts to evaluate personality functioning in "real life situations," especially those where examiners stand around taking notes, had negligible predictive validity. Interviews by clinical psychologists and by psychiatrists of candidates for becoming trainees in these professions had little value in identifying the students who later proved successful. Even more remarkable, the more confident a clinician had been in his judgments, the less accurate his predictions turned out to be. What seemed to be at least temporarily reassuring was that these studies had neglected to ascertain, before demanding clinical predictions, those characteristics that are necessary for later success and those that insure failure.

Results with the Rorschach, TAT, MMPI, and other personality techniques were not particularly helpful in indicating those persons who would benefit from psychotherapy. One ray of sunshine, though a negative one, was the fact that global tests of personality were less predictive of some specified characteristic than the tests specially devised for that purpose. After reviewing over one hundred studies having to do with the prognostic usefulness of psychological tests with neurotic and psychotic patients, Fulkerson and Barry concluded: "The variables which appear to have the strongest relationship to outcome (of psychotherapy and other forms of treatment) have been nontest variables, severity and duration of illness, acuteness of onset, degree of precipitating stress, etc." The consensus that was finally reached was that, not isolated test scores, but the analysis and understanding of the individual's total behavior in the testing situation integrated with what was known about his past seemed to be of most value in making predictions.

It appeared that the clinician's race, sex, and bodily size produced only minor interactive effects on projective test results under ordinary circumstances. What seemed to be crucial in altering responses was the person's attitude toward the total test situation, and in turn this attitude was affected by the personality characteristics of the psychologist, particularly his friendliness or hostility. "Thus," concluded Masling, "the procedure (the Rorschach) that many clinicians hoped would serve as an X-ray proves, on close examination, to function also as a mirror, reflecting impartially the S(ubject), the E(xperimenter), the situation, and their interactions."

Test results, unless gross screening was intended, were also not found to be very useful for the prediction of psychiatric categories. However, recognition of the arbitrariness of psychiatric diagnoses and groupings vitiated, for the time being, the importance to be attached to failures to demonstrate concurrent validity. Clinicians tended to draw away from psychiatric labeling as the goal of a psychological evaluation and definitely moved toward a preference for descriptions of personality functioning. Whether a diagnosis of brain damage or schizophrenia was substantiated was now thought to be of less importance than an accurate understanding and representation of the person's behavior.

The task of the clinician in diagnosis, as he saw it, had become to grasp the uniqueness of the individual. For this purpose he employed a variety of diagnostic techniques, of which the Rorschach, Draw A Person, TAT, Bender-Gestalt, Stanford-Binet, WAIS, MMPI, Draw A Man, and WISC were high in popularity. But he and other psychologists wondered if his testing, even assuming that it assisted a valid understanding of the person, was of any practical value.

There seemed little doubt that psychological testing had an established and significant place in education, but whether or not it had any real merit for psychiatry was still questioned. The de-emphasis of psychiatric nosology was welcomed by those proponents of testing who had been disappointed by studies failing to demonstrate the concurrent validity of their instruments as well as by those who had also recognized the unreasonableness of the task they had set for themselves. But becoming aware of the futility of a goal could be no completely satisfactory substitute for reaching it, and some psychologists were compelled, in good conscience, to continue wondering just how seriously results of personality tests should be taken in arriving at meaningful decisions about a patient.

That they may play a minor role in influencing the course of psychotherapy was indicated in a thought-provoking report by Meehl, who noted that only 17 percent of the therapists polled in one study claimed that a diagnostic evaluation based on tests was helpful in accelerating treatment. Nor did there appear to be any economy in having a patient tested as far as an understanding of him was concerned, since therapists in any case usually reached a fairly accurate and stable impression of their patients after about four interviews. Moreover, Rogers argued that a psychological evaluation as a prelude to treatment is unnecessary and may even hinder progress in psychotherapy because it implies that the responsibility for self-knowledge and growth belongs, not to the client, but to the psychologist-expert.

As if these criticisms were not enough, psychological testing was also under fire from antagonists outside psychology who flayed it, for the most part unjustly, as an invasion of privacy, a devious method for imposing conformity in thought and behavior, and an obstacle that stood between a good man and the attainment of some worthwhile position. Psychologists in general rallied to the defense of tests when they were under such attacks, but a most significant point, emphasized by Meehl, is that the true value of what the clinical psychologist accomplishes is to be found above and beyond the particular instruments he happens to employ: "If there is anything that justifies our existence . . . it is that we think scientifically about human behavior and that we come from a long tradition . . . of being critical of ourselves as cognizing organisms and of applying quantitative methods to the outcomes of our cognitive activity."

Actually, most clinicians did not feel that matters had reached the point where the situation had to be viewed so starkly. Quite a few of them, even those working in psychiatric settings, asserted that their diagnostic appraisals are useful and have practical value, and cited that this estimate is shared by their colleagues in other disciplines who are in a position to know what clinical psychologists are doing. Admittedly, they contended, psychological testing has little importance in those situations where, regardless of test findings, patients are handled in about the same way.

Yet the fact remained that for reasons of urgency and necessity the use of certain tests had come to pass before their usefulness had been rigorously demonstrated. This kind of acceptance did not relieve clinicians of their obligation to evaluate the worth of their instruments, but, if anything, made it all the more imperative for them to do so. Clinical psychologists in the fifties agreed that they had this responsibility, and some discharged it, in part, through research, much work in the development of new techniques, and by acting as their own most severe critics.

DIAGNOSTIC FORMULATIONS

Although progress had unquestionably been made toward improved diagnostic formulations, these advances had consisted more frequently in reaching a better understanding of the complexity of a problem rather than in its solution. The structure of intelligence, the relative weightings of hereditary and environmental variables in psychological functioning and malfunctioning were still matters for debate and investigation. Moreover, the definitions of terms whose meanings had formerly been taken for granted were called into question. Here, too, advances were to be measured not so much by the attainment of final answers as by difficulties more fully appreciated.

Since clinical psychologists had come to agree that nonintellective personality characteristics affect intellectual functioning, much of their interest at this time centered on evaluating the effects of various psychiatric disturbances, levels of anxiety, and a felt need for achievement on intelligent behavior. In general, the results indicated that there are optimum levels of anxiety and need for achievement. Above such an optimum, there are disruptions of functioning, while below it, the individual seems unmotivated to put forth his best efforts.

There was also general agreement that intellectual functioning is a complex process dependent on satisfactory interpersonal relationships for normal development. Although some question was raised as to whether the studies of maternal deprivation might after all be considered more accurately studies of sensory deprivation, there was overwhelming evidence to justify the conclusion that disturbances in family interactions could adversely affect a child's learning.

In 1955, Nancy Bayley reported. that the scores on intelligence tests connected with an ability to use verbal concepts and abstractions continued to increase in adulthood in the case of superior adults. Thus determining the age when highest intellectual capacity is reached appeared to be a complex issue dependent upon what functions are being assessed, on the procedures used to evaluate those functions, and on the intellectual level of the population being studied.

The structure of intelligence was regarded by most clinicians, at least implicitly, in accordance with Spearman's two factor formulation. As elaborated by A. W. Stern in 1956 the primary mental abilities, in the view of an up-to-date adherent of Spearman, are thought to possess characteristics somewhat analogous to those of nuclear particles, i.e., they exhibit collective as well as independent behaviors and possess group as well as individual properties. Their duality of function, both discrete and interactional, may be attributed to the fact that the brain is an interacting system. Stern called their collective characteristic *connectivity*, referring to a coupling among separate factors. He defined intelligence as "the resultant collective behavior among the intellective factors," and g as "the measure of the strength of the resonance evoked by the coupling process."

On the basis of the formulations of Stern and others, Wechsler was led to the following conclusion about the construction of intelligence scales: "In order completely to measure intelligence, it is insufficient to extend the range of abilities measured, . . . we must also find tests which manifest both greater coupling potential and greater resonance characteristics." In other words, Wechsler advocated the construction of intelligence scales in which there are relatively high intercorrelations between an extensive variety of subtests, or a relatively high saturation of g.

To some extent Wechsler's conclusion was echoed by J. P. Guilford in 1959. Following his factor analytic investigations into the structure of intelligence, Guilford erected a model of intellect in the shape of a 5 × 4 × 6 cube. He listed five major factors—cognition, memory, convergent thinking, divergent thinking, and evaluation; four content factors—figural, symbolic, semantic, and behavioral; and six products factors—units, classes, relations, systems, transformations, and implications. Thus there were 120 predicted unique abilities, e.g., cognitive figural units, cognitive figural classes. However, Guilford's cube model or factor analysis or both were soon called into question when later studies revealed that some cells contained more than one factor. Therefore, Guilford concluded somewhat tautologically, to know an individual's intellectual resources thoroughly, psychologists would have to obtain many scores from him on many tests, or perhaps not so many, since a number of the factors seemed to be intercorrelated.

As a result of what he found in his studies into the structure of intelligence Cyril Burt came to favor the views of Spearman. One of his findings was that this structure seems to be a function of age. Although g appears to account for 50 percent of the variance in childhood, as the person matures specific group factors contribute more to the variance. Burt's finding is in keeping with a generally accepted principle in developmental psychology, namely that growth tends to progress from a general or relatively undifferentiated matrix toward greater differentiation and specialization in functioning and behavior. This is also in keeping with Garrett's hypothesis referred to in the previous chapter.

The crudely put question of whether heredity or environment is more important had now become virtually a dead issue. In the course of time the question had become *how* or *in what way* do heredity and environment influence the individual's functioning. It was agreed that every observable characteristic is the product both of heredity and of environment, that what the individual inherits are only tendencies to develop in certain directions, and that these tendencies require the appropriate environmental conditions in order to be manifested. Given a society in which adequate nutrition, good health, and opportunities for advanced education are the rule, it is possible to estimate, as Burt did, that most of the variance in intelligence is due to heredity and to conclude that "Improved environmental amenities can of themselves ensure no lasting results; but the changes in a nation's genetic constitution are likely to prove irreversible." However, in a society which is undernourished, impoverished, or unable to provide what would ordinarily be considered a satisfactory education, it seems quite likely that favorable modifications of the environment can, for all practical purposes, bring about lasting improvements in the intellectual functioning of its people.

It had long been held that there are 48 chromosomes in the human cell. Now Joe Hin Tjio and Albert Levan reported the discovery that the correct number is 46. Later, Jérome Lejeune found that persons afflicted with mongolism have 47 chromosomes, and subsequent research indicated the presence of a metabolic disorder in this form of subnormality. Lejeune believed that because, in part, of the extra chromosome mongoloids produce an excess of an enzyme that acts to break down tryptophan, an essential component of the proteins involved in brain functioning.

Other metabolic anomalies, probably genetic in origin, found to impair effective brain function are: a deficiency of ceruloplasmin or copper protein, apparent in Wilson's disease; a deficiency of galactose in the disorder galactosemia; and the previously mentioned phenylalanine hydoxylase in phenylpyruvic oligophrenia. Naturally, it is not unreasonable to expect any metabolic anomaly to have some effect on brain functioning in an intricately interrelated system such as the human organism.

Psychologists were still hoping to clarify the issue of whether differences in scores on mental tests between Negroes and whites are primarily a function of hereditary or environmental variables, though it is no secret that they thought it was probably the latter. Dreger and Miller reviewed approximately two hundred studies concerning this topic covering the period from 1943 through 1958. In general, higher intelligence and achievement scores were found for whites, and a higher incidence of psychosis was found for Negroes. Still, no unequivocal conclusion could be reached in view of the Negroe's inferior social status. Unfavorable environmental conditions seemed to confront him regardless of where in the United States he lived. Until equality exists in fact as well as in words, it is unlikely that any definitive answer to the question can be obtained. At any rate it is clear from the high accomplishments of many Negroes, both in the United States and in Africa, that a broad range of intellectual functioning exists within that race as well as within the white race.

Although Franz Kallman did not overlook the influence of environmental variables, his research strongly suggested to him the presence of some gene-specific metabolic deficiency at the heart of schizophrenia. His primary evidence was an observed trend toward an increase in the frequency of schizophrenia among the relatives of a schizophrenic in proportion to the degree of consanguinity with the known case. Given a schizophrenic patient, the probability that a relative suffers from the same disorder is higher if that relative is an identical twin than if he is a full sibling, higher for a full- than for a half-sibling, and higher for a half-sibling than for a step-sibling. Nevertheless, it was still argued that environments also tend to be more similar in proportion to the degree of consanguinity to the schizophrenic relative. While most clinicians were willing to assume, as did Freud, the likelihood of constitutional predispositions to various psychiatric disturbances, they were unwilling to assume that these tendencies were transmitted in the germ plasm (It is possible that the physiological changes which accompany a mother's disturbance affect the developing organism within her before birth.) or that they were ordinarily of much practical significance.

Clinical psychologists gave a considerable amount of their attention to a large number of psychological explanations for schizophrenia, all more or less explicitly focusing on childhood and family interactions. Arieti attributed the disorder to some severe trauma in childhood which, by being repeatedly experienced, leads progressively to retreat into archaic forms of thinking, emotional detachment, and desocialization. He regarded the metabolic and endocrine changes associated with schizophrenia as psychosomatic aspects of the psychologically initiated disease process. Lidz thought a person who became schizophrenic was probably raised in a severely disturbed family whose members distort the shared meanings, particularly the linguistic meanings, of the culture. Faced by conflict between the demands of his society and the demands of his family, such a child withdraws from the culture's imposed semantics and logic. This withdrawal eventuates in further isolation and immersion in the distortions of his family.

Margaret Mahler thought the two major symptoms of childhood psychosis or schizophrenia are a severe disturbance of self-identity and an alienation or withdrawal from reality. The first symptom is obvious in a symbiotic psychosis, where the child and mothering person have been virtually inseparable and may be seen as extensions of one another. The second symptom is prominent in early infantile autism, where the child has apparently not progressed to that stage of development in which people are differentiated from other objects in his environment. In connection with this disorder Kanner, who at first had been impressed by the autistic child's compulsive desire for sameness and his relating to others as though they were inanimate things, thought the disturbance might be produced by a cold, emotionally unresponsive mother. Later, impressed by the early onset of the illness, its resistance to significant amelioration, and the genuine concern of some of the parents for their child, Kanner thought it probable that organic factors are involved in the etiology of infantile autism, and that it should be classed as one of the schizophrenias.

Cameron and Magaret suggested that virtually all behavior disorders are the end products of cumulative learning resulting from patterns of reaction that have become overlearned, overgeneralized, and self-perpetuating. Therefore, these reactions or symptoms have not been, nor would they be, abandoned under altered circumstances when they are no longer appropriate. It follows that the withdrawal pattern of the schizophrenic, for example, might have been initiated and perpetuated by traumatic experiences, but that with the passage of time the symptom becomes intrinsically satisfying to the person and thus persists even in the safety of the mental hospital.

It was suggested that two groups of patients could be distinguished among adult schizophrenics. One, the reactive group, evidence a satisfactory prepsychotic adjustment, extraverted behavior, a sudden onset of the disturbance in association with some trauma, and a favorable response to treatment. This form of schizophrenia is supposedly psychogenic. The other group of schizophrenics, the process group, evidence a lifelong history of maladjustment, introverted behavior, a gradual onset of psychosis, and a poor response to treatment. This form of the disorder is supposedly organic. An obvious distinction between the two groups is the duration of schizoid symptoms prior to hospitalization. The reactive cases are those who supposedly show psychotic symptoms only just prior to psychiatric intervention, while the process cases are those believed to have manifested symptoms of maladjustment over a long period of time which eventually became so severe that hospitalization was required.

After reviewing some fifty studies in this area, W. G. Herron concluded that the process-reactive formulation clarifies many heterogeneous reactions found in investigations of schizophrenia. Yet, despite the merit of the distinction, he considered that the dichotomy is to some extent artificial and that it would be an error to believe that all schizophrenics can be easily classified as members of one or the other of these disparate groups. Usually a schizophrenic is found to have both process and reactive signs, which suggests a continuum of personality organization or, perhaps, an imprecise method of classification.

A diagnostic category called "pseudoneurotic schizophrenia" was proposed by Hoch and Polatin. This refers to a schizophrenic disorder which appears like, and may be mistaken for, a neurosis. The symptoms of the disturbance are pan-anxiety, pan-neurosis, and pan-sexuality. Along similar lines, Dunaif and Hoch suggested a diagnostic category which they termed "pseudopsychopathic schizophrenia" for an apparent psychopathic personality with an underlying schizophrenic process. The symptoms of this disturbance are pan-neurosis, pan-sexuality, an acting out of antisocial behavior, and indications in the case history that after imprisonment full-blown psychotic episodes occurred. At about the same time clinicians seemed to become apprehensive lest these pseudo- (Fill in blank) schizophrenias become portents of a diagnostic trend which has *post hoc, ergo propter hoc* reasoning as its major symptom.

The failures of experiments to support Goldstein's contention that schizophrenic functioning is concrete led him to offer some clarification by way of defense of his view. He suggested that the motivation in schizophrenia can only be explained if one carefully considers the patient's situation and determines whether this set of circumstances is likely or not to arouse his anxiety. Given an anxiety-arousing situation, the schizophrenic does perform concretely. Otherwise, the schizophrenic's behavior may be either concrete or abstract. By abstract behavior, Goldstein meant symbolic behavior, or the ability to transcend immediate sense impressions and react appropriately. He illustrated this by saying that a person entering a dark room, but not immediately turning on the light because there might be someone in it asleep is an instance of abstract behavior, which in this example has to do with contemplating the consequences of one's actions.

Impairments of abstract behavior, or the abstract attitude, seem to occur not only in schizophrenia but in patients with known brain damage. Goldstein believed this impairment among the brain-damaged could not be obviated, although each patient was not equally handicapped, the severity depending upon the location of the lesions and the extent of the cortical damage. But regardless of whether the disturbance is organic or psychogenic, Goldstein emphasized that the symptoms have to be considered as performances of the total personality. The symptoms are not caused directly, but are the results of the affected organism's attempts to cope with the inner and outer demands confronting it as it struggles to realize its capacities to the highest degree possible.

In the same way, Agostino Gemelli, an Italian priest and psychologist, pointed out that psychoses are both organic *and* mental diseases since: "What we call 'personality' . . . is the whole man considered in the light of his organic factors and activities." Therefore, a mental disease is not psychogenic *or* organic, but rather it is to be thought of as "organic alterations, regressions or modification which are necessarily accompanied by psychopathological disintegrations." From this frame of reference, Gemelli believed it reasonable to consider psychology as a biological science concerned with man in his entirety.

According to these formulations, schizophrenia appears to be a disturbance toward which a child is constitutionally predisposed. However, the probability that he will develop schizophrenia increases as a function of both the degree of the constitutional predisposition and the degree to which he is compelled to adjust to circumstances which are deviant. In any case, the symptoms of the disorder are to be regarded as not only expressions of a defect, but as reactions to it, including attempts to somehow overcome it. Similar conclusions could be drawn for neuroses.

During this decade practically every explanation of neurosis previously entertained remained viable, either in its original form or in one that was somewhat modified though still recognizable. In 1950, Dollard and Miller had published their integration of psychoanalysis and Hullian learning principles. They saw transference as a special case of stimulus generalization. Repressed conflicts became those that the individual simply cannot "label," while maladjustments are attributed to conflicts between two strong drives producing incompatible responses. Unfortunately, both learning theorists and psychoanalysts had misgivings or reservations about the Dollard-Miller integration. From the point of view of learning theory, there were those who believed that Hullian principles were outmoded; on the psychoanalytic side, David Rapaport criticized their proposals as "clinically unsophisticated" and modeled after the Freudian theory of pre-1923.

Mowrer claimed that maladjustments arise from a learning deficit that results from a failure to incorporate parental and social values into the structure of the ego. Thus the neurotic feels he has committed some transgression, or actually has "sinned," because he is lacking in superego or conscience. In Mowrer's view, the neurotic is not a sick person but a "sinful" person. Mowrer interpreted the great interest in existentialism as a reflection, on a broad scale, of this loss of moral values, one which had led many individuals to question just what is their identity and the meaning of their lives. Although psychologists were critical of Mowrer's introduction of the concept of "sin," they noted that in practice the therapeutic approach that he advocated was not markedly different from most. Since the "sinner" or neurotic has a rejecting attitude toward himself, the task of Mowrer's therapist is to accept him as a person and especially to help him recognize his "sins" rather than refuse to acknowledge them.

Hans Eysenck (b. 1916), who received his Ph.D. from the University of London in 1940 and was still connected with that institution, was using factor analysis to gain an understanding of personality. He suggested that "psychoticism" and "neuroticism" are two independent dimensions of personality, each a continuous variable in normals and abnormals. Introversion-extraversion appears to be a third dimension with its basis, he hypothesized, in constitutional differences in the capacity for developing and dissipating cortical inhibition. Eysenck thought that extraverts generate stronger cortical inhibitions more quickly, but dissipate them more slowly, than introverts. It follows from Pavlovian learning theory and Eysenck's assumptions that extraverted neurotics, which he believed to be hysterics and psychopathic personalities, should evidence quick, strong, lasting inhibitory processes, but weak, slow excitatory processes. He predicted that just the reverse would be the case with introverted neurotics, a group that he suggested is composed of reactive depressions, anxieties, and obsessive disorders.

Since social training is thought to consist largely of conditioned anxiety reactions, Eysenck supposed that extraverts are undertrained and so exhibit a tendency to act out their impulses, while introverts are overtrained and overcontrolled. But when experimental attempts were made to test these predictions they yielded unimpressive and conflicting results. Diligence is often rewarded in this fashion, as the next two topics will also demonstrate.

A consistent finding in extraversion-introversion research has been a positive relationship between extraversion and various measures of satisfactory adjustment, and between introversion and various measures of unsatisfactory adjustment. (We may recall at this point that evidence of extraverted behavior is a criterion for judging which patients are of the good prognosis reactive schizophrenic group, and that introverted behavior is an indicator of membership in the poor prognosis process schizophrenic group.) The usual explanation given for this relationship is that within the culture of the United States the extraverted pattern is more highly valued by the public than the introverted. But then it is fair to ask whether this relationship would also hold in cultures where introversion is more highly valued. In such a culture is extraversion associated with an unsatisfactory adjustment? Furthermore, is it possible to state whether these two personality patterns are wholly learned or based in large part on constitutional differences? After surveying many years of research on extraversion-introversion Patricia Carrigan concluded that many fundamental questions still remain unanswered and as challenging as ever.

The nature of hypnosis continued to be a topic of interest and controversy. Many effects associated with the trance state were now thought to be epiphenomena. Persons who are not hypnotized can, if given appropriate suggestions to do so, tolerate pain, "regress" in their behavior, produce alterations in gastric and pancreatic secretions, recall memories, and even produce localized blisters and alter their blood glucose levels. There seemed to be no physiological way to differentiate "the hypnotic state" from "the waking state."

Studies indicated that what the individual knows about hypnosis has a significant bearing upon his behavior when hypnotized. It also appeared clear that what the person thinks is being demanded of him and the nature of the demand characteristics of the experimental procedure are important determiners of his performance while in the trance. The question seems to be this: does hypnosis actually consist of a unique kind of functioning or is the person playing a role based on his conception of what a hypnotized subject is supposed to do?

On one side of the question, M. T. Orne suggested four characteristics of hypnosis which distinguish it from an individual's "normal" state. *One,* the person who has experienced a deep trance feels that the trance is discontinuous from his "normal waking" behavior. *Two,* the person reports he is unable to resist the hypnotist's suggestions. *Three,* the person claims he actually experiences the alterations, distortions, or denials of reality which are suggested to him, such as "not seeing" an individual who is clearly visible in the room. *Four,* the person appears able to tolerate logical inconsistencies in the trance which would "normally" disturb him or which he would not accept. Obviously the value of these characteristics depends upon how much confidence we can have in the validity of such self-reports.

On the other side of the issue, T. E. Barber, following his review of over a hundred studies of hypnosis, asserted that its nature is still elusive. Rather than continue to focus directly on hypnosis, he proposed that psychologists would find it more profitable to direct research efforts toward uncovering those biographical and situational variables that may possibly explain why some people exhibit hypnotic behavior while others do not.

Before we proceed to the remainder of this section, which introduces some additional problems, it is well for us to pause and to emphasize the significance of the fact that questions were being asked that would stimulate investigation and experimental research. In and of itself this represents some progress—though no doubt not as much as would be represented by arriving at conclusive answers. Charles Darwin commented upon a similar situation in this way: "False facts are highly injurious to the progress of science, for they often endure long; but false views, if supported by some evidence, do little harm, for every one takes a salutary pleasure in proving their falseness."

The American Psychiatric Association published a revised nomenclature in 1952. In it neurasthenia, hypochondriasis, and hysteria were dropped as separate diagnostic categories, and hysteria was broken down into phobic, conversion, and dissociated reactions. Personality disorders, transient reactions to special stress, and the adjustment reactions of childhood, adolescence, and later life were added to the general class of psychiatric disturbances. The number of schizophrenic reactions was increased to allow more detailed diagnoses. Manic-depressive reactions were reduced in number and grouped under "Affective Reactions." The use of IQ limits to distinguish mild, moderate, and severe mental deficiency was abandoned. Psychosomatic disorders became a separate category under a different name, "psychophysiologic autonomic and visceral disorders." Psychopathic personality was replaced by "sociopathic personality," but the use of either label was discouraged.

Quite sensibly, in view of the fact that the information furnished by psychiatric diagnoses is both limited and likely to be only transitorily applicable, the goal of the clinical psychologist veered almost completely from putting a diagnostic label on a patient to an effort to understand how his unique personality functions and to predict his behavior. Additional support for this position came from the observation that some psychiatric disorders, the "classical" neuroses (hysteria and obsessive-compulsive neuroses), formerly quite common, were now almost rare, while personality trait disturbances (passive-aggressive personality, compulsive personality, emotionally unstable personality, etc.) were now frequently reported "illnesses." Most clinicians were inclined to think the changing picture of the neurotic could be attributed to the relatively more permissive methods of rearing children and to a relaxation of moral standards. Both changes may have been, in part, produced by the impact of psychoanalytic formulations, directly and indirectly, on the public. Whatever the reasons, the "new" neurotic, unhappy and dissatisfied with his life and/or himself, seemed even more difficult to help than his hysterically paralyzed and perplexingly ritualistic predecessors.

Along with a recognition of the blurring between the normal and abnormal came an attempt to conceptualize what constitutes positive mental health. Marie Jahoda suggested the following criteria are involved in the concept: growth and self-actualization; accepting attitudes toward the self; integration; perception of reality; autonomy; and mastery of the environment.

But the question may be raised as to whether positive mental health is such an eminently desirable condition. After all, it cannot be denied that out of the psychological sufferings of some people have emerged creative productions whose unique worth can be traced to their origins in their creator's pathology. Is it wise to encourage individuals like these to undertake psychotherapy? Moreover, is it possible that some day in the future man may have to decide whether or not to continue what is grotesquely beautiful, tragic, and pathetic as viable forms of human expression? The conclusion of M. Brewster Smith was that "It (mental health) is a cluster of values that compete with other values in the arena of personal and social choice. We will not always want to give it priority." However, other psychologists were not so certain that the matter was still not open to considerable debate.

TREATMENT FORMULATIONS

The comments with which the preceding section opened will serve equally well here. What progress was being made in psychotherapy came not so much from the resolution of differences and from answers to questions as it did from recognition of additional variables which have to be taken into account. Unlike forms of physical therapy, where some may fall into disuse and become completely abandoned, the basic methods of psychotherapy all seem to thrive, with proliferations of apparently limitless variety.

At the beginning of the decade electric and insulin shock therapies were the primary forms of psychiatric treatment employed with psychotic patients. Electro-shock seemed most effective with those depressed patients who were agitated and anxious, but did not seem to work well with depressed patients who reported somatic complaints and who were openly guilt-ridden. Attempts had been made to use electro-shock with neurotics and children, but their improvements in behavior tended to be temporary and so the practice was not encouraged. However, this is not a sufficient explanation since temporary improvements were also not uncommon with psychotic patients. It seems likely that psychiatrists regarded the procedure as too drastic to be employed routinely with nonpsychotics in view of its hazards, the availability of other kinds of treatment, and the outcome.

A fourteen-year follow-up study of 781 schizophrenic patients who had been given courses of insulin coma therapy showed that approximately 68 percent of the group had responded favorably to the initial course, but of this group benefited, 63 percent suffered a relapse. A second course of insulin treatment produced improvement in 52 percent of the relapsed patients. Thus of an original group of patients, about 47 percent benefited from either one or two courses of insulin shock. Favorable response seemed to be associated with the following factors,—a psychosis of less than six months duration, comas totaling thirty to sixty hours, and a gain of approximately thirty pounds in the patient's weight during the course of the therapy.

Some psychiatrists were trying ether and carbon dioxide inhalations as a method of treatment and reporting encouraging results. Studies on the outcomes of lobotomies, topectomies, and transorbital leucotomies, however, were discouraging. Few or no significant differences were found between patients who had undergone these forms of surgery and their controls. In consequence the practice of these surgical procedures sharply declined.

Doses of glutamic acid were administered to mental defectives in the hope of raising the level of their intellectual functioning. There was some early enthusiasm for this form of medication, but later it was sadly concluded that what mental stimulation it provided was not sufficient to alter in any marked degree the prospects of the intellectually subnormal.

Around 1952 a major change in the treatment of psychiatric disturbances did indeed begin. A pharmacological agent, resperine, extracted from the roots of the rauwolfia plant, seemed to have a beneficial effect on psychotic patients, calming them, and helping them to maintain better contact with their environment and to become more cooperative. Two years later another drug, chlorpromazine, which had been used earlier in Europe, was introduced in the United States. It seemed to alleviate anxiety and to make psychotic symptoms less intense and disturbing. A related development was the discovery that lysergic acid diethylamide (LSD) could produce transient psychotic symptoms. This touched off a search for drugs which would counteract the effects of LSD and which thus might prove useful in the treatment of psychoses.

Within a relatively short period of time a large variety of ataractic or tranquilizing drugs were produced and their effects in treating psychotics and neurotics of all ages were extensively studied. Of particular interest was the question as to just how these drugs worked to bring about the benefits associated with their use. Resperine was connected with the release of serotonin in the brain, but the significance of this association, if any, was conjectural. Some psychologists and psychiatrists wondered if the modifications in symptoms might be due less to the drugs themselves and more to the warm interest in their patients by those who administered them. Or perhaps, on a more analytic level, what was involved was the gratification of the patients' dependency needs when they received and took their pills from the giving therapist. In any case, and regardless of how the drugs worked, beneficial effects were being produced.

In just a few years 4500 studies were reported in the world's medical literature on just one of these drugs, chlorpromazine. There seemed to be general agreement that it accelerated the termination of acute psychotic episodes, that it could rapidly produce a reduction in motor activity and aggressiveness, and that it contributed to more logical thinking and to a feeling of "distance" from their hallucinations in some paranoid and catatonic patients.

It was also generally agreed that these pharmacologic agents made patients more accessible to individual psychotherapy, though in the first wave of enthusiasm there was expressed the almost exultant hope that the drugs might do away with any need to resort to such expensive and time-consuming "traditional" methods. Yet another benefit, and one by no means to be ignored, was the virtual disappearance from mental hospitals of disturbed wards with screaming, babbling patients milling about. The hospitals were more quiet than they had ever been and the patients more easily managed. Whatever might be said of the drugs from the patients' point of view, they raised the morale among nurses, physicians, and attendants by making their working conditions less clamorous.

Since the drugs were relatively cheap and easily administered, it became feasible to discharge patients whose psychoses were, so to speak, controled and have them continue their medication outside the hospital . . . in the same way, for example, that persons who suffer from convulsive disorders (epilepsy) can control their illnesses by barbiturates or other drugs. The tendency in state hospitals, therefore, was to step up greatly the turnover of patients by returning them to their families as quickly as possible, even though some might to some degree continue to show disturbed behavior.

As far as the public was concerned, tranquilizers just seemed to be one of the "miracle drugs" invented by man to make his life a little more palatable. Magazines and newspapers described their wonder-working effectiveness in glamorous, overdrawn reports, and endorsed their use as though there were no side effects or failures to respond favorably. People feeling "nervous" and "tense" were encouraged to take them to gain a feeling of relief and relaxation in the face of onrushing stress. From these accounts it appeared that the mental hospitals would soon be emptied, that immediate and lasting comfort for all neurotics was at hand, and that the *Brave New World* predicted by Aldous Huxley with its contentedly drugged society and its blithe motto of "Half a gram is worth ten damns" was already tiptoeing into the twentieth century.

Understandably, there were at this time signs of concern and even anxiety over the future of psychotherapy. This uneasiness was largely confined to the professional men and women engaged in this form of treatment. In contrast to their distressing malaise, the only problems about psychoanalysis and psychotherapy seen by the public were their cost and their limited availability. There was little question that going to one's analyst had become virtually a symbol of status in American society, but psychologists were less inclined to be so easily impressed.

Although the books that described any method of psychotherapy usually recorded only morale-inspiring instances of success, soberly conducted empirical studies of outcomes reported, on the average, that one-third of the patients had not improved. Nor did it seem likely that any therapist had avoided, or would be able to avoid, experiencing moments of ineptitude and failure. On a purely intellectual level, furthermore, all psychotherapists could agree that it was unreasonable to expect any one form of treatment to be completely effective in treating even just one form of illness, not to speak of the heterogeneous assortment of maladies for which psychotherapy was prescribed—ranging from vague feelings of dissatisfaction to pronounced psychoses, from transistory problems in making an adjustment to entrenched patterns of life-long maladaptive behavior, from disturbances in which the person eagerly seeks help to those in which he fights it with every resource he can command, from a child's difficulties in accepting toilet training to an elderly man's difficulties in accepting death. On the intellectual level, then, it could be agreed that psychotherapy is of limited effectiveness and that psychotherapists are limited both in their skills and what they can reasonably hope to achieve. Yet when failures and limitations were pointed out, some psychotherapists responded not intellectually, but self-critically, and perhaps even with a sharply defensive attitude which opposed any criticism of this method of treatment.

With the stage thus set and remembering that many forms of the psychotherapies we have described, and particularly psychoanalysis, were still vigorously believed in and practiced, we shall consider some of the variants in method espoused in this period. We shall see that a major distinction between them is that they vary along a continuum of depth of interpretation.

At the part of the continuum that is "less deep," Frieda Fromm-Reichmann (1889–1957), who had been influenced greatly by the ideas of Sullivan, joined with others in recommending modifications in psychoanalytic technique, such as the use of a chair instead of the traditional couch and seeing a patient less often than once a day. She strongly urged her colleagues to consider the patient as a person of his present age and not to insist that he must have somehow regressed and become fixated at some infantile stage of development. And along with other analytically oriented therapists, Fromm-Reichmann desexualized the Oedipus complex into a wish for "closeness" and "tenderness" with one parent, while feeling "envious resentment" toward the other.

Near the "very deep" end of the continuum, Marie Sechehaye believed it is helpful when the therapist participates directly in the psychotic reality of the schizophrenic patient. Instead of necessarily endeavoring to interpret the patient's symbols to him, Sechehaye often used them directly as a means of communicating with him and demonstrating her understanding of his needs. Therefore she might present her patient with food to symbolize that she was prepared to gratify the oral needs that had been frustrated in his early life. Or perhaps she might offer a patient a book to signify that she realized his yearning for definite limits and self-control. In these concrete and symbolic ways Sechehaye attempted to establish a therapeutically meaningful relationship, though she hoped that eventually she would be able to provide interpretations of this material that her patient would accept.

Although Sechehaye regarded interpretations as necessary during the course of treatment, a view shared by most analysts, Carl Rogers believed that they should be avoided. In his book *Client-centered Therapy* (1951), Rogers explained that the aim of the counselor should be to perceive his client's perceptual field and to communicate his understanding of it to the person. He believed that this aim is best accomplished through attending to the client's feelings and then clarifying them, which, if followed faithfully, precludes a probing, interpretative approach. Rogers further assumed that since, supposedly, the client is the one who introduces whatever material comes up in the session, he (the client) will be capable of dealing with it, for otherwise he would not have been free to bring it up in the first place. This belief in the capability and strength of the client is the cornerstone of Roger's method: "the counselor chooses to act consistently upon the hypothesis that the individual has a sufficient capacity to deal constructively with all those aspects of his life which can potentially come into awareness."

It is a credit to Rogers that he consistently endeavored to subject his ideas to empirical investigation. A study made by him and his colleagues at the Counseling Center of the University of Chicago indicated some of the changes that occur during a course of psychotherapy. The person seems to become more satisfied with himself, not only in meeting his own standards, but also in terms of his feeling of how he "stacks up" against others. Indications of such changes were found in higher correlations between Q sorts for self and ideal self, and between self and the "ordinary person." The general trend was that the person in therapy moved toward less rigid conceptualizing, and more inner comfort, optimism, self-confidence, spontaniety of feelings, and comfortable relations both with others and himself.

Rogers felt that the counselor, as well as the client, gains from the therapeutic relationship. What he had learned from his many clients was that the individual tends toward positive growth, that the counselor should be genuinely himself in the relationship, that the counselor should feel free to enter into an understanding of another person, and that the facts of scientific inquiry, whatever they might be, are friendly.

In 1957, Rogers accepted a professorship in the Departments of Psychology and Psychiatry at the University of Wisconsin. Part of his purpose in leaving Chicago for Madison was to be able to conduct a research program evaluating the effectiveness of his therapeutic approach with schizophrenic patients. Regardless of the outcome of such a program, Rogerian therapy had now become an internationally recognized and widely adopted form of treatment.

Markedly different from Rogerian therapy was Albert Ellis' rational-emotive therapy. According to Ellis, neurotic behavior is a product of illogical or irrational assumptions. The job of the very active rational psychotherapist, then, was to examine the patient's assumptions, to demonstrate that these beliefs are both at the root of his disturbed behavior and that they are without any sensible foundation, to persuade the patient to work against his neurotic attitudes, and to help him to substitute new attitudes that will be more serviceable. Ellis reported that his approach was the most effective of any that he had tried.

Let us now look at two methods of treatment that make little attempt to deal specifically with unconscious conflicts. George Kelly described an integration of diagnosis and psychotherapy which he called "fixed-role therapy." The procedure he recommended calls for: First, a diagnosis of the person's psychological constructs in significant interpersonal relations by means of his responses on the Role Construct Repertory Test (REP test). Second, using the diagnostic information gained from the REP test, the counselor prepares a personality sketch of the kind of person the client may reasonably be expected to become if favorable changes occur. Third, this personality sketch, under a pseudonym as a label, is discussed with the client in the light of its becoming a possible role he might be able to play for the next several weeks. Fourth, perhaps after the role has been tailored, the client play-acts it with the therapist and then is encouraged to play-act it in significant situations outside the counseling sessions. Fifth, the client reports to the counselor and discusses the progress he seems to be making in playing the role, describing his feelings while playing it and the responses it seems to elicit from other persons. Kelly believed that the person was helped to bring about changes in his personality which he himself desires through his practice of such a role, and he reported encouraging results from the use of his method.

John Wolpe advocated a therapy for neurotics based on learning theory, called variously "reciprocal inhibition," "desensitization," and "deconditioning." In essence, it consisted of efforts to elicit responses which would be incompatible with, and thus inhibit, the neurotic symptoms. The techniques used by Wolpe and his followers for doing this were similar to those proposed by Watson when he attempted to eliminate fears of furry objects and by Dunlap when he tried to remove habits through negative practice. However, Wolpe's theoretical framework was Hullian.

In the practice of desensitization the therapist arranges the patient's anxiety-arousing stimuli in a hierarchical list from the most to the least feared. After the patient has been helped to relax somewhat, either by means of hypnosis or verbal suggestions, the least frightening stimulus on the list is presented. Following this the next higher up on the list are presented in order until the patient signals that he is feeling distress. Wolpe reported that after a number of similar sessions, the vast majority of his patients, about 90 percent, became able to tolerate what had previously been the most anxiety-arousing of all the stimuli without any alarm. By treating symptoms alone, and without attempting to ascertain any particular causes for the neurotic behavior, improvements appeared to be obtained.

Before we examine some of the variables and problems that make the evaluation of treatment difficult we are going to complete this survey by taking a look at group therapy, which was now more popular than ever. Few professionals any longer regarded it solely as an expedient, and many preferred it as the treatment of choice for certain kinds of disturbance under certain conditions. One of its leading advocates, Slavson, defined it as: "a special application of the principles of individual therapy to two or more persons simultaneously which also brings into the situation the phenomena and problems of interpersonal relations." But this definition did not please everyone because it made group therapy seem more an extension of individual psychotherapy than a unique method requiring its own distinctive principles and techniques.

Corsini expressed his belief that the growth in the practice of group therapy might be a reflection of a cultural demand for a treatment procedure which almost immediately alleviated feelings of being alone and socially isolated. Whatever the reason, there could be no doubt about the growth. During the years from 1931 to 1940, 89 publications concerning group therapy appeared. From 1941 to 1950 there were 739. During the years 1951 to 1955 the number of publications rose to a total of 879 books, articles, and dissertations in the treatment of people in groups and by groups.

One of the interesting developments in group therapy was the attempt to extend residential treatment to delinquent children. These efforts were inspired by the success reported by the psychoanalyst August Aichhorn (1878–1949), who shortly after World War I arranged to have twelve adolescent delinquent boys live together in a house in Vienna. He reasoned that the antisocial behavior of the boys were due, putting it in psychoanalytic terms, to failures on the part of their egos to integrate the reality principle, i.e., to postpone gratifications and to evaluate their environments realistically. These ego weaknesses had led, Aichhorn believed, to deficiencies in the growth of their superego functions, or to put it another way, they did not feel guilty after they did something wrong. Consequently, he decided it would be of most therapeutic value to allow these boys to gratify their impulses with virtually no restrictions and thus let them experience in full the consequences of their own behavior. At first the boys responded to their freedom with a period of almost wild destructiveness. But then, receiving no punishment from external sources, they became seemingly depressed and self-reproachful. Following this period of open expressions of sadness, grief, and a sense of worthlessness, they accepted appropriate modes of social behavior and became receptive to reeducation.

Fritz Redl and David Wineman tried to use an approach similar to Aichhorn's with severely disturbed, hyperaggressive, pre-adolescent children in Detroit, Michigan. Just as in the case of the Viennese boys there was at first a period of destructiveness. Unfortunately it went on and on. There appeared to be no end to the hatred and the aggression shown by the children, and the professional staff experienced considerable difficulty in dealing with the impulsiveness and lack of emotional control displayed by their charges. Redl and Wineman concluded that their boys not only had deficient egos but also "solidification of their hatred into an organized department of shrewdly developed defenses" and thus were protected from realizing the moral implications of their behavior. What these boys seemed to need were environmental supports and "a counterbalanced design" to help them perceive their world realistically and maintain self-control in their dealings with it. Moreover, such growth had to take place before the usual therapeutic approaches could even be attempted. How, exactly, this was to be accomplished was a subject for further investigation and research, for as Redl and Wineman observed: "Our trouble is that we don't know enough about Hate."

Despite admitted gaps in their knowledge, Redl and Wineman and practically all others engaged in residential treatment for children agreed on several basic principles for the construction of a therapeutic milieu. *One* is that the children should be completely protected from any traumatic handling by personnel. A *second* is that they should be provided with gratifications regardless of whether they earned, "deserved," them or not. *Three,* there should be tolerance of symptomatic and regressed behavior, although the staff should have techniques for dealing with the children in order to prevent them from harming themselves or someone else. *Four,* the physical design of the milieu should be such as to allow the boys as much freedom as possible, e.g., fragile, expensive furnishings should be avoided. These principles seemed to make sense in general, and so whenever possible they were incorporated in the construction of treatment centers, clinics, and mental hospitals, and in the policies of these institutions.

Morita therapy, named for Shoma Morita (1874–1952), a Japanese psychiatrist, was widely used in Japan. It was based on the principles of Zen Buddhism. The patient was encouraged to stop thinking about himself and his problems, and instead to take an interest in the activities going on in the world about him while maintaining a realistic attitude toward life. Included in this "realism" was an acceptance of the belief that problems and unhappiness are a part of life shared by everyone. The patient was encouraged to recognize that we must live at times with suffering, and so it is to bear one's troubles with equanimity.

Within the Soviet Union psychiatric treatment was guided by traditional Pavlovian formulations about conditioning and brain functioning and consisted chiefly of occupational therapy or plain "work," physiotherapy, and "active therapy." The last, so-called active therapy, included insulin shock and electroshock, sulphotherapy, and the induction of sleep and relaxation by means of sodium amytol and other drugs. Psychosurgery or leucotomy had been introduced as a procedure in 1947, but was banned three years later on grounds that it was "unsoviet," "cruel," and "ineffective." Psychotherapy, either in a psychoanalytic or a Rogerian form, was not practiced to any considerable extent.

A vast mass of thoughtful attention and research was devoted to counseling and psychotherapy during the fifties. These efforts succeeded in shedding light on a number of complex variables, but if anything made the task of evaluating the outcomes of treatment methods appear to be even more stygian in perplexity. The individual came to be seen as part of an interpersonal matrix or system in which efforts to ameliorate his condition may become disruptive to, and elicit resistances from, those other members of the network who are dependent upon his pathology for the gratification of their own needs. For example, an alcoholic's wife may interfere with rehabilitation because her husband's recovery would deprive her of the satisfactions of being a compassionate, long-suffering "mother." If we grant that this point has merit, then this question is raised: Is it appropriate to attribute some cases of lack of improvement following psychotherapy, not to defects in the method, but to a failure to take into account, and to deal adequately with, the actions of persons of significance to the patient that thwart his growth?

The personality of the therapist came to loom as ever greater in importance. His friendliness and genuine interest and concern for his patient were seen to be variables of major significance in helping the person to feel positively toward the treatment relationship. Yet it was found that the therapist's embedment in his own culture, usually middle class, appeared to impair his ability to understand and accept patients with different standards and values. His preference for seeing in therapy persons who shared his frame of reference was recognized, as was the fact that he also tended to feel that they were the kind of people who would benefit most from his help. It now became essential to discover whether a therapist's middle-class cultural biases precluded his being able to help to a significant degree those whose status was low but whose need for assistance was undeniable.

At the same time there was much discussion about the "arousal" value of each of the persons involved in the therapeutic interaction, i.e., the nature and intensity of the feelings the therapist tends to arouse in his patient, and of those the patient tends to arouse in the therapist. All therapists could agree that if either party almost immediately arouses negative feelings in the other, psychotherapy becomes more difficult than when the feelings are positive.

Edward Bordin emphasized the variable of ambiguity-structuredness in the counseling situation. He suggested that counseling can be distinguished from psychotherapy by reference to this factor. At the beginning and during the course of the relationship the counselor (therapist) structures the topics appropriate for discussion, the closeness and character of the interactions, and the goals to be attained by means of the sessions. In counseling, as compared with psychotherapy, the relationships tend to be more structured and less ambiguous, the topics discussed more specific and circumscribed, and the goals more limited.

Further, Bordin thought it likely that as the situation becomes more ambiguous, the client is more apt to experience anxiety and to react in a more personal and affective manner. Therefore, if desired, anxiety and the intensity of the transference may be increased by increasing ambiguity, and, on the other hand, as the client shows evidences of benefitting from the counseling or treatment, his tension and investment can be diminished even more by reducing the ambiguity of the situation.

A cynical view of psychotherapy was offered by the psychiatrist Jules Masserman, who believed that this method might actually be dedicated to the establishment or strengthening of what he called "ur-defenses." These ur-defenses were regarded as certain delusions necessary to all men in order to help them adjust to the harsh realities of life. One such delusion assists the person to deny the constant threat to his existence and his eventual death; the patient, by being seen in therapy, is encouraged to believe that he possesses a self that is of value and significance, a self that has momentous effects upon the selves of others which can reverberate and persist through countless generations. A second ur-defense is the delusion of the omnipotent servant; the patient is led to feel that he must indeed be a very worthy and important person since he has at his command the powerful, deeply involved, all-wise, and all-understanding therapist. A third ur-defense is the fiction that man is kind to his fellow men; in the unreal world of the therapist's office an attempt is made to build up the delusion that the patient can hope to find help, warmth, and concern outside the therapeutic milieu similar to what he has experienced within it.

It was one of Masserman's contentions that these false beliefs are fostered by denials on the part of the patient and therapist that their relationship is an economic transaction in which a fee is paid for services rendered. The patient wishes to deny the fee so that he can believe more easily that he is a person of worth who would be listened to by the therapist regardless of whether or not he has money. The therapist denies the fee so that he can see his work as noble, pure, and altruistically motivated, even though he would probably be quite distressed if his clients did not pay their bills.

Not too many psychotherapists were aware of Masserman's sardonic analysis of their profession, but even without it they gave signs of experiencing uncertainties enough over what was found in studies of therapeutic outcomes. The results of a number of investigations indicated that degree of improvement depended more on the acuteness of onset and the subtype of the illness than on the method of treatment, whether insulin or electroshock or psychotherapy. Though on the other hand, Lauretta Bender did believe she had found evidence that with brain-damaged children the prognosis and behavior manifestations are far more dependent on the way in which the children are accepted and helped than upon the degree, or even the presence, of organic factors.

Kanner and Eisenberg reported a follow-up study of sixty-three children diagnosed as early infantile autism. Approximately nine years had elapsed between the time of their original diagnoses and follow-up evaluations. Thirty-four of the children were then in residential treatment, while twenty-nine were still living at home. Of thirty-one children who had been mute at the age of five years, only one showed any improvement. Of thirty-two children who could speak at least some words at five years of age, sixteen showed later improvement. Most discouraging to Kanner and Eisenberg were the signs of disturbance and the need for close supervision even among those children who had made some progress. They noted that no one of the various treatments was superior to any other, which in this case is a way of saying that all were equally ineffective.

In 1952, Hans Eysenck published the results of his survey of the literature on the effects of psychotherapy. Different investigators had adopted different standards for what they would consider "improvement," with psychoanalysts being more demanding of themselves in this regard than others. Estimates of the percentage of patients who had improved from psychotherapy ranged from 39 percent to 77 percent, with 66 percent about a fair average estimate. But it also appeared that anywhere from 66 percent to 72 percent of neurotic patients improved who had had custodial care but no psychotherapy. Therefore, Eysenck concluded, the research failed to justify rejecting the hypothesis that the results of psychotherapy are due to chance or random effects. In other words, whatever supposed "effects" are observed after psychotherapy are probably not uniquely related to or specific to the therapy itself.

Eysenck's conclusion touched off an outburst of dismay and indignation. Despite the soundness of many of the objections raised to his survey, such as his throwing together of a conglomeration of studies with widely differing frames of reference and patient populations as if they were of equal merit and relevance, the fact remained that the responsibility for demonstrating the effectiveness of psychotherapy rested upon those who asserted that it is effective, and to that date that responsibility had not been met in an unequivocal and completely convincing manner.

Perhaps due to myriad difficulties that stood in the way of a demonstration of the effectiveness of psychotherapy, the responsibility for doing so seemed to be avoided. Somewhat symptomatic of those troubled years was the proposal brought forward to use multiple therapy; two or more therapists would see a single patient, and the patient might play the role of a participant-observer while his therapists analyzed one another.

A meeting of some of the leading figures engaged in research in psychotherapy was held in Washington, and a report of that meeting was published by the American Psychological Association in 1959. Rubenstein and Parloff, who summarized the proceedings of the conference, were impressed by the ingenuity of the research designs and methods for investigating the *process* of psychotherapy. They were puzzled, however, by the glaring neglect of any attempt to deal with the issue of its *outcome,* and concluded that despite monumental effort, "there has been relatively little progress in establishing a firm and substantial body of evidence to support very many research hypotheses."

Zax and Klein, following their review of studies of the measurement of personality and behavior changes during and after psychotherapy, concluded that no relationship had been demonstrated between measures of process or reported concepts of self and the everyday behavior of the person.

In a study based on a survey of the literature up to 1958, Eyseck was led to an even more forceful conclusion than the one he had reached in 1952: "With the single exception of the psychotherapeutic methods based on learning theory, results of published research with military and civilian neurotics, and with both adults and children, suggest that the therapeutic effects of psychotherapy are small or non-existant."

Thus by the close of the fifties psychotherapy was being severely criticized and yet simultaneously advocated for a variety of disturbances from infancy through senility. Its proponents were convinced of its worth and of the success of their methods despite the lack of any quantitative evidence obtained by adequately controled research that would support their convictions. Though the burden for demonstrating the effectiveness of psychotherapy rested on them, and though it would have testified to their confidence and their prudence had they essayed such a thorough-going and soundly designed demonstration, those who investigated psychotherapy seemed satisfied with concentrating their efforts on examining antecedent variables and the process itself.

Raimy's appraisal of psychotherapy was as valid in 1959 as it had been in 1952 when he observed that "the field of psychotherapy appears to have an enormous but somewhat leaderless vitality." Though perhaps it would have been more accurate to charge, not that the field was "leaderless," but that it was of such heterogeneity and vitality that no one person could pass a judgment upon it which a majority of his colleagues could endorse. There were many leaders, yes, but no Leader.

Turning to the problem of evaluating the effectiveness of physical methods of treatment we find a similar situation. After the first wave of enthusiasm for the ataractic drugs had ebbed, it appeared that 65 percent to 75 percent of schizophrenic patients remained severely handicapped, a percentage approximately the same as had been reported years earlier during the time of Bleuler. Robert White, in concluding a report in 1959, made a statement in reference to a psychotic population that might have been said of the entire spectrum of mental illness: "Thus we are left with a curious uncertainty concerning what it is that improves chronic hospital patients. One is almost tempted to think of a single scale of improvement on which a patient's position can be bettered by a given unit of chlorpromazine, or L-glutavite, or respect, or structured tasks."

PROFESSIONAL DEVELOPMENT

Each year of this period was marked by growth in numbers, influence, status, and prestige. In 1950, the APA had 7250 members; in 1959, 16,644. After 1958, there were only two classes of voting membership, fellows and members, both requiring a doctoral degree based on a psychological dissertation and continued professional work psychological in nature.

During the fiscal year 1952–1953, the United States government appropriated $11,000,000 for contracts and grants for psychological research. During the fiscal year 1958–1959, $31,300,000 was appropriated for research in psychology and closely related areas. In 1950, *Psychological Abstracts* took note of 6563 publications; in 1959, 11,242, and the APA journals alone published approximately 870 original articles. The National Institute of Mental Health in 1956 awarded $1,674,664 in graduate training grants for clinical psychology, a sum approximately eight times what was allocated in 1948.

Further evidence of growth is provided by the increase in legal recognition and status. In 1950, Kentucky passed a certification bill and in 1951, the Georgia legislature passed a licensure law for psychologists. That same year, 1951, Minnesota passed a certification law and the New York legislature passed a licensing bill, subsequently vetoed by Governor Dewey of New York because of strong opposition from the medical profession. Despite the temporary setback in the Empire State, legislation elsewhere marched on: Maine's certification law and Tennessee's licensure law in 1953; a certification law in Washington and a licensure law in Arkansas in 1955; at last New Yorkers had their certification law in 1956; certification followed in California, Florida, New Hampshire, and Maryland in 1957; and certification in Utah in 1959.

The competence of the profession was given legal recognition by the Supreme Court of the State of Michigan when it ruled, as did various other courts, that the testimony of a clinical psychologist on questions of mental illness could be admitted as that of an expert witness.

Judging by their actions, psychiatrists seemed torn by disagreements within their profession over the stance that they should take with regard to the certification of psychologists. Although it had consistently resisted such measures over the years, in 1952, the Council of the American Psychiatric Association passed a resolution favoring the certification of clinical psychologists. But when, in 1957, the American Psychiatric Association rescinded this resolution, understandably enough, relations between the two professions, at least on the formal level, could fairly be said to have become "strained."

However psychiatrists were not alone in feeling ambivalent about licensure and certification. Within the profession of psychology there were psychologists who feared that legislation designed primarily to be applicable to clinicians in private practice might have the effect of restricting or hampering the activities of other psychologists. In order to circumvent such possible discrimination, they urged upon their colleagues a policy of voluntary certification, i.e., certification by the psychologists themselves rather than the state, and this policy was adopted in

Illinois, Louisiana, Massachusetts, Nebraska, New Jersey, Ohio, Oregon, and West Virgina.

Finally, to close this survey of certification, we should note that the number of states certifying school psychologists had risen from eleven in 1949 to twenty-three by 1959. Newcomers to the list, in addition to the District of Columbia, were: Colorado, Hawaii, Illinois, Indiana, Iowa, Kansas, Massachusetts, Michigan, Missouri, Oklahoma, Oregon, and Rhode Island.

Our review thus far has focused on developments between psychology and society in general, principally in terms of support and recognition by the public. However, of direct pertinence to the growth of the profession itself, and as evidence of its maturity, was the preparation of a code of ethics. As a beginning, in 1951, the APA published a tentatively formulated ethical code only for clinical and consulting psychologists. But in the following years a more complete formulation of the ethical standards which should apply to all forms of practice by psychologists was adopted. This code was not considered fixed, of course, but as subject to continuing revisions and amplifications as demanded by new and changing circumstances.

To complete the accouterments of maturity, in 1955, the APA initiated the practice of conferring Gold Medal Awards upon those psychologists who had made an outstandingly significant contribution to the science. The first recipient of a Gold Medal Award was Robert Woodworth. A similar honor, the APA's Distinguished Scientific Contribution Award was bestowed upon two clinical psychologists, Carl Rogers in 1956 and Paul Meehl in 1958.

Incontestably, the United States had attained leadership in the profession. In 1952, it was estimated that there were 18,000 psychologists in the United States, 2500 psychologists in England, 700 in Japan, and 24 in all South America. In Austria and Western Germany in 1953, there were 209 graduate students working for doctorates in psychology at fifteen universities. However, neither of these countries had any formulated clinical psychology training program, although some psychologists were functioning as clinicians. In Turkey and the Arab countries, psychology was still almost exclusively an academic discipline. Egypt did have about forty psychologists, a handful of whom worked as clinicians at an outpatient child and student clinic affiliated with the Institute of Higher Education for Men in Cairo. They were using an adaptation of the Binet, and the Egyptian army employed intelligence and aptitude tests. There were some teaching of clinical psychology at the Syrian State University in Dasmascus. Aside from Egypt and Syria, there was little to report about the profession in the Arab states.

By 1959, there were approximately 2000 psychologists in the Japanese Psychological Association. Six centers in Japan were devoted to teaching the Rorschach, there was a modification of the TAT in use, and the method of psychotherapy identified with Carl Rogers was very popular. Great Britain had about 400 clinical psychologists, many of whom were expressing interest in the practice of psychotherapy. Clinical psychology appeared to be growing in France, Germany, and elsewhere on the west European continent.

In the United States, there were fifty-six APA approved doctoral training programs in clinical psychology and twenty-seven in counseling. During the four-year period from 1957 through 1960, 3074 Ph.D.'s were awarded in psychology, of which 1047 were in clinical psychology. ABEPP diplomas had been awarded to 1403 psychologists, of whom 965 were clinicians. The Clinical Division of the APA, largest in the association, had 2736 members.

It was by now generally agreed that an internship program had to be an integral part of doctoral training for a clinical psychologist. Such an internship had to include at least one year of supervised experience in clinical settings with persons demonstrably in need of diagnosis and psychotherapy. The student in training was to be insured the opportunity to maintain intensive, intimate, long-term contacts with clinical problems. He was to be encouraged and aided in developing professional independence, self-confidence, and facility in communication with the members of allied professions. His immersion in the vital problems of human beings was, in addition to sharpening his clinical skills, to acquaint him with the raw data of a field in which he must be prepared later to undertake relevant, sophisticated research.

At the same time there was a need, not only for proficiency, but for flexibility. Clinical psychologists were extending their services in new directions. Some were working closely with neurosurgeons to evaluate the fitness of patients to undergo operations intended to alleviate the symptoms of Parkinson's disease. Some were assessing the effects, direct and indirect, of surgical and other medical procedures. Some were participating in the training of physicians in comprehensive or humanistic medicine. Some were in the area of executive appraisal, leadership counseling, and the analysis of man-machine systems.

But all this expansive vigor and recognition, rather than marking a final stage in the development of clinical psychology, is better seen as marking a later phase of its beginning. We are confident that there is still much to come, and we are certain that as clinical psychologists continue to further the growth of their profession, they should be aware of, but not bound to, their history. For although a great number of words speak to us from the past, there are other voices that must wait upon our advances before they can be heard.

Lightner Witmer died in 1956. Even his name sounds a bit anachronistic, and so, not too surprisingly, his death was for the most part overlooked, as he had been, in all the forward rush of the profession he had named, and amid all the celebrations commemorating the centennial of Freud's birth. Yet fifty years before, in the article which introduced the field of clinical psychology, Witmer concluded with words that retain their importance today: "But in the final analysis the progress of clinical psychology, as of every other science, will be determined by the value and amount of its contributions to the advancement of the human race."

References

Aichhorn, A. *Wayward youth*. New York: Viking, 1935.

Allport, G. W. *Becoming: basic considerations for a psychology of personality.* New Haven: Yale U. Press, 1955.

American Board of Examiners in Professional Psychology. *Amer. Psychol.,* 1959, 14, 827–829.

APA Committee on Ethical Standards for Psychology. Ethical standards in clinical and consulting relationships. *Amer. Psychol.,* 1951, 6, 57–64, 145–166.

APA Committee on Test Standards. *Amer. Psychol.,* 1952, 7, 461–475.

Anastasi, Anne. Heredity, environment, and the question "how?" *Psychol. Rev.,* 1958, 65, 197–208.

Arieti, S. *Interpretation of schizophrenia*. New York: Brunner, 1955.

Atkinson, J. W. Personality dynamics. *Ann. rev. Psychol.,* 1960, 11, 255–290.

Barber, T. E. Physiological effects of "hypnosis." *Psychol. Bull.,* 1956, 53, 210–226.

Barron, F. An ego-strength scale which predicts response to psychotherapy. *J. consult. Psychol.,* 1953, 17, 327–333.

Bateson, G., *et al.* Toward a theory of schizophrenia. *Behavioral Science,* 1956, 1, 251–264.

Bayley, Nancy. On the growth of intelligence. *Amer. Psychol.,* 1955, 10, 805–818.

Bender, Lauretta. *Psychopathology of children with organic brain disorders.* Springfield, Ill.: Charles C Thomas, 1956.

Bettelheim, B. *Love is not enough*. Glencoe, Ill.: Free Press, 1950.

Billingslea, F. Y. The Bender-Gestalt: a review and a perspective. *Psychol. Bull.,* 1963, 60, 233–251.

Blake, R. R. & Mouton, Jane S. *Personality. Ann. rev. Psychol.,* 1959, 10, 203–232.

Brackbill, G. A. Studies of brain dysfunction in schizophrenia. *Psychol. Bull.,* 1956, 53, 210–226.

Buros, O. K. *The fourth mental measurements yearbook.* Highland Park, N.J.: Gryphon Press, 1953.

Burt, C. The inheritence of mental ability. *Amer. Psychol.,* 1958, 13, 1–15.

Buss, A. H. & Durkee, Ann. Conditioning of hostile verbalizations in situation resembling a clinical interview. *J. consult. Psychol.,* 1958, 22, 415–418.

Buss, A. H. & Gerjuoy, Irma R. Verbal conditioning and anxiety. *J. abnorm. soc. Psychol.*, 1958, 57, 249–250.

Cameron, N. & Magaret, Ann. *Behavior pathology*. Boston: Houghton Mifflin, 1957.

Carrigan, Patricia M. Extraversion-introversion as a dimension of personality: a reappraisal. *Psychol. Bull.*, 1960, 57, 329–360.

Challman, R. C. Clinical methods: psychodiagnostics. *Ann. rev. Psychol.*, 1951, 2, 239–258.

Chauncey, H. Some notes on education and psychology in the Soviet Union. *Amer. Psychol.*, 1959, 14, 307–312.

Cofer, C. N. Motivation. *Ann. rev. Psychol.*, 1959, 10, 173–202.

Committee on Nomenclature and Statistics of the American Psychiatric Association. *Diagnostic and statistical manual*. Washington: APA Mental Health Service, 1952.

Corsini, R. J. *Methods of group psychotherapy*. New York: McGraw-Hill, 1957.

Cronbach, L. J. Assessment of individual differences. *Ann. rev. Psychol.*, 1956, 7, 173–196.

Cronbach, L. J. & Meehl, P. E. Construct validity in psychological tests. *Psychol. Bull.*, 1955, 52, 281–302.

Crutchfield, R. S. Conformity and character. *Amer. Psychol.*, 1955, 10, 191–198.

Daily, J. M. Verbal conditioning without awareness. Unpublished doctoral dissertation. State U. of Iowa, 1953.

David, H. P. Clinical psychology aboard. *Amer. Psychol.*, 1959, 14, 601–605.

Dement, W. & Kleitman, N. The relation of eye movements during sleep to dream activity: an objective method for the study of dreaming. *J. exp. Psychol.*, 1957, 53, 339–346.

Deutsch, Cynthia P. After legislation—what price psychology? *Amer. Psychol.*, 1958, 13, 645–652.

Dollard, J. & Miller, N. E. *Personality and psychotherapy*. New York: McGraw-Hill, 1950.

Dreger, R. M. & Miller, K. S. Comparative psychological studies of Negroes and whites in the U.S. *Psychol. Bull.*, 1960, 57, 361–402.

Dunaif, S. & Hoch, P. H. Pseudopsychopathic schizophrenia. In Hoch, P. H. & Zubin, J. (Eds.). *Psychiatry and the law*. New York: Grune & Stratton, 1955.

Edwards, A. L. Edwards Personal Preference Schedule. New York: Psych. Corp., 1954.

Ellis, A. Rational psychotherapy. *J. gen. Psychol.*, 1958, 59, 35–49.

English, H. B. & English, Ava C. *A comprehensive dictionary of psychological and psychoanalytic terms*. New York: Longmans, Green, 1958.

Erikson, E. H. *Childhood and society*. New York: Norton, 1950.

Erikson, E. H. Identity and the life cycle. *Psychological Issues*, 1959, Vol. 1, No. 1.

Ethical standards of psychologists. *Amer. Psychol.*, 1959, 14, 279–282.

Eysenck, H. J. *The scientific study of personality.* New York: Macmillan, 1952.

Eysenck, H. J. The effects of psychotherapy: an evaluation. *J. consult. Psychol.,* 1952, 16, 319–324.

Eysenck, H. J. The effects of psychotherapy. In H. J. Eysenck (Ed.). *Handbook of abnormal psychology.* New York: Basic Books, 1961.

Fordham, Frieda. *An introduction to Jung's psychology.* London: Penguin Books, 1953.

Foster, A., Benton, A. L., & Rabin, A. I. The internship in clinical psychology: three alternative plans. *Amer. Psychol.,* 1952, 7, 7–13.

Fromm, E. *The sane society.* New York: Rinehart, 1955.

Fromm-Reichmann, Frieda. *Principles of intensive psychotherapy.* Chicago: U. of Chicago Press, 1950.

Fulkerson, S. C. & Barry, J. R. Methodology and research on the prognostic use of psychological tests. *Psychol. Bull.,* 1961, 58, 177–204.

Garner, Ann M. Abnormalities of behavior. *Ann. rev. Psychol.,* 1958, 9, 391–418.

Gemelli, A. Autobiography. In E. G. Boring, *et. al.* (Eds.). *A history of psychology in autobiography.* Vol. IV. Worcester, Mass.: Clark U. Press, 1952.

Gill, M. The present state of psychoanalytic theory. *J. abnorm. soc. Psychol.,* 1959, 58, 1–8.

Glueck, S. & Glueck, E. *Unraveling juvenile delinquency.* New York: Commonwealth Fund, 1950.

Goldstein, K. Functional disturbances in brain damage. In S. Arieti (Ed.). *American handbook of psychiatry.* Vol. 1. New York: Basic Books, 1959.

Goldstein, K. Concerning the concreteness in schizophrenia. *J. abnorm. soc. Psychol.,* 1959, 59, 146–148.

Guerton, W. H., *et al.* Research with the Wechsler-Bellevue Intelligence Scale: 1950–1955. *Psychol. Bull.,* 1956, 53, 235–257.

Guerton, W. H., *et. al.* Research with the Wechsler intelligence scales for adults: 1955–1960. *Psychol. Bull.,* 1962, 59, 1–26.

Guilford, J. P. Creativity. *Amer. Psychol.,* 1950, 5, 444–454.

Guilford, J. P. Three faces of intellect. *Amer. Psychol.,* 1959, 14, 469–479.

Harlow, H. F. The nature of love. *Amer. Psychol.,* 1958, 13, 673–685.

Harmon, L. R. Production of psychology doctorates in the United States. *Amer. Psychol.,* 1961, 16, 717–717.

Hathaway, S. R. & Meehl, P. E. (Eds.) *An atlas for the clinical use of the MMPI.* Minneapolis: U. Minn. Press, 1951.

Hartmann, H. *Ego psychology and the problem of adaptation.* New York: International Universities Press, 1958.

Hebb, D. O. The motivating effects of exteroceptive stimulation. *Amer. Psychol.,* 1958, 13, 109–113.

Hebb, D. O. Alice in Wonderland, or psychology among the behavioral sciences. In H. F. Harlow & C. N. Woolsey (Eds.). *Biological and biochemical bases of behavior.* Madison: U. Wisconsin Press, 1958.

Herron, W. G. The process-reactive classification of schizophrenia. *Psychol. Bull.,* 1962, 59, 329–343.

Hess, W. R. *Das Zwischenhirn: Syndrome, Lokalisationen, Functionen.* Basel: Schwabe, 1954.

Hoch, P. H. & Polatin, P. Pseudoneurotic forms of schizophrenia. *Psychiat. Quart.,* 1949, 23, 248.

Hodges, W. L. State certification of school psychologists. *Amer. Psychol.,* 1960, 15, 198–200.

Horney, Karen. *Neurosis and human growth.* New York: Norton, 1950.

Jahoda, Marie. *Current concepts of positive mental health.* New York: Basic Books, 1958.

Jensen, A. R. Personality. *Ann. rev. Psychol.,* 1958, 9, 295–322.

Jersild, A. T. Self-understanding in childhood and adolescence. *Amer. Psychol.,* 1951, 6, 122–126.

Joint report on relations between psychology and psychiatry. *Amer. Psychol.,* 1960, 15, 198–200.

Kallman, F. J. The genetics of mental illness. In S. Arieti (Ed.). *American handbook of psychiatry.* Vol. I. New York: Basic Books, 1959.

Kanner, L. The conception of wholes and parts in early infantile autism. *Amer. j. Psychiat.,* 1951, 108, 23–26.

Kanner, L. & Eisenberg, L. Chapter 13. In P. H. Hoch & J. Zubin (Eds.). *Psychopathology of childhood.* New York: Grune & Stratton, 1955.

Kantor, R. E., Wallner, J., & Winder, C. L. Process and reactive schizophrenia. *J. consult. Psychol.,* 1953, 17, 157–162.

Kelly, E. L. Theory and techniques of assessment. *Ann. rev. Psychol.,* 1954, 5, 281–310.

Kelly, E. L. Consistency of the adult personality. *Amer. Psychol.,* 1955, 10, 659–681.

Kelly, E. L. & Fiske, D. W. The prediction of success in the VA training program in clinical psychology. *Amer. Psychol.,* 1950, 5, 395–406.

Kelly, G. A. *The psychology of personal constructs.* Vol. 1. *A theory of personality.* Vol. 2. *Clinical diagnosis and psychotherapy.* New York: Norton, 1955.

Kendler, T. S. Contributions of the psychologist to constitutional law. *Amer. Psychol.,* 1950, 5, 505–510.

Kora, T. & Sato, K. Morita therapy: a psychotherapy in the way of Zen. *Psychologia,* 1958, 1, 219–225.

Lehner, G. F. J. Psychological training facilities in Austria and West Germany. *Amer. Psychol.,* 1955, 10, 79–82.

Lidz, T. Schizophrenia and the family. *Psychiatry,* 1958, 21, 21–27.

Lidz, T., *et. al.* The intrafamilial environment of the schizophrenic patient: VI. The transmission of irrationality. *Arch. Neurol. Psychiat.,* 1958, 79, 305–316.

Littell, W. M. The WISC: review of a decade of research. *Psychol. Bull.*, 1960, 57, 132–156.

Liverant, S. Intelligence: a concept in need of re-examination. *J. consult. Psychol.*, 1960, 24, 101–110.

Loevinger, Jane. Theory and technique of assessment. *Ann. rev. Psychol.*, 1959, 10, 287–316.

London, I. D. Therapy in Soviet psychiatric hospitals. *Amer. Psychol.*, 1953, 8, 79–82.

Lowenfeld, Margaret. *The Lowenfeld Mosaic Test.* New York: Psych. Corp., 1954.

MacKinnon, D. W. Fact and fancy in personality research. *Amer. Psychol.*, 1953, 8, 138–146.

Margaret, Ann. Clinical methods: psychodiagnostics. *Ann. rev. Psychol.*, 1952, 3, 283–320.

Mahler, Margaret S. Autism and symbiosis: two extreme disturbances of identity. *Internat. j. Psychoanal.*, 1958.

Masling, J. The influence of situational and interpersonal variables in projective testing. *Psychol. Bull.*, 1960, 57, 65–85.

Masserman, J. H. *The practice of dynamic psychiatry.* Philadelphia: W. B. Saunders, 1955.

Maupir, E. W. Zen Buddhism: a psychological review. *J. consult. Psychol.*, 1962, 26, 362–378.

May, R., Angel, E., & Ellenberger, H. F. (Eds.). *Existence.* New York: Basic Books, 1948.

McCary, J. L. The psychologist as an expert witness in court. *Amer. Psychol.*, 1956, 11, 8–13.

McConnell, J. V., *et. al.* Subliminal stimulation: an overview. *Amer. Psychol.*, 1958, 13, 229–242.

McGinnies, E. Psychology in Japan. *Amer. Psychol.*, 1960, 15, 556–562.

McKinney, F. Psychology in Turkey. *Amer. Psychol.*, 1960, 15, 717–721.

Meehl, P. E. The cognitive activity of the clinician. *Amer. Psychol.*, 1960, 15, 19–27.

Miller, G. A. What is information measurement? *Amer. Psychol.*, 1953, 8, 3–11.

Miller, J. G. Toward a general theory for the behavioral sciences. *Amer. Psychol.*, 1955, 10, 513–531.

Miller, N. E. Central stimulation and other new approaches to motivation and reward. *Amer. Psychol.*, 1958, 13, 100–108.

Mowrer, O. H. *Learning theory and personality dynamics.* New York: Ronald, 1950.

Mowrer, O. H. The psychologist looks at language. *Amer. Psychol.*, 1954, 9, 660–694.

Mowrer, O. H. "Sin," the lesser of two evils. *Amer. Psychol.*, 1960, 15, 301–304.

Orne, M. T. The nature of hynosis: artifact and essence. *J. abnorm. soc. Psychol.,* 1959, 58, 277–299.

Pervin, L. A. Existentialism, psychology, and psychotherapy. *Amer. Psychol.,* 1960, 15, 305–309.

Price, A. C. & Deabler, H. L. Diagnosis of organicity by means of spiral after-effect. *J. consult. Psychol.,* 1955, 19, 299–302.

Protho, E. T. & Melikan, L. H. Psychology in the Arab Near East. *Psychol. Bull.,* 1955, 52, 303–310.

Rabin, A. I. & Guertin, W. H. Research with the Wechsler-Bellevue test, 1945–1950. *Psychol. Bull.,* 1951, 48, 211–248.

Rachman, S. The treatment of anxiety and phobic reactions by systematic desensitization psychotherapy. *J. abnorm. soc. Psychol.,* 1959, 58, 259–263.

Raimy, V. C. (Ed.). *Training in clinical psychology.* Englewood Cliffs, N.J.: Prentice-Hall, 1950.

Raimy, V. C. Clinical methods: psychotherapy. *Ann. rev. Psychol.,* 1952, 3, 321–350.

Rapaport, D. *Personality and psychotherapy:* an analysis in terms of learning, thinking, and culture. *Amer. j. Orthopsychiat.,* 1953, 23, 204–208.

Redl, F. & Wineman, D. *Children who hate.* Glencoe, Ill.: Free Press, 1951.

Rogers, C. R. *Client-centered therapy.* Boston: Houghton Mifflin, 1951.

Rogers, C. R. A process conception of psychotherapy. *Amer. Psychol.,* 1958, 13, 142–149.

Rogers, C. R. & Dymond, Rosalind F. (Eds.). *Psychotherapy and personality change.* Chicago: U. Chicago Press, 1955.

Rotter, J. B. Clinical methods: psychodiagnostics. *Ann. rev. Psychol.,* 1953, 4, 295–316.

Rubenstein, E. R. & Parloff, M. B. (Eds.). *Research in psychotherapy.* Washington: APA, 1959.

Sanford, F. Psychology and the mental health movement. *Amer. Psychol.,* 1958, 13, 80–85.

Sarason, S. B. *The clinical interaction, with special reference to the Rorschach.* New York: Harper, 1954.

Schafer, R. *Psychoanalytic interpretation in Rorschach testing.* New York: Grune & Stratton, 1954.

Sechehaye, Marie A. *Symbolic realization.* New York: International Universities Press, 1951.

Selye, H. *The stress of life.* New York: McGraw Hill, 1956.

Shaffer, L. F. Of whose reality I cannot doubt. *Amer. Psychol.,* 1953, 8, 608–623.

Shoben, E. J., Jr. Counseling. *Ann. rev. Psychol.,* 1956, 7, 147–172.

Siegel, Norma & Bernreuter, R. G. Foreign language requirements for reading current psychological literature. *Amer. Psychol.,* 1951, 6, 179.

Skinner, B. F. Reinforcement today. *Amer. Psychol.,* 1958, 13, 94–99.

Slavson, S. R. *The practice of group therapy.* New York: International Universities Press, 1951.

Smith, M. B. Research strategies toward a conception of positive mental health. *Amer. Psychol.,* 1959, 14, 673–681.

Stern, A. W. The nature of g and the concept of intelligence. *Acta Psychologia,* 1956, 12, 282–289.

Stone, H. K. & Dellis, N. F. An exploratory investigation into the levels hypothesis. *J. proj. Tech.,* 1960, 24, 333–340.

Strong, E. K., Jr. Satisfactions and interests. *Amer. Psychol.,* 1958, 13, 449–456.

Summerfield, A. Clinical psychology in Great Britain. *Amer. Psychol.,* 1958, 13, 171–176.

Sundberg, N. D. A note concerning the history of testing. *Amer. Psychol.,* 1954, 9, 150–151.

Sundberg, N. D. The practice of psychological testing in clinical services in the U.S. *Amer. Psychol.,* 1961, 16, 79–83.

Taylor, Janet. A personality scale of manifest anxiety. *J. abnorm. soc. Psychol.,* 1953, 48, 285–290.

Tryon, R. C. Psychology in flux: the academic-professional bipolarity. *Amer. Psychol.,* 1963, 18, 134–143.

Wechsler, D. Cognitive, conative, and non-intellective intelligence. *Amer. Psychol.,* 1950, 5, 78–83.

Wechsler, D. *Manual for the WAIS.* New York: Psych. Corp., 1955.

Wechsler, D. *The measurement and appraisal of adult intelligence.* Fourth edition. Baltimore: Williams & Wilkins, 1958.

White, R. W. Abnormalities of behavior. *Ann. rev. Psychol.,* 1959, 10, 265–286.

Windle, C. Psychological tests in psychopathological prognosis. *Psychol. Bull.,* 1952, 49, 451–482.

Wolpe, J. *Psychotherapy by reciprocal inhibition.* Stanford: Stanford U. Press, 1958.

Wright, M. E. Abnormalities of behavior. *Ann. rev. Psychol.,* 1957, 8, 269–308.

Yarrow, L. J. Maternal deprivation: toward an empirical and conceptual re-evaluation. *Psychol. Bull.,* 1961, 58, 459–490.

Young, Marguerite L. & Odbert, H. S. Government support of psychological research. *Amer. Psychol.,* 1960 ,15, 661–664.

Zaidi, S. M. H. Pakistan psychology. *Amer. Psychol.,* 1959, 14, 532–536.

Zax, M. & Klein, A. Measurement of personality and behavior changes following psychotherapy. *Psychol. Bull.,* 1960, 57, 435–448.

Zimmerman, F. T. & Burgemeister, B. B. Permanency of glutamic acid treatment. *Arch. Neurol. Psychiat.,* 1951, 65, 291–298.

INDEX